INTRODUCTION
TO
COMPUTER
OPERATIONS

INTRODUCTION TO COMPUTER OPERATIONS

WILLIAM M. FUORI, Ph.D.

CHAIRMAN, DATA PROCESSING DEPARTMENT
NASSAU COMMUNITY COLLEGE

ANTHONY D'ARCO, M.S.

DATA PROCESSING DEPARTMENT
NASSAU COMMUNITY COLLEGE

LAWRENCE ORILIA, Ph.D.

DATA PROCESSING DEPARTMENT
NASSAU COMMUNITY COLLEGE

McGRAW-HILL BOOK COMPANY

New York	Kuala Lumpur	Panama
St. Louis	London	Rio de Janeiro
San Francisco	Mexico	Singapore
Düsseldorf	Montreal	Sydney
Johannesburg	New Delhi	Toronto

Library of Congress Cataloging in Publication Data

Fuori, William M.
  Introduction to computer operations

  Bibliography: p.
  1. Electronic data processing. 2. Electronic
digital computers. I. D'Arco, Anthony, joint author.
II. Orilia, Lawrence, joint author. III. Title.
QA76.5.F86   001.6′4   73-1695
ISBN 0-07-022619-9

INTRODUCTION TO COMPUTER OPERATIONS

567890 DODO 798

*The editors for this book were Alan W. Lowe
and Alice V. Manning, the designer was Marsha
Cohen, and its production was supervised by
James E. Lee. It was set in Optima by York
Graphic Services, Inc.*

CONTENTS

UNIT IV   INPUT/OUTPUT DEVICES

APPENDIXES

PREFACE

Today's educator who must prepare a student to enter the field of data processing faces one of the most challenging educational tasks of his career. He must anticipate the ever-changing needs of this field up to five years hence so that his students will be adequately prepared to obtain a position in this field and carry out the responsibilities of that position in the most efficient and productive manner possible.

The educator's major considerations, then, are to determine those skills which will be essential to the student's employment two to five years hence *and* to provide the student with sufficient skills to make him capable of entering the data processing field in one of several capacities. He should be prepared to accept such positions as a computer operator trainee, a programmer trainee, and a junior programmer.

Today, it is not sufficient to simply train the data processing student in the uses and operational aspects of unit record equipment; he must also be educated in the uses, advantages and disadvantages, and operational aspects of the computer.

All too often, the two- or four-year data processing graduate must prove himself in an operations role within a company before he will be considered for a position in the programming or systems area. It is therefore essential that he be exposed to the concepts of computer operations early in his educational career. He must also be made to realize that his role as a computer operator within the business organization is as essential as that of the programmer or systems analyst to ensure that the computer is utilized in the most efficient and productive manner. It is for these reasons that this text was written.

In addition to providing the student with a basic and initial exposure to computer operations and the role of the computer operator, this text will give the student a basic understanding of what a computer is, what it can do, and what equipment is generally found in a medium- or large-scale computer complex.

This text is recommended for a one-semester course prior to, corequisite with, or as a replacement for the standard Introduction to Computers course. In many schools, this course will serve as a substitute for the Punched Card or Unit Record Equipment Operations and Wiring course.

**Structure of
the Text**

This book is organized to facilitate the student's comprehension of the uses and operational aspects of the computer and its associated peripheral equipment. To accomplish this end, the text has been subdivided into six units as follows:

Unit I.   This unit serves to introduce the student to the historical development of the computer so that he may more clearly understand recent trends and innovations in their proper perspective. In addition the student is exposed to what data processing is and to fundamental data processing operations and functions.

Unit II.   This unit provides a detailed introduction to the basic punched card concept and to the machines which process these cards and support the computer. The operational concepts of each machine presented are also discussed. Selected wiring diagrams, coupled with an overview of the concepts of wiring, are introduced and illustrated.

Unit III. This unit contains an introduction to the components of a data processing system which the student will encounter in subsequent sections in the text. The student will learn what is involved in preparing an application for programming as well as the types of programming languages that are available for use on virtually every modern medium- or large-scale computer. In this unit the student will also be introduced to computer number systems and the concepts of program execution in order to clarify how the computer stores and processes data.

Unit IV.   This unit will expose the student to the various peripheral devices which are used to input data to, and output from, the computer. For each device discussed, the student is presented with sufficient detailed information for him to be able to understand the functions, as well as any operational considerations, of the device.

Unit V.   This unit introduces the components employed by the operator in interacting with a computer system—the console and console typewriter. The pushbuttons, display lights, and switches composing each unit are detailed and discussed. Each of these components is utilized in storage and display operations.

Unit VI.   This unit will acquaint the student with some of the more common methods of processing jobs, together with providing him with an understanding of his role in each of these methods. This unit also discusses the various clerical tasks that the student will be called on to perform as a computer operator.

Uniqueness and Special Features

1. This text is unique in that it is the first text ever to introduce the data processing major to the concepts of computer operations even though a large percentage of all such graduates enter the data processing field as a computer operator or operator trainee.

2. There is a continuity from one chapter to the next as a result of the unit concept discussed above. Thus, the student is able to view the subject matter as a whole, instead of as a series of disjointed topics.

3. The material in this text has been successfully "field-tested" at Nassau Community College by data processing students for several semesters. The extremely enthusiastic response of the students has convinced the authors that this text will provide an interesting, informative, and easy-to-read approach to teaching the fundamentals of computer operations to data processing students.

4. This text provides certain topics in asterisked sections. These sections supply more depth on the basic material presented in addition to supplying the instructor with the ready availability of more complex topics in the same general subject matter areas. The instructor is thus free to gear the level of the course to the interests and backgrounds of his students.

5. This text includes a number of exercises at the end of each chapter. These exercises are far in excess of the number and scope of exercises normally found in introductory textbooks. For this reason, and also to decrease the financial burden on the student, it is felt that a laboratory manual would serve no useful purpose and has therefore not been provided.

6. Programmed instruction–type questions are provided throughout the text to reinforce previously presented material. In this way, the student obtains many of the advantages of a programmed instructional type of presentation as well as those of a lecture-type presentation.

Instructor's Manual

An instructor's manual is available to aid in structuring the course to fit within existing time and hardware constraints, and to fit the interests, and backgrounds of the students. Included in the instructor's manual are illustrations which can be used directly for the production of overhead projector foils, complete and detailed solutions to text exercises and discussion questions, and suggested quiz questions.

ACKNOWLEDGMENT

The authors wish to thank the American Telephone Corporation, Applied Digital Data Systems, Burroughs Corporation, Friden Business Machines division of Singer Corporation, Honeywell Corporation, National Cash Register Corporation of America, Teletype Corporation, and Univac Division of the Sperry Rand Corporation for graciously granting permission to use the charts, diagrams, illustrations, photos, and tables that made this text more meaningful. In particular, the authors wish to thank the International Business Machines Corporation for their aid and assistance, and for the granting of permission for the use of photos and illustrations contained in the below listed publications.

R20 4115-1	229 2141-0
GA 22 6866-5	229 2135-1
F22 6517	C28 2017-3
GA 26 5756-7	Y 24 3518-0
C20 1649-2	GA 24 1431-3
D22 6508-2	A24 10007-0
GR 29 0256-3	224 6384-2
GR 29 0256-2	A24 1010-0
A24 3144-2	A24 1002-2
A24 3373-2	GA 21 9033-3
GA 24 3523-2	R20 4115-1

The authors also wish to thank the persons listed below for their assistance and constructive criticism during the development of this text.

Mrs. C. Blanche Adinolfi, Secretary to the Data Processing Department, Nassau Community College, Garden City, N.Y.

Mr. Martin Deitch, Systems Engineer, Nesconset, N.Y.

Mr. John Shaner, Technical Assistant, Nassau Community College, Garden City, N.Y.

Mr. Dominick Tedesco, Adjunct Professor, Nassau Community College, Garden City, N.Y.

UNIT I
INTRODUCTION TO DATA PROCESSING

AUTOMATION AND DATA PROCESSING

CHAPTER 1

Introduction   Data processing is by no means a new or even recent endeavor. Data processing, or the processing of facts, can be traced back thousands of years. Now, as then, every business is concerned with the processing of facts, or data, about its operations in order to provide the most current and accurate information to management. Such information might include a summary and analysis of operation expenses, market statistics, inventory levels and controls, and other quantitative factors.

In order to provide such information to management as quickly and accurately as possible, business has continuously sought more improved and sophisticated manual, mechanical, and electronic means of processing data to produce useful information. Unprocessed facts or data are of little use to a business until they can be analyzed, combined, and manipulated into a usable form. Only then can these data be considered information. Devices to convert raw data into usable information can be traced back several thousand years.

This need for faster and cheaper methods of processing data in shorter and shorter times became even more apparent with the advent of the industrial revolution. To fill this void, various types of automated devices were introduced in the business world. Most recent and foremost among these was the introduction of the electronic computer, the fastest and most sophisticated device yet devised by man. When the electronic computer was first introduced, it was capable of processing approximately 35,000 instructions for a cost of about $1, whereas today, only two decades later, the same $1 will pay for the processing of over 1 million instructions.

A Brief History   Let us briefly trace the development of calculating devices from their humble beginnings to their current level of sophistication.

The abacus   We shall begin our discussion of calculating devices with what was probably the first mechanical device ever used—the *abacus*. This device is said to have been used by the Babylonians as early as 2200 B.C. The most widely used form of the abacus is illustrated in Figure 1-1. The abacus was clearly limited in its applications since it did not possess a capability for multiplication or division. In addition, its accuracy and speed were heavily dependent on the capability of the operator using the device, not on the device itself.

Pascal's machine   In 1647, approximately 4,000 years after the first known uses of the abacus,
arithmétique   a French philosopher and mathematician named Blaise Pascal invented one of the first practical adding machines, the *Machine Arithmétique*. The basis of this machine's operation was a series of gear-driven counter wheels, similar in operation to the odometer (mileage indicator) used in an automobile. This principle of operation was employed in calculators developed over the next 300 years.

Figure 1-1
Abacus

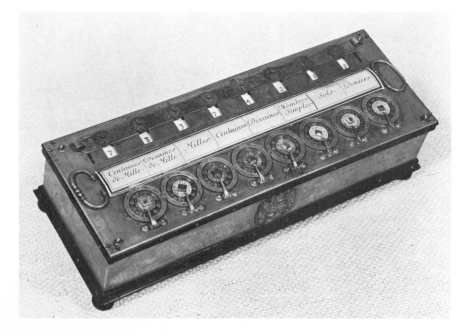

Figure 1-2
Pascal's Machine
Arithmétique

Babbage's difference and analytical engines

Just after the turn of the nineteenth century, an English mathematician named Charles Babbage designed a calculator for the purpose of producing ballistic tables, the *Difference Engine*. Being dissatisfied with the limited uses of the Difference Engine, Babbage set out to design a device capable of performing general purpose calculations. Unfortunately, however, due to financial, engineering, and design problems, this brilliant conception was never made operational during Babbage's lifetime. The design concepts set forth by Babbage in his *Analytical Engine* were, however, used as the basis for a calculator developed by Howard H. Aiken at Harvard University in 1937, the *MARK I Automatic Calculator*.

The birth of the electronic computer

Toward the end of World War II, at the University of Pennsylvania, two electrical engineers named Eckert and Mauchly designed and built the world's first all-electronic computer, the *ENIAC* (Electronic Numerical Integrator And Calculator). This computer was used on a limited basis for the production of tables and was programmed by means of a series of switches and plug-in connections. Several years later, at Cambridge University in England, the first computer capable of storing data and instructions was designed and built, the *EDSAC* (Electronic Delay Storage Automatic Computer).

Both of these computers, however, were not available commercially, but were used exclusively by the government or for research purposes. It wasn't until the early 1950s that a computer was developed and made available commercially. This computer was developed by the Sperry Rand Corporation and called the *UNIVAC I* (UNIVersal Automatic Computer). This computer was first used in 1954, at General Electric Park, Louisville, Kentucky.

Subsequent developments

From the introduction of the UNIVAC I in 1954, over 50,000 computers have been installed in virtually every size and type of business. Developments in computer design over these two decades have been so significant and numerous that they have been categorized by generations, with each generation being initiated by a significant advance in the design of *computer hardware* or *computer software*.[1]

First-generation computers (1942-1959). The first generation of computers was characterized by the use of vacuum tubes. Because of the bulkiness, heat problems, and the large number of failures of the vacuum tube, the first generation of computers was never as reliable as their intended applications required. Programming of first-generation computers was principally done in *machine language*.[2]

[1] See Appendix A for a definition of these terms.
[2] See Chapter 7 for a detailed explanation of this term. A brief definition of this term can be found in Appendix A.

Second-generation computers (1959–1965). The second generation of computers introduced the transistor, a switchlike device with no moving parts. The use of the transistor resulted in computers capable of processing instructions in millionths of a second. Programming of second-generation computers was principally done in *symbolic* or *assembly language*.[3]

Third-generation computers (1965–1970). Third-generation computers were characterized by the incorporation of microminiaturized integrated circuits with components so small that they were barely visible to the naked eye. In addition to the more sophisticated components used in their construction, third-generation computers possessed greater input/output, storage, and processing capabilities than any previous computers. Third-generation computers made the nanosecond (1/1,000,000,000 second) a reality in computer processing speeds. Programming was principally done in *problem-oriented* and *procedure-oriented languages* in addition to symbolic and machine languages.[4]

Fourth-generation computers (1970–   ). Fourth-generation computers promise to offer even greater input/output, storage, and processing capabilities than seen with the third generation of computers. For example, the laser storage device recently developed is capable of storing greater amounts of data with faster access speeds than previously possible. Capabilities such as this have made available to the small business computing power previously available to only the very large business enterprise.

Self-study exercise 1-1

1. Every business is concerned with the processing of _____ about its operations in order to provide the most current and accurate _____ to management.

◆ ◆ ◆

> *facts, or data,*
> *information*

2. Only after raw facts (or data) have been analyzed, combined, and manipulated can they be considered _____.

◆ ◆ ◆

> *information*

---

[3] Ibid.
[4] Ibid.

3. Probably the first mechanical device ever used was the _____ .

◆ ◆ ◆

abacus

4. The abacus was limited in that _____ .

◆ ◆ ◆

it did not possess a capability for multiplication and division, and its speed and accuracy were heavily dependent on the skill of its operator

5. The first practical adding machine was designed by _____ in 1647 and called the _____ .

◆ ◆ ◆

Blaise Pascal
Machine Arithmétique

6. Pascal's calculator was designed around a series of _____ used in calculators for the next 300 years.

◆ ◆ ◆

gear-driven counter wheels

7. Charles Babbage is credited with having designed two machines: the _____ and the _____ .

◆ ◆ ◆

Difference Engine
Analytical Engine

8. The _____ designed by Babbage was intended to be a(n) _____ and formed the basis for a calculator developed at Harvard by Howard H. Aiken which was called the _____ .

◆ ◆ ◆

Analytical Engine
general purpose computer
MARK I Automatic Calculator

9. The first electronic computer was designed by _____ from the University of Pennsylvania and called the _____ .

♦ ♦ ♦

Eckert and Mauchly
ENIAC (Electronic Numerical Integrator And Calculator)

10. The first computer capable of storing data and instructions was the _____ .

♦ ♦ ♦

EDSAC (Electronic Delay Storage Automatic Computer)

11. It was not until the introduction of the UNIVAC I that _____ .

♦ ♦ ♦

computers were available commercially

12. Because of the significant and numerous advances made in the design of computers, they have been categorized by _____ .

♦ ♦ ♦

generations

13. The first generation of computers was characterized by the _____ , the second generation by the _____ , and the third generation by _____ .

♦ ♦ ♦

vacuum tube
transistor
microminiaturized integrated circuits

14. Computers presently on the market are generally considered as _____ -generation computers.

♦ ♦ ♦

fourth

15. The fourth generation of computers has made available to the small business computer capabilities previously found only in _____.

♦ ♦ ♦

larger business enterprises

What Is Data Processing? As a student of data processing, one should be thoroughly familiar with the meaning of the words *data processing* and possess an understanding of those operations involved in the processing of data.

Let us begin our discussion of data processing by stating what data processing is. Data processing can simply be defined as the manipulating and using of facts. In recent years, however, business concerns have relied heavily on automated devices such as the electrical accounting machine (EAM) and computers for the processing of data. This reliance on, and heavy use of, electronic equipment in the processing of data has led to the introduction of the term *electronic data processing*.

Fundamental data processing operations Whether the system used to process data is manual, mechanical, or electronic, there are certain fundamental operations that must be performed. These operations are:

1. Recording
2. Classifying
3. Sorting
4. Calculating
5. Summarizing
6. Reporting

Recording. Recording is the transcribing of data into some permanent form. In a computerized application, recording would consist of transcribing *source,* or raw, *data* onto some machine-readable form such as a punched card or a magnetic tape similar to that used with home tape recorders.

Classifying. Classifying is the grouping of like items into predefined classes. Generally, data are classified according to some code. In a furniture warehouse inventory system, for example, stock items could be classified according to the type of room in which the item would be utilized (i.e., kitchen, living room, bedroom, etc.).

Sorting. Sorting can be described as the arranging of data into a given sequence according to a common characteristic. This arrangement is generally in either an alphabetic or numeric sequence. Customer information in a retail company, for example, is generally sorted numerically according to customer account number.

Calculating. Calculating involves the adding, subtracting, multiplying, and dividing of raw facts, or data, to produce usable results. In a payroll calculation, for example, this might involve the determination of appropriate employee deductions and then the subtracting of these deductions from the employee's gross pay to yield his net pay.

Summarizing. Summarizing consists of the consolidating of results, emphasizing main points and tendencies. That is, summarizing is concerned with accumulating totals or results together with printing these results and appropriate descriptive data necessary for the proper identification of the totals or results. A student's report card at the end of a semester, for example, contains a summary of the student's performance during the semester.

Reporting. Once the data have been summarized, they must be reported to the proper individual(s). Summarized output or results are of little value unless they can be communicated to the concerned individual(s) in a timely and effective manner.

The above operations of recording, classifying, sorting, calculating, summarizing, and reporting, when performed on an automated device such as an electrical accounting machine or computer, can be combined into three very basic functions, namely,

Data processing functions

1. Input
2. Processing
3. Output

Input. Input can be described as data recorded on a computer-acceptable medium to be transferred to an electrical accounting machine or computer for subsequent processing. The medium used to record these data for future processing is known as the *input medium.*

Processing. Processing consists of logical and arithmetical operations performed on input to produce meaningful results.

Output. Output consists of the results of processing input data in its finished or edited form. The medium used to record these results is known as the *output medium.*

Self-study exercise 1-2

1. Data processing can be defined as _____.

◆ ◆ ◆

the manipulating and using of facts

2. Electronic data processing refers to the processing of data on _____.

♦ ♦ ♦

electronic equipment

3. The basic operations performed in any data processing application are _____.

♦ ♦ ♦

recording, classifying, sorting, calculating, summarizing, and reporting

4. Recording can be described as the _____.

♦ ♦ ♦

transcribing of data into some permanent form

5. Sorting involves the _____.

♦ ♦ ♦

arranging of data into a given sequence according to a common characteristic

6. _____ involves the consolidating of results, emphasizing main points and tendencies.

♦ ♦ ♦

Summarizing

7. The above operations, when performed via computer, can be combined into _____ basic functions, namely, _____.

♦ ♦ ♦

three
input, processing, and output

8. Input involves the _____.

♦ ♦ ♦

recording of data on a computer-acceptable medium and the transferring of these data to an electrical accounting machine or a computer

9. Processing involves the _____ .

◆ ◆ ◆

performance of logical and arithmetical operations on input data to produce meaningful results

10. Output consists of _____ .

◆ ◆ ◆

the results of the processing of input data in finished or edited form

True-false exercise

1. Data processing is a relatively new process.
2. Raw facts can be considered data, not information.
3. The need for automated devices to process data became more critical after the industrial revolution than at any previous time.
4. With the increased complexity and sophistication of computers, the cost of processing an instruction has increased.
5. The abacus is probably the oldest known mechanical calculator.
6. Pascal incorporated many of the principles discovered by Babbage in his Machine Arithmétique.
7. Babbage never actually constructed a working model of his Analytical Engine.
8. The first all-electronic computer was the EDSAC.
9. The second generation of computers employed microminiaturized integrated circuits.
10. Problem-oriented languages were used extensively with third-generation computers.
11. Data processing refers to the processing of data by electrical accounting machines or computers.
12. Analysis is one of the fundamental data processing operations.
13. The basic data processing operations are designed to be performed using only manual methods.

End-of-chapter Exercises

14. The three basic data processing functions are input, processing, and output.
15. Input data are initially recorded on a computer-acceptable input medium before they can be processed.

Multiple-choice exercise

1. Raw data only takes on real value to management after it has been
   a. examined
   b. compared
   c. classified
   d. analyzed
   e. all the above
2. As compared to the early 1950s, $1 today will pay for the processing of
   a. ½ million instructions
   b. 1 million instructions
   c. 1 billion instructions
   d. 10 billion instructions
   e. none of the above
3. Pascal's Machine Arithmétique was similar in operation to
   a. the abacus
   b. modern-day calculators
   c. an automobile odometer
   d. an electronic calculator
   e. none of the above
4. Charles Babbage was responsible for the design of the
   a. Difference Engine
   b. Analytical Engine
   c. ENIAC
   d. a and b above
   e. a and c above
5. The first truly all-electronic computer was the
   a. EDSAC
   b. MARK I
   c. UNIVAC I
   d. Analytical Engine
   e. ENIAC
6. Sperry Rand Corporation was responsible for the production of the
   a. EDSAC computer
   b. MARK I computer
   c. UNIVAC I computer
   d. Analytical Engine computer
   e. ENIAC computer

7. The principal problem associated with the vacuum tube was
   a.   poor reliability
   b.   heat
   c.   bulkiness
   d.   all the above
   e.   none of the above
8. Second-generation computers saw the introduction of the
   a.   microcircuit
   b.   transistor
   c.   vacuum tube
   d.   all the above
   e.   none of the above
9. Which of the following is not a fundamental data processing operation?
   a.   Reporting
   b.   Analyzing
   c.   Summarizing
   d.   Sorting
   e.   None of the above
10. Summarizing can be defined as the
   a.   reporting of data
   b.   consolidating of facts
   c.   grouping of all calculations
   d.   all the above
   e.   none of the above

Problems

1. Discuss the fundamental data processing operations associated with the processing of data.
2. The computer revolution has often been called a second industrial revolution. Support or refute this statement.
3. Discuss the effect that the computer has had on business.
4. Briefly trace the development of computers from the abacus to modern-day computers.
5. What had Babbage hoped to accomplish with his Analytical Engine that he had not accomplished with his Difference Engine?
6. Why do you think that the development of the computer was so small between the time of Babbage and Aiken?
7. What do you believe were some of the motivating forces responsible for the development of computers?

UNIT II

UNIT RECORD SYSTEMS

IBM PUNCHED CARD AND CODE

CHAPTER 2

Introduction   The punched card was one of the earliest media and is still perhaps the most common medium used to transmit data to automatic data processing devices. It was first used by an inventor named Joseph Marie Jacquard who, in 1801, in Lyons, France, invented a textile loom which was controlled by a strip of paper with a series of holes punched in it. For all practical purposes this remained the only application of the punched card for almost a century.

In 1880, the taking of a ten-year census was initiated as required by law. By 1885, the Census Bureau found itself in the midst of a deluge of collected facts and figures relating to the census. With an anticipated population increase of approximately 20 to 25 percent by 1890, it was apparent that this chore would become even more difficult and time-consuming in the future.

As the census is the basis for the allocation of seats in the Congress, it was essential that some means be devised for the timely completion of the 1890 census. To this end, Herman Hollerith, a statistician with the U.S. Census Bureau, applied his genius. By 1887, Hollerith had invented a code for recording data on strips of paper. This was accomplished by punching a series of holes in a planned pattern into the paper strips. Each hole had a unique and specific meaning. For better durability and ease of handling, the paper strips were soon replaced by thin cardboard cards of a fixed size and shape. Each card was used to record data relative to a single individual or family, a *unit record*. To process these coded punched cards or unit records, Hollerith devised a keypunch machine capable of punching source data onto cards in this newly discovered code, a sorter which would sort the coded punched cards into various classes, and a tabulator which could process these cards by accumulating data and printing the resulting totals.

This code and the machines designed to interpret and process cards punched with this code were used in the processing of the 1890 census, a feat which was completed in approximately three years. Punched card processing had now become a reality.

Self-study exercise 2-1

1. The punched card was first used to control the operations of _____.

◆ ◆ ◆

textile looms

2. The punched card acquired its present form as a result of the efforts of _____, a statistician with the Census Bureau.

◆ ◆ ◆

Herman Hollerith

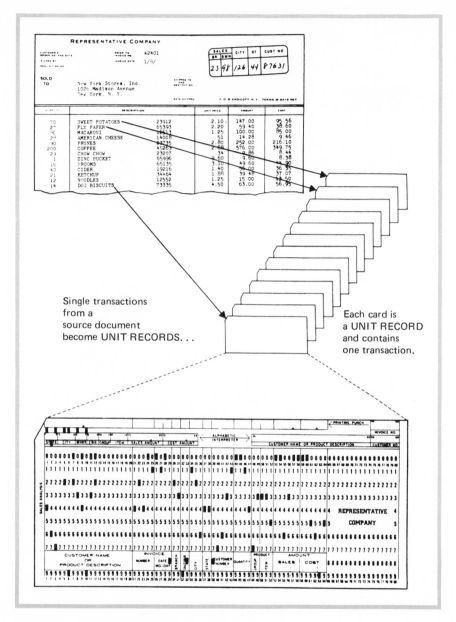

Single transactions
from a
source document
become UNIT RECORDS. . .

Each card is
a UNIT RECORD
and contains
one transaction.

Figure 2-1
The Punched Card as a
Unit Record

3. In each of its applications, the punched card was used to record data
   relative to a single individual or family, a(n) _____.

◆ ◆ ◆

unit record

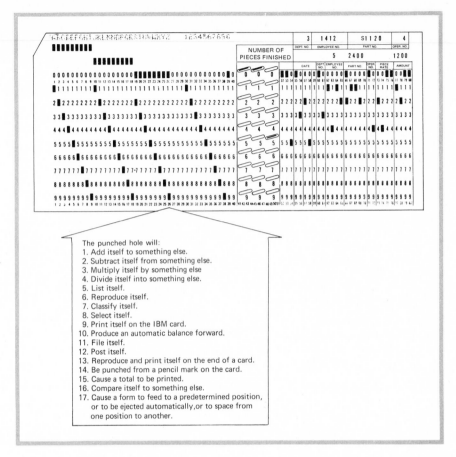

Figure 2-2
What the Punched Hole
Will Do

4. The punched card became firmly established after its use in the calculation of the _____.

♦ ♦ ♦

1890 census

IBM 80-column Card The IBM 80-column card, often referred to as the standard card, is rectangular in shape and measures $3\frac{1}{4}$ by $7\frac{3}{8}$ in. You will notice that in the punched card illustrated in Figure 2-3, the upper left corner has been cut off. Punched cards are, however, available with any or no corner cut off. The purpose of cutting off one corner of a card is to facilitate the alignment of a group of punched cards and to clearly point out any card(s) which may be misaligned with the remaining cards in the group. Such a group of punched cards is commonly referred to as a *deck* of punched cards.

In Figure 2-3, you will notice that the card is divided into 80 vertical spaces or *columns,* each being assigned a unique column number beginning at the left of the card with column 1 and progressively increasing to column 80 at the righthand side of the card. Each column is capable of storing *1* character, thus providing a maximum storage capacity of *80* characters on *one* punched card. A character may be a letter of the alphabet, a digit, or a special character (decimal point, comma, dollar sign, etc.).

Figure 2-3 illustrates a standard card containing information punched into it. Upon careful examination, you will note that in addition to being divided vertically into 80 columns, this card is also divided horizontally into 12 spaces or *rows.* The upper three rows are conjunctively called the *zone punching area,* and beginning at the top of the card, these rows are individually referred to as the 12 row, 11 row or *X row,* and 0 row. The lower nine rows constitute the *digit punching area* and are called the 1 row to 9 row, respectively, beginning with the first row below the zone punching area. As a result of these row designations, the top and bottom edges of the card are referred to as the 12 edge and 9 edge, respectively.

A character (letter, digit, or special character) is recorded in one card column as an organized pattern of machine-readable, rectangular punched holes in the zone and digit punching areas. Some of these character representations are illustrated in Figure 2-3.

Figure 2-3
IBM Punched Card
Containing Digits, Letters,
and Special Characters

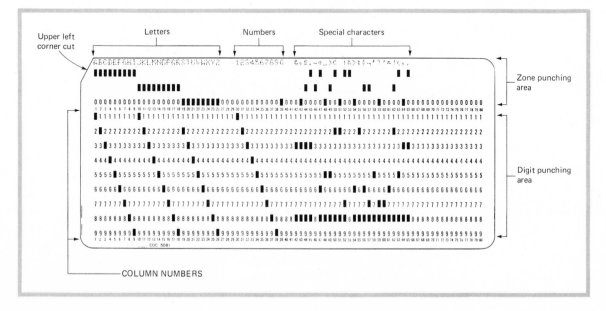

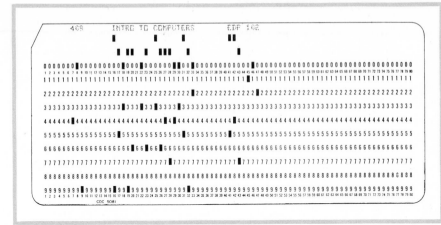

Figure 2-4
Punched Card Containing
Numeric and Alphabetic
Data Punched into It

Numeric characters and fields

A digit can be punched into any given column by punching a hole into the digit punching row corresponding to the particular digit to be punched. For example, the digit 4 would be recorded in a card as a rectangular hole punched in the 4 row of the desired column, while a 9 would be recorded as a rectangular hole punched in the 9 row of the desired column. That is, with the exception of the digit 0 (zero), a digit is recorded in a column as a single punch in the appropriate row of the digit punching area of that column. The digit 0 (zero), however, is recorded by a single punch in the 0 row of the zone punching area in the column desired.

In Figure 2-4, you will note that the digits 4, 0, and 9 have been punched in columns 7, 8, and 9 of the card, respectively. Since these digits appear in consecutive or adjacent columns, they could represent the single number 409, or they could represent other possibilities such as the numbers 40 and 9 or the numbers 4 and 09 or the numbers 4, 0, and 9. Should these digits be intended to represent the number 409, for example, these columns would be referred to as a card field. A *card field* is defined as a fixed number of consecutive card columns assigned to a unit of information. More specifically, since in this case the field consists of only numbers, as opposed to letters of the alphabet or special characters, these columns would represent a *numeric field*.

Alphabetic and special characters

Letters of the alphabet are punched into a given column by punching two holes in that column, one in the zone punching area and one in the digit punching area. The letters A through I consist of a punch in the 12 row of the zone punching area *and* a punch in the 1 row to the 9 row, respectively. The letters J through R consist of a punch in the 11 row of the zone punching area *and* a punch in the 1 row to the 9 row, respectively, while the letters S through Z consist of a punch in the 0 row of the zone punching area, *and* a punch in the 2 row to the 9 row, respectively.

Table 2-1. Examples of Different Types of Fields

Alphabetic	Numeric	Alphanumeric
JAMES	473	A47200
CREDIT	14	23 HARRIS PL
EDP	31406	CREDIT 45
INTRO TO COMP	4001	6 TABLES

In Figure 2-4, a group of letters of the alphabet and blanks have been punched into adjacent card columns to form the title INTRO TO COMPUTERS. Since these characters are contained in consecutive card columns and represent a unit of information, this area of the card qualifies as a card field. Furthermore, since the data contained in this card field consists of letters of the alphabet and blanks, it can more specifically be termed an *alphabetic field*. Referring again to Figure 2-4, the field containing the characters EDP 102 would be referred to as an *alphanumeric field* since it contains only alphabetic and numeric characters and no special characters. It is noteworthy that, within a field, numeric data is *right-justified* (placed as far right as possible within the field) and that alphabetic or alphanumeric data is *left-justified* (placed as far left as possible within the field). Table 2-1 illustrates the possible contents of alphabetic, numeric, and alphanumeric fields.

To demonstrate your understanding of the field concept, identify the nonblank fields punched in the card illustrated in Figure 2-5, and determine the specific data punched into each nonblank field.

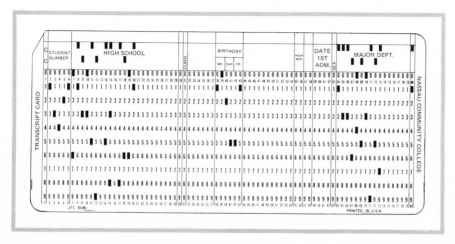

Figure 2-5
IBM Punched Card
Containing No Printing

You should have determined that the above card contained four nonblank fields, specifically:

Student number
High school
Birthday
Major department

You should have also determined that the actual data contained in each of these fields is:

Student number: 13421
High school: WALTER E. HOWARD
Birthday: 102551
Major department: ACCOUNTING

Self-study exercise 2-2

1. The purpose of the cut corner on a punched card is to _____.

◆ ◆ ◆

facilitate the alignment of a group of punched cards and to clearly point out any card(s) which may be misaligned with the remaining cards in the group

2. A group of punched cards is referred to as a(n) _____ of punched cards.

◆ ◆ ◆

deck

3. A standard punched card is divided into _____ columns and _____ rows.

◆ ◆ ◆

80
12

4. The upper three rows on the 80-column punched card are conjunctively referred to as the _____ and beginning at the top of the card, individually referred to as the _____ row, _____ row, and _____ row.

◆ ◆ ◆

zone punching area
12
11 or X
0

5. The lower nine rows of a punched card constitute the _____.

◆ ◆ ◆

digit punching area

6. Each column of a card is capable of recording one _____ as a series
of machine-readable _____.

◆ ◆ ◆

character
rectangular punched holes

7. A(n) _____ is a fixed number of consecutive card columns assigned
to a unit of information.

◆ ◆ ◆

card field

8. A field may be classified as _____, _____, or _____ depending on
the type of data to be recorded in the field.

◆ ◆ ◆

numeric
alphabetic
alphanumeric

9. Numeric fields are _____-justified, while alphabetic or alphanumeric
fields are _____-justified.

◆ ◆ ◆

right
left

10. Data right-justified in a field is data that is placed _____, while data left-justified in a field is placed _____.

◆ ◆ ◆

as far right as is possible within the field
as far left as is possible within the field

IBM 96-column Card
From the introduction of the punched card into automated processing and until the late 1960s, the standard 80-column card was used virtually exclusively by IBM, the largest computer manufacturer in the world, as the card input medium to their product line. In the late 1960s, IBM introduced a new computer system, the IBM System/3 computer. The System/3 computer utilized a completely new punched card design, a 96-column card. This card is uniquely different in both physical appearance and in the manner in which data is encoded into it.

Physically, it is smaller than the 80-column standard card and is square in appearance. It is subdivided horizontally into three tiers, each capable of holding 32 characters. The top of the card can accommodate three lines of print, one for each punching area or tier.

The encoding scheme employed is based on the BCD[1] (Binary Coded Decimal) code, as opposed to the Hollerith code used with the 80-column standard card. In the BCD code, a character is represented by a unique

[1]There are slight variations between the standard BCD code pattern and the BCD code used with the 96-column card of System/3. These variations occur in the codes for the digit 0 (zero) and for certain special characters.

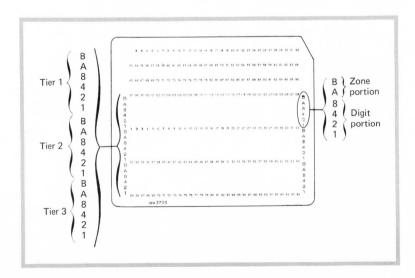

Figure 2-6
Punch Positions on IBM
System/3 96-column Card

Table 2-2. Comparison of Zone Punches in Hollerith and BCD Codes

Hollerith	BCD
12 punch	B punch and A punch
11 punch	B punch only
0 punch	A punch only

combination of up to six punches, two of which are used to represent the zone portion of the character, while the remaining four punches are used to represent the numeric portion of the character. Each of the six punching rows in a tier of the 96-column card is assigned a unique name, as are the rows in the 80-column standard card. The names of these punching rows are the B row, A row, 8 row, 4 row, 2 row, and 1 row as illustrated in Figure 2-6. The relationship between the zone and numeric punch combinations in the BCD and Hollerith codes is illustrated in Tables 2-2 and 2-3.

Employing Tables 2-2 and 2-3, one can determine the BCD code for any given character from the Hollerith representation for that character. For example, for the character G (12 punch and a 7 punch in Hollerith code) we would determine from Table 2-2 that the BCD zone configuration would consist of a punch in each of the B and A rows. From Table 2-3, we can ascertain that the numeric configuration of the character G would consist of a punch in each of the 4, 2, and 1 rows. Similarly, one could

Table 2-3. Comparison of Digit Punches in Hollerith and BCD Codes

Hollerith	BCD
9 punch	8 punch and 1 punch
8 punch	8 punch only
7 punch	4 punch and 2 punch and 1 punch
6 punch	4 punch and 2 punch
5 punch	4 punch and 1 punch
4 punch	4 punch only
3 punch	2 punch and 1 punch
2 punch	2 punch only
1 punch	1 punch only
0 punch	no punches

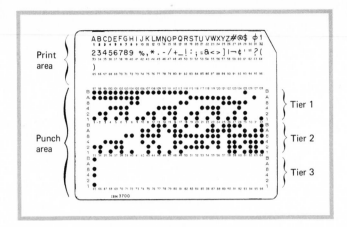

Figure 2-7
IBM System/3 96-column
Punched Card

determine that the BCD configuration of the character Z would consist of a punch in each of the A, 8, and 1 rows. The complete 96-column card character set is given in Figure 2-7.

Self-study exercise 2-3

1. In the late 1960s, IBM introduced the System/3 computer together with a completely new punched card design, a(n) _____.

♦ ♦ ♦

96-column card

2. The 96-column card is subdivided into three _____, each capable of holding _____ characters.

♦ ♦ ♦

tiers
32

3. The coding scheme employed with the 96-column card is _____.

♦ ♦ ♦

BCD (Binary Coded Decimal)

4. Each character in BCD consists of up to _____ punches, _____ of which represent the zone of the character and _____ of which represent the numeric portion of the character.

◆ ◆ ◆

six
two
four

5. The BCD representation of the character R would consist of punches in the _____ row(s).

◆ ◆ ◆

B, 8, and 1

There are three general classifications of punched cards: detail cards, master cards, and summary cards. Each of the three types of punched card is used for a particular purpose.

Classifications of Punched Cards

A detail card generally contains facts or data pertaining to a single transaction. That is, one detail card represents one sale, charge, invoice, etc. Detail cards are usually punched directly from the source document. For example, in preparing a detail card for a sales transaction, items such as sales slip or invoice number, customer name or account number, date of the sale, name or number of the item sold, quantity of items sold, and amount of the sale would be recorded into a punched card directly from the invoice or sales slip.

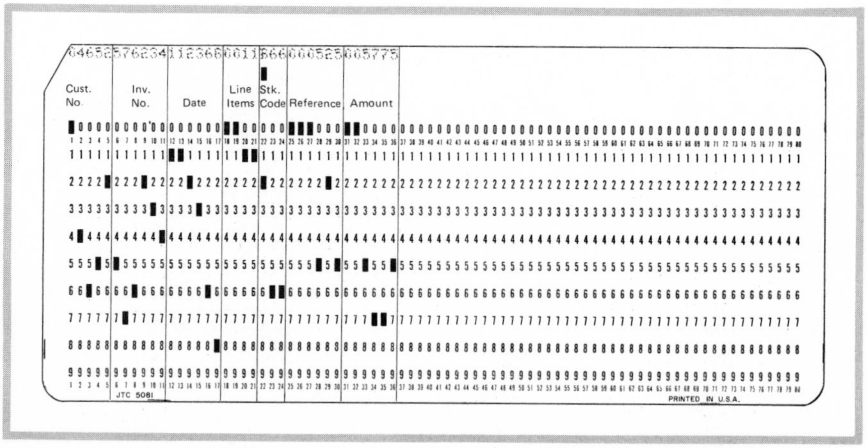

Detail cards

Figure 2-8
Typical Detail Card

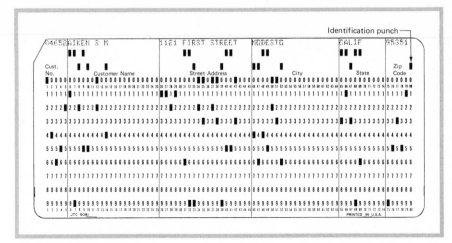

Figure 2-9
Typical Master Card

Master cards A master card is one which contains relatively fixed or nonvariable data. For example, a customer master card to be used in an automated charge account would contain such information as the customer's name, address, account number, etc. Specific data relating to the individual transactions of a customer would be contained on a series of detail cards which would be processed with the master card for that account. To accomplish this, it would be essential that both the master and detail cards contain an account identification field in order that they may be properly matched before processing.

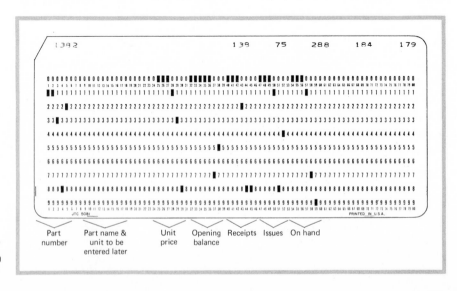

Figure 2-10
Typical Summary Card

A summary card contains a compilation or summary of the transactions from a group of similar detail cards. For example, a summary card could be used to contain the end-of-month summary totals pertaining to all the transactions for a particular customer for that month. This summary card could then be used for customer billing and as the starting point of the subsequent month's processing. In this manner, it is only necessary to process the detail cards once—to produce the summary card.

Summary cards

There are many types of punched cards that the computer operator may encounter in the performance of his duties. Some of these are:

Types of punched cards

1. General purpose cards
2. Document cards
3. Dual cards
4. Mark-sensed cards
5. Stub cards

General purpose cards. Cards with no special printing; a general purpose card is illustrated below.

Document cards. Punched cards that also serve as an output document. Checks and invoices are common examples of document cards.

Dual cards. Punched cards that provide space on the face of the card to record handwritten information. In this case, the punched card contains both handwritten and punched information. Physical inventory cards are examples of this type of card.

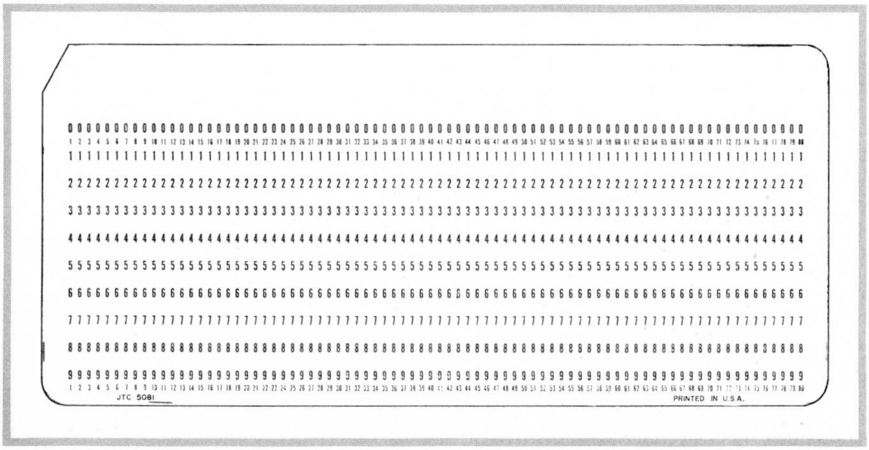

Figure 2-11
General Purpose Card

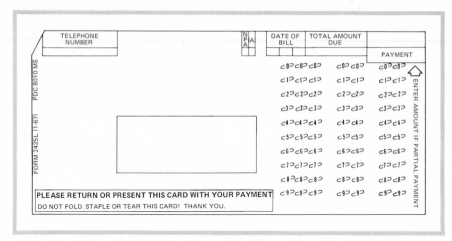

Figure 2-12
Document Card

Mark-sensed cards. Cards which allow a limited quantity of data to be recorded directly onto the card by means of a special pencil with a magnetic-type lead. A specially equipped machine then "reads" the special pencil marks and automatically punches the read information onto the same card. This card can then be input to a computer via a punched card reader.

Stub cards. Special form of document cards with a small tear-off section attached. Public utility invoices are popular examples where the stub portion is to be torn off by the customer and returned with his payment.

The development of the punched card and the methods and machines with which to process it have been substantially responsible for the

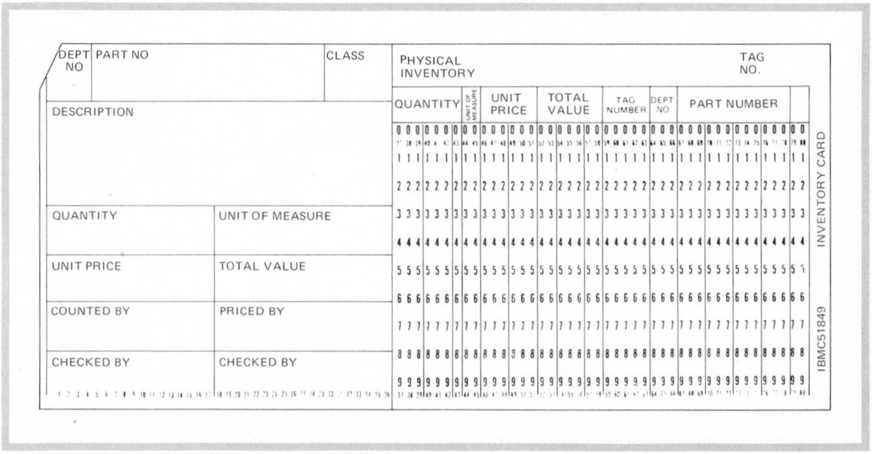

Figure 2-13
Typical Dual Card

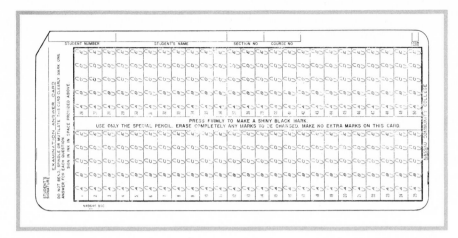

Figure 2-14
Typical Mark-sensed Card

economical and efficient processing of the accounting operations of many a business enterprise or government agency. From its first full-scale application with the U.S. Census Bureau in 1890, punched card applications have increased in scope and level of sophistication. Its use has been responsible for significant reductions in paperwork handling and processing, as well as being responsible for the more efficient use of company resources through production planning techniques.

It must also be pointed out, however, that there are limitations and disadvantages associated with the use of the punched card as an input medium. For example, punched cards are bulky to handle, relatively sensitive to warping and swelling due to high-humidity conditions, not reusable, and subject to wear relatively quickly with heavy usage; and they require a great deal of space for storage.

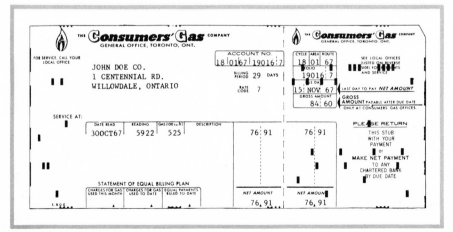

Figure 2-15
Typical Stub Card

As you will see in subsequent chapters, many of these disadvantages and limitations have been overcome by the introduction of more modern input media, such as magnetic tape, punched paper tape, and magnetic discs, to name but a few of the media which have been introduced into automated processing to complement the punched card.

Self-study exercise 2-4

1. A detail card generally contains facts or data pertaining to _____.

♦ ♦ ♦

a single transaction

2. A(n) _____ card contains relatively fixed or nonvariable data.

♦ ♦ ♦

master

3. A summary card contains _____.

♦ ♦ ♦

a compilation or summary of the transactions from a group of similar detail cards

4. Some of the various types of punched cards include _____.

♦ ♦ ♦

general purpose cards, document cards, dual cards, mark-sensed cards, and stub cards

5. Many of the limitations and disadvantages of using the punched card have been virtually eliminated with respect to modern input media such as _____.

♦ ♦ ♦

magnetic tape, punched paper tape, and the magnetic disk

End-of-chapter Exercises

True-false exercise

1. Punched cards consist of up to 80 columns into which data can be punched.
2. In Hollerith code, a character is represented by a zone and a numeric punch.

3. A punched card often serves as a unit record.
4. Herman Hollerith originated the concept of the punched card.
5. Alphanumeric data is generally right-justified in a field.
6. The upper lefthand corner of a punched card is cut off to facilitate card handling.
7. Each card column can record one character of information.
8. A character can be a digit, a letter of the alphabet, or a special character (period, comma, parenthesis, asterisk, etc.).
9. A card field must consist of adjacent card columns.
10. The 96-column card is essentially used with many computer systems.
11. The 96-column card employs the BCD coding scheme.
12. A maximum of two punches is required to represent digits or letters on the 96-column card.
13. Detail cards generally contain more information than master cards.
14. A summary card is often used for customer billing purposes.
15. The punched card has, for all practical purposes, been replaced by more modern input/output media.

Fill-in exercise

1. The first practical punched card tabulator was designed by _____.
2. The 80-column punched card is _____ in shape.
3. The 0 row on an 80-column punched card is contained in the _____ punching area.
4. The character K recorded on an 80-column card would consist of a(n) _____ and a(n) _____ punch.
5. A(n) _____ is a fixed number of consecutive card columns assigned to a unit of information.
6. The 96-column card is _____ in size than the 80-column card.
7. The names of the rows on a 96-column card are _____ , _____ , _____ , _____ , _____ , and _____ .
8. A K punch on a 96-column card would consist of punches in the _____ and _____ rows.
9. The three classes of punched cards are _____ , _____ , and _____ .
10. Five commonly used types of punched cards are _____ , _____ , _____ , _____ , and _____ .

Problems

1. Describe the Hollerith code used in recording data on punched cards.
2. Give the Hollerith and BCD codes for each of the characters below.
   - a. B   d. 4
   - b. X   e. R
   - c. M   f. 0

3. What are some of the differences between the recording of alphabetic data on the 80- and 96-column cards?
4. List and discuss some of the advantages and disadvantages of using the punched card medium.
5. What restrictions exist concerning the size of and material used in the manufacturing of punched cards? Discuss why these restrictions are necessary.

CARD PUNCH MACHINE

CHAPTER 3

Introduction   In the previous chapter we learned that the punched card is one of the most common input media used in the automated processing of data. We also learned of the various coding schemes employed to record data onto punched cards. The one area that we did not discuss is how data is actually recorded onto the punched card.

In general, the data to be recorded on the punched card is contained within an existing form. This form or document is referred to as a *source document*. It might be a ledger, a time sheet, an invoice, a sales slip, or a registration form. The operator then transcribes the desired data from the source document to the punched card by depressing the corresponding keyboard keys of the card punch machine. As each character is keyed in, via the keyboard, the data is actually punched onto the card in Hollerith code. Thus, the finished card now provides a computer-acceptable record of the given data, using the Hollerith code format.

The card punch machine is also frequently referred to as a *keypunch*. This term is derived from the fact that a character is *punch*ed into a card as a result of the operator's depressing a *key* on the keyboard of the card punch machine. Since this term is commonly used in data processing installations, we shall use it in the remainder of the chapter.

For purposes of our discussions, we shall consider the IBM Model 029 keypunch (Figure 3-1), a commonly used keypunch device. We shall concern ourselves with its operational characteristics, forms of operator usage, and operator error-handling procedures. We shall also discuss some other commonly used keypunch machines.

The IBM Model 029
Keypunch

Introduction

The principal use of the keypunch is for the preparation of a large quantity of cards. In the hands of an experienced keypunch operator, this device can serve to produce such quantities of punched cards. In order that the keypunch be used to its fullest potential, the keypunch operator must possess a detailed knowledge of 029's operating characteristics. Many of these details, however, are of little concern to the computer operator since the applications to which he would apply the keypunch are relatively limited. This limitation applies both to the volume of cards produced and to the extent that the keypunch is used.

In general, the computer operator's limited use of the keypunch would consist of such functions as punching control cards to be used in directing the activities of the computer system, repunching lost or damaged cards, duplicating a card, etc. It should be apparent from this partial list that punched cards prepared on the keypunch by a computer operator are those cards utilized by the operator in the normal performance of his duties. Therefore, we shall confine our discussions to only those operational aspects of the Model 029 which concern the computer operator.

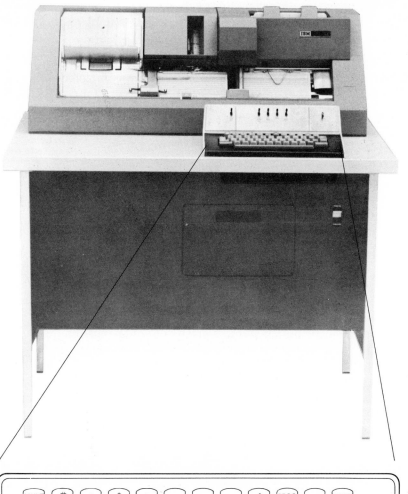

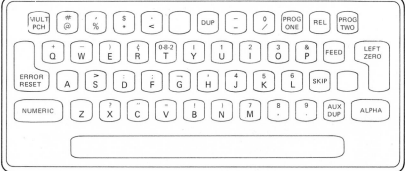

Figure 3-1
IBM 029 Keypunch and
Keyboard

Let us begin our discussion of the keypunch by studying the path traveled by a card being punched as it moves through the keypunch.

Path of the card The path of the card refers to the actual movement of the punched card through the keypunch, from an unpunched to a completed state. Figure 3-2 denotes, with the aid of a dotted line, the path the card will follow through Model 029. In traversing this path, the card must pass through each of four areas, namely,

1. Card hopper
2. Punching station
3. Reading station
4. Card stacker

The card hopper holds the cards which are to be keypunched. Approximately 500 cards can be held in the card hopper. From the card hopper, cards are fed to the punching station one at a time. Once the card has been seated at the punching station, keypunching may begin in the first column of the seated card.

Data may be punched into a given column of a card only when that card column is located directly beneath the punching station. As the operator strikes a key on the keyboard, that character's code is punched

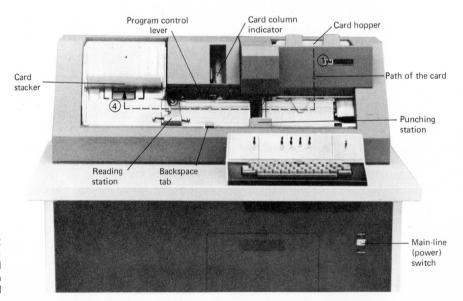

Figure 3-2
The MAIN-LINE (Power)
Switch, Path of the Card
Areas, and Column
Indicator Noted

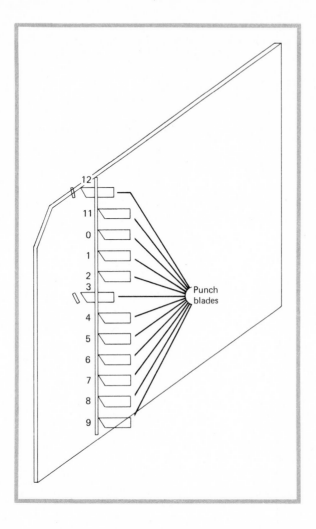

Figure 3-3
The Letter C Punched
onto a Card

into the given card column. Thus, characters are punched one card column at a time, or *column by column.*

To facilitate the punching of any combination of digit and zone punches into any one card column, the punching station is composed of a series of 12 *vertical punch knives*—one punch knife corresponding to each row on the punched card. Depression of the desired character's key on the keyboard will activate the appropriate punch knives (see Figure 3-3). Each time a character is punched, the card advances so as to position the punch knives over the next column so that they are ready to punch the character corresponding to the key depressed by the operator. This process continues until the card has been completely punched. At this point, the card passes from the punching station to the reading station.

As its name implies, the reading station is used to read data, coded in the form of punched holes, from a card. This reading operation is accomplished by a series of 12 vertical *reading brushes,* one for each row of the card. These reading brushes are only utilized during an operation which is referred to as *duplication.* In this operation, data from a card, being read at the reading station, is copied, column by column, onto a second card being punched at the punching station. Thus, for duplication to occur, cards must be seated beneath both the punching and reading stations. Both cards move *simultaneously* through their respective stations, one column at a time. Data received from the reading station is punched onto *only* the card passing beneath the punching station at that instant. As a result of the duplication operation, an entire card or a portion of a punched card may be reproduced.

As cards pass from the reading station, they are placed in the card stacker—the final position in the path of the card. The card stacker has a capacity to hold approximately 500 cards.

During the keypunching or duplicating operations, the operator may utilize the *column indicator* to determine the particular card column he is about to punch. This red-tipped indicator, shown in Figure 3-4, notes the card column into which data will be punched. The operator relies quite heavily on the column indicator when duplicating sections of cards or keying data into fields that are irregularly spaced.

Should the operator bypass a particular card column, the BACK-SPACE tab, shown in Figure 3-2, is used. A momentary depressing of this tab will cause cards at both the reading and punching stations to "back up" one card column each. If the BACKSPACE tab is held down, both cards will continue to backspace until the tab is released or card column 1 is reached.

Major control over the movement of a card is exercised through the Model 029's keyboard. By depressing specific keys on the keyboard, the operator may, for example, cause a card to be moved from one station to another or data to be "duped" (duplicated) from one card to another. An understanding of correct keyboard usage is important to the operator. This knowledge will save the operator from wasted efforts and the making of minor but infuriating and time-consuming mistakes.

Keyboard   The keyboard of the Model 029 is laid out very similarly to the key format of a typewriter, and it is depicted in Figure 3-1. However, in the case of the 029 keypunch, the keyboard is color-coded. Control keys are blue, while keys representing characters are gray. Examination of the keyboard reveals a set of characters composed of 26 alphabetic, 10 numeric, and

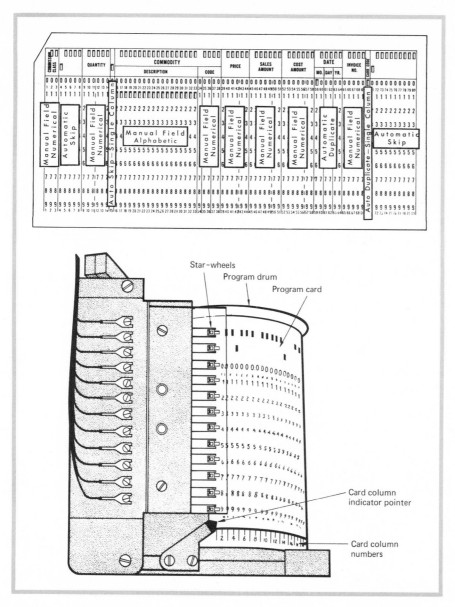

Star-wheels
Program drum
Program card

Card column
indicator pointer

Card column
numbers

Figure 3-4
A Completed Program
Control Card Before and
After Being Wrapped
around the Program
Drum

various special characters (i.e., comma, period, asterisk, dollar sign, etc.).
In addition, many keys represent more than one character. Let us examine
the key representing characters L and 6.

In a secretary's terminology, the character L would be described as
"lowercase" and the character 6 "uppercase." When the keyboard is used

Table 3-1. Major Control Keys on the IBM 029

Key	Key Name	When the Key Is Depressed
FEED	Feed	A card is fed from the hopper to punching station.
REG	Register	The card is seated properly within the punching station.
REL	Release	The card is released from the reading or punching station.
DUP	Duplicate	Duplication of data read at the reading station is permitted.
. . .	Space Bar	The card moves column by column with no data being punched.
MULT PCH	Multiple Punch	The card is prevented from advancing to the next column, thereby permitting more than one punch code to be entered in that column.

to punch lowercase characters, it is said to be in *alphabetic* mode, the *normal* operating mode of the 029's keyboard.

To punch an uppercase character, the keyboard must be set in *numeric* mode—its second operational mode. The keyboard is shifted to numeric mode from alphabetic mode (referred to as a *keyboard shift*) by depression of the NUMERIC key. Thus, for the character key in our example, alphabetic mode would produce the character L (an 11 punch and a 3 punch), and numeric mode would produce the character 6 (a 6 punch only).

The NUMERIC key is a control key and, therefore, colored blue. Control keys are employed to effect the movement of the card or alter the keyboard's state. Table 3-1 reviews some of the major control keys associated with the Model 029 keypunch.

Functional control switches Our discussions, to this point, have centered about the keyboard and the movement of a punched card. Whereas the keyboard controls the movement of a card, a series of switches referred to as the *functional control switches* affect the operation of the keypunch. The Model 029's functional control switches, located directly above the keyboard and illustrated in Figure 3-5, are:

Switch	Label
Clear	CLEAR
Leading zero print suppression	LZ PRINT
Print	PRINT
Automatic feed	AUTO FEED
Program select	PROG SEL
Automatic skip duplication	AUTO SKIP DUP

Depending upon the quantity of cards to be keypunched, the operator may choose between feeding cards automatically or manually. Control over the manner in which cards are fed is exercised through the AUTO FEED switch. In its ON (up) setting, cards are automatically fed to and moved between the punching and reading stations. With the AUTO FEED switch set to off (down), the Model 029 is placed under the operator's manual control, and cards must be individually advanced from station to station.

Whether cards are fed manually or automatically, the operator may or may not elect to use the 029's printing capability. The PRINT and LZ PRINT switches afford the operator this option. With the PRINT switch set to ON (upward), every character keypunched will be printed. That is, as the key is struck on the keyboard, the holes are punched into a card column, and that character's representation is printed in the same card column, above the 12 row. With the PRINT switch off (down), keypunching may continue, but absolutely *no* printing of any type will occur.

The LZ PRINT switch controls the printing of extraneous leading zeros when the keypunch is under control of the *program control card*. When set ON, though the card is punched as 00279, the printing above those card columns would read bb279 (where the b denotes a blank, or unprinted space). If the LZ PRINT option is not used, for the same field the numbers printed would be 00279.

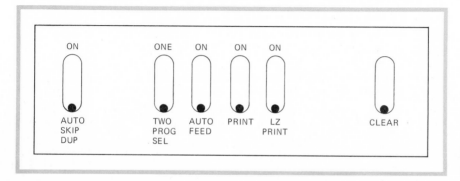

Figure 3-5
The Functional Control
Switches on the IBM 029

The operator may desire to clear all cards from the reading and punching stations. If so, the CLEAR switch would be used, causing all cards along the path of the card to be transferred to the card stacker. The CLEAR switch, though lifted upward to initiate the clearing of cards, will always return to its downward position.

The remaining functional control switches, PROG SEL and AUTO SKIP DUP, like the LZ PRINT switch, are employed *only* when the key-punch is placed under the control of a program control card. Their usage will be discussed after the introduction of the program control card.

Program control card   The program control card, also referred to as a *program* or *control* card, is designed to simplify and ease the keypunch operator's task. Through its use, the 029 can be "programmed" to perform specific routine tasks auto-matically. The program card can control the skipping between data fields, the shifting between keyboard modes, the correct placement of a card in the initial column of a data field, the automatic duplication of data between successive cards, and the release of cards from the reading or punching station. Thus, the keypunch operator, relieved of these control tasks, can concentrate his efforts on the accurate keying of data.

The control card is a standard punched card into which a series of predefined control codes have been punched. The most commonly used of these codes, discussed in Table 3-2, direct the Model 029 in the perform-ance of specific operations.

One might question the functions of two of the codes—the 1 punch or blank (no punches in a card column) since it was previously stated that normal operation of the keyboard is in alphabetic mode. This is true; however, it is also true that the use of the program card causes the key-punch to shift its keyboard completely to numeric mode. Therefore, to

Table 3-2.   Program Control Card Codes

Type of Punch	Function
Blank	Indicates the beginning of a numeric field to be punched
11 (−)	Indicates the beginning of a field to be skipped
0	Indicates the beginning of a field to be duplicated
12 (&)	Signifies the remaining positions of the field defined by the blank, 12, 11, or 0 codes
1	Used in combination with the above punches to designate alphabetic fields; otherwise, the card punch will be in numeric mode

enable the automatic shifting between modes while the keypunch is under control of a program card, the latter two codes are necessary.

The completed program card containing the desired control codes is wrapped around a magnetic cylinder referred to as the *program drum* (see Figure 3-4). This drum is then seated within the keypunch. The control punches on the program card are read by a set of spurlike (five-pointed) reading wheels referred to as *star-wheels* (see Figure 3-4). These wheels ride over the face of the program card, sense the control punches, and transmit them to a control unit which directs the 029's operation.

On the Model 029, there are two sets of four star-wheels each. The top set, reserved for program card format 1, rides above card rows 12, 11, 0, and 1. However, should the operator elect to place a second program card format on the same card, a second set of star-wheels is provided. This set would ride above card rows 4, 5, 6, and 7, where the second control format would be punched. Generally, this option is very rarely employed, as the common practice is to place only one control format on the program control card. Figure 3-4 illustrates the mounted program card, drum, and star-wheels. The functional control switch PROG SEL determines the program format that will be followed (see Figure 3-5). In its up position (ON), program format ONE is sensed from card rows 12, 11, 0, and 1. The downward setting, TWO, permits use of the second control format, with card rows 4, 5, 6, and 7 being read.

With the program control card correctly mounted in the 029 keypunch and the desired format chosen, two further conditions must be satisfied for use of the program card. First, the functional control switch AUTO SKIP DUP must be set in its ON (upward) position. In doing this, the keypunch is readied for operation under the control of a program card, and the selected set of star-wheels is activated. This switch's off (down) setting renders the program card and star-wheels inoperative.

Second, the star-wheels must be lowered until they touch the face of the program card. In their raised position, the star-wheels are inoperative, since they cannot sense any of the punches on the surface of the program card. The star-wheels are lowered to, or raised from, the surface of the card by means of a butterflylike switch—the *program control lever* (see Figure 3-2). It should be noted that, with the star-wheels lowered, the removal of the program card will dislodge the star-wheels from their mountings.

Self-study exercise 3-1

1. A _____ represents a commonly used input medium.

♦   ♦   ♦

punched card

2. To activate the keypunch, the _____ switch must be turned to POWER ON.

◆ ◆ ◆

main-line power

3. Data is punched onto a card _____.

◆ ◆ ◆

column by column

4. The four predetermined positions in the path of a card are _____, _____, _____, and _____.

◆ ◆ ◆

card hopper
punching station
reading station
card stacker

5. For data to be keypunched onto a card, the card must be positioned under the _____.

◆ ◆ ◆

punching station

6. To cause a card to be fed from the card hopper, the _____ key must be depressed.

◆ ◆ ◆

FEED

7. To seat a card correctly at the punching station, the _____ key must be depressed.

◆ ◆ ◆

REG

8. The REL key _____ a registered card from the reading or punching station.

♦ ♦ ♦

releases

9. Duplication requires the transfer of data from the card at the _____ to the card at the _____ .

♦ ♦ ♦

reading station
punching station

10. Cards at the reading and punching stations move _____ during duplication.

♦ ♦ ♦

simultaneously

11. To perform the operation of duplication, the _____ key is depressed.

♦ ♦ ♦

DUP

12. Should the operator decide to back up to a specific column on a card undergoing punching, the _____ tab is used.

♦ ♦ ♦

BACKSPACE

13. The column indicator arrow indicates the card column _____ .

♦ ♦ ♦

into which data will be punched

14. Control keys are distinguished from character keys by their _____ color.

♦ ♦ ♦

blue

15. The keyboard's two operating modes are _____ and _____.

♦ ♦ ♦

alphabetic
numeric

16. Normal operating mode of the keyboard is _____. To switch from alphabetic mode to numeric mode, the operator must depress the _____ key.

♦ ♦ ♦

alphabetic
NUMERIC

17. If more than one set of characters is to be punched into one card column, the _____ key is depressed while the desired character keys are being depressed.

♦ ♦ ♦

MULT PCH (multiple punch)

18. Functional control switches are used to control _____.

♦ ♦ ♦

the operations of the keypunch

19. To remove all cards from the reading and punching stations of the keypunch, the _____ switch is used.

♦ ♦ ♦

CLEAR

20. Using the LZ PRINT switch, the keypunched data 00200 would be printed atop the card as _____.

♦ ♦ ♦

bb200 (where b indicates a blank space)

21. With the AUTO FEED switch ON, as a card is released from the punching station, a second card is _____ at the punching station, and a third card is _____ from the card hopper.

◆ ◆ ◆

seated
fed

22. The PRINT switch (will/will not) affect the feeding of cards.

◆ ◆ ◆

will not

23. The _____ and _____ switches are used in conjunction with the program control card.

◆ ◆ ◆

PROG SEL (program select)
AUTO SKIP DUP (automatic skip duplication)

24. The program control card is designed to _____ the keypunch operator.

◆ ◆ ◆

assist

25. Using the program control card, the operator can perform numerous tasks on the keypunch, namely, _____ .

◆ ◆ ◆

automatically duplicate data from card to card, automatically skip between data fields, switch between operating keyboard modes, automatically position the card at the first column of a data field

26. Using a program control card, the operator can _____ the entire keypunch's operation.

◆ ◆ ◆

affect

27. Using a program control card, the keypunch operator can devote his full attention to _____.

◆ ◆ ◆

reading data from the source document and keying the data onto the keyboard correctly

28. Control information is conveyed on the program control card as _____.

◆ ◆ ◆

a series of predefined punches

29. When the keypunch is under the control of the program control card, the keyboard is set in _____ mode.

◆ ◆ ◆

numeric

30. The code punched into the program control card and used to shift the keyboard to numeric mode, while under program card control, is a(n) _____.

◆ ◆ ◆

blank or no punches

31. The remaining four program control card codes with their functions are _____, _____, _____, and _____.

◆ ◆ ◆

12 punch—defines the size of a field
11 punch—permits automatic skipping between fields
0 punch—controls automatic duplication of data
1 punch—shifts the keyboard to alphanumeric mode

32. Before the program control card can be used, it must be wrapped around the _____.

◆ ◆ ◆

program drum

33. When placed around the program drum, the program control card is read by four _____ which pass over the _____ of the card.

◆ ◆ ◆

star-wheels
surface

34. The star-wheels may be _____ , where they are inoperative, or _____ to their operational position.

◆ ◆ ◆

raised
lowered

35. Before the program drum can be removed, the star-wheels must be _____ .

◆ ◆ ◆

raised

36. Using the PROG SEL switch, the operator may select between two _____ .

◆ ◆ ◆

program formats

37. The second program control card format utilizes rows _____ of the program control card.

◆ ◆ ◆

4, 5, 6, and 7

The manner in which the operator utilizes the keypunch will dictate how cards are fed to the punching station. If, for example, a large quantity of cards require punching, the operator would probably favor the automatic feeding of cards. But, should only a few cards require punching, the operator may elect to manually control the keypunch and individually feed cards as they are needed. In either case, once a card is seated at the punching station, keypunching may begin.

Card Feeding and Insertion

At the punching station

As we stated previously, for cards to be automatically fed to the punching station, the AUTO FEED control switch must be set ON. In addition, to permit the automatic feeding of cards, the 029 requires that two cards be initially fed to the punching station. This is accomplished by depressing the FEED key twice. The first card will be directly seated, or *registered,* beneath the punching station while the second card is held in an *unregistered* position awaiting its placement at the punching station. That is, when the FEED is depressed the first time, a card advances from the card hopper to the unregistered position just before the punching station. When the FEED key is depressed the second time, the first card advances from its unregistered position and is registered at the punching station, while the second card is fed from the card hopper to the unregistered position just before the punching station. Figure 3-6 depicts the card's movement to the punching station.

At this point, data may be keypunched onto only the first, or registered, card. When the keypunching of this card has been completed, the card may then be released from the punching station by simply depressing the REL key. The depressing of this key causes three actions to occur simultaneously: (1) the first card is released from the punching station and registered at the reading station; (2) the second (unregistered) card is registered beneath the punching station; and, (3) a new card is fed from the card hopper and placed in an unregistered position.

Data may now be keyed onto the card just registered at the punching station. By utilizing the keypunch in this manner, a steady stream of cards may be punched without the keypunch operator having to both feed and register each of the cards.

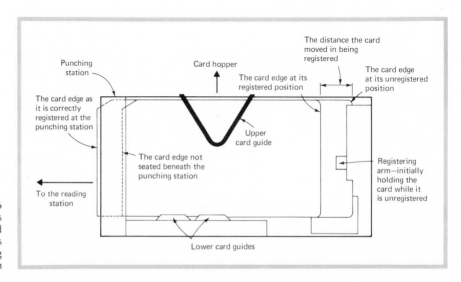

Figure 3-6
The Punch Card in Its Registered and Unregistered Positions as It Enters the Punching Station

In some cases, however, it is desirable to manually feed cards through the keypunch. In such cases, the AUTO FEED switch is turned off (down position). Individual cards must now be fed and registered as needed by the operator. Thus, while the keypunch is being operated manually, he may exercise more direct control over the movement of the card.

In order to manually register a card at the punching station, both the FEED and REG keys must be utilized. The depressing of the FEED key will cause *one* card to advance from the card hopper to its unregistered position, prior to the punching station. Momentarily depressing the REG key will now cause *only* this card to be registered at the punching station and *no* other card to be fed from the card hopper. Once this single card is registered at the punching station, the keypunching operator may proceed as previously described.

One of the major reasons for manually feeding cards through the keypunch is that this process facilitates the keying of additional data into a card into which information has previously been punched. To accomplish this

1. The card, into which the additional data is to be punched, is inserted behind the card guides until the left (column-1) edge of the card just touches the punching station (see Figure 3-6). Thus, the card is manually placed in an unregistered position.
2. Depression of the REG key will cause the 029 to correctly seat or register the card at the punching station.
3. The operator may now space to the desired card column and key in the additional data. It should be noted that during this operation no cards need be fed from the card hopper.

Quite frequently, the computer operator is faced with a different problem. While processing a computer program, he may be required to duplicate a portion of or an entire card. Through manual control of the Model 029, utilizing the capabilities of the reading station, the operator can eliminate the necessity of having to rekeypunch an entire card. Instead, this type of task may be completed in the following manner: **At the reading station**

1. Place an unpunched card in the unregistered position prior to the punching station. This is accomplished by either depressing the FEED key or manually inserting a card behind the card guides. (See Figure 3-7.)
2. Place the card containing the data to be duplicated in an unregistered position at the reading station. That is, the card to be duplicated is inserted through the plastic slot provided until its left (column-1) edge just touches the reading station (see Figure 3-7).

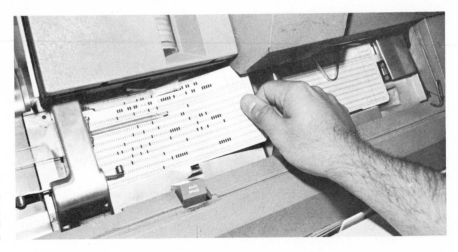

Figure 3-7
Cards Inserted at Both
the Reading and
Punching Stations

3. Depress the REG key. Both cards will be properly registered at the punching and reading stations, respectively.
4. Depress the space bar as necessary until the cards are positioned at the first of the columns to be duplicated.
5. Depress the DUP key for the desired number of card columns. The operator can duplicate the entire card or up to a given card column. Should the operator elect to key in new data after "duping" a few columns, the keyboard is used in the normal manner.
6.[1] Depress the REL key. The original data card will advance from the reading station but *will not* move to the card stacker. The duplicated card advances from the punching station, but will not be registered at the reading station. *No* cards will be fed from the card hopper.
7.[1] Depress the REG key. This will cause the original data card to enter the card stacker and register the duplicated card at the reading station.
8.[1] Repeat steps 5 and 6 to remove the duplicated card from the reading station.

This sequence of steps is also used when a master card, containing data to be duplicated on a series of successive cards, must be inserted at the 029's reading station. After properly registering the master card at the reading station, the duplicating operation can commence.

[1]These combined steps may be replaced by lifting the CLEAR switch.

Prior to commencing keypunching, the operator should determine whether an adequate supply of cards exists within the card hopper. It is usually a good idea to place a sufficient number of cards in the card hopper before initiating a keypunching operation. It is important that cards be properly placed in the card hopper, as cards that are haphazardly or sloppily loaded may result in *card jams*. Card jams, resulting from the improper feeding of cards, will render the keypunch unusable as the card(s), in general, will not be properly seated at either the punching or the reading station.

At the card hopper

The operator can reduce the possibility of such machine stoppages resulting from the improper feeding of cards by adhering to the following simple procedure:

1. Remove a handful of cards from their shipping carton or card storage rack.
2. Examine this group of cards, discarding all cards that are unserviceable, damaged, bent, etc.
3. Fan and joggle the remaining cards, thereby removing any static electricity and aligning the cards (see Figure 3-8).
4. After loading these cards, feed one card to the punching station, ensuring that at least the first few cards are feeding correctly.

When a card jam does occur, it is sometimes necessary for the computer operator to rectify this problem. For this reason, we shall now discuss some operational troubleshooting techniques which will prove useful on the Model 029.

Figure 3-8
The Fanning, Joggling, and Aligning of Punched Cards Prior to Their Insertion into the Card Hopper

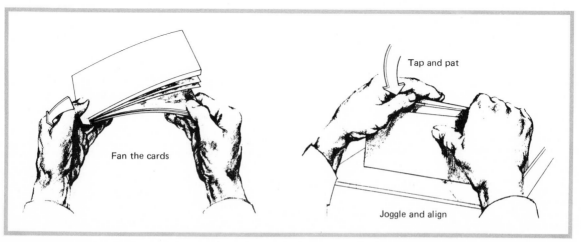

Fan the cards

Tap and pat

Joggle and align

Self-study exercise 3-2

1. Cards may be fed by the operator either _____ or _____ . (The manner of card feeding is determined by the operator.)

◆ ◆ ◆

automatically
manually

2. To permit the automatic feeding of cards, the _____ switch must be set to ON.

◆ ◆ ◆

AUTO FEED

3. When a card is correctly seated beneath the punching station, the card is said to be _____ .

◆ ◆ ◆

registered

4. Depression of the FEED key will advance a card from the card hopper and place it in a(n) _____ position, awaiting registering at the punching station.

◆ ◆ ◆

unregistered

5. With the 029 under manual mode, a card may be placed in an unregistered position at the punching station by sliding the card _____ at the punching station.

◆ ◆ ◆

behind the card guides

6. Employing the automatic feeding option requires that two cards be _____ fed to the punching station.

◆ ◆ ◆

initially

7. The _____ key is used to free a card from the punching station.

♦ ♦ ♦

REL (release)

8. Under manual operation and depressing the REL key, a card (will/will not) be fed from the card hopper.

♦ ♦ ♦

will not

9. With the 029 in manual use, to release a card from the punching station to the reading station or to release a card to the card stacker, the _____ and _____ keys are hit.

♦ ♦ ♦

REL (release)
REG (register)

10. To manually duplicate a card, the data card to be duplicated must be inserted at the _____ and a blank card inserted at the _____.

♦ ♦ ♦

reading station
punching station

11. To duplicate data in a series of consecutive card columns, the _____ key is held down.

♦ ♦ ♦

DUP (duplicate)

12. To manually duplicate data, cards at the reading and punching stations must be _____.

♦ ♦ ♦

registered

13. With manual duplication, the operator may elect to "dup" _____,
_____, or _____ .

♦ ♦ ♦

an entire card
only a portion of a card
a portion of card, followed by newly keyed-in data

14. Before commencing any keypunching, the operator should check the
_____ of cards in the card hopper.

♦ ♦ ♦

number

15. When cards are carelessly handled and placed in the card hopper, a(n)
_____ may result.

♦ ♦ ♦

card jam

16. Cards being placed within the 029's card hopper should always be
_____, thereby aligning the cards and removing _____ .

♦ ♦ ♦

fanned and joggled
static electricity

Handling Machine Stoppages The Model 029 keypunch is a fairly reliable and dependable machine. Considering the extent of its use, the 029's durability is truly remarkable. When difficulty is encountered within the Model 029, it is normally in the form of a card jam. In general, jams are of a variety that the operator should be able to handle easily. On the other hand, it is possible that a card, or pieces of a card, will become tightly wedged beneath the punching station. This case may require the operator to spend several minutes in removing the jammed card. It is, therefore, important that we discuss how some of the more common card jams should be handled.

Card jams Card jams will generally occur at the punching or reading station. In such cases punched cards become wedged within the particular station and block the path of subsequent cards.

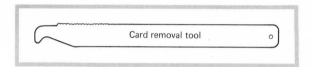

Figure 3-9
The Card Removal Tool

When a card jam is noticed by the operator, no additional cards should be fed since this will only further complicate the situation. Instead, the operator should immediately attempt to remove the jammed card(s) by hand, paying careful attention not to tear any of these cards. Quite often, however, in spite of the degree of care exercised, the jammed card will tear, and a portion of the card will remain lodged under that station. A metal slide, called a *card removal tool,* shown in Figure 3-9, can be utilized to free the pieces of the wedged card. The hooked tip of this tool will prove to be useful when dislodging the bits of cards stuck beneath the blocked station. Upon clearing the station, a few cards should be fed to it, ensuring that cards may freely pass through it, before the actual keypunching operation is resumed.

Stoppages may also occur as cards are initially fed from the card hopper. In these stoppages, however, the card becomes wedged at the point where it leaves the hopper. Once again, the operator should attempt to remove the card without tearing it. If it is not possible to clear the card, the operator should:

1. Remove the faceplate which shields the card hopper.
2. Lift the RELEASE lever which will enable the easy removal of any jammed cards. (See Figure 3-10.)
3. Check the cards remaining for damage, and reseat them in the card hopper.
4. Feed one or more cards to the punching station.

The card jam represents one form of machine stoppage. In some cases, however, the problem is not so easily diagnosed. In these cases, the keypunch will simply appear to react erratically while being used. Should the operator become aware of this type of situation, he should first make certain that the keypunch is being used properly. The "apparent" malfunction of the keypunch represents the second most frequent form of machine stoppage.

The above use of the word *apparent* is deliberate. Frequently, the keypunch will not react in the manner expected. Initially it might appear as if the keypunch is malfunctioning, but after a more careful investigation, we often find that the operator has not properly prepared the keypunch for use. In particular, this situation arises quite frequently when the keypunch is operating under the control of a program card.

Apparent malfunctions

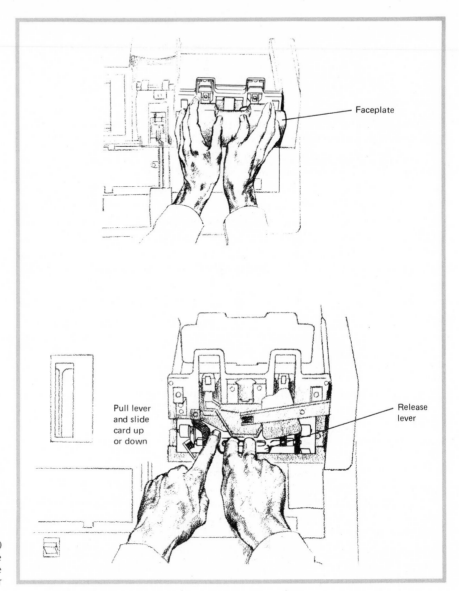

Faceplate

Pull lever
and slide
card up
or down

Release
lever

Figure 3-10
Removal of the Faceplate
and Raising the Release
Lever

When it is reported that a keypunch is acting erratically under control of a program card, the operator should:

1. Ensure that the program card is correctly wrapped around the program drum and that no bumps, creases, or wrinkles exist.
2. Check all the functional control switches. The AUTO FEED,

AUTO SKIP DUP, and PROG SEL switches must be correctly positioned.

3. Ensure that the star-wheels are lowered to the surface of the card. Also, count the number of star-wheels in each set. Often a star-wheel is unseated when the program drum is removed improperly.

4. Ensure that the program drum is seated directly atop its spindle.

Generally, correcting one of the conditions in the outlined steps will return the keypunch to normal operation.

When attempting to correct a reported malfunction, the operator should initially examine all functional control switches. With the keypunch *not* under program card control, it may simply be that a misset switch has caused the apparent malfunction. By simply resetting the switch, the operator can correct the error condition.

If, after performing these initial checks, the operator is unable to return the keypunch to its normal operating state, no further repairs of any type should be attempted. Instead, the operations manager or manufacturer's service representative should be contacted and alerted to the problem.

Self-study exercise 3-3

1. When a card jam occurs, it is usually at the _____ .

◆ ◆ ◆

punching and reading stations

2. After noting the stoppage, the operator should attempt to _____ .

◆ ◆ ◆

remove the jammed cards by hand

3. If, after step 2 above, a portion of a card remains wedged under the station, a(n) _____ is used to remove the wedged pieces.

◆ ◆ ◆

card removal tool

4. In addition to stoppages which occur at the reading and punching stations, stoppage may also occur at the _____ .

◆ ◆ ◆

card hopper

5. In order to clear a card jammed at the card hopper, the operator should first attempt to _____ .

♦ ♦ ♦

remove the card by hand

6. If the jammed card cannot be easily removed from the card hopper by hand, the operator should _____ and lift the _____ .

♦ ♦ ♦

remove the hopper's faceplate
feed spring

7. Before using the program control card feature, the operator should ensure that _____ , _____ , _____ , and _____ .

♦ ♦ ♦

the star-wheels are lowered
each set of star-wheels consists of four wheels
the functional control switches are correctly set
the program drum is properly seated atop its spindle

Verification of Punched Data   There always exists the possibility that errors may occur during the keypunching operation. These errors can be the result of the operator's being distracted and striking the wrong key or simply the result of the operator's incorrectly reading the source document. If such an error should occur and is detected by the keypunch operator, a new correct card could be immediately punched and the old card destroyed. However, many errors occur during keypunching of which the operator is unaware. To check for such errors visually would be both an extremely costly and a time-consuming task. Therefore, a device was developed to facilitate this operation mechanically. This device is referred to as a *verifier*. An example of an IBM 059 Card Reader, a verifier, is shown in Figure 3-11.

The IBM 059 verifier is very similar in appearance and method of use to the 029 keypunch. Both devices have the same card path, feed cards from a card hopper, store completed cards in a card stacker, and employ their respective keyboards in the same manner. The major operational difference between these devices lies in the fact that the keypunch is used to punch data, whereas the verifier is used to check the accuracy of previously punched data.

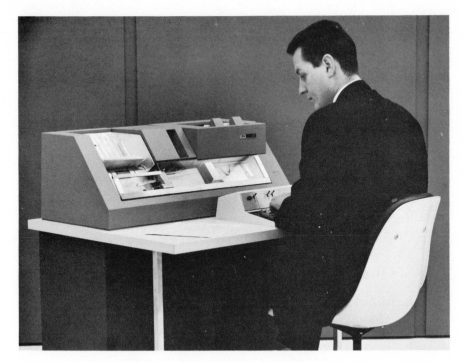

Figure 3-11
IBM 059 Verifier in Use

As a result, the 059 and 029 are internally constructed differently. The verifier has a series of 12 *sensing pins* (not punch knives) that are used to read data that has been *previously* punched onto a card. As characters are keyed in, column by column via the verifier's keyboard, the verification process compares these keyed-in impulses against the data contained on the original card and being sensed by the sensing brushes. In essence, we are duplicating the original keypunching operation, since the same source document is being used and the same data is being keyed. The only difference is that *no* punching is actually taking place. The verifier merely *compares* the data that was originally punched into the card against the data currently being keyed in.

If no errors are sensed, a notch is placed in the right (column-80) edge of the card, between the 0 and 1 rows. (See Figure 3-12.)

When an error is detected, the verifier alerts the operator by lighting an indicator lamp and preventing further data from being keyed. The character in the indicated card column, thought of as being incorrect, is keyed in twice more. This procedure ensures that the operator performing the verifying operation has not made the error (i.e., a mis-hit key or data keyed into the wrong column). After the third unsuccessful attempt at verifying the character on the source-punched card, a notch is placed above

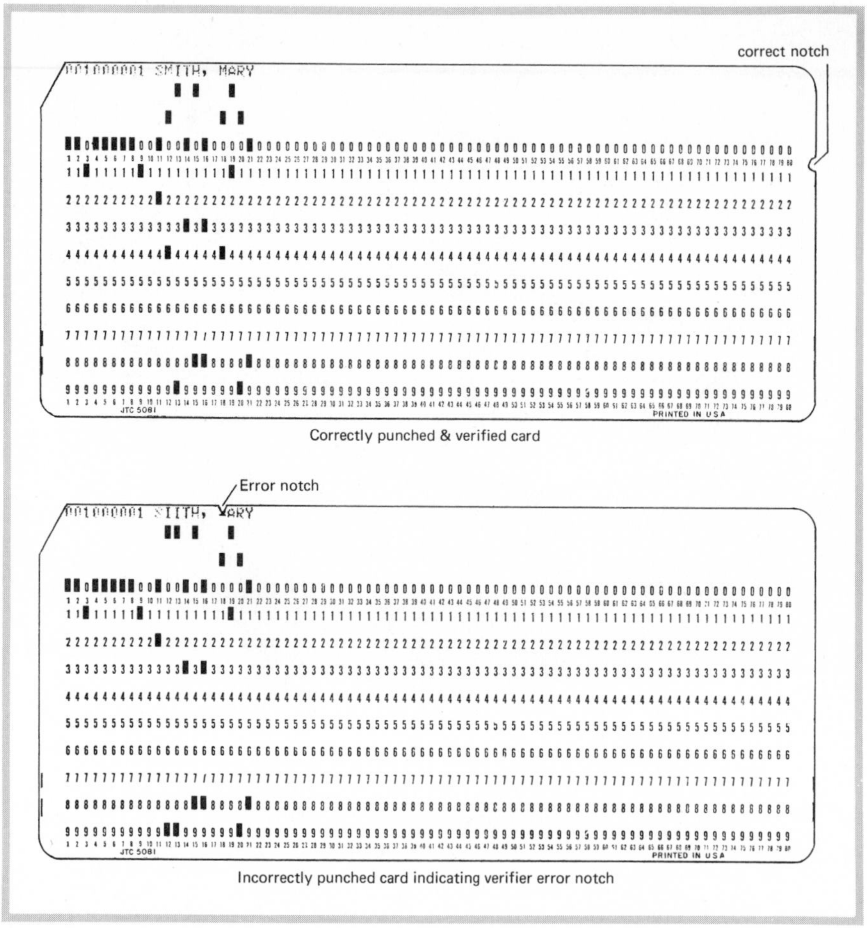

Figure 3-12
Correctly and Incorrectly
Verified Punched Cards

the 12 row in the card column in which the error exists (see Figure 3-12). This verification process is repeated for each column of the card. Should an irreconcilable error have occurred in any card column, the card is then set aside and subsequently rekeypunched.

It is good practice not to have the same operator keypunch and verify the same set of data cards. The operator would be prone to make the identical mistake twice (once during keypunching and once in verifying the data).

The IBM 059 verifier is subject to the same type of operational difficulties as the 029 keypunch. Thus, card jams, as well as any problems inherent in use of a program control card, would be handled in the same way on the verifier as they were on the keypunch.

Self-study exercise 3-4

1. Verification is performed to _____ the accuracy of keypunched data.

   ◆ ◆ ◆

   check

2. The verifier uses _____, not punch knives.

   ◆ ◆ ◆

   sensing pins

3. Whereas the keypunch punches data onto a card, the verifier _____ the data already on the card.

   ◆ ◆ ◆

   senses or reads

4. The punches sensed on the card, during verification, are _____ against the data being keyed _____.

   ◆ ◆ ◆

   compared
   column by column

5. If no errors are detected on a card after verification, a notch is placed _____. If an error is noted, a notch is placed _____.

   ◆ ◆ ◆

   on the column-80 edge of the card, between rows 0 and 1
   in the card column where the error was detected, above the
   12 row

6. After detection of an error, the operator should rekey the data _____.

   ◆ ◆ ◆

   twice more

7. Verification (should/should not) be performed by the same operator that keypunched the original deck of cards.

◆ ◆ ◆

should not

Other Card Punch Units

The IBM 129 card data recorder

The IBM 129 Card Data Recorder (Figure 3-13) is a multifunction device in that it serves as both a keypunch and verifier in the same physical unit. The significant difference between the 129 and 029 is not a visible one. The 129 has an internal storage capability; the 029 does not. Each of the 129's two storage units (Input and Output storage) has a capacity to store 80 characters of data. During keypunching, these storage units are used as follows:

1. Data keyed from the source document is stored magnetically in input storage. The column indicator notes the input storage position into which the next character is to be placed.
2. If a character is keyed incorrectly, the machine is backspaced, and the correct character keyed in. Thus, the incorrect magnetic character image is replaced, within input storage, by the new character image.

Figure 3-13
The IBM 129 Card Data
Recorder

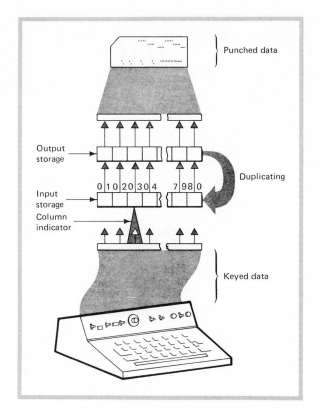

Punched data

Output storage

Duplicating

Input storage

0 10 20 30 4   7 98 0

Column indicator

Keyed data

Figure 3-14
The Keypunching Process
Used on the IBM 129

3.   When all data for the given card has been correctly keyed, the data record is transferred from input storage to output storage, and the next card record can be keyed into input storage.

This process is depicted in Figure 3-14.

For the duplication of cards, data stored at output storage is transferred to input storage. The duplicate card is then punched, using the normal keypunching sequence.

For verification, the card to be verified is physically read into input storage. The data that is then keyed in is compared with that data already kept in input storage. If an error is found, it may be easily corrected within input storage and using the corrected format, a new card may immediately be punched.

The Model 129 is controlled through use of the keyboard and functional control switches illustrated in Figure 3-15. Though the keyboard and control switches are used in a manner similar to that of the Model 029, there are some noteworthy operating differences.

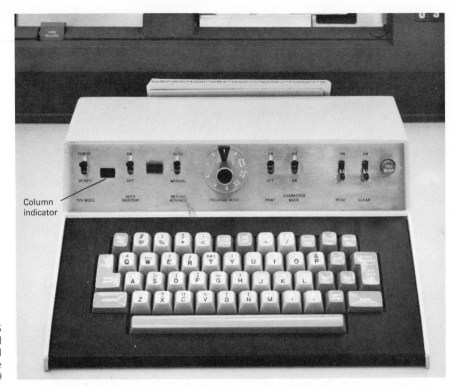

Figure 3-15
The Keyboard and
Functional Control
Switches Available on the
IBM 129

Using the PUNCH/VERIFY switch, the operator may select the 129's mode of operation. Its up position, PUNCH, renders the Model 129 a keypunch, while in the down setting, VERIFY, the 129 is employed as a verifier. The column indicator, acting as a digital counter, denotes the card column into which data is to be punched.

When the *PROGRAM MODE* dial is set on 0, the Model 129 is controlled via the keyboard and switches. On the mode dial, settings 1 to 6 are set aside for storing up to six program control card formats. Since the 129 does not have a program drum, the desired program control card formats must be read in and stored. The operator may then select from six different formats stored within the 129. The PROGRAM MODE dial is used with the keyboard's PROG SEL key to accomplish this selection.

For further details of operation, the operator should consult the Model 129 operating manual.

The UNIVAC 1701 verifying punch (VP)

As its name implies, the UNIVAC 1701 VP (Figure 3-16) is also a multifunction device, serving as both a keypunch and a verifier. The internal storage component of the 1701, called *core storage,* is composed of three units: program storage, data input storage, and data output storage. Each of these units has a capacity to magnetically store 80 columns of data.

For keypunching, data keyed into data input storage is transferred to data output storage and subsequently punched onto a card. Errors made during the keying operation are corrected by backspacing to the appropriate data column and rekeying the correct characters. The new character images merely overlay the old images, destroying them.

Verifying and duplicating operations are performed using the UNIVAC's core storage units. The 1701's method of performing both these operations is similar to that of the IBM 129. The 1701 may be placed under control of a program card. However, only *one* format, stored within the program storage unit, may be retained in the device at a time.

The major difference in operation of the UNIVAC 1701, when compared to the IBM 129, is the use of its keyboard. Whereas the IBM 129's

Figure 3-16
The UNIVAC 1701
Verifying Punch (VP) and
Its Keyboard

keyboard is normally in alphabetic mode, the UNIVAC 1701 keyboard's normal operating mode is numeric. This difference may cause some confusion in an installation where a keypunch operator will be called upon to use both units.

For the complete list of operating procedures, consult the UNIVAC 1701 operating instructions manual.

Self-study exercise 3-5

1. The IBM 129 and the UNIVAC 1701 VP are _____ devices. They can operate as either a(n) _____ or _____.

♦ ♦ ♦

multifunction
keypunch
verifier

2. A card is not punched on the IBM 129 until data is transferred to _____.

♦ ♦ ♦

output storage

3. For the Model 129, the operator may select from _____ possible program card formats.

♦ ♦ ♦

six

4. On the Model 129, the PROG SEL key is found on the machine's _____, while on the IBM 029 the program-select option is exercised through a(n) _____.

♦ ♦ ♦

keyboard
functional control switch

5. The core storage capacity of the UNIVAC 1701 is composed of _____ units, namely, _____.

♦ ♦ ♦

three
program storage, data input storage, and data output storage

6. To correct an error on the UNIVAC 1701 or IBM 129, the operator _____ to the desired column and _____ the corrected data.

◆ ◆ ◆

backspaces
keys in

True-false exercise

1. The names *card punch machine* and *keypunch* are used interchangeably.
2. Data is keypunched into a card row by row.
3. Data can only be punched into the card positioned beneath the punching station.
4. The DUP key is used to initiate keypunching.
5. The BACKSPACE tab is employed to return to a previous card column.
6. All keyboard keys on the IBM 029 Card Punch are gray in color.
7. The PRINT switch is used when only numbers are to be printed.
8. Each code punched into a program control card has a predefined meaning.
9. The program drum may be removed with the star-wheels lowered.
10. When a card has been properly seated at the punching or reading station, it is said to have been registered.
11. The IBM 059 verifier is similar in outward appearance to the IBM 029 keypunch.
12. A correctly verified card has a notch in card column 1.
13. The same operator should be used to verify a group of punched cards that keypunched them.

Fill-in exercise

1. In a computer system, the punched card is a commonly used _____ medium in processing large volumes of data.
2. To feed a card from the card hopper, the _____ is depressed.
3. Duplication requires the transfer of data from the _____ to the _____.
4. The operating keyboard modes are _____ and _____.
5. Control of the 029 is accomplished through use of the _____.
6. To suppress the printing of unwanted leading zeros in a numeric field, the _____ switch is used.
7. The program card codes consist of _____, _____, _____, and _____ punches.
8. Star-wheels must be _____ to the surface of the card before they can be used.

9. Cards should be _____ prior to their placement in the 029's card hopper.
10. Card jams may result when cards become _____ beneath the punching or reading station.
11. The verifier is used to _____ previously punched cards.
12. Both the IBM 129 and UNIVAC 1701 use internal magnetic _____ units, to facilitate their multipurpose functioning.
13. Corrections are made on the IBM 129 or UNIVAC 1701 by rekeying data into their respective magnetic _____ storage area.

Multiple-choice exercise

1. The complete path of the card is composed of
   a. card hopper, punching and reading stations
   b. punching and reading stations, card stacker
   c. card hopper, reading station, card stacker
   d. card hopper, card stacker, punching station
   e. none of the above
2. During duplication, cards at the reading and punching station will move
   a. one card at a time
   b. with the card at the reading station moving first
   c. simultaneously
   d. with the card at the punching station moving first
   e. none of the above
3. The column indicator notes
   a. the column into which data was punched
   b. the column into which data will be punched
   c. the column to be moved to for punching
   d. all the above
   e. none of the above
4. The MULT PCH key is used when
   a. two cards are to be punched at once
   b. more than one character's code is punched in a given card column
   c. a code is to be punched in consecutive columns
   d. punching codes into successive card columns
   e. none of the above
5. The program card is used to
   a. ease the operator's task
   b. control the overall operation of the keypunch
   c. duplicate cards
   d. a and b
   e. none of the above
6. Two switches that are only used in conjunction with the program card are

    a. CLEAR and PROG SEL
    b. AUTO SKIP DUP and PRINT
    c. PRINT and CLEAR
    d. PRINT and AUTO FEED
    e. AUTO SKIP DUP and PROG SEL

7. Star-wheels read
    a. data keyed into the keypunch
    b. data from the reading station
    c. data from the card wrapped around the program drum
    d. data on the program card passed beneath the reading station
    e. none of the above

8. A card may be placed in an unregistered position
    a. manually
    b. by depressing the FEED key
    c. by depressing the REL key, with the AUTO FEED switch ON
    d. all the above
    e. none of the above

9. When the IBM 029 acts erratically under control of the program control card, the operator should
    a. check the star-wheels
    b. check the functional control switches
    c. ensure that the drum is correctly seated
    d. all the above
    e. none of the above

10. Card jams
    a. never occur on the IBM 029
    b. represent a form of machine stoppage
    c. occur quite frequently on the IBM 029
    d. *a* and *b*
    e. *b* and *c*

11. The IBM 129 and the UNIVAC 1701 can
    a. verify cards
    b. punch cards
    c. duplicate cards
    d. all the above
    e. none of the above

Discussion questions

1. Discuss the procedure used to insert a card at
    a. the punching station.
    b. the reading and punching stations.
2. List the program control card codes and their purposes.

3. List and discuss three reasons why the keypunch might malfunction while under control of the program control card.
4. Briefly discuss the operator technique for handling card jams at the punching station and at the card hopper.
5. Discuss those characteristics common to the IBM 129 and UNIVAC 1701.

OTHER UNIT RECORD MACHINES

CHAPTER 4

Classifying and Arranging Data

Sorter

Collator

IBM 85 collator

IBM 87 collator

IBM 88 collator

Accounting Machine

Operational capabilities

IBM 402 accounting machine

IBM 403 and 419 accounting machines

IBM 407 accounting machine

End-of-chapter Exercises

Thus far, we have discussed the punch card and its use in an automatic data processing system. We learned in Chapter 2 that the development of the punch card by Dr. Herman Hollerith was accompanied by machines designed to create and process these cards—*unit record machines.* This chapter will be devoted to a discussion of machines of this type. This chapter will also include a brief introduction to basic wiring principles. A knowledge of these fundamentals will facilitate the learning of more complex wiring techniques from manufacturers' supplied reference manuals.

Introduction

Unit record machines include a series of data processing devices which utilize the punched card medium. These machines derive their name from the fact that they utilize punched cards which contain a single but complete record, a *unit record* of data. Although varying in appearance and function, all unit record machines share the use of the punched card as the basic medium for data storage. As you will see later in this chapter, these machines perform a wide variety of operations. Together, these machines constitute a unit record data processing system which enables businesses to electromechanically produce reports, payroll checks, invoices, and other documents.

Unit record machines represent a large advance in data processing capability over their predecessors, the manually operated calculating machines. Unlike these key-driven calculating machines, unit record machines are able to continuously read punched cards and perform repetitive operations with a minimum of manual intervention.

Some unit record machines, such as the calculator and accounting machine, are called EAM (Electrical Accounting Machine) equipment. The term *EAM systems* is often used to describe data processing systems which process data directly from punched cards.

Despite the great increases in the use of electronic computers, there are still certain areas where unit record equipment is practical as well as economical. The machines which we shall discuss in this chapter are principally used to complement a computer system or are employed by smaller companies that cannot justify a computer system.

There are three basic classifications of tasks which can be handled by a unit record system:

1. Recording data
2. Classifying or arranging data
3. Summarizing and printing data

The recording of data has been discussed in Chapter 1. Recording is accomplished with the aid of a card punch machine and checked on the verifier. The classifying or arranging of data can be done on the sorter or the collator. The summarizing and printing is accomplished on the calculator or accounting machine.

Unit record

Card punches

Verifiers

Sorters

Interpreters

Reproducers

Collators

Accounting machines

Figure 4-1
Various Unit Record
Machines

In addition to these major tasks, there are several machines that perform auxiliary functions which are not always essential to the system's output but which can save a great deal of human effort. These are the reproducer, which can duplicate or copy punched cards, and the interpreter, which translates holes previously punched onto a card into printed information on the face of that card.

Self-study exercise 4-1

1. Machines designed to create and process punched cards are referred to as _____ machines.

◆ ◆ ◆

unit record

2. A punched card is also referred to as a(n) _____.

◆ ◆ ◆

unit record

3. A major advantage of unit record machines over their predecessors, the manually operated calculating machines, is _____.

◆ ◆ ◆

their ability to continuously read punched cards and perform repetitive operations with a minimum of manual intervention

4. The term _____ is often used to describe data processing systems which process data directly from punched cards.

◆ ◆ ◆

EAM (Electrical Accounting Machine) system

5. The _____ basic tasks handled by unit record systems are _____.

◆ ◆ ◆

three classifications of
recording data, classifying or arranging data, and summarizing and printing data

6. The classifying or arranging of data can be accomplished using either the _____ or the _____ .

♦ ♦ ♦

sorter
collator

7. Summarizing and printing is accomplished on the _____ .

♦ ♦ ♦

calculator or electrical accounting machine

8. Machines that perform auxiliary functions which are not always essential to the system's output but which can save effort and time include _____ .

♦ ♦ ♦

the reproducer and the interpreter

9. The reproducer _____ punched cards while the interpreter _____ .

♦ ♦ ♦

duplicates or copies
translates holes punched into a card into printed information on the face of the card

Basic Principles of Unit Record Machine Operation Most unit record machines can perform more than a single function. However, each piece of equipment must be directed in the particular function it is to perform as well as in the manner in which the input data must be handled. As with a computer system, the method of handling data must be predetermined. The manner by which the programmer's instructions are conveyed to the particular unit record device will be discussed subsequently.

Read impulses With the exception of the card punch and verifier, operations performed on all unit record machines may be characterized as reading a card, performing an operation, and then reading another card. This is a continuous process until all the specified data cards have been read.

The reading of a punched card is performed mechanically as the card passes beneath a series of metal reading brushes and above a contact roller

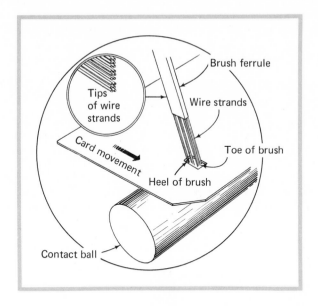

Figure 4-2
Punched Card Reading
Brushes

or through a *photoelectric unit*. As the card passes beneath the reading brushes, punched holes are sensed as the brush penetrates the hole and makes contact with the metal roller beneath the card. In the case of the photoelectric unit, punched holes are sensed as the light beam passes through the card to a light cell beneath the card. In both instances, the impulses produced represent characters punched into the card. A composite of the resulting electric impulses represents an image of the data punched into the card being read.

The impulses received are of a short duration, lasting only as long as the brushes remain in contact with the roller. In the absence of a hole, the circuit is not completed, and an impulse is not produced. Machines determine what character is punched by *timing*. For example, if a card were fed in with the 12 edge first and if a hole were punched in the 4 row, as shown in Figure 4-3, the impulse received would be a 4. If an impulse were received slightly later, it would be interpreted as a 5. The machine determines which hole was read by the amount of time that passed from the instant the leading edge passed under the brush until the brush dropped into a punched hole and produced the impulse.

Most machines contain 80 brushes, one brush for each column of a card, so that an entire card can be read on one pass through the machine. (See Figure 4-4.)

Machine cycle

All unit record machines perform their functions within a fixed period of time referred to as a *machine cycle*. During any given machine cycle, the

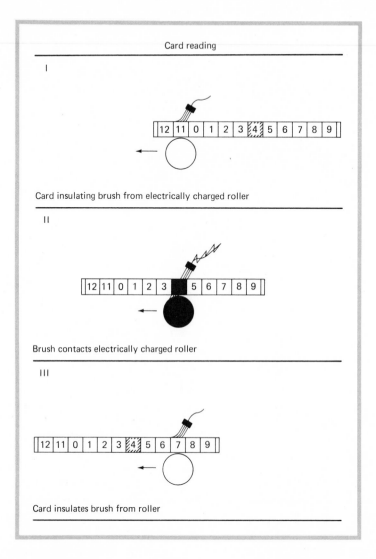

Figure 4-3
Schematic of Punched
Card Reading Process

machine moves completely through an operation. This includes the feeding of cards, reading in the read cycle, punching in the punch cycle, etc.

The specific operations which a machine can perform are controlled by its design and the electronic circuits wired into it. Many unit record machines offer increased flexibility of operation through the use of externally wired control panels. These panels allow the machine operator to control the internal circuitry of the machine and thereby alter the operation performed by the machine.

After the control panels are wired to perform the required operation,

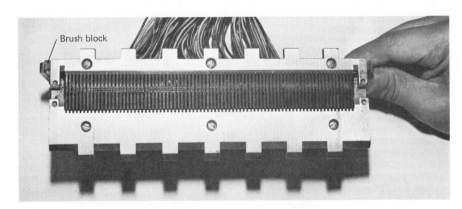

Brush block

Figure 4-4
An 80-column Brush
Assembly

they must be inserted into a special compartment in the machine, as shown in Figure 4-5.

There are two general types of control panels. One type has *metal jacks* that press against metal prongs in the machine, as in Figure 4-6*b*. The second type of control panel consists of *hubs* into which the external wires are inserted, as shown in Figure 4-6*a*. Both types of panel may be *fixed* or *manual*. Fixed control panels are wired with permanent wires, that is, wires which expand when inserted, making them impossible to remove without

Control panels

Figure 4-5
Control Panel Being
Inserted into Machine

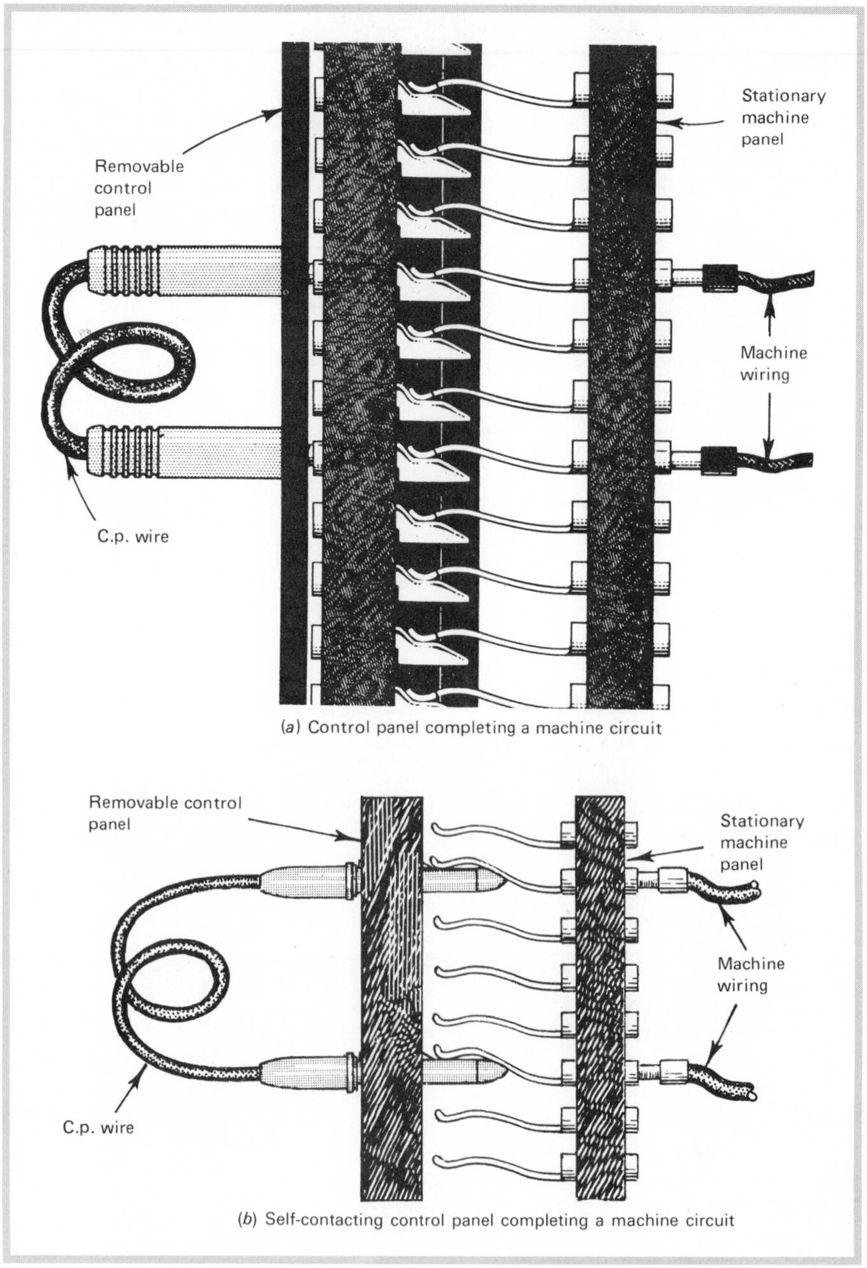

(a) Control panel completing a machine circuit

Removable control panel

C.p. wire

Stationary machine panel

Machine wiring

(b) Self-contacting control panel completing a machine circuit

Removable control panel

C.p. wire

Stationary machine panel

Machine wiring

Figure 4-6
Circuits Completed by
External Wiring

cutting off the end. These panels are used for jobs of a recurring nature that do not require alteration of the wiring. Manual control panels are wired with temporary wires that can be easily removed. We will refer to only manual panels for the remainder of this chapter. The wires used in this type panel are normally called *self-contacting wires* and fit into four basic types of hubs.

Hubs

Exit Hubs emit electric impulses from within the machine. Some exit impulses originate during the read cycle, while others are generated under specific conditions or at a particular time.

Entry Hubs accept electric impulses from one point on the panel to another. Some entry hubs are used primarily to accept card-generated impulses, and others accept impulses occurring at other than the read cycle.

Common Hubs are identified by a white line connecting the hubs on the control panel. These hubs are internally joined together. If they are exit hubs, the exit impulse is available at both hubs. If they are entry hubs, the impulse wired to one is sent into the machine and is available out of the other, making the common hub an exit.

Bus Hubs are internally connected to one another but not to an internal circuit. Any impulse plug into one hub is available out of all others. This is used primarily to avoid the necessity of splitting wires.

There are two other types of hubs you may encounter. Hubs that are connected by a straight arrow indicate that these two hubs are a switch—a method of turning on a particular device within the machine. When wired, the switch is ON. The other type of hub is shown with a curved arrow, as in Figure 4-7, which indicates that a switch is used via a *selector,* which will be discussed later in the chapter.

Wires

Electricity requires a path to follow. This path on a control panel is provided by external wires. Wires come in various lengths, each length designated

Figure 4-7
Switch Hubs

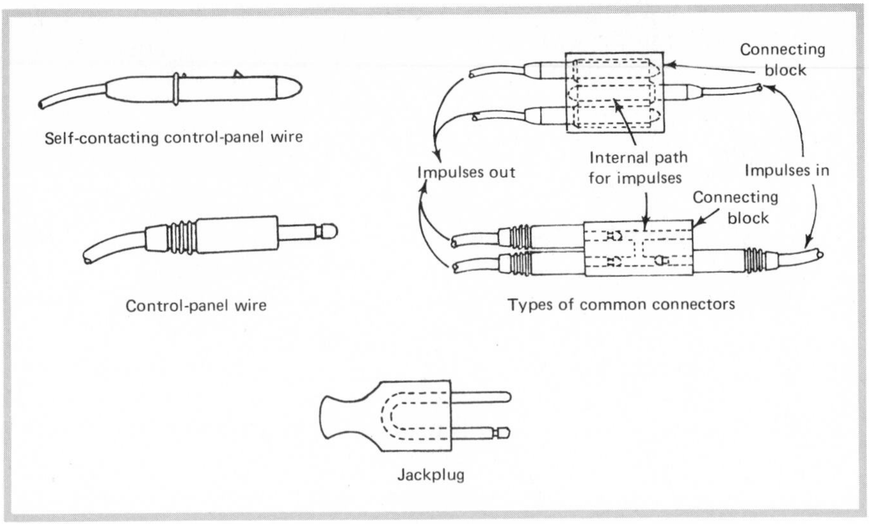

Figure 4-8
Control Panel Wires and
Wiring Aids

by a different color. The different lengths are provided for convenience of wiring and have no other significant meaning. There are two types of wires used: the one-way wire, which by the use of a *diode* allows electricity to pass in only the one direction indicated on the wire by an arrow, and the second and most commonly used wire, which allows an impulse to travel in either direction. If bus hubs are not available and if it is necessary to get several of the same impulses, common *connectors* are used. By placing a wire into one end of a connector, as shown in Figure 4-8, two may exit. In some instances, you may need to put two impulses together to form a third. As an example, a 12 impulse and a 2 impulse put into a connector would form an alphabetic B impulse.

When two adjacent hubs are to be connected, you may use a *jackplug* or any length wire. The shorter the wire, the neater and easier to follow the panel. The jackplug, as shown in Figure 4-8, is basically a short wire.

Diagraming conventions
Throughout this chapter, you will be exposed to control panel wiring diagrams. The following wiring conventions will be used. When wiring several hubs or a field from one point in a panel to another, the entire field should be connected by a single line as identified by 1 and 2 in Figure 4-9. Arrows indicate in which direction the impulses are traveling, identified by 3 in Figure 4-9. When it becomes necessary to cross a direction line, the line should be broken as identified by 4 in Figure 4-9. When a field carries from one line to another, a small half-circle is used to indicate that the remainder of the field is on the next line, identified by D in Figure

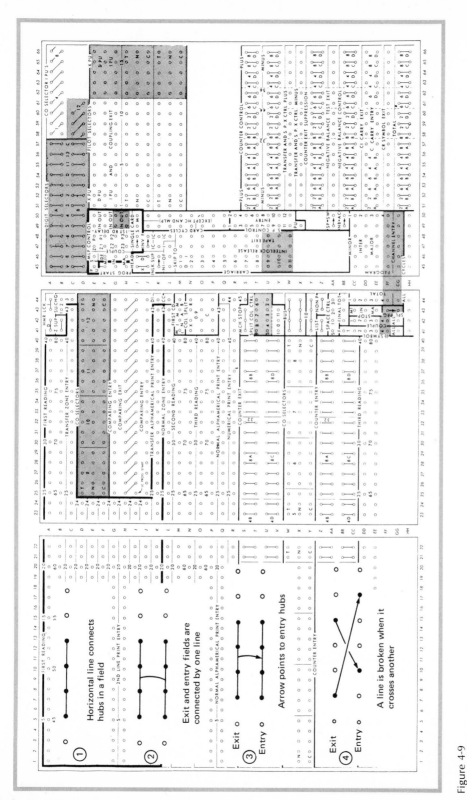

Figure 4-9
Diagraming Conventions
and a Typical Wiring
Diagram

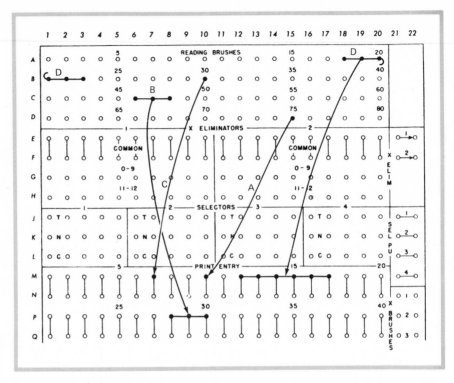

Figure 4-10
Wiring Diagram for
Printing Fields

4-10. You should place on the diagram exactly what is to be accomplished, for the diagram is the blueprint of what the control paneling must look like.

Self-study exercise 4-2

1. Most unit record machines are capable of performing _____ function.

♦   ♦   ♦

more than one

2. Unit record machines other than the card punch and verifier may be characterized by the operations of _____, _____, and _____.

♦   ♦   ♦

reading a card
performing an operation
reading another card

3. The reading of a punched card may be accomplished as the card passes under a(n) _____ or through a(n) _____ unit.

◆   ◆   ◆

series of wire brushes
photoelectric

4. Unit record machines determine what character is punched by _____.

◆   ◆   ◆

timing

5. Most machines contain _____ brushes, one brush for each _____ of a card, so that an entire card can be read in one pass through the machine.

◆   ◆   ◆

80
column

6. Unit record machines perform their functions within a fixed period of time referred to as a(n) _____.

◆   ◆   ◆

machine cycle

7. The specific operations which a machine can perform are controlled by _____.

◆   ◆   ◆

its design and the electronic circuits wired into it

8. Many unit record machines offer increased flexibility of operation through the use of _____.

◆   ◆   ◆

externally wired control panels

9. There are two types of control panels. One has _____ that press against metal prongs in the machine, while the other has _____ into which external wires can be inserted.

◆ ◆ ◆

metal jacks
hubs

10. _____ control panels are wired with permanent wires and are used for jobs _____, whereas _____ panels are used _____.

◆ ◆ ◆

Fixed
of a recurring nature that do not require alteration of wiring
manual
for applications subject to change or of a nonpermanent nature

11. There are _____ basic types of hubs, namely, _____.

◆ ◆ ◆

four
exit hubs, entry hubs, common hubs, and bus hubs

12. There are two general types of wires used in wiring a control panel. These are _____ and _____.

◆ ◆ ◆

one-way wires, which by the use of a diode allow electricity to pass through them in only one direction,
two-way wires, which allow electricity to pass in either direction

13. If bus hubs are not available and it is necessary to have several of the same impulses, then _____ may be used.

◆ ◆ ◆

connectors

14. When two adjacent hubs are to be connected, a(n) _____ may be used.

◆ ◆ ◆

jackplug

15. You should place on a wiring diagram _____.

♦ ♦ ♦

exactly what is to be accomplished

16. When drawing a wiring diagram of several hubs or a field from one point to another, the entire field should be _____ on the diagram.

♦ ♦ ♦

connected by a single line

Interpreters

In Chapter 3, we learned that the card punch machine punches holes in a card and at the same time is capable of printing, or interpreting, the punched character directly over the card column punched. Once the punched card is printed, it takes the form of a readable document such as a check, a utility bill, an identification card, a warehouse location card, etc. However, in many cases cards are punched without printing, making them difficult to read by eye. To allow these cards to be printed on, or interpreted, the interpreter was devised. The only purpose of the interpreter is to translate alphabetic, numeric, or certain special characters punched into a card to printed characters on that card. This device will be the first machine discussed in this chapter requiring control panel wiring.

The IBM 548 alphabetic interpreter

The wiring principles of most interpreters are basically alike. This section will show the control panel wiring for the IBM 548 Alphabetic Interpreter and discuss the capabilities and operating features of other models.

Operating features. The IBM 548 Alphabetic Interpreter, as shown in Figure 4-11, can read, or sense, up to 80 card columns and print a maximum of 60 interpreted characters on one line. If the printing of all 80 characters is desired, the card is passed through the machine a second time. Data can be printed on the card on either of two lines—one above the 12 row (called the upper line) and the other between the 12 and 11 rows (called the lower line). Line selection can be made by setting a two-position knob at the rear of the machine as shown in Figure 4-12. The positions are marked U for upper and L for lower. Cards are placed in the hopper (see Figure 4-11) with the 12 edge first, face up. This hopper can accommodate up to 700 cards.

Once the cards are placed in the machine, the MAIN LINE POWER switch is turned to the ON position which supplies power to the device. A green READY light will then go on, indicating that the machine is ready for operation. The START key can then be depressed to start the automatic feeding of data cards. This key should be held depressed until at least three cards have been fed into the machine to ensure continuous card feeding. The STOP key can be depressed at any time to stop card feeding. Once the operation begins, cards are fed in through the hopper, pass a set of early read brushes, and then pass under an 80-column reading brush assembly which reads all 80 card columns. This information is then routed by the wires in the control panel to the print mechanism where printing is accomplished. The cards then proceed into a stacker which holds approximately 900 cards. When either the stacker is full or the hopper is empty, the interpreter will automatically shut off. Emptying the stacker or inserting additional data cards into the hopper and pressing the START key

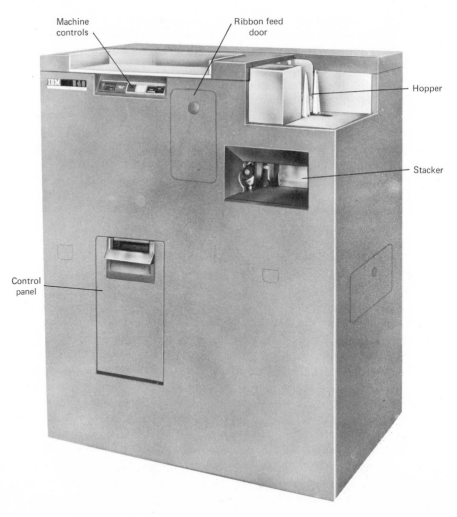

Figure 4-11
IBM 548 Alphabetic
Interpreter

Figure 4-12
Print Position Knob

will resume the processing. Cards may be removed or replaced while the operation is in progress without stopping the machine.

The printing mechanism consists of 60 typebars, each containing 39 printing characters—10 numeric (0 through 9), 26 alphabetic (A through Z), and 3 special characters. These special characters are identified by a 12, 11, or a combination of 0-1 punch as seen in Figure 4-13.

Straight and offset printing. The arrangement of printing is determined by the control panel wiring. For example, if a field were located in card columns 1 to 5, and if it were desired to have the printing accomplished on the left side of the card, then wires would be inserted in READING BRUSHES hubs 1 to 5 and PRINT ENTRY hubs 1 to 5. This is called *straight interpreting* (see Figure 4-14). If you wanted to print characters punched in card columns 11 to 15 in a different location from that where they were punched, in print positions 55 to 59 for example, then you would wire READING BRUSH hubs 11 to 15 to PRINT ENTRY hubs 55 to 59. This is called *offset interpreting* (see Figure 4-14).

X elimination. In order to conserve space on the card, a coded punch or *overpunch* is sometimes used. This would be the placing of a control punch, the 11 or 12 punch, over one of the columns of a numeric field. For example, 4579M might be punched in card columns 11 to 15. This would mean the negative number 45794, or that this number was a debit rather than a credit. If the field punched were wired directly to the PRINT ENTRY hubs, then the characters punched would be interpreted exactly as these were. The control punch can, however, be prevented from reaching the PRINT ENTRY hub by using X elimination. Each X eliminator consists of three sets of hubs: the common hub, the 0-9 hub, and the 11-12 hub. At 12 and 11 time, the impulse into the common hub is available at the 11

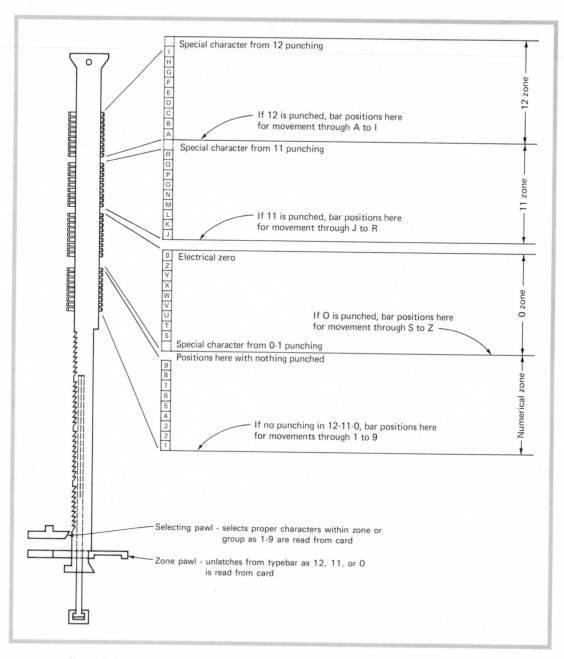

Figure 4-13
Schematic of Typebar

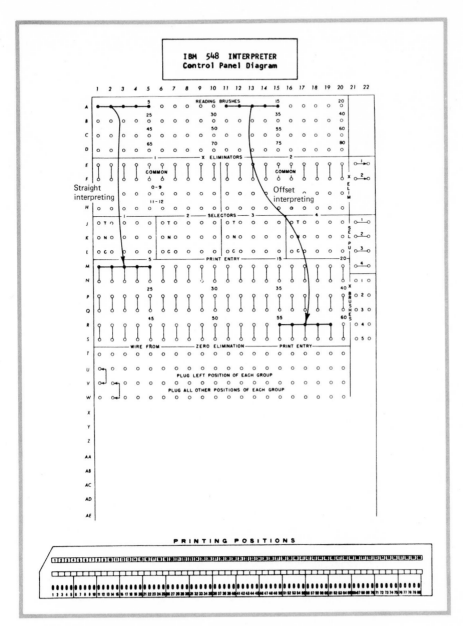

Figure 4-14
Straight and Offset
Interpreting

or 12 hub. At 0 time, the connection is broken and made between the common and the 0-9 hubs. The inverse of this is also true. At 5 time, an impulse in the 0-9 hub is available in the common hubs. In order to print the example above, columns 11 to 14 would be wired directly to the PRINT ENTRY, while column 15 would go to the common hub and the

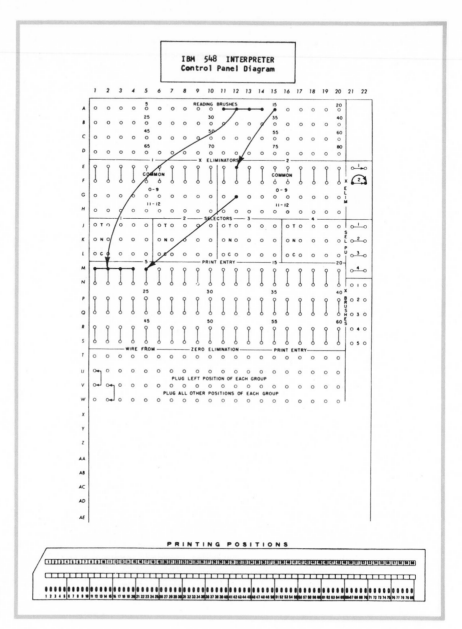

Figure 4-15
IBM 548 Wiring Diagram
Illustrating X Elimination

0-9 to the PRINT ENTRY. The X ELIMINATORS are operative only if they are wired as shown in Figure 4-15. Hubs on line E or F in columns 21 and 22 of the diagram should be wired in the direction of the arrow. The two switches correspond to the two sets of X eliminators. You will encounter the X eliminator on other machines, even though it may be referred to by another name such as a *column split*.

Selection. Selection means making a choice or decision. For example, you may decide to print information in one place for a credit invoice and in another place for a debit invoice. In this way, a clerk, when using this document, could instantly tell whether he had a credit or debit item.

The principle of selection can be applied to operations performed with data processing machines through the proper wiring of selectors at the control panel. The use of selection is similar in most machines, although they differ slightly in their basic operation.

Two selectors are provided for on the IBM 548 Alphabetic Interpreter. Each selector has three sets of hubs: *common, normal,* and *transfer,* which are sometimes called C, N, and T. The selectors work basically the same way as the X eliminators. When an impulse is received in the common, it may exit by the normal or the transfer, depending on the situation. Let us consider the railroad track example shown in Figure 4-16. In this example, if a train were moving down the main track and it came to a fork in the track, a switch would be required to alter the course of the train. Within the internal wiring of the SELECTOR, there is a connection or switch between the common and normal and between the common and the transfer. The machine must have some method of determining when to make this change. This method uses a control punch contained in the card being processed. This control punch is sensed by the *early read brush,* and the connection between the common hub and the transfer hub is made.

Figure 4-16
Similarity between
Railroad Depot and
Selector

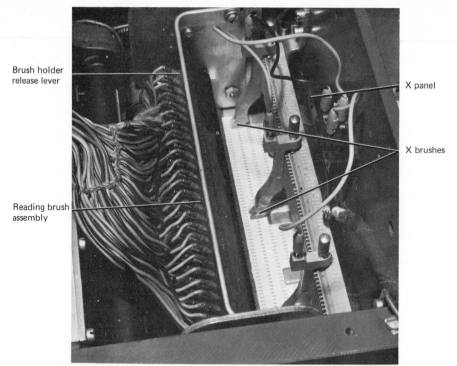

Brush holder
release lever

X panel

X brushes

Reading brush
assembly

Figure 4-17
X Brushes and X Panel

The control punch is sometimes referred to as the X punch. The lack of an X punch or an "NX" will maintain the normal connection (not transferred) that is between the common hub and the normal hub. Figure 4-17 shows three of five possible early read or *X brushes* that can be placed over up to five selected card columns by the operator. The X read brushes are positioned before the 80 READING BRUSHES, and as a result they sense an impulse one cycle earlier. This allows the SELECTOR to be set to a particular condition. If a card has an X punch located in column 75, the operator would place an X brush over column 75 and then wire that to one of five positions on the X panel, as shown in Figure 4-17. The impulse is then passed to the control panel and exits from the X brushes located in hubs N through S and 21 and 22 of the panel. A control wire is then placed from the X brush to the selector pickup (SEL PU) which in turn sets the switch in SELECTORS 1, 2, 3, or 4 as desired.

Thus, selection by two different methods is possible. One method is called *class selection,* while the other is called *field selection.* Class selection would be used when a field is to be printed in one of two places, depending upon the presence or absence of the X punch (11 punch). Field selection is the opposite of class selection. In field selection, there are two different fields, one of which will be printed in a given location, again depending upon the presence or absence of the X punch. Let us assume that we wish to interpret a statement card for a large department store. The customer's balance is punched in card columns 16 to 20. It is to be printed in print positions 1 to 5 if there is a credit (no X punch) and in print positions 55 to 59 if a payment is due (X punch). The wiring required to accomplish this task (class selection) is illustrated in Figure 4-18. Wiring for field selection is shown in Figure 4-19.

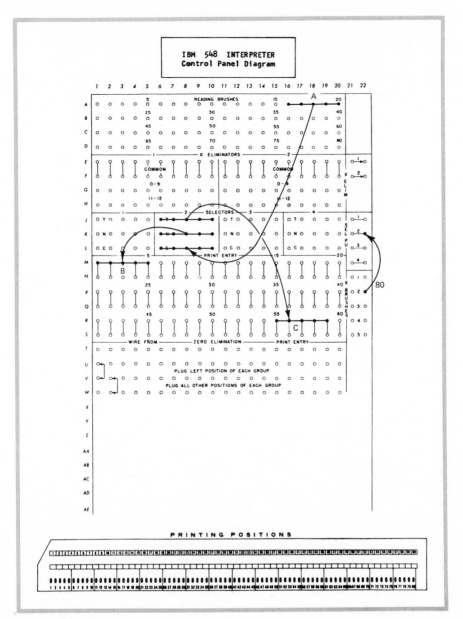

Figure 4-18
Wiring Diagram for Class
Selection

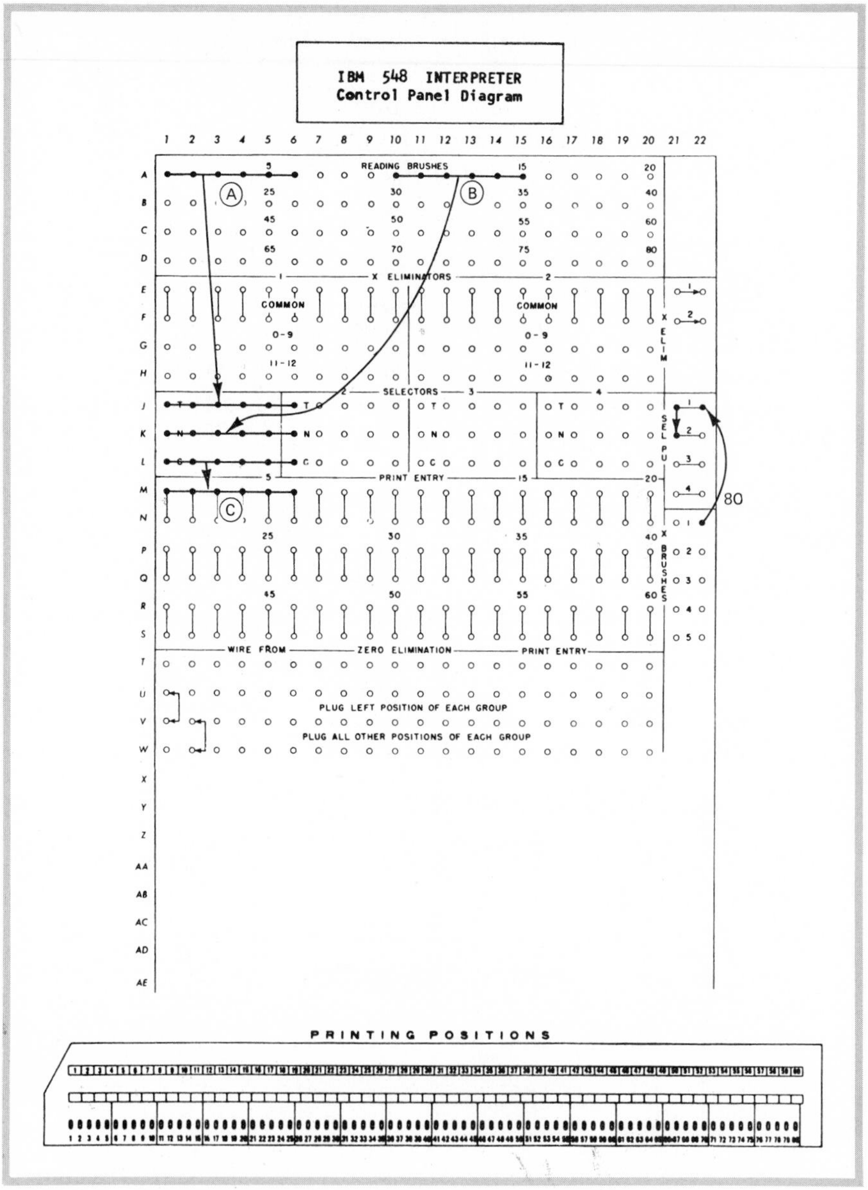

Figure 4-19
Wiring Diagram for Field
Selection

For the class selection the amount field is located in card columns 16 to 20 with a possible control punch in column 80. The operator places an X brush directly over column 80 and plugs that to X panel number 2. Then on the control panel, field A, as shown in Figure 4-18, is wired to the common of the selector. The normal is wired to field B, and the transfer is wired to field C. The X brush is wired to SEL PU 2.

For field selection two possible fields are available: one located in card columns 1 to 6 with a control punch in card column 80, the other in card columns 10 to 15 without a control punch. The operator must place an early read brush over card column 80 and plug it into X panel number 1. Now field A is wired to the transfer, field B to the normal, and the common to the PRINT ENTRY field C. The X brush is then wired to SEL PU 1, and SEL PU 1 to SEL PU 2 (since the field has exceeded the 5 available hubs in 1 selector), as shown in Figure 4-19.

Zero elimination. The last feature of the 548 is called zero elimination, that is, the elimination of the printing of unwanted zeros. It is often the case that when a field is not entirely used, zeros are punched into the unused leftmost positions. For example, a salary field is located in card columns 45 to 50. The actual salary is $97.03. It would be punched 009703. When this field is interpreted, the elimination of the leading zeros would facilitate the reading. Thus the interpretation printed on the card should be 9703. The wiring for this, shown in Figure 4-20, would be to simply wire the entire field A from the PRINT ENTRY to the ZERO ELIMINATION area B. The jackplugging of the leftmost position C in hubs on lines U and V of Figure 4-20 indicates that this is the first position of the field, and here zero elimination begins. The remainder of the field is then jackplugged onto hubs on lines V and W (position D). When a card is now interpreted, all leading zeros of this field will not be printed. This leading zero print elimination ceases when the first significant digit is sensed, causing all remaining zeros to be printed.

The following operating suggestions, with slight deviations, could be applied to most machines discussed in this chapter.

Operating suggestions

1. Joggle all cards before placing them into a hopper. This is to arrange them in perfect alignment and to reduce the possibility of card feed failures.
2. Check to see if cards are in the proper direction—with the 12 edge face up. If the cards are reversed, then the wrong fields will be interpreted.
3. Check the print position knob and/or switches before starting each job.
4. Always use a few test cards before starting the main operation. This will determine that you have the right control panel, that you have wired the panel correctly, and that the machine is functioning properly.
5. If the machine stops before either the stacker is full or the hopper is empty, check the last card fed into the stacker for a possible card jam. Remove the cards causing the jam, and determine whether or not they should be repunched. *Remember:* if re-

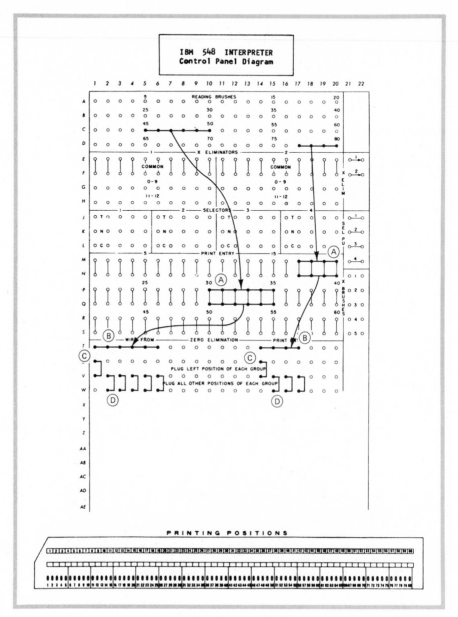

Figure 4-20
Zero Elimination

punching is necessary, ensure that the repunched card has been punched exactly the same as the original.

The IBM 552 interpreter   The IBM 552 interpreter is an early model that lacks some of the features of the 548. However, the wiring and operation are essentially the same.

The selectors are installed only as an optional feature, and there is no zero elimination feature.

The IBM 557 Alphabetical Interpreter prints at a rate of 100 cards per minute, allowing for a printing of a maximum of 60 characters on one line in one pass of the machine. A total of 25 lines can be printed. Cards must be passed through the machine one time for each line to be printed. The print line dial, shown in Figure 4-21, controls the line to be printed. The hopper has a capacity of 800 cards, while the stacker holds 900 cards. Cards are fed in 12 edge first, face down.

The IBM 557 Alphabetical Interpreter

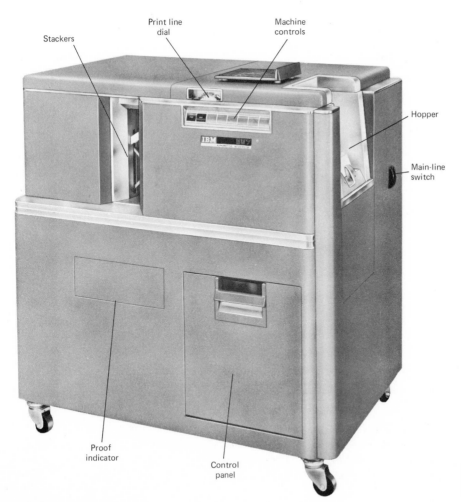

Figure 4-21
IBM 557 Alphabetical
Interpreter

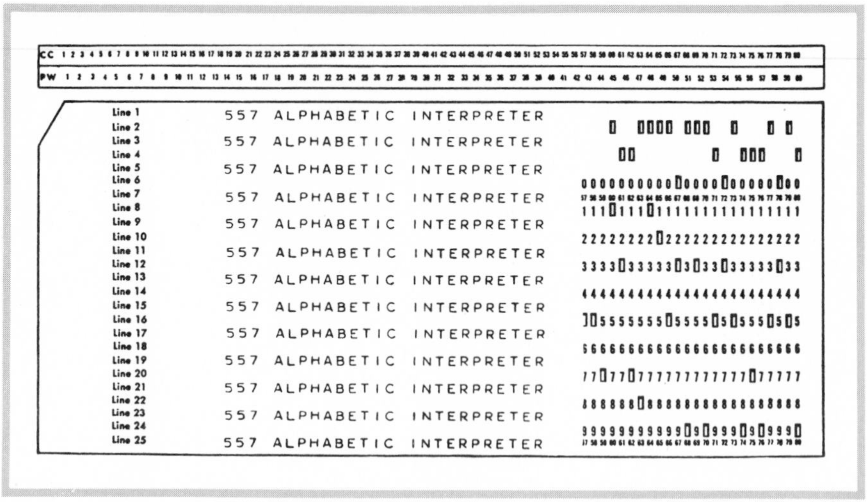

Figure 4-22
Punched Card Interpreted
on IBM 557 Alphabetical
Interpreter

Additional features. The IBM 557 interpreter offers the following additional features:

Selective Line Printing	a device by which card printing can be controlled on each of 25 lines, as shown in Figure 4-22.
Repeat Print	a device which enables data read from a master card to be printed on that card and the detail cards following it. At the same time, each card can be compared to ensure that printing occurs on the proper cards.
Selective Stackers	a feature which enables cards to be directed to four separate stackers by proper control panel wiring. As an example, master and detail cards could be separated by wiring to select cards with the X punch (either master or detail, according to design).
Interpret Emitter	a device that can emit an impulse for each character which can be punched on a card. This makes it possible to print emitted characters in addition to characters punched on a card.
Proof	a device that verifies data printed on the card to ensure that the proper characters were in fact printed. If an error is indicated, card feeding stops.
Card Counter	a means to count all cards processed.
PRINT ENTRY 2	a device using 60 print wheels, rather than type-bars. Either of two control panel entries

(PRINT ENTRY 1 and PRINT ENTRY 2) can be manually selected by a switch located in front of the machine. The operator now can wire two separate jobs on the same panel, thus reducing operation time.

Presensing a function similar to that of the X ELIMINATOR and SELECTOR which also can be used to control the repeat print device.

Self-study exercise 4-3

1. The only purpose of the interpreter is to _____ .

translate alphabetic, numeric, or certain special characters punched on a card into printed characters on that card

2. The IBM 548 Alphabetic Interpreter can read up to _____ card columns and print up to _____ of these characters on one line in one pass through the machine.

♦ ♦ ♦

80
60

3. Completely interpreting a card (all 80 columns) would require _____ passes through the machine (the IBM 548) and would yield _____ lines of print located _____ .

♦ ♦ ♦

two
two
above the 12 row and between the 12 and 11 rows

4. Straight interpreting would require that data read in card columns 1 to 7 be interpreted in print positions _____ , whereas offset interpreting would require that this data be interpreted in _____ .

♦ ♦ ♦

1 to 7
any print positions except 1 to 7

5. _____ involves restricting a control or X punch impulse from being transmitted to the PRINT ENTRY hubs.

◆ ◆ ◆

X elimination

6. Selection involves the making of a(n) _____.

◆ ◆ ◆

choice or decision

7. Each selector on the IBM 548 has _____ hubs, namely, _____.

◆ ◆ ◆

three
common, normal, and transfer

8. The two types of selection are _____ and _____.

◆ ◆ ◆

class selection
field selection

9. _____ selection would be used when _____, whereas in _____ selection there are two different fields, one of which will be printed, depending on the presence or absence of a control punch.

◆ ◆ ◆

Class
a field is to be printed in one of two places, depending upon the presence or absence of a control punch
field

10. _____ facilitates the suppression of printing leading zeros.

◆ ◆ ◆

Zero elimination

11. The IBM 552 is a(n) (earlier/later) model than the IBM 548.

◆ ◆ ◆

earlier

12. The IBM 557 is capable of printing at a rate of _____ cards per minute with a maximum of _____ characters per card on up to _____ lines on the card.

◆ ◆ ◆

100
60
25

13. Some of the additional features of the IBM 557 not found on the 548 or 552 are _____ .

◆ ◆ ◆

selective line printing, repeat printing, selective stackers, interpret emitter, proof, card counter, PRINT ENTRY 2, and presensing

Reproducers

The primary function of the reproducer is to sense the holes punched in a card and duplicate these punches in other cards. For example, this type of device can be used for updating a card file when the file design of the system has been changed.

The IBM 514 reproducing punch

The IBM 514 Reproducing Punch shown in Figure 4-23 contains two feed units: the reading unit and the punching unit. Cards may be fed from either or both units, depending upon the job being performed. Each hopper can contain about 800 cards, and cards are fed in 12 edge first, face down. There are two stackers, each capable of holding up to 1,000 cards before shutting off the machine. Hoppers may be filled and stackers emptied while the machine is automatically feeding cards. The standard machine operates at a speed of 100 cards per minute, regardless of how many card columns are to be punched. An exception to the rule is summary punching, which requires 1.2 seconds per card.

Read unit. Referring to Figure 4-24, you will notice that as cards pass from the hopper through the read unit, they must first pass under five read X brushes. As with the interpreter, they can be set by the operator to read up to 5 of the 80 card columns, thereby controlling the reading of data

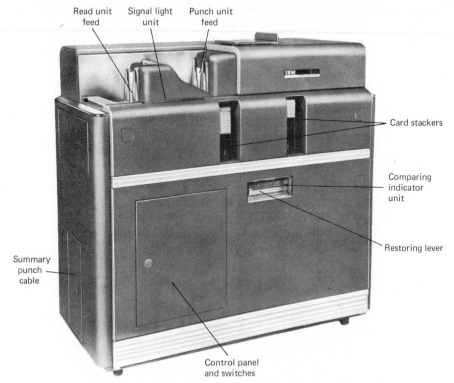

Read unit feed   Signal light unit   Punch unit feed

Card stackers

Comparing indicator unit

Restoring lever

Summary punch cable

Control panel and switches

Figure 4-23
IBM 514 Reproducing
Punch

from the card. The next station contains two sets of 80 reading brushes each. The first set, called the REPRODUCING BRUSHES, reads the entire card, whereas the second set, called the COMPARING BRUSHES, is used to read the card a second time (which can be used to verify the first reading).

Punch unit. Referring again to Figure 4-24, we can see that after passing from the feed hopper, cards must pass six punch X brushes which must be set by the operator, just as the read X brushes were. This affords the operator control over which cards will be punched. If a *mark-sense* option is installed, cards are read after this set of brushes and then passed under the punching dies. Here, there is a set of 80 blades (knives) which are used to punch the card in parallel, or row by row. During the last cycle the cards are read by a set of 80 brushes called PUNCH BRUSHES (which can be used to verify the punching operation).

Keys and lights. The operational state of the reproducer is controlled and indicated by a series of switches, controls, and lights. Table 4-1 shows the operating functions of the switches, controls, and lights available with the reproducer.

Operational capabilities

REPRODUCING
Cards may be reproduced either straight or offset. To accomplish this, cards to be reproduced are placed in the read unit hopper, blank cards or cards with blanks in the fields to be reproduced are placed in the punch hopper, and the REPRODUCING BRUSHES are wired to the PUNCH MAGNETS (knives), as shown in Figure 4-25.

GANGPUNCHING
Some situations require that a given data item be punched into each card of a deck of punched cards. This can be accomplished by placing the card containing the data item on top of the deck of cards to be punched and then placing them into the punch unit hopper. The first card containing the data item is read by the PUNCH BRUSHES, and the information is passed to the PUNCH MAGNETS via external wiring connecting the PUNCH

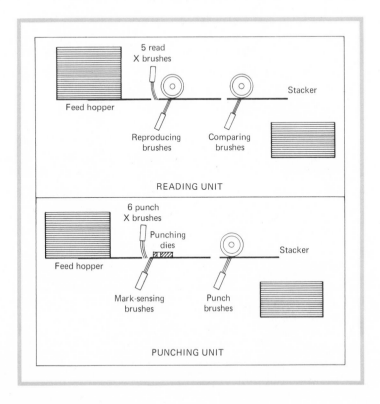

Figure 4-24
Schematic of IBM 514
Reproducing Punch

Table 4-1. Keys, Lights, and Switches

Key, Light, or Switch	Operating Function
MAIN LINE Switch	The MAIN LINE switch is located on the right end of the machine and is used to provide power to the machine.
START Key	When depressed, this key initiates the reading of cards. It must, however, be depressed and held until three cards have passed from the hopper, to commence automatic feeding.
STOP Key	The STOP key, when depressed, causes the machine to stop card feeding.
RESET Key	This key must be depressed to reset the *double punch* and *blank column detection circuits* and to put out the DP & BC DETECT light.
Comparing Indicating Lever	When lifted, this lever extinguishes the *COMPARE light,* and card feeding may proceed after the START key is depressed.
Green Light	When illuminated, this light indicates that the machine is ready to commence operations.
COMPARE Light	When illuminated, this light indicates that an error in verification has been detected, and the machine stops the card feeding process.
DP (Double Punch) & BC (Blank Column) Detect Light	This light indicates that a double punch or blank column has been detected or that the machine has stopped the card feeding process.
COMPARING Indicator	This lights up and shows the area in which an error has occurred during the *comparing function.*

BRUSHES to the PUNCH MAGNETS, as shown in Figure 4-26. This operation is called gangpunching.

COMPARING
Verification of the reproducing operation can be accomplished using the reproducer's comparing unit. After the reproducing operation has been

completed, the cards pass under the comparing brushes and the punch brushes simultaneously. By externally wiring both the COMPARING BRUSHES and the PUNCH BRUSHES to the comparing unit (COMPARING MAGNETS), as shown in Figure 4-27, verification can be accomplished. In the event that an unequal comparison occurs, card feeding is ceased, and a COMPARING INDICATOR flags the card column in which the unequal comparison occurred by a pointer as shown in Figure 4-28.

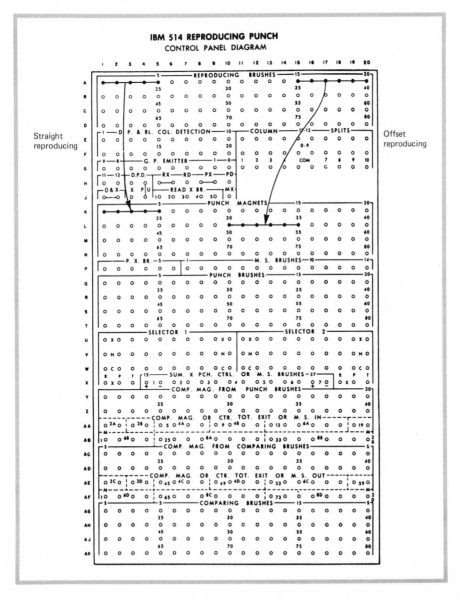

Figure 4-25
Straight and Offset
Reproducing

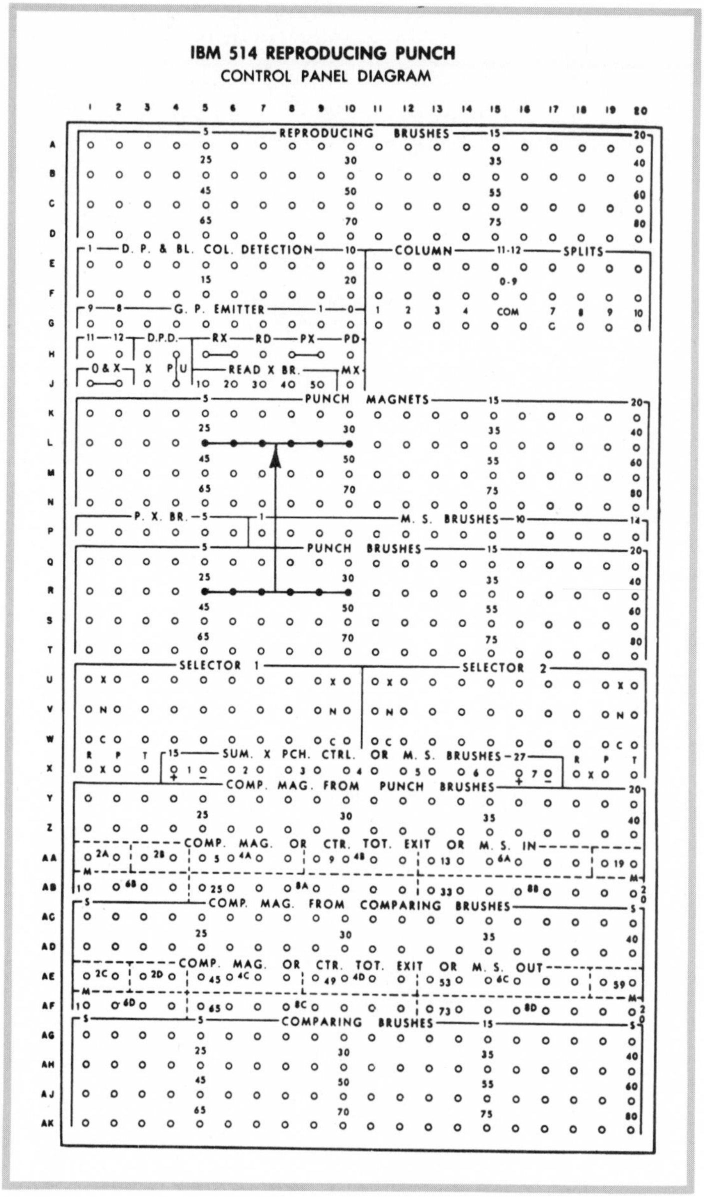

Figure 4-26
Gangpunching

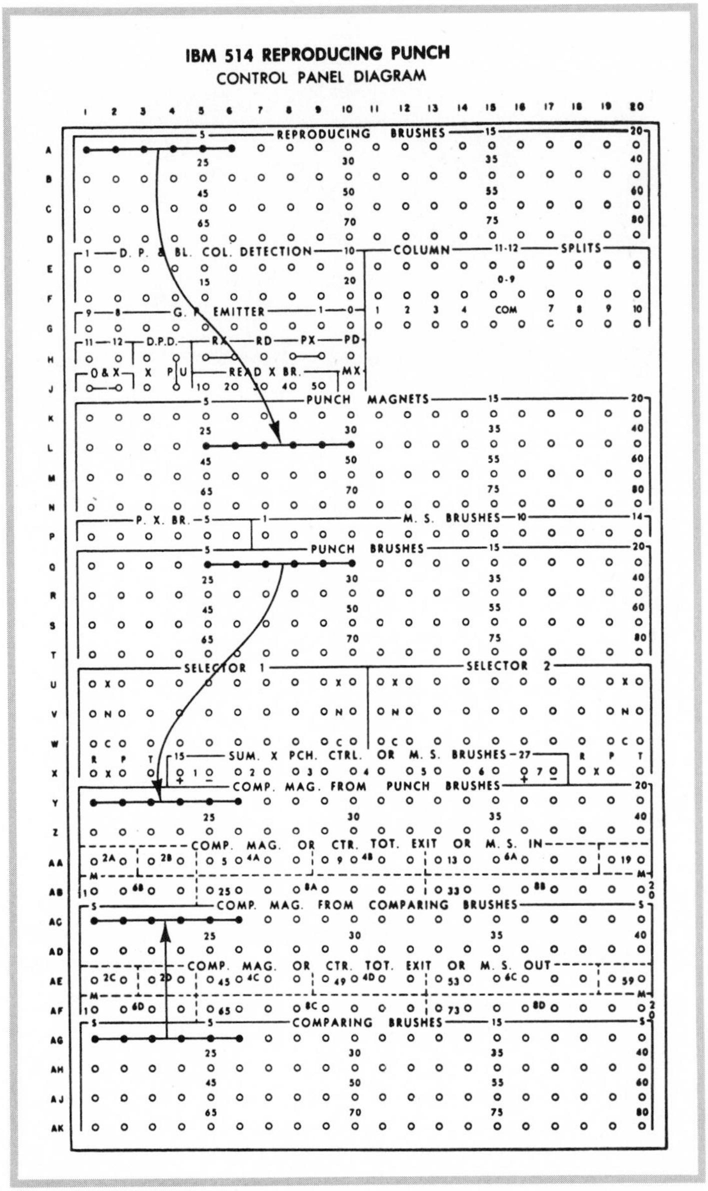

Figure 4-27
Offset Reproducing with
Comparing

Figure 4-28
Comparing Indicator Unit

SELECTIVE REPRODUCING
Selective reproducing is the process whereby only one type of card (X or NX) will be reproduced. We shall discuss this operation no further except to state that it is accomplished with the aid of SELECTORS.

INTERSPERSED GANGPUNCHING
When information to be gangpunched is changed during the gangpunch operation, the operation is referred to as interspersed gangpunching.

ILLUSTRATIVE EXAMPLE
An example would be when five dates are to be punched into 5,000 cards, one date for each 1,000 cards. To accomplish this, the first card would have an X punched together with the desired date, followed by 1,000 NX blank cards, another X-punched date card, and 1,000 NX blank cards, etc. The machine would reproduce the first date onto the first 1,000 cards. The selector would then hold the punching long enough to pass the next X-punched master. Once this master has passed below the punching dies unpunched, its code is then punched into the following 1,000 cards. If this master detection should fail for some reason, for example due to a broken wire, then the last card would have all the dates punched into it. This error condition is called *lacing*.

COLUMN SPLIT
The column split functions exactly as the X eliminator on the interpreter.

EMITTING

The gangpunch emitter is an optional device that is capable of generating impulses. That is, this feature affords the opportunity to create characters that have not been read and cause them to be punched into a card.

MARK-SENSING

This optional device may be installed in the punch unit and is used to automatically convert special pencil marks into punched holes. The pencil used must contain special leads with a high graphite content to be sensed by this device.

DOUBLE-PUNCH (DP) AND BLANK-COLUMN (BC) DETECTION

The DP & BC DETECT light is generally installed with the mark-sensing device, but may be added separately. With this device, any field may be checked for double punches or blank columns. For example, should two digits be punched in a card column or should a blank column occur in a salary field, the machine would immediately stop feeding cards, and the DP & BC DETECT light would go on.

SUMMARY PUNCHING

In this operation, the reproducer is connected to the *accounting machine* by a wire cable. As the accounting machine produces a total or summary, this total or summary is passed to the reproducer, where it is punched into a card.

Functional switches. Machine operations are controlled by a series of functional switches located inside the control panel compartment, as shown in Figure 4-29. These switches are discussed in Table 4-2.

Figure 4-29
IBM 514 Control Panel
and Functional Switches

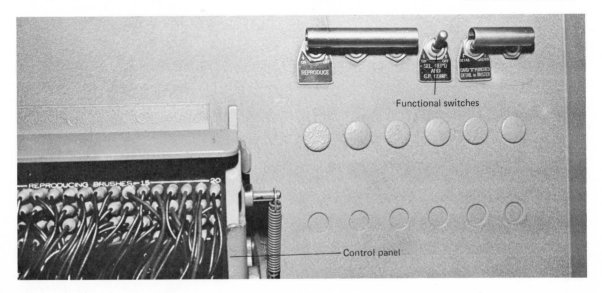

Functional switches

Control panel

Table 4-2. Functional Switches

Switch	Function
REPRODUCE Switch	This switch synchronizes the read and punch unit so that they work together for any given operation. When the switch is OFF, each unit may be used independently to perform separate operations.
SEL REPD AND GP. COMP. Switch	This allows continuous feeding in the read and punch units separately. When OFF, the read unit feeding is suspended.
CARD "X" PUNCHED DETAIL or MASTER Switch	This switch controls the handling of X or NX cards. This switch is set to MASTER when the master card contains the controlling or X punch or when reproducing from the NX card is desired. It is set to DETAIL when detail cards contain the X punch or when reproducing from the NX cards is desired.
MARK-SENSING Switch	This must be ON during mark-sensed operations.
MASTER CARD PUNCHING Switch	In a combination reproducing and gang-punch operation in which mark-sensed master cards are used, this switch should be ON to permit mark-sensed information to be punched into the master card. It should be OFF for all other operations.
BLANK COLUMN CHECK Switch	A switch is provided for each card column of DP and BC detection. When the switch is ON, a DP or BC condition will stop card feeding. When this switch is OFF, only double punches will be detected.

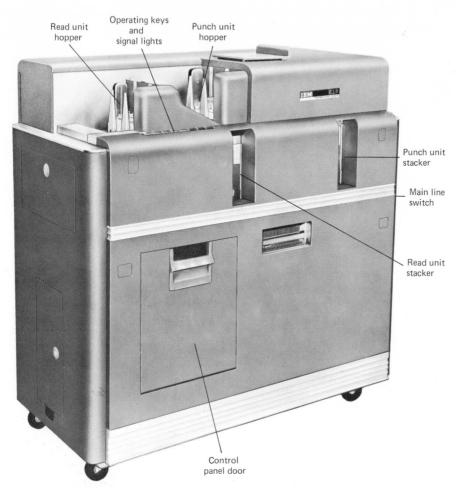

Read unit hopper

Operating keys and signal lights

Punch unit hopper

Punch unit stacker

Main line switch

Read unit stacker

Control panel door

Figure 4-30
IBM 519
Document-originating
Machine

The IBM 519 Reproducing Punch, shown in Figure 4-30, is similar in appearance to the IBM 514 reproducer and is designed to perform all functions previously described for the 514. However, in addition its print unit provides a capability for printing as many as eight digits across the end of a card as the card passes through the punch unit (see Figure 4-31). If the information is printed from the same card as when gangpunching, it is called *interpreting*. If it is printed from a card in the read unit, it is called *transcribing*.

**The IBM 519
Reproducing Punch**

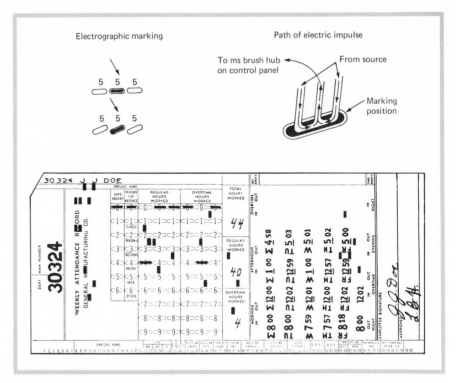

Figure 4-31
Mark-sensing

Self-study exercise 4-4

1. The primary function of the reproducer is ———.

♦   ♦   ♦

to sense the holes punched in a card and duplicate these punched holes in other cards

2. The IBM 514 contains two feed units: the ——— unit and the ——— unit.

♦   ♦   ♦

read
punch

3. The 514 normally operates at a speed of ——— cards per second, but when summary punching, the 514 takes approximately ——— seconds to process one card.

♦   ♦   ♦

100
1.2

4. The read unit of the 514 contains _____ set(s) of brushes, namely, _____ .

◆ ◆ ◆

three
read X brushes (5) and reproducing and comparing brushes (80)

5. The punch unit of the 514 contains _____ set(s) of brushes, namely, _____ .

◆ ◆ ◆

three
the punch X brushes (6), the mark-sensing brushes, and the punch brushes (80)

6. Operations which can be performed on the reproducer include _____ .

◆ ◆ ◆

straight and offset reproducing, gangpunching, comparing, selective reproducing, and interspersed gangpunching

7. In order to perform a summary punching operation, the reproducer must be connected to a(n) _____ .

◆ ◆ ◆

accounting machine

8. The mark-sensing device is an (optional/standard) device on the reproducer and is located in the _____ unit.

◆ ◆ ◆

optional
punch

9. The _____ is an optional device on the reproducer capable of generating impulses.

◆ ◆ ◆

gangpunch emitter

10. The _____ on the reproducer functions exactly the same as the X eliminator on the _____ .

◆ ◆ ◆

column split
interpreter

11. To synchronize the read and punch units to work together, the _____ switch must be _____ .

◆ ◆ ◆

REPRODUCE
ON

12. The IBM 519 is capable of performing all the functions available on the 514 and the additional function of _____ .

◆ ◆ ◆

printing up to eight digits across the end of the card as the card passes through the punch unit

Classifying and Arranging Data The end result of the punched card accounting cycle is usually a printed report. Information in these reports is generally grouped according to some predetermined arrangement or sequencing of unit records. Since the cards produced by a card punch operator are seldom in any particular order, the classifying or arranging of these cards must be performed on a separate unit record machine. Machines capable of such operations are the sorter and collator.

Sorter Before a report can be prepared on an accounting machine, the input data must be placed in some sort of order or sequence. For example, customer charges in a retail concern must be grouped in customer account number sequence prior to the calculation of customer account balances. The sorting of punched cards into groups or into a desired sequence can be performed easily and rapidly by card sorting machines.

Four methods used during such operations are:

Numeric Sorting cards arranged into either ascending or descending numeric sequence by sorting each column of the field being sorted.

Alphabetic Sorting cards arranged into alphabetic order by sorting each column of a field twice, once on the digit punch of that column and then once on the zone punch of that column.

Selective Sorting not all cards of a file need to be processed. Some applications may require that only those cards with a particular prefix or department number be processed. *Selective switches* provide a means of selecting only those desired cards without disturbing the sequence of the remainder of the cards in the file.

Block Sorting when the volume of cards is so large that it would require a great deal of time to sort them on one machine, or when the total number of cards is unwieldy, the card file can be divided into groups called blocks. Then each block can be sorted by a different machine at the same time, or on the same machine at different times.

Components of the sorter:

1. The *hopper* holds the cards to be read by the sorter. Cards are fed in 9 edge first, face down.
2. The COLUMN SELECTOR knob selects the card column to be sorted on.
3. The *control switches* detect the sorter functions to be performed.
4. The SELECTOR switch determines either zone punch or numeric punch sorting.
5. The DIGIT SUPPRESSION switch causes the presence of numeric punches to be ignored when sorting.
6. Thirteen *pockets* hold the cards which have passed through the sorter. Twelve of the pockets correspond to the twelve possible card rows. The thirteenth or R pocket is the rejection pocket for cards not directed into one of the other twelve pockets.

The sorter operates by reading cards from the hopper and, depending on the setting of the switches, passes the cards into one of the 13 pockets. Reading is accomplished by a single read brush which is positioned over the desired card column by the COLUMN SELECTOR knob. Under normal operation, the first hole sensed by the read brush determines the pocket to which the card will be sent. This operation is shown schematically in Figure 4-32.

If no punch is detected in the card column, the card is sent to the reject pocket.

The most common functions of the sorter are the sorting of cards numerically or alphabetically and selecting certain cards from a deck of cards. As an example, let's see how cards can be sorted when we wish

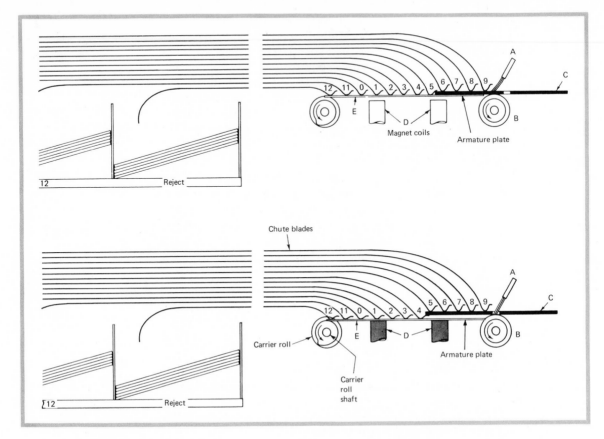

Figure 4-32
Sorter Schematic Diagram

to sort into ascending numeric sequence on columns 32 and 33. The procedure for performing this sort is as follows:

1. Turn the COLUMN SELECTOR knob to column 33.
2. Place the cards to be sorted into the hopper, and press the START button. After all the cards have been run through the sorter, the cards will be sorted into pockets corresponding to their punch in column 33.
3. Pull the cards from the pockets from right to left, placing the pulled cards on the bottom of the card deck. Now the cards are in sequence for column 33.
4. Turn the COLUMN SELECTOR knob to column 32, and repeat the operation. At the end of this pass, the cards will be in correct numeric sequence for the two-digit field.

The important fact to note is that a sorting operation is initiated in the unit's position (or rightmost column) of a field being sorted unless the field is being sorted by block.

To sort fields alphabetically, two passes are required for each column. The first pass sorts on digit punches and the second on zone punches. This is accomplished by setting the SELECTOR switch to either numeric or zone sorting. When set to zone sorting, the numeric punches are ignored, and only the zone punches are sorted. As in numeric sorting, alphabetic fields must be sorted column by column from the right to the left of the field being sorted.

Cards can also be selected from a card deck using the sorter. For example, suppose all the cards with a 5 punch in column 10 were to be selected out of a card deck. By setting the COLUMN SELECTOR knob to column 10 and turning on all the DIGIT SUPPRESSION switches except the 5, cards containing a 5 punch would be fed into the 5 pocket, whereas all other cards would be sent to the reject (R) pocket in exactly the same order that they were placed into the machine.

Figure 4-33
Sorter Brush Column Indicator

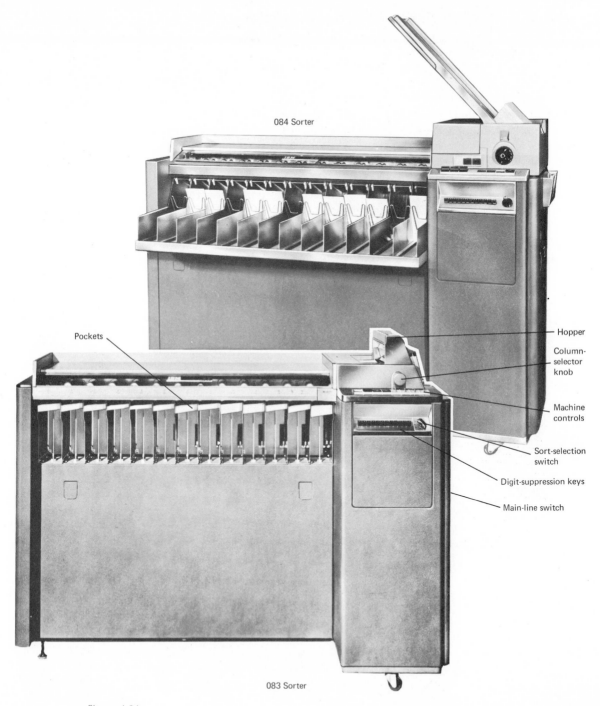

084 Sorter

Pockets

Hopper

Column-
selector
knob

Machine
controls

Sort-selection
switch

Digit-suppression keys

Main-line switch

083 Sorter

Figure 4-34
IBM Sorters

IBM 084

IBM 082

Figure 4-35
Sorter Selection Switches

Two of the available sorting machines are shown in Figure 4-34. The IBM Model 82, for example, can sort up to 650 cards per minute, while Models 83 and 84 can sort up to 1,000 and 2,000 cards per minute, respectively. The operational capabilities of each of these machines are basically the same except for the sorting switches. The 83 and 84 are controlled by depressing buttons, while the switches on the 82 are activated by moving them into the center of the dial as shown in Figure 4-35.

As we have discussed previously, one of the basic requisites of preparing a report is that the data be arranged in some kind of sequence, either alphabetic or numeric. We have learned that after cards have been punched, they can be arranged into the desired sequence on a sorter. Now, let us assume that we now wish to verify that these cards are in sequence and that we wish to merge other cards into this sequenced deck. This operation is only one of many that can be accomplished with the aid of the collator.

Collator

The operation principle of the collator is to read and compare two files (decks of cards) simultaneously in order to *match* them, check their sequence, or combine them into one file. At the same time, cards in each file that do not have a matching card in the other file may be *selected*.

Operational capabilities. Operations which can be performed on the collator fall into five general categories:

1. Sequence checking
2. Selection
3. Merging
4. Merging with selection
5. Matching

SEQUENCE CHECKING

After a file of cards has been sorted into the desired sequence, it can be checked on the collator to verify that the cards are in proper order. The collator performs this function by comparing each card with the one ahead of it. If any cards are found to be out of sequence, the machine can be directed, by control panel wiring, to stop and turn on the error light or to *select* the cards that are out of sequence.

SELECTION

Particular types of cards can be selected from a file without disturbing the sequence of the others. The type selected may be an X or NX card, the first card of a group, the last card of a group, a single-card group, a zero-balance card, a card with a particular number, or cards containing numbers between two control numbers. Single cards or groups of cards out of sequence may also be selected. The type of card(s) selected depends upon the operation being performed and the control panel wiring.

MERGING

This is the operation in which two files of cards, both in either ascending or descending sequence, are combined into one file. In a merging operation, the feeding from each feed unit is controlled by the comparison of the cards fed from one feed with the cards fed from the other. The result of this operation will be one combined file in proper sequence.

MERGING WITH SELECTION

The operation of merging two files into one can be controlled so that if either file contains cards that do not match cards in the other, these cards can be selected out. Thus, at the end of a merging operation, there will probably be three groups of cards: one group of merged cards and two groups of selected cards.

MATCHING

Suppose that, instead of merging two files of cards, one wishes to select from one file only those cards that have a match in the other. Cards in either file that do not have a match in the other file can be selected, and the unmatched cards can be stacked into two groups, one for each original file. Thus, when the operation is completed, there will probably be four groups of cards: two groups of matched and two groups of unmatched.

The IBM 85 Collator, shown in Figure 4-36, performs all the basic functions listed above. The number of cards fed per minute will range from 240 to 480, depending upon control panel wiring and the job being performed. There are two hoppers—primary and secondary—and four stackers. Stackers 1 and 2 can receive cards from the primary hopper. Stackers 2, 3, and 4 receive cards from the secondary hopper. In addition to the basic operational capabilities, the IBM 85 Collator employs selectors and blank column detection, which were discussed for previous machines. These additional features may be used separately or in conjunction with any other function.

IBM 85 collator

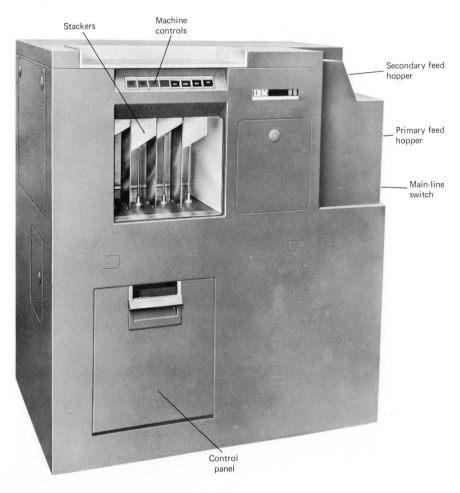

Stackers

Machine controls

Secondary feed hopper

Primary feed hopper

Main-line switch

Control panel

Figure 4-36
IBM 85 Collator

IBM 87 collator   The IBM 87 Collator functions with essentially the same operational capabilities as the IBM 85. The major difference is that the IBM 87 can process numeric, alphabetic, and special character data, while the IBM 85 can only handle numeric data.

IBM 88 collator   The IBM 88 Collator, pictured in Figure 4-37, performs all numeric operations previously described for the IBM 85. In addition, an editing feature facilitates the checking of cards in both feeds for accuracy of numeric punching. Card feeding may be stopped whenever a double punch or blank column is detected. Each feed is capable of handling 650 cards per minute, providing a combined capability to collate up to 1,300 cards per minute. The IBM 87 and 88 have two feeds and five stackers. Stackers 1, 2, and 3 can receive cards from the primary feed, whereas 3, 4, and 5 can receive cards from the secondary feed. The IBM 188 Collator is the alphabetic version of the IBM 88 Collator.

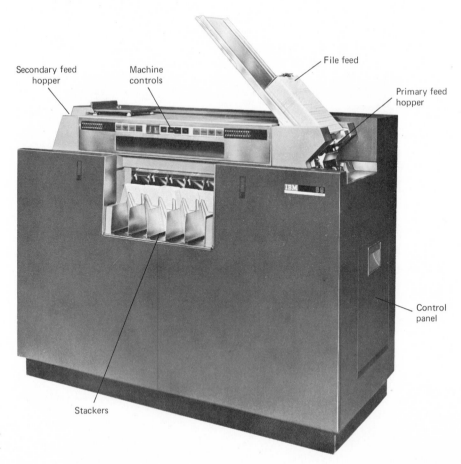

Figure 4-37
IBM 88 Collator

Self-study exercise 4-5

1. Machines capable of classifying and arranging punched cards are
   _____ .

♦ ♦ ♦

   the sorter and the collator

2. Four methods used by sorters are _____ .

♦ ♦ ♦

   *numeric sorting, alphabetic sorting, selective sorting, and block
sorting*

3. Selective sorting enables one to _____ certain cards from a deck of
   cards.

♦ ♦ ♦

   select

4. Sorters generally contain _____ pockets, each one corresponding to
   _____ and one called a(n) _____ pocket.

♦ ♦ ♦

   13
   a row on a punched card
   reject

5. _____ column(s) of a card may be sorted at a time.

♦ ♦ ♦

   One

6. A six-digit numeric field would require _____ passes through most
   sorters, whereas a six-character alphabetic field would require _____
   passes through the machine.

♦ ♦ ♦

   6
   12

7. All cards containing a 6 punch could be selected from a deck of cards without disturbing the sequence of the remainder of the deck by _____.

♦ ♦ ♦

turning off all SELECTOR switches or buttons except the 6-punch switch or button

8. The operation principle of the collator is _____.

♦ ♦ ♦

to read and compare two files (decks of cards) simultaneously in order to match, sequence-check, or combine them

9. Operations which can be performed on the collator fall into _____ general categories: _____.

♦ ♦ ♦

five
sequence checking, selection, merging, merging with selection, and matching

10. Sequence checking involves _____.

♦ ♦ ♦

verifying that a deck of cards is in the proper sequence

11. Merging is an operation in which _____.

♦ ♦ ♦

two files of cards, both in either ascending or descending sequence, are combined into one file in sequential order

12. Matching is an operation in which _____.

♦ ♦ ♦

cards are selected from one file that have a match in a second file

13. The IBM 85 and 88 Collators can process _____ data while the 87 can process _____ data.

◆ ◆ ◆

numeric
numeric, alphabetic, and special character

One of the most important functions of a manual or automatic data processing system is the preparing of reports. Reports and analyses form the basis for all administrative actions. In order that management may make pertinent and timely decisions, there must be a constant flow of current information in sales analysis, inventory and production reports, payrolls, and many other areas. In preparing these documents, many computations must be made, checked, and summarized before the results can be printed. With the basic data previously recorded onto punched cards, these reports can be prepared quickly and accurately on the accounting machine or, as it is sometimes termed, the tabulator.

Accounting Machine

Accounting machines are designed to print and accumulate data contained in punched cards at speeds ranging from 50 to 150 cards per minute, depending on the type or model machine and the particular job being performed. These capabilities can be grouped in five general categories:

Operational capabilities

1. Detail printing
2. Group printing
3. Accumulating
4. Programming
5. Summary punching

Detail printing. Detail printing is the printing, or listing, of selected fields from each card passed through the machine. This can be accomplished in any format desired through appropriate control panel wiring.

Group printing. Group printing involves the printing of identifying data from the first card (master) of a group and accumulations or summaries from the remaining cards (detail) of that group. For example, in an inventory analysis run, the name and stock number of a spare part would be printed from the master card together with a total of the parts issued in a 30-day period, where each issue is punched on a separate card.

Accumulating. Data may be added to or subtracted from counters until a final total or result is obtained.

402-519 Connecting Assembly

402 Accounting Machine   519 Document-originating Machine

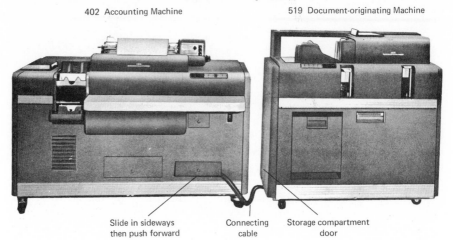

Figure 4-38
Summary Punching

Slide in sideways   Connecting   Storage compartment
then push forward   cable   door

Programming. This is the process by which the machine can determine the difference between one control group and another. This is needed to determine the end of one group and the beginning of another. For example, in processing the weekly sales of a company, the programming feature allows us to process sales by department, and simultaneously by salesman within each department to determine departmental sales and individual sales commissions.

Summary punching. In this operation, the reproducer is attached to the accounting machine by cable, as shown in Figure 4-38. Totals accumulated on the accounting machine can then be transmitted to the reproducer through the connecting cable and there punched into summary cards.

There are several types of accounting machines which may be used to perform the operations listed above. Some of these machines are the IBM 402, 403, 419, and 407 Accounting Machines.

IBM 402 accounting machine

The IBM 402 Accounting Machine, shown in Figure 4-39, is capable of printing up to 88 characters per line. This is accomplished with a series of 88 typebars, the first 43 of which are capable of printing alphabetic and numeric characters in addition to the special character & (ampersand). These typebars control the printing in the first or leftmost 43 positions of the page. The remaining and rightmost 45 typebars are capable of printing the digits 0 to 9, the special character * (asterisk) on odd-numbered typebars, and CR (credit symbol) on the even-numbered typebars.

In addition to the above-mentioned five general operational capabilities, the IBM 402 is capable of printing (using selectors as in the interpreter), emitting, column splitting, leading zero print suppression, and space control. Space control is performed by the carriage control unit, which designates lines to be skipped, when to start a new page, and so forth.

The IBM 403 and 419 are similar in operation to the IBM 402. They differ only in that the 419 can print only numeric information, and that the 403 can print three lines from one card, whereas the 402 and 419 are limited to one line of printing for each card read. For this reason the IBM 403 is sometimes called a Multiple-Line Print (MLP) machine. In all other respects, these machines are alike, and the same basic principles of operation apply to each.

IBM 403 and 419 accounting machines

The IBM 407 Accounting Machine, illustrated in Figure 4-40, can perform all the operations previously listed for the IBM 402 including the MLP of the IBM 403. In addition, the 407 is equipped with storage units capable of storing information which can be used later in its operation. The 407 has 120 type wheels in place of the 88 typebars available on the 402, each of which is capable of printing any of the 26 letters of the alphabet, 10 numerals (0 to 9), and 11 special characters. The appropriate type wheels rotate to the desired character positions and then are pressed toward the paper, causing their printing.

IBM 407 accounting machine

Figure 4-39
IBM 402 Accounting Machine

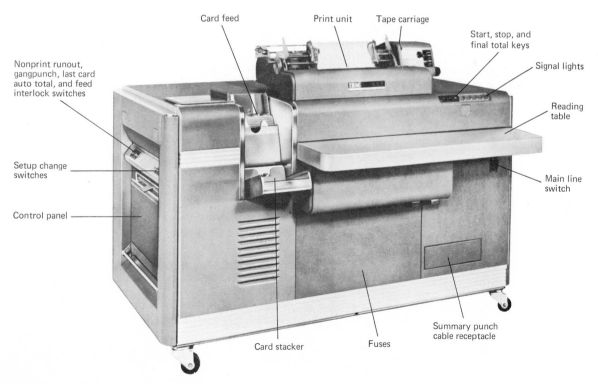

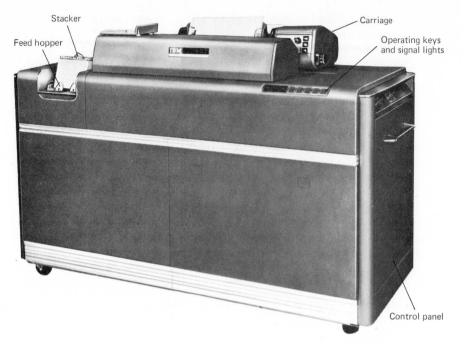

Stacker
Feed hopper
Carriage
Operating keys
and signal lights
Control panel

Figure 4-40
IBM 407 Accounting
Machine

Self-study exercise 4-6

1. Accounting machines are designed to _____.

♦ ♦ ♦

print and accumulate data contained in punched cards at speeds ranging from 50 to 150 cards per minute

2. The specific capabilities of the accounting machine include _____.

♦ ♦ ♦

detail printing, group printing, accumulating, programming, and summary punching

3. _____ printing involves the printing of identifying data from the first card (master) of a group and accumulations or summaries from the remaining cards (detail) of that group.

♦ ♦ ♦

Group

4. In _____, data may be added to or subtracted from counters until a final total or result is obtained.

♦ ♦ ♦

accumulating

5. The IBM 402 Accounting Machine is capable of printing _____ characters per line, _____ of which are alphanumeric and print on the _____ side of the page and _____ of which are numeric and print on the _____ side of the page.

♦ ♦ ♦

88
43
lefthand
45
righthand

6. The IBM 403 and 419 differ in capabilities from the 402 in that _____.

♦ ♦ ♦

the 419 can print only numeric information and the 403 can print up to three lines per card input

7. In addition to the features possessed by the IBM 402 and 403, the IBM 407 can _____.

♦ ♦ ♦

store information for later use

8. Available with the 407 are _____ in place of the 88 typebars available with the 402, each of which is capable of printing _____.

♦ ♦ ♦

120 type wheels
26 letters of the alphabet, 10 numerals, and 11 special characters

End-of-chapter Exercises

True-false exercise

1. Unit record machines utilize the punched card medium.
2. The term *EAM systems* is often used to describe data processing systems which process data directly from punched cards.

3. The classifying of data can be performed on the accounting machine.
4. The summarizing and printing of data is accomplished on the reproducer.
5. The primary function of the interpreter is to reproduce punched cards.
6. The reading of cards can be performed electrically as the card passes beneath a series of reading brushes.
7. The photoelectric unit interprets and prints on all cards that pass beneath the reading brushes.
8. There are 60 reading brushes on the interpreter.
9. Printing can be accomplished on the interpreter on from 2 to 25 possible lines, depending on the model.
10. The interpreter can interpret either straight or offset.
11. X eliminators are also known as column splits.
12. There are two types of selection possible: class and field.
13. Reproducing is the transferring of information from a master card to many subsequent detail cards.
14. Gangpunching involves the punching of information from one master card to one or more detail cards.
15. The reproducer contains two punching units.
16. Summary punching can be performed when the reproducer is connected by cable to the accounting machine.
17. A standard feature of the reproducer is mark-sensing.
18. The document-originating machine is sometimes called a tabulator.
19. A basic operation that can be performed on the collator is the selection of specified cards from a card file.
20. Sequence checking can only be performed using numeric fields.
21. After a file of cards has been sorted into sequence, this sequence can be verified on the collator.
22. To arrange a group of cards into alphabetic order, each column of the field being sorted must be sorted twice, first on the zone portion and second on the digit portion.
23. Failure to joggle cards could cause a card jam in any of the unit record machines.
24. The sorter has two reading brushes: one for the zone and one for the digit punching areas.
25. When sorting on a numeric field, the high order or leftmost column is sorted first.
26. The accounting machine can automatically feed cards, accumulate data in predetermined fields, and print the results of these accumulations.
27. Information printed on a report by the accounting machine can also be simultaneously punched into cards.
28. Programming the accounting machine can determine the first card of one group and the last card of another.
29. There are no storage areas on any model accounting machine.

30. All accounting machines are capable of printing both alphabetic and numeric information.

Multiple-choice exercise

1. Interpreters can be used to
   a. summarize data and print it on the same card
   b. print data punched in a card on that card
   c. print information from the accounting machine
   d. all the above
   e. none of the above
2. The print positions on the IBM 548 Alphabetic Interpreter are located as follows:
   a. The upper line is above the 12 row on the card
   b. The lower line is located between the 0 and 11 rows
   c. The upper line is located between the 11 and 12 rows
   d. The lower line is located below the zone area and above the digit punching area
   e. None of the above
3. The following operations can be performed on the IBM 557 Alphabetic Interpreter:
   a. Information can be read from a master card and printed on successive detail cards
   b. Printing may be performed on up to 25 lines
   c. Characters may be printed that were not read from cards
   d. All the above
   e. None of the above
4. The reproducer will stop reading cards and the comparing indicator will turn on when
   a. the machine has run out of cards in either hopper
   b. the wrong control panel has been inserted
   c. an incorrect comparison of punching has been detected
   d. all the above
   e. none of the above
5. The primary functions of the reproducer are
   a. reproducing, end punching, and gangpunching
   b. reproducing, gangpunching, and summary punching
   c. reproducing, gangpunching, and accumulating
   d. reproducing, selecting, gangpunching, and merging
   e. none of the above
6. To successfully reproduce cards on the IBM 514 reproducer
   a. the punch brushes are wired to the punch magnets
   b. the comparing brushes are wired to the punch magnets
   c. the reproducing brushes are wired to the punch magnets

    d.   the reading brushes are wired to the punch magnets

    e.   none of the above

7. The capabilities of the collator are

    a.   merging, matching, sorting, selecting

    b.   merging, matching, listing, selecting

    c.   merging, matching, sequence checking, selecting

    d.   merging, selecting, and sorting

    e.   any combination of the above

8. Hubs that emit electronic impulses from within the machine are called

    a.   entry hubs

    b.   exit hubs

    c.   common hubs

    d.   bus hubs

    e.   none of the above

9. The interpreter is capable of printing up to

    a.   40 characters on a line

    b.   60 characters on a line

    c.   20 characters on a line

    d.   all the above

    e.   none of the above

10. The main function of the sorter is to

    a.   merge two files into one

    b.   arrange cards into a predetermined pattern

    c.   sequence-check a file of cards

    d.   all the above

    e.   none of the above

11. Selection switches make it possible to

    a.   sort alphabetically

    b.   separate certain types of cards without upsetting the sequential arrangement of the remainder of the deck

    c.   select cards with a specific punch

    d.   all the above

    e.   none of the above

12. The operating capabilities of the accounting machine do not include

    a.   group printing

    b.   detail printing

    c.   mark-sensing

    d.   programming

    e.   summary punching

13. An additional feature of the accounting machine is

    a.   emitting

    b.   zero suppression

    c.   space control

    d. all the above

    e. none of the above

14. The IBM 407 Accounting Machine is capable of printing alphabetic characters in

    a. the leftmost 43 positions

    b. all 88 positions

    c. the leftmost 45 positions

    d. all 120 positions

    e. none of the above

Problems

1. Describe the three basic data processing tasks and the unit record machines used to perform these tasks.
2. Discuss the principle of selection using control panel wiring.
3. Discuss column splits as used with unit record machines.
4. Discuss zero elimination.
5. Explain the operation of summary punching as it relates to the accounting machine and the reproducer.
6. List and discuss the operational capabilities of the reproducer.
7. Discuss four methods of sorting a card file.
8. List and discuss the operational capabilities of the collator.
9. Explain the difference between group and detail printing.
10. Discuss this statement: Punched card machines are obsolete and will soon disappear from the data processing scene.
11. What is the unit record concept? How did it arise?
12. Explain the similarities and differences between reproducing and gang-punching.
13. Discuss why it is necessary for punched cards to have restrictions as to size of the card, paper composition, etc.

UNIT III
COMPUTER SYSTEMS

COMPUTER NUMBER SYSTEMS

CHAPTER 5

Introduction   As the name *computer* would lead one to believe, it is a device designed for the express purpose of computing in the most efficient and economical manner possible. To this end, the designers of computers have applied their efforts and expertise. One of the conclusions reached as a result of their efforts is that it is essential to the development of an efficient, economical, and reliable computer that physical quantities be represented within the computer in forms other than in the traditional decimal number system. Therefore, since computers internally represent physical or numerical quantities in a nondecimal system, it is essential that the computer operator understand these nondecimal number systems in order that he may carry out his duties most efficiently. But, before we turn our attention to these nondecimal number systems, let us first review the meaning of the term *number system.*

What Is a Number System?   A *number system* is a convenient way of representing quantities of physical items. For example, in the decimal number system with which we are familiar, a box containing a dozen articles could also be described as containing 12 articles. The number 12, however, is meaningless unless one understands the decimal number system, just as a dozen articles is meaningful only to those who know what is meant by a *dozen.*

Let us just review what the decimal number 12 actually means. First, it contains two digits—the digit 1 and the digit 2. There are 10 possible digits which may be used in any decimal number, namely, the digits 0, 1, 2, 3, 4, 5, 6, 7, 8, and 9. Each digit in a number serves as a counter. The digit immediately to the left of the decimal point—the digit 2 in the case of the number 12—counts the number of 1s or units in the number. That is, in the number 12 there are two 1s. The next digit to the left counts the amount of 10s in the number. In the case of the number 12, there is one 10 in the number. Putting these facts together, we have that:

The number 12 contains one 10 and two 1s. Expressing this in mathematical form, we have

$$12 = 1 \times 10 + 2 \times 1$$

If we were to consider the number 3,864 in a similar manner, we would conclude that:

$$3,864 = 3 \times 1,000 + 8 \times 100 + 6 \times 10 + 4 \times 1$$

which is referred to as the *expanded form* of the number 3,864. You will note that the weights or multipliers associated with each digit form a definite pattern. Beginning with the weight 1, each subsequent weight is determined by multiplying the previous weight times 10. Thus, the weights are:

$$1 = 1$$
$$1 \times 10 = 10$$
$$(1 \times 10) \times 10 = 100$$
$$[(1 \times 10) \times 10] \times 10 = 1,000$$

. . . .

The fact that the weights associated with the various digits are determined by multiplication by 10, together with the fact that there are 10 distinct digits available, is responsible for our number system being called the *dec*imal number system.

Self-study exercise 5-1

1. A number system can be described as a(n) _____ .

◆ ◆ ◆

convenient way of representing quantities of physical items

2. The _____ of the number 497 would be $4 \times 100 + 9 \times 10 + 7 \times 1$.

◆ ◆ ◆

expanded form

3. The expanded form of the number 4,719 would be _____ .

◆ ◆ ◆

$4 \times 1,000 + 7 \times 100 + 1 \times 10 + 9 \times 1$

4. The weights used in the decimal number system are related in that they are determined by _____ .

◆ ◆ ◆

multiplication by 10

The concepts on which the decimal number system is based also form the foundation of nondecimal number systems. That is, nondecimal number systems also consist of a distinct set of digits and weights. The binary number system, for example, utilizes only two digits—1 and 0. Beginning with the weight 1, each subsequent weight is determined by multiplying the previous weight times 2. Thus, the binary weights are:

Binary Number System

. . .	2 × 16	2 × 8	2 × 4	2 × 2	2 × 1	1
. . .	32	16	8	4	2	1

Utilizing these weights, one could represent the decimal number 23 as follows:

$$23 = 1 \times 16 + 0 \times 8 + 1 \times 4 + 1 \times 2 + 1 \times 1$$

Eliminating the weights and writing just the digits, as we do in the decimal system, we have

$$23 = 1\ 0\ 1\ 1\ 1 \qquad \text{(in binary)}$$

That is, the decimal number 23 is equivalent to the binary number 10111. Each digit within this binary number is called a *binary digit* or *bit* (*bi*nary dig*it*).

As an additional example, let us consider the binary representation of the number 57. To determine the binary equivalent of 57, we must select those binary weights which, when added together, equal 57. We shall begin with the binary weight just larger than the number to be converted—in this case, the binary weight 64.

Binary Weights	Decision to Accept or Reject	Cumulative Total	Total Remaining Unaccounted For
64	No	0	57
32	Yes	32	25
16	Yes	48	9
8	Yes	56	1
4	No	56	1
2	No	56	1
1	Yes	57	0

Summarizing and converting each yes to a 1 and each no to a 0, we have

$$57 = 1 \times 32 + 1 \times 16 + 1 \times 8 + 0 \times 4 + 0 \times 2 + 1 \times 1$$

In the shorthand notation, we have

$$57 = 1\ 1\ 1\ 0\ 0\ 1 \qquad \text{(binary)}$$

An alternate method of determining the binary equivalent of a decimal number is by the *division algorithm*.[1] In this process the decimal number is repeatedly divided by 2, recording the remainder from each division, until a quotient of 0 (zero) is obtained. The remainders of each division by 2, recorded in the reverse order from that in which they were obtained, represent the binary equivalent of the original decimal number.

In the case of the decimal number 57, this process would appear as follows:

Remainder

2)57		
2)28	1	
2)14	0	
2)7	0	
2)3	1	
2)1	1	
0	1	

Thus, in shorthand notation, we have

$$57 = 111001 \quad \text{(binary)}$$

If one wished to determine the decimal equivalent of a given binary number, it would be necessary only to express the number in its expanded form and then to evaluate the expanded form. As an example, let us evaluate the binary number 1101101. The expanded form of this number is

1101101 (binary)
$$= 1 \times 64 + 1 \times 32 + 0 \times 16 + 1 \times 8 + 1 \times 4 + 0 \times 2 + 1 \times 1$$

Performing the indicated operations yields

1101101 (binary) $= 64 + 32 + 0 + 8 + 4 + 0 + 1 = 109$

That is, the binary number 1101101 is equivalent to the decimal number 109.

Self-study exercise 5-2

1. The binary number system utilizes _____ digits, namely, _____.

♦ ♦ ♦

two
0 and 1

---

[1] The division algorithm should not be used with other than *whole numbers,* a whole number being one which has no decimal places.

2. The binary equivalent of the decimal number 13 is _____ .

◆ ◆ ◆

1101

3. The binary equivalent of a decimal number can be determined by selecting the _____ which, when added together, equal the number or by employing a process known as the _____ .

◆ ◆ ◆

binary weights
division algorithm

4. The decimal equivalent of the binary number 1101011 is _____ .

◆ ◆ ◆

107

Hexadecimal Number System

In the hexadecimal number system there are 16 digits. Since we are familiar with only the 10 digits 0, 1, 2, 3, 4, 5, 6, 7, 8, and 9, it is necessary to create an additional 6 digits, namely, A, B, C, D, E, and F, where A = 10, B = 11, C = 12, D = 13, E = 14, and F = 15.

The weights in the hexadecimal system begin with 1, as in other number systems, but with subsequent weights being determined by multiplying the previous weight times 16. Thus, the hexadecimal weights are 1, 16, 256, etc. In order to determine the decimal equivalent of a hexadecimal number, we proceed as we did with conversions from binary—we evaluate the expanded form of the hexadecimal number. In the case of the hexadecimal number 3AC, for example, this would be as follows:

$$
\begin{aligned}
3AC &= 3 \times 256 + A \times 16 + C \times 1 \\
&= 3 \times 256 + 10 \times 16 + 12 \times 1 \\
&= 768 + 160 + 12 \\
3AC &= 940 \quad \text{(decimal)}
\end{aligned}
$$

If we examine the binary equivalent of 940, we note a unique relationship between this binary number and the hexadecimal number 3AC. We see that each group of four binary digits, beginning at the decimal point, is exactly equal to a corresponding digit in the equivalent hexadecimal number.

This relationship is illustrated below.

3   A   C   (hexadecimal equivalent of 940)

001110101100   (binary equivalent of 940)

A complete list of the binary-to-hexadecimal digit conversions is given in Table 5-1.

Utilizing Table 5-1, we can convert the hexadecimal number 1A4.B3 to its binary equivalent.

0001   (binary) = 1   (hexadecimal)
1010   = A
0100   = 4
1011   = B
0011   = 3

Putting these equivalences together, we have

1A4.B3 = 000110100100.10110011

Table 5-1. Binary-to-hexadecimal Conversions

Binary Digits	Hexadecimal Digit
0000	0
0001	1
0010	2
0011	3
0100	4
0101	5
0110	6
0111	7
1000	8
1001	9
1010	A
1011	B
1100	C
1101	D
1110	E
1111	F

Let us consider two additional examples.

1. 101101001001.01001010 (binary) = ? (hexadecimal equivalent)

1011	0100	1001	0100	1010	(binary number)
B	4	9	4	A	(hexadecimal equivalent)

Therefore

101101001001.01001010 (binary) = B49.4A (hexadecimal)

2. A34B.F (hexadecimal) = ? (binary equivalent)

A	3	4	B	F	(hexadecimal number)
1010	0011	0100	1011	1111	(binary equivalent)

Therefore

A34B.F (hexadecimal) = 1010001101001011.1111 (binary)

Self-study exercise 5-3

1. The hexadecimal number system consists of the _____ digits _____ .

◆ ◆ ◆

16
0, 1, 2, 3, 4, 5, 6, 7, 8, 9, A, B, C, D, E, F

2. Each hexadecimal weight after the weight 1 is found by multiplying the previous weight by _____ .

◆ ◆ ◆

16

3. The decimal equivalent of the hexadecimal number A6 is _____ .

◆ ◆ ◆

166

4. The binary equivalent of the hexadecimal number A4BF is _____.

♦ ♦ ♦

1010010010111111

You will recall we stated earlier that, within a computer, numbers or physical quantities are represented in a form other than decimal. In actuality, numbers or physical quantities are represented within the computer as a series of bits (*binary digits*). In the IBM 360 or 370 computer, for example, the smallest unit of information which can be stored in its memory is a bit. However, data can be accessed only in groups of 8 bits. Such a group of 8 bits is referred to as a *byte*. The memory of a computer can be thought of as a string of bytes with each byte being assigned a unique address by which it can be identified and by which the number contained within it can be accessed. The first byte in the memory of the computer is assigned the address 0; the second byte, the address 1; the third byte, the address 2; etc., for each byte in the computer's memory.

*Bits, Bytes, and Words[2]

    Bytes are combined into units called *half-words* (2 bytes, or 16 bits), *fullwords* (4 bytes, or 32 bits), and *doublewords* (8 bytes, or 64 bits). The address associated with half-words, fullwords, and doublewords is the address assigned the first byte within the given half-word, fullword, or doubleword.

    It is noteworthy that, as a result of assigning to a half-word, fullword, or doubleword the address associated with the first byte within it, half-word addresses will always be multiples of 2, fullword addresses multiples of 4, and doubleword addresses multiples of 8.

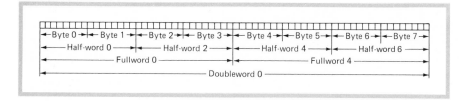

Figure 5-1
Relationship between a Byte, Half-word, Fullword, and Doubleword

Self-study exercise 5-4

1. The term *bit* is a contraction of the words _____.

♦ ♦ ♦

binary digit

---

[2]Unless otherwise stated, the concepts discussed in the remainder of this chapter will refer directly to the IBM 360 and 370 Series computers and will be generally applicable to other models and manufacturers' computers.

2. A byte consists of _____.

◆ ◆ ◆

8 binary digits or bits

3. Bytes are combined in the memory of the computer into larger units called _____, _____, and _____.

◆ ◆ ◆

half-words
fullwords
doublewords

4. A half-word consists of _____ bits, a fullword of _____ bits, and a doubleword of _____ bits.

◆ ◆ ◆

16
32
64

Data Storage Formats

We have stated that computers generally do not store data in decimal. The question then arises, "What does the computer do if a decimal number is input to it?" The answer is a relatively simple one. Should a decimal number be input, it must first be translated into binary, or some other form, before it can be stored and subsequently utilized. Within the IBM 360 or 370 Series computer, there are four possible modes into which data can be translated for subsequent storage and processing. These are:

1. Binary
2. Packed decimal
3. Zoned decimal
4. Floating point

Binary

In general, when a quantity is stored in binary, it utilizes one fullword of storage (4 bytes, or 32 bits). Since in the binary number system we have only the digits 1 and 0, each bit of the fullword is necessarily a 1 or a 0. If we were to store the binary number 101101101 (equivalent to the decimal number 365) in fullword 0, it would appear as:

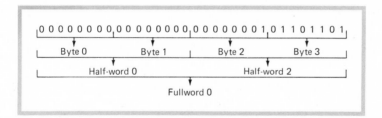

Figure 5-2
Fullword 0 Containing
the Binary Number
101101101

It should be noted that although the binary number was only 9 bits long, when stored in the computer it occupied an entire fullword, or 32 bits.

Suppose now that we wish to store the binary number −101101101. It is clear that some means must be provided to store the equivalent of the minus (−) sign. We know we cannot store it directly, since each bit is capable of storing only a 1 or a 0. What the computer does is manipulate the actual binary number itself by taking the 2's complement of the original binary number. This can be thought of as a three-step process.

Step 1.   Store the binary number without consideration of the negative (−) sign in a fullword.

00000000000000000000000101101101

Step 2.   Change each 1 in the above to a 0 and each 0 in the above to a 1.

11111111111111111111111010010010

Step 3.   Add a binary 1 to the binary number obtained in step 2 above.

11111111111111111111111010010011

This now represents the 2's complement of the binary number 101101101, and most importantly, it represents the binary number −101101101.

You are probably wondering why such a complicated process is necessary. The answer is twofold. First, for the computer this is a very simple operation which can be accomplished quickly and easily. Second, this process allows the computer to easily handle the addition of *signed numbers*[3] and also to accomplish a subtraction without actually having to

[3] A signed number is a number preceded by either a + (positive) or − (negative) sign.

subtract. For example, should the computer be required to add the binary numbers −10110 and 11001, it could accomplish this by *adding* the 2's complement of the binary number 10110 to the binary number 11001. How the computer actually accomplishes this is not relevant to our study at this time. All that need concern us is that what normally would have involved a subtraction is accomplished as the result of performing a 2's complement and an addition, thus eliminating the necessity for a computer to contain a separate device capable of subtracting. As another example, let us subtract the binary number 1011 from the binary number 10111.

$$
\begin{array}{r}
10111 \\
-\ 1011 \\
\hline
\end{array}
$$

This is accomplished by *adding* the binary number 10111 to the 2's complement of the binary number 1011. It is important to remember that this process involves fullwords, not just the bits in the binary number.

As you have probably realized, the bit configuration of a given half-word, fullword, and especially a doubleword is cumbersome to read, interpret, or write down. To simplify these processes, a shorthand method of indicating the bit configuration of a half-word, fullword, or doubleword is utilized. The method is simply to convert the binary number to its hexadecimal equivalent. As we discussed earlier in the chapter, a binary number can be converted to its hexadecimal equivalent by simply converting the binary digits, in groups of four, to hexadecimal digits. Thus, the binary number 10110101101, stored in a fullword as

00000000000000000000010110101101

would appear in this shorthand or hexadecimal notation as follows (see Table 5-1):

00000000000000000000010110101101

0　0　0　0　0　5　A　D

Thus, only 8 hexadecimal digits are now required, where previously 32 binary digits were necessary. To determine the binary equivalent of a number expressed in this notation, one simply assigns 4 binary digits to each hexadecimal digit. For example, the hexadecimal number

0　0　0　4　A　B　3　7 would equal

00000000000001001010101100110111 in binary

(See Table 5-1)

Table 5-2. Comparison of Zone Codes in Hollerith, BCD, and EBCDIC Coding Schemes

Hollerith	BCD		EBCDIC				Hex. Equiv.
12 punch	1	1	1	1	0	0	C
11 punch	1	0	1	1	0	1	D
0 punch	0	1	1	1	1	0	E
No zone punch	0	0	1	1	1	1	F

As a character is represented on a card as a combination of zone and digit punches, so can it be represented within the computer as a combination of zone and digit bits. Specifically, when a character is stored in the zoned decimal format, 4 bits each are required for the zone and digit portions. That is, one character, be it a letter of the alphabet, a digit, or a special character, can be stored in zoned decimal format in each byte of storage. The code which is utilized to represent characters in zoned decimal is referred to as the Extended Binary Coded Decimal Interchange Code (EBCDIC). Tables 5-2 and 5-3 illustrate the relationship between the Hollerith, BCD, and EBCDIC zone and digit coding schemes.

Zoned decimal

Using Tables 5-2 and 5-3, we can determine that the letter G, for example, which consists of a 12 punch and a 7 punch in Hollerith code, consists of 1100 in the zone portion and 0111 in the digit portion in EBCDIC.

Table 5-3. Comparison of Digit Codes in Hollerith, BCD, and EBCDIC Coding Schemes

Hollerith	BCD	EBCDIC	Hex. Equiv.
0 punch	0000	0000	0
1 punch	0001	0001	1
2 punch	0010	0010	2
3 punch	0011	0011	3
4 punch	0100	0100	4
5 punch	0101	0101	5
6 punch	0110	0110	6
7 punch	0111	0111	7
8 punch	1000	1000	8
9 punch	1001	1001	9

Representing this letter in a single byte, we have

11000111

Employing the shorthand hexadecimal notations yields

11000111

C   7

That is, in zoned decimal format the letter G would appear within the computer as 11000111 with a hexadecimal equivalent of C7.

As a practice exercise, let us determine the hexadecimal code in zoned decimal format for the word *MIKE*.

	M	I	K	E
Hollerith	11–4	12–9	11–2	12–5
EBCDIC	11010100	11001001	11010010	11000101
Hexadecimal	D4	C9	D2	C5

That is, the word *MIKE* would be contained in one fullword of storage as

D4C9D2C5

It should be noted that data stored in zoned decimal format must consist of an even number of bytes and cannot exceed 16 bytes in length. That is, a maximum of 16 characters may be stored in zoned decimal. Should the data not consist of an even number of characters, the hexadecimal code for a blank is inserted in the zoned decimal representation of the data so that it will occupy an even number of bytes.

Numbers in zoned decimal. The only difference between the representation of numeric quantities in zoned decimal, as opposed to letters, is that numeric quantities *must be* stored with an algebraic sign, be it positive (+) or negative (−). This is accomplished by utilizing the rightmost byte of the zoned decimal representation to contain both the sign of the entire number *and* the rightmost digit of the number. In the case of the number

−384

this would mean that the rightmost byte would contain a code both for the negative (−) sign of the number and for the digit 4.

This is accomplished by placing a code for the negative (−) sign in the zone (first 4) bits of this byte and the code for the digit 4 in the digit (last 4) bits of this byte. The codes for the algebraic signs + and − are:

Algebraic Sign	Code	
	EBCDIC	Hexadecimal
+	1100	C
−	1101	D[4]

Utilizing the above code, the number − 384 would appear as follows:

Characters	3	8	(−) & 4
EBCDIC	11110011	11111000	11010100
Hexadecimal	F 3	F 8	D 4

That is, the zoned decimal representation of the number − 384 would be F3F8D4. Some additional examples are:

Number	EBCDIC	Hexadecimal
3,452	11110011111101001111010111000010	F3F4F5C2
814	111110001111000111000100	F8F1C4
−1,736	11110001111101111111001111010110	F1F7F3D6
−2	11010010	D2
4	11000100	C4

In recording alphabetic or alphanumeric data, one must use the zoned decimal format. However, with numeric data, several options are available. We have already seen two of these options—zoned decimal and binary. Let us now investigate a third possibility—packed decimal.

Packed decimal

You will note that when numeric data is represented in zoned decimal, with the exception of the rightmost byte which carries the sign, the zone bits of each byte are 1111 (hexadecimal F). They are carrying virtually no information. To make better use of these bits, the packed decimal format was devised. When storing a number in packed decimal, each digit of the number to be stored need be allocated only 4 bits ($\frac{1}{2}$ byte) as opposed to the 8 bits (1 byte) required to store a digit in zoned decimal format. As with zoned decimal, packed decimal also requires that 4 bits be used

[4]Note that the hexadecimal character D utilized as a zone in representing alphabetic characters is also utilized to represent a negative (−) sign in the case of a negative number.

to represent the sign of the number. There is, however, a difference in the relative position of the sign bits within the number. While the sign bits were the first 4 bits in the rightmost byte in zoned decimal, they are the last 4 bits in the rightmost byte in packed decimal.

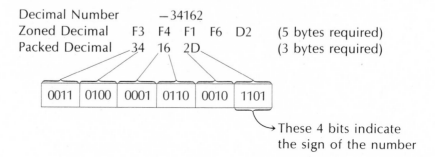

Decimal Number   −34162
Zoned Decimal   F3 F4 F1 F6 D2   (5 bytes required)
Packed Decimal   34 16 2D   (3 bytes required)

| 0011 | 0100 | 0001 | 0110 | 0010 | 1101 |

These 4 bits indicate
the sign of the number

Let us apply this to a practical example. For example, let us determine the packed decimal representation of the number −487:

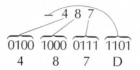

−4 8 7
0100 1000 0111 1101
4   8   7   D

Note that in packed decimal the sign is carried after the number, while in the decimal representation the sign is carried before the number. Thus, the only difference in appearance between the packed decimal format of this number in hexadecimal notation and the number in decimal notation is the symbol used to indicate the algebraic sign of the number (+ or −) and the placement of this symbol.

One exception to this rule arises when the number (counting the algebraic sign as a digit) contains an odd number of digits. In this case, a leading zero would appear in the packed decimal representation in order to utilize a whole number of bytes. That is, the decimal number −87 would appear as

087D

in packed decimal, thus completely utilizing 2 bytes (16 bits) of storage. Some additional examples of packed decimal representations of decimal numbers are:

−4	01001101	4D
6	01101100	6C
−15	0000000101011101	015D
15	0000000101011100	015C

Packed decimal representations are restricted to a maximum size of 16 bytes (31 digits plus an algebraic sign) as were zone decimal representations.

* Floating point

Occasionally, it is desirable to process numbers which are larger or fractionally smaller than is possible in a binary or packed decimal format. This is accomplished by representing the numbers in exponential notation. In exponential notation, a number consists of two parts—a *mantissa* and a *characteristic*. The mantissa contains the significant digits (all digits excluding leading and/or trailing zeros) in the number, while the characteristic refers to the placement of the decimal point. For example, the number 314.159 could also be represented in exponential notation as $.314159 \times 10^3$ ($10^3 = 1,000$). In this representation, the mantissa is .314159 and the characteristic is 3. Reconstructing the number from this exponential notation to decimal notation, we simply need move the decimal point in the mantissa the number of places to the right or left as is indicated in the characteristic. A positive (+) characteristic means that the decimal point in the mantissa should be moved to the right, while a negative (−) characteristic means that the decimal point in the mantissa should be moved to the left. In our case, we have

$$.3 \ 1 \ 4. \ 1 \ 5 \ 9 = 314.159$$
$$+1 \ +2 \ +3$$

Other examples are shown in Table 5-4.

Within the computer, however, there is a slight variation in representation from what has just been illustrated. That is, within the computer,

Table 5-4. Examples of Numbers Stored in Floating Point Format

Decimal Number	Exponential Form	Mantissa	Characteristic	Reconstruction
4783.9	$.47839 \times 10^4$	.47839	+4	4 7 8 3.9 +1+2+3+4
.00437	$.437 \times 10^{-2}$	.437	−2	.0 0437 −2−1
3900000	$.39 \times 10^7$	.39	+7	3 9 0 0 0 0 0. +1+2+3+4+5+6+7

floating point numbers are represented in 32-bit words as follows:

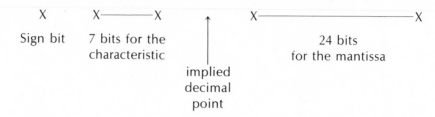

The sign bit is 0 if the number is positive or 1 if the number is negative.

The interpretation of the 7-bit characteristic requires some explanation. To determine the actual value of the characteristic, one must subtract 64 from the decimal equivalent of the 7 bits. For example, if the 7 bits were

$$1000101$$

then the characteristic would be determined as follows:

$$1000101 = 69 \qquad \text{and} \qquad 69 - 64 = 5$$

Therefore, the characteristic is 5. And, since the IBM System/360 is a hexadecimal machine, the characteristic indicates how many hexadecimal digits, or groups of 4 binary digits, the decimal point must be moved from its assumed position in the mantissa. That is, a characteristic of 5 refers to moving the decimal point to the right 5 hexadecimal places, or 20 bits.

The 24-bit mantissa contains the equivalent of the decimal mantissa, except that it is expressed in binary (or hexadecimal if interpreted in groups of 4 bits).

Let us put together all these concepts to interpret the meaning of the 32-bit floating point fullword below.

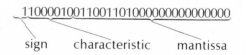

Table 5-5. Interpretation of a Number Stored in Floating Point Format

Item	Bit Configuration	Interpretation
Sign	1	negative number
Characteristic	1000010	$1000010 = 66 - 64 = 2$
Mantissa	011001101000000000000000	668000 (in hexadecimal)
	assumed decimal point	

Table 5-6.   Binary and Hexadecimal Equivalents
of Selected Decimal Numbers Less than 1

Decimal	Binary	Hexadecimal
0.05	.000011001100	.0CC
0.10	.000110011001	.199
0.15	.001001100110	.266
0.20	.001100110011	.333
0.25	.010000000000	.400
0.30	.010011001100	.4CC
0.35	.010110011001	.599
0.40	.011001100110	.666
0.45	.011100110011	.733
0.50	.100000000000	.800
0.55	.100011001100	.8CC
0.60	.100110011001	.999
0.65	.101001100110	.A66
0.70	.101100110011	.B33
0.75	.110000000000	.C00
0.80	.110011001100	.CCC
0.85	.110110011001	.D99
0.90	.111001100110	.E66
0.95	.111100110011	.F33

Putting these facts together, we can conclude that the given fullword is equal to -66.8000 in hexadecimal or -102.5 in decimal.

Other examples are found in Table 5-7.

Floating point numbers can, in special cases, be 64 bits (doubleword) in length. Such numbers are called *double-precision* floating point numbers. The additional 32 bits are added to the mantissa of the single-precision floating point number. Thus, double precision allows up to a maximum of 14 decimal places of accuracy as opposed to the maximum of 6-decimal-place accuracy which is possible in single precision (32-bit single word).

Computational and output formats

You have seen thus far that it is possible to store data in any of four possible formats, namely, binary, zoned decimal, packed decimal, and floating point. It is, however, not possible for a computer to perform computations on data stored in zoned decimal. This data must first be converted to packed decimal before any arithmetic operations can be performed. If only limited computations will be performed, they can be performed in packed decimal. However, if a substantial number of calculations will be performed with

Table 5-7.   Conversions of Decimal Numbers to Floating Point Format

Decimal Number	Binary Equivalent	32-bit Floating Point Equivalent			Interpretation of Floating Point Equivalent		
		Sign Bit	Characteristic	Mantissa	Sign	Mantissa (in Hexadecimal)	Characteristic
49	110001	0	1000010	00110001000000000000000	+	310000	2
13	1101	0	1000001	11010000000000000000000	+	D00000	1
−8	1000	1	1000001	10000000000000000000000	−	800000	1
−254	11111110	1	1000010	11111110000000000000000	−	FE0000	2
49.5[1]	110001.1	0	1000010	00110001100000000000000	+	318000	2
−254.75[1]	11111110.11	1	1000010	11111110110000000000000	−	FEC000	2

[1]See Table 5-6 for the conversion of fractional parts of numbers to and from decimal and binary or hexadecimal.

data input in zoned decimal, it would be beneficial to convert this input data from zoned decimal to packed decimal and then from packed decimal to binary. The reason is simply that binary is, by far, the fastest and most efficient format in which to perform arithmetic operations.

It should be noted, however, that before data can be printed out, it must be in zoned decimal format. Should the data for output be in any other format, it must be converted to zoned decimal prior to being output.

Self-study exercise 5-5

1. Within the IBM 360 and 370 Series computers, there are _____ possible modes into which data can be stored, namely, _____ .

◆   ◆   ◆

four
binary, packed decimal, zoned decimal, and floating point

2. In general, a quantity stored in binary utilizes _____ of storage, or _____ bytes of storage.

◆   ◆   ◆

one fullword
4

3. The binary number 11011011, equal to the decimal number _____,
   would appear as _____ in binary mode.

   ◆   ◆   ◆

   219
   00000000000000000000000011011011

4. If, on the other hand, the negative of the number referred to in Problem 3 (−11011011) were to be stored, it would appear in binary mode
   as _____.

   ◆   ◆   ◆

   11111111111111111111111100100101

5. In a modern computer such as the IBM 360 or 370, subtraction of
   numbers in the binary mode can be accomplished by adding _____.

   ◆   ◆   ◆

   the 2's complement of the number to be subtracted

6. The 2's complement of a number in binary mode can be determined
   in two steps, namely, _____.

   ◆   ◆   ◆

   Step 1.   Change each 1 to a 0 and each 0 to a 1
   Step 2.   Add binary 1 to the binary number obtained in step 1

7. To simplify the reading, interpreting, and writing of the bit configurations of half-words, fullwords, and doublewords, the bit configurations
   are generally converted to an equivalent _____ notation.

   ◆   ◆   ◆

   hexadecimal

8. The equivalent hexadecimal notation of the binary number
   11011110110000110111101001000001 is _____.

   ◆   ◆   ◆

   DEC37A41

9. In zoned decimal format, characters are coded using _____.

◆ ◆ ◆

EBCDIC (Extended Binary Coded Decimal Interchange Code)

10. Digit codes in the EBCDIC and BCD coding schemes are _____.

◆ ◆ ◆

identical

11. The BCD coding scheme utilizes _____ bits to represent the various zones, while _____ bits are required in EBCDIC.

◆ ◆ ◆

2
4

12. The EBCDIC representation of the letters in the name *LIZ* is _____.

◆ ◆ ◆

L 11010011
I 11001001
Z 11101001

13. The hexadecimal code in zoned decimal format for the word *HELP* contained in one fullword of storage is _____.

◆ ◆ ◆

C8C5D3D7

14. The maximum number of characters that can be stored in zoned decimal is _____.

◆ ◆ ◆

16

15. In zoned decimal format, numbers must be stored with a(n) _____.

◆ ◆ ◆

algebraic sign

16. The algebraic sign of a number is stored in the _____ of the _____ byte of the zoned decimal representation of the number.

◆ ◆ ◆

zone bits (or first 4 bits)
rightmost

17. A + or − algebraic sign is indicated by the hexadecimal digits _____, respectively.

◆ ◆ ◆

C or D

18. The zoned decimal representation of the number −492 is _____.

◆ ◆ ◆

EBCDIC: *11110100*   *11111001*   *11010010*
Hexadecimal: *F4*   *F9*   *D2*

19. The packed decimal format may be used with only _____ data.

◆ ◆ ◆

numeric

20. In packed decimal, except for the byte containing the sign of the number represented, each byte is used to store _____.

◆ ◆ ◆

two digits

21. The sign in packed decimal is located in the _____ bits of the _____ byte.

◆ ◆ ◆

rightmost 4
rightmost

22. The packed decimal representation of the number −178 is _____.

◆ ◆ ◆

178D

23. If the number of digits in a given number, counting the algebraic sign as a digit, is odd, a(n) _____ will appear in the packed decimal representation of the number so that this representation will satisfy the requirement that it consist of _____.

◆ ◆ ◆

leading zero
an even number of bytes

24. The packed decimal representation of the number 3462 is _____.

◆ ◆ ◆

03462C

25. The maximum number of digits that can be represented in packed decimal is _____ plus an algebraic sign.

◆ ◆ ◆

31

26. In exponential notation, a number consists of a(n) _____ and a(n) _____.

◆ ◆ ◆

mantissa
characteristic

27. In exponential form, the number −3,847.1 would be _____.

◆ ◆ ◆

−0.38471 × 10⁴

28. Floating point numbers are represented in _____-bit words in the general form _____.

◆ ◆ ◆

32

$$\underset{\substack{\text{sign} \\ \text{bit}}}{\underbrace{x}} \quad \underset{\substack{\text{7 bits for the} \\ \text{characteristic}}}{\underbrace{x\text{_____}x}} \quad \underset{\substack{\text{implied} \\ \text{decimal} \\ \text{point}}}{\uparrow} \quad \underset{\substack{\text{24 bits for} \\ \text{the mantissa}}}{\underbrace{x\text{_____}x}}$$

29. If the 7 bits representing the characteristic of a number in floating point mode were 1001010, then the actual characteristic would be _____.

◆ ◆ ◆

10, since 1001010 = 74 and 74 − 64 = 10

30. The hexadecimal equivalent of the floating point number 1100001100010111011010000101000 is _____.

◆ ◆ ◆

1	1000011	0001	0111	0110	1000	0101	0000
sign	characteristic				mantissa		
−	3=67−64	1	7	6	8	5	0

Thus $-\underbrace{1\,7\,6}.850 = -176.850$ *(in hexadecimal)*

31. A floating point number, in special cases, can be as large as _____ in length.

◆ ◆ ◆

64 bits, or a doubleword

32. Numeric data stored in zoned decimal must first be _____ before this data can be used in computations.

◆ ◆ ◆

converted to packed decimal

33. If a substantial number of computations are to be performed with data stored in zoned decimal, it would be beneficial to convert this data _____.

◆ ◆ ◆

to packed decimal and from packed decimal to binary

34. Before data can be output, it must be converted to _____ mode, if it is not already in this mode.

◆ ◆ ◆

zoned decimal

End-of-chapter Exercises

True-false exercise

1. Computers generally represent data internally in decimal.
2. The basic concepts on which the decimal number system is based also form the foundation for nondecimal number systems.
3. The binary number system utilizes only two digits, 1 and 2.
4. The binary equivalent of the decimal number 27 is 11001.
5. The division algorithm is a process which can be used to convert a decimal number to binary.
6. The hexadecimal number system utilizes 16 digits, namely, 0, 1, 2, 3, 4, 5, 6, 7, 8, 9, A, B, C, D, E, F.
7. A binary number can be converted to hexadecimal by equating each group of four binary digits to one hexadecimal digit.
8. A fullword consists of 8 bytes, or 64 bits.
9. Within the IBM 360 and 370 Series computers, data may be represented internally in one of four possible modes.
10. Alphabetic data may be represented internally in the computer only in the zoned decimal format.
11. Data may be output from the computer only in zoned decimal format.

Fill-in exercise

1. The _____ of a number represents the number with the weight associated with each digit in the number being explicitly represented.
2. A contraction for the words *binary digit* is _____.
3. The binary equivalent of the decimal number 84 is _____.
4. The hexadecimal equivalent of the binary number 1101111010011010 is _____.
5. A byte consists of _____ bits, while a fullword consists of _____ bits.
6. Half-words, fullwords, and doublewords are identified by numbers which are multiples of _____, _____, and _____, respectively.
7. The possible modes into which data can be translated for subsequent storage and processing are _____, _____, _____, and _____.
8. The _____ mode, in general, most closely resembles the appearance of a number in decimal.
9. The _____ of a floating point number refers to the relative placement of the decimal point in the number.
10. _____ format may be used to represent both alphabetic and numeric characters.

Problems

1. Define each of the terms below.
   a. number system   d. mantissa
   b. half-word   e. division algorithm
   c. byte   f. signed number

2. Determine the decimal equivalent of the numbers below.
   a. 101101   (binary)
   b. 1101101101   (binary)
   c. 3A4B   (hexadecimal)
   d. 47A   (hexadecimal)

3. Express each of the numbers below in the expanded form.
   a. 3146   (decimal)
   b. 101101   (binary)
   c. A3FB   (hexadecimal)

4. Represent each of the terms below in BCD and EBCDIC.
   a. ELIZABETH
   b. COMPUTERS 1
   c. 314AC
   d. 890,462

5. Determine the binary equivalent for each of the numbers below.
   a. 47   c. 1,041
   b. −3,142   d. 38,472

6. Convert the binary numbers below to hexadecimal.
   a. 10110101
   b. −10110110
   c. 11011.11001111
   d. −10101000.1110100011

7. Convert the hexadecimal numbers below to binary.
   a. A34B   c. −3A4B.FE
   b. −FE04   d. E0BC.AD

8. Represent each of the numbers below in binary, packed decimal, zoned decimal, and floating point.
   a. 346
   b. 1,347
   c. 3,084,762

9. Determine the 2's complement of the numbers below.
   a. 101101
   b. 10111101011

10. Convert the numbers below to floating point mode.
    a. 3,874.6
    b. 0.4782×10^3
    c. A479.B   (hexadecimal)

COMPONENTS OF A DATA PROCESSING SYSTEM

CHAPTER 6

Introduction A computer system can be thought of as a complex of various diverse machines working together to a common end—to solve problems. Within this complex of machines, one would usually find three types of devices: one which actually accomplishes the processing of data (Central Processing Unit, or CPU), one which is used to store input data for subsequent use (storage), and one which facilitates the input and output of data (input/output devices).

In this chapter, we shall discuss the functions and capabilities of the CPU, the concepts and types of storage, and some of the various types of input/output devices associated with computer systems.

Central Processing Unit (CPU) The CPU is the control center of the entire computer system. It accepts data from the input device(s), processes this data, and outputs the results via the appropriate output device(s).

In general, the processor or CPU of a computer system consists of two subunits:[1]

    1.   Arithmetic and Logic Unit (ALU)
    2.   Control Unit

Arithmetic and logic unit (ALU) The ALU contains those electronic circuits which perform the basic arithmetic operations of addition, subtraction, multiplication, and division. This unit also contains the circuitry necessary to perform such logical operations as comparing, the moving of data within storage, editing, and various other operations on data stored within the computer.

Control unit The control unit of the CPU controls and coordinates the activities of the computer system in much the same manner as the human brain coordinates and controls the activities of the human body. Within the computer it controls the input/output devices, the storing and retrieving of data, the routing of data between storage and the ALU, and the execution of instructions. This unit is principally responsible for integrating the various components or devices within a computer system into a functionally cohesive whole.

Registers As shown in Figure 6-1, the CPU also contains a number of registers. A *register* is a device capable of storing a specified amount of data, generally one or more fullwords (one fullword = 32 bits). Registers are used for arithmetic operations, logical operations, and with computer instructions. In the IBM 360, for example, there are 16 general registers, each with a

---

[1] In some computer systems, the storage unit is considered an integral part of the CPU; however, in the case of the IBM Series 360 and 370 computers, this is not so.

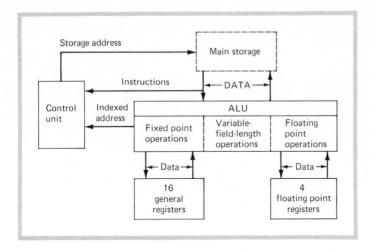

Figure 6-1
Central Processing Unit,
Subunits, and Logic Flow

capacity of one fullword, identified by the numbers 0 to 15, respectively. Registers are utilized in the performance of certain arithmetic operations in addition to holding data to be operated upon. Data contained within a register may consist of numbers, letters of the alphabet, or codes utilized by the programmer.

Four additional floating point registers are provided to facilitate operations dealing with floating point numbers. These registers are each a doubleword (64 bits) in length and are identified by the numbers 0, 2, 4, and 6, respectively.

In some instances, it is possible to display on the console of the CPU, via a group of small lights, register contents and various program conditions.

Self-study exercise 6-1

1. A computer system can be thought of as a(n) _____ .

♦ ♦ ♦

complex of various diverse machines working together to a common end of solving problems

2. The CPU is the _____ of the entire computer system.

♦ ♦ ♦

control center

3. In general, the CPU consists of _____ subunits, namely, _____ and _____ .

♦ ♦ ♦

two
Arithmetic and Logic Unit (ALU)
Control Unit

4. The ALU contains _____ .

♦ ♦ ♦

those electronic circuits which perform the basic arithmetic operations of addition, subtraction, multiplication, and division

5. The Control Unit of the CPU _____ .

♦ ♦ ♦

controls and coordinates the activities of the computer system

6. A(n) _____ is a device capable of storing a specified amount of data, generally _____ .

♦ ♦ ♦

register
one or more fullwords

7. Registers are used for _____ .

♦ ♦ ♦

arithmetic operations, logical operations, and with computer instructions

8. Data contained within a register may consist of _____ .

♦ ♦ ♦

numbers, letters, or codes utilized by the programmer

9. In the IBM 360, there are _____ general registers and _____ floating
   point registers.

◆ ◆ ◆

16
4

In addition to possessing a CPU, a computer system must also possess a   **Storage**
capability to store data for subsequent use.

Such a storage capability is as essential to the operation of a computer system as our memory is to us in the performance of routine everyday
activities.

In addition to storing data, the storage facility associated with a
computer system must be capable of storing instructions necessary to direct
the computer in the solution of problem applications. Once stored, these
instructions (stored program), and the data required by these instructions,
can then be accessed and executed in a predetermined sequence.

There are two general types of storage utilized by computers. They
are:

1. Primary storage
2. Secondary storage

Primary storage, referred to by numerous other names, such as main storage,   **Primary storage**
core, or memory, is under the direct control of and commonly an integral
part of the CPU of the computer. Access time[2] is minimal when data is
located in primary storage.

The relationship that exists between primary storage and the computer is almost identical to the relationship in the human being between
the body and the human memory. In both cases, information is directly
and easily accessed at great speed. In the case of the human being, data
input via the senses is stored in the memory before subsequent analysis
can be made and action based on this data can be taken. And so it is the case
with a computer system. Data must be placed in primary storage before
it can be processed or otherwise utilized within the computer system.

As we learned in the previous chapter, data is stored as bits (binary
digits) or bytes (groups of eight binary digits). This is physically accomplished with the aid of high-speed electronic circuits (monolithic circuits)
or by less expensive, lower-speed physical devices such as magnetic cores,
thin film, or plated wire. The most common of those used in the design

---

[2]Access time is the time interval between the instant at which information is called
from storage and the instant at which delivery is completed.

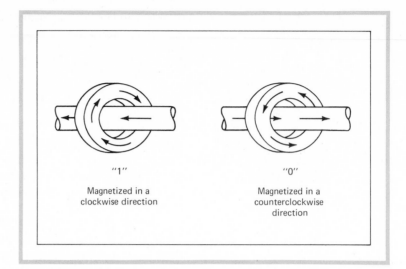

"1"

Magnetized in a
clockwise direction

"0"

Magnetized in a
counterclockwise
direction

Figure 6-2
Two States of a Ferrite
Core

of primary storage is the magnetic core. For this reason, primary storage is often referred to as *core,* or *core storage.*

As illustrated in Figure 6-2, the magnetic core is a tiny doughnut-shaped iron ring capable of being magnetized in one of two directions, clockwise or counterclockwise. The direction of magnetization indicates whether a 1 bit or a 0 bit is stored on the core.

Secondary storage   Many data processing applications require a larger storage capacity than is available in primary storage. In these cases, the storage capability of a computer system can be augmented by one or more secondary storage devices.

Secondary storage is located outside of the CPU and may or may not be connected to the CPU. In either case, in order to process an item of data contained in secondary storage, it would first have to be transferred or moved to the CPU (primary storage), at which point it would be processed as any other data in primary storage. Thus, access times are generally greater for secondary storage than for primary storage. Therefore, frequently accessed data is commonly stored in primary storage. Less frequently used data, or data whose great volume makes its placement in primary storage impractical, if not impossible, is stored in secondary storage.

Secondary storage is classified as one of two types, depending upon whether or not it is connected to the CPU. If it is connected to the CPU, it is referred to as *auxiliary storage;* if it is not connected to the CPU, it is referred to as *external storage.*

Using the previously mentioned parallel between the human memory and internal storage, auxiliary storage corresponds to information stored in a person's wallet. It is always with the person, but not as quickly accessed as information from a person's memory. External storage, on the other hand, is to the computer as a file cabinet is to an individual. In general, it takes a significantly longer period of time to retrieve data from external storage (file cabinet) than from auxiliary storage (wallet) or internal storage (memory).

Auxiliary storage devices include magnetic disk, magnetic drum, and magnetic tape units, while common external storage devices, which service the computer *offline* (not connected to the CPU), include punched cards, punched paper tape, and in some cases magnetic tape readers. These devices will be discussed in detail in subsequent chapters.

A magnetic tape unit, for example, is often connected offline to a printer. In this case, the computer outputs data to be printed onto an online magnetic tape at high speed. The magnetic tape is then dismounted from the online tape drive and mounted on an offline tape drive unit connected to the printer. The time-consuming operation of printing can then proceed while the computer goes about processing the next job.

Table 6-1. Comparison of Primary and Secondary Storage

Characteristic	Primary Storage	Secondary Storage	
		Auxiliary	External
Location with respect to the CPU	Within CPU	Outside of, but connected to, CPU	Outside of and not connected to the CPU
Cost[1]	Most expensive	Less expensive than primary storage	Least expensive
Capacity[1]	Up to several million bytes (8 bits)	Billions of bytes	Virtually infinite
Access time[1]	In billionths of a second	In millionths of a second	Not applicable
Means of storing data	Magnetic core Monolithic circuit film	Magnetic disk Magnetic tape Magnetic drum Data cell	Punched card Punched paper tape Magnetic tape

[1]These items will vary with manufacturers and computer systems.

Self-study exercise 6-2

1. In addition to possessing a CPU, a computer system must also possess a capability to _____ for subsequent use.

◆ ◆ ◆

store data

2. The storage facility associated with a computer system must be capable of storing both _____.

◆ ◆ ◆

data and instructions

3. There are two general types of storage utilized by computers, namely, _____ and _____ storage.

◆ ◆ ◆

primary
secondary

4. Primary storage, sometimes also called _____, is under the direct control of and often an integral part of the _____ of the computer system.

◆ ◆ ◆

main storage, core, or memory
CPU

5. Primary storage is associated with the _____ speed of access.

◆ ◆ ◆

fastest

6. The most common physical device used in the construction of primary storage is the _____.

◆ ◆ ◆

magnetic core

7. Secondary storage is located _____ and _____ be connected to the CPU.

♦ ♦ ♦

outside of the CPU
may or may not

8. Secondary storage is classified as one of _____ types, namely, _____.

♦ ♦ ♦

two
auxiliary, external

9. Auxiliary storage _____ connected to the CPU, while external storage _____ connected to the CPU.

♦ ♦ ♦

is
is not

10. Auxiliary storage devices include _____, while common external storage devices include _____.

♦ ♦ ♦

magnetic disk, magnetic drum, and magnetic tape units
punched cards, punched paper tape, and in some cases magnetic
tape readers

11. A device is said to be offline if _____.

♦ ♦ ♦

it is not connected to the CPU

Modern-day computers are capable of accepting input from numerous types of devices via a multitude of media, either one at a time or simultaneously, depending on the particular computer system employed. However, there is one thing that is common to all computer systems—there must be some means to input data and to output meaningful and useful information.

Input/Output Devices

Input devices   Regardless of the type, size, shape, color, or manufacturer of the computer, there is one thing about which we can be certain: there must be some means by which data can be input. Some of the devices used for this purpose are described below.

Punched card readers. The punched card reader is one of the most common input devices to the computer. The principal function of this device is to transmit data contained on punched cards to the memory of the computer. Modern punched card readers perform this function at speeds ranging from 200 to over 1,000 cards per minute. In most cases, accuracy in reading is checked by a complete second reading of the card and a comparison of the two readings before the data read is transmitted to the computer.

Character readers. Character readers are input devices which are capable of both accepting data from source documents in printed or written form and converting this data into a computer-acceptable code. Modern character readers can read and interpret a maximum of approximately 1,000 docu-

Figure 6-3
IBM 2501 Card Reader

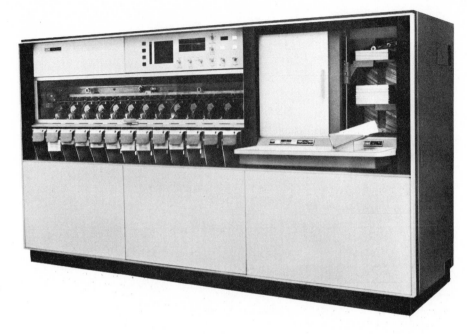

Figure 6-4
Magnetic Ink Character
Reader

ments per minute. Character readers are classified into two basic types: *magnetic ink character readers* and *optical scanners.*

Magnetic ink character readers read source documents containing data recorded with a special ferrite-impregnated ink. Characters recorded in this magnetic ink can be read and directly processed, thus eliminating the need to convert the data contained on the source document to the punched card medium.

Optical scanners read data printed with regular ink on a source document and convert it directly to a machine-readable code. These devices, although promising a great future, are presently used to a limited extent. This is due to the poor reliability of character interpretation which results from source-document typewriter inconsistencies, erasures, etc.

Tape readers. Tape readers were among the first input devices to be used with a computer. In their early days, they were used to read data punched onto a reel of paper tape. More recently, however, they are used to read data recorded on a reel of coated plastic tape (as with a home tape recorder) in the form of a series of magnetized spots. This tape has come to be known as magnetic tape. Magnetic tape has several advantages over punched paper tape, such as reusability, increased speed, and increased storage capacity. As a result, magnetic tape is currently used far more heavily than punched paper tape.

Figure 6-5
IBM 2420 Magnetic Tape
Unit

Other input devices. In recent years many new and innovative input devices have been introduced. Some of the more common of these devices are:

Terminals a device similar in appearance and operation to a typewriter and with which data can be keyed directly into the computer. Terminals are also available with a display tube, similar to that used with a television set, on which input and output data can be pictured.

Film Device a device capable of accepting data prerecorded on microfilm for input to the computer.

Audio Device a device capable of accepting data input by human voice for input to the computer.

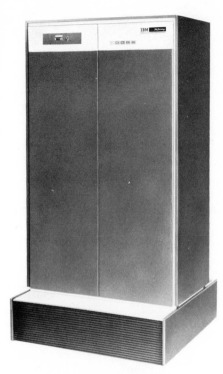

(a) Audio Response Unit

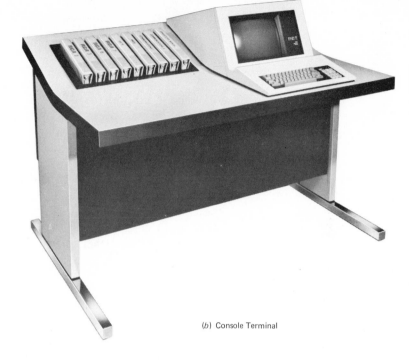

(b) Console Terminal

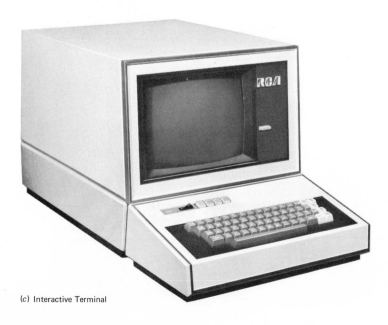

(c) Interactive Terminal

Figure 6-6
Other Input
Devices—Interactive
Terminal, Audio Response
Unit, and Console
Terminal

Output devices   Many devices used with computers serve as both input and output devices. For example, with the exception of the punched card reader, each of the input devices discussed above can also serve as an output device. In addition to these dual-function devices, there are two other commonly used output devices—card punches and printers.

Card punches.   Card punches are used to encode output data into punched cards for future processing. This operation can take place at speeds ranging from 50 to 500 cards per minute. Punch verification is accomplished by reading the card punched and comparing the read data with the data intended to be punched. Card punches are utilized in many business concerns to produce two-part, punched card bills or invoices, one part of the invoice to be retained by the customer and the other part returned to the company for processing. Many computer systems utilize a device which is both a card reader and a card punch in one physical unit. An IBM 2540 Card Read Punch is an example of such a multipurpose device.

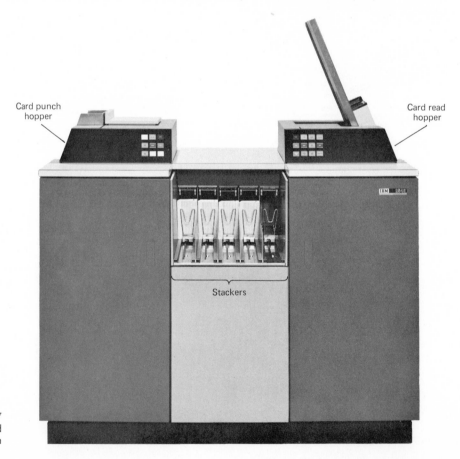

Card punch hopper

Card read hopper

Stackers

Figure 6-7
IBM 2540 Card Read
Punch

Figure 6-8
IBM 1403 Printer

Printers. The printer is the most common of all output devices in use today because it provides the user with a permanent visual record of the data output from the computer. Printer rated speeds range from 150 to 2,500 lines of output per minute, with each line consisting of up to 150 characters. Printers are capable of printing on ordinary paper, on specially prepared forms, and even on punched cards.

Printers are also available which do not print by the line but by the character. Such devices include console typewriters and teletypewriters capable of printing from 10 to 100 characters per second. Character printers, by virtue of their slow speeds, are used only for the printing of limited output.

Self-study exercise 6-3

1. Every computer system must have some means to _____.

◆ ◆ ◆

input data and output meaningful and useful information

2. Among the input devices used with computers are _____.

◆ ◆ ◆

punched card readers, character readers, tape readers, terminals, film devices, and audio devices

3. Character readers are classified into _____ basic types: _____.

◆ ◆ ◆

two
magnetic ink character readers and optical scanners

4. The most common input device is the _____.

◆ ◆ ◆

punched card reader

5. Some of the advantages of magnetic tape over punched paper tape are _____.

◆ ◆ ◆

reusability, increased speed, and increased storage capacity

6. Most input devices also serve as _____.

◆ ◆ ◆

output devices

7. Devices used exclusively for output are the _____.

◆ ◆ ◆

card punch and printer

8. The most common of all output devices is the _____.

◆ ◆ ◆

printer

* Input/Output Communications

In recent years, the internal speeds of computers increased at a much more rapid rate than the speeds of most input/output devices. As a result, it often happens that the CPU is waiting for the completion of an input or output operation before resuming processing. In such cases, the computer system is said to be *I/O-bound*. The result is poor utilization of the capabilities of the computer system. Therefore, it became necessary to devise a method

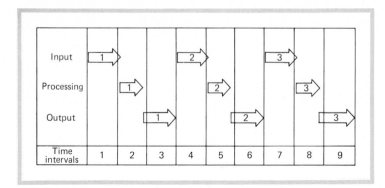

Figure 6-9
Nonoverlapped
Processing

which would eliminate the necessity for the CPU to remain idle during a low-speed I/O operation and which would expand the capabilities of computer systems to handle more and more input/output devices more efficiently. Attempts to solve the above problems have led to a concept known as *overlapped processing.*

All data processing applications involve the operations of input, processing, and output, with each of these operations requiring a specific amount of time for its completion. The time required to completely solve a problem, then, will be a combination of the times required to complete each of the above operations. The total required time, however, will be heavily dependent on what is meant by "a combination of the times required to complete each operation." If, for example, only one of these operations could be performed at a time, then the total required time for the job would be the sum of the times required to complete each input, processing, and output operation (nonoverlapped processing). Figure 6-9 illustrates how this might take place. In this illustration, you will notice that only three input-processing-output cycles were possible in the time period represented. In Figure 6-10, however, in the same time period it was possible to perform more than seven input-processing-output cycles. This was accomplished by performing more than one operation at a time (overlapped processing). As you can clearly see, overlapped processing is more efficient than nonoverlapped processing. It is for this reason that most computers today employ overlapped processing.

   You are probably wondering how it is possible for a computer to do more than one thing at a time. The answer is relatively simple. Attached to the computer are special devices called *channels* that control the input/output operations, thereby freeing the processing unit to perform other operations. Thus, at any given time one channel can be controlling an input

Overlapped processing[3]

[3]William Fuori, "An Introduction to the Computer: The Tool of Business," pp. 186–189. Prentice-Hall, Inc., Englewood Cliffs, N.J., 1973.

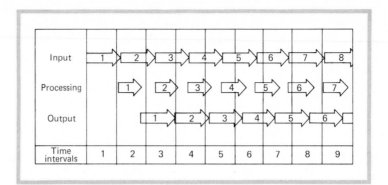

Figure 6-10
Overlapped Processing

operation while a second channel is controlling an output operation and the computer is possibly performing an arithmetic calculation. A computer system may have many channels attached to it, with each channel being responsible for controlling several input or output devices. Figure 6-11 illustrates one of many possible arrangements and uses of channels.

What actually takes place between the input/output device, the channel, and the computer is as follows. Let us assume that we wish to read some data from cards, perform a detailed calculation, and output the results. To begin with, the channel causes the input device to read one or more cards and store their contents in a temporary storage area called a *buffer*. This operation can be performed while the computer is busy with another operation. When this data is needed for processing, it is called for by, and transferred to, the processing unit at a very rapid rate. While this data is being processed in the CPU, the channel is causing the buffer to be filled for ready availability. When the processing of the previously read data is completed, the computer causes this output data to be rapidly transferred, via another channel, to an output buffer. From the output buffer the channel controls the slower operation of printing, thus freeing the CPU to accept more data from the input buffer via its channel and to begin

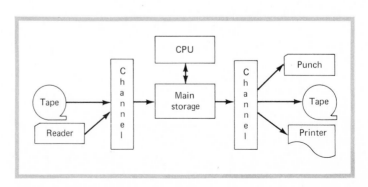

Figure 6-11
Overlapped Computer
System

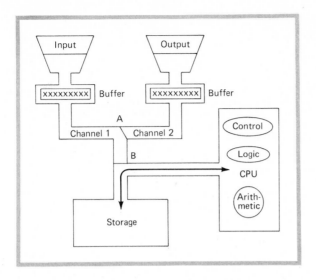

Figure 6-12
Overlapped Computer
System Employing
Input/Output Buffering

processing this data. What we have, then, is a condition where the relatively slow operations of reading cards and printing are controlled by the channels, allowing the processing unit to communicate only with the channels and at high speeds. In this manner the processing unit is operating as much as possible and is not constantly waiting for the card reader or the printer to become available.

Self-study exercise 6-4

1. When the CPU is waiting for the completion of an input or output operation before it can resume processing, the computer system is said to be _____ .

◆   ◆   ◆

I/O-bound

2. Attempts to eliminate or reduce CPU idle time have led to a concept known as _____ .

◆   ◆   ◆

overlapped processing

3. In overlapped processing _____ operations can take place simultaneously.

◆   ◆   ◆

input, output, and processing

4. Channels are used to control _____ operations.

◆ ◆ ◆

input and output

5. A(n) _____ is a temporary storage area used to increase the transfer rate between an I/O device and the CPU.

◆ ◆ ◆

buffer

End-of-chapter Exercises

True-false exercise

1. Primary storage is generally contained within the CPU.
2. The control unit controls the order of execution of program instructions.
3. Within an IBM 360 Series computer, there are 15 general registers and 4 floating point registers.
4. Only numeric data may be stored in general registers.
5. Cores may be magnetized in only one direction.
6. Character readers convert images read from a source document into computer-acceptable codes.
7. Input/output devices have faster internal speeds than computers.
8. During overlapped processing, only one channel may be simultaneously used for both input and output operations.

Fill-in exercise

1. The CPU is the _____ center of the entire computer system.
2. The CPU is composed of two subunits: the _____ and the _____.
3. A device capable of storing specific amounts of data is called a(n) _____.
4. A general register is, at minimum, _____ bits long, whereas a floating point register is _____ bits in length.
5. The general types of computer storage are _____ and _____ storage.
6. Magnetizable, doughnut-shaped iron rings used in the construction of primary storage are referred to as _____.
7. External storage units are auxiliary storage units that are _____ to the CPU.
8. Character readers that require the use of specially prepared magnetic inks are classified by the term _____.
9. When the computer system must wait for the completion of an input or output operation in order to begin processing, it is said to be _____.
10. A special device used in controlling I/O operations, freeing the CPU for other tasks, is called a(n) _____.

Multiple-choice exercise

1. The ALU can perform the following operations.
    a.   Control the activities of the I/O devices
    b.   Basic arithmetic operations
    c.   Moving data stored in the computer
    d.   b and c
    e.   a and b
2. The control unit is used to
    a.   control the activities of the I/O devices
    b.   add data in registers
    c.   route data between storage and the ALU
    d.   a and b
    e.   a and c
3. The primary storage capability of a computer
    a.   may not be altered or added to
    b.   may be augmented by secondary storage units
    c.   remains fixed in size
    d.   all the above
    e.   none of the above
4. Secondary storage within a computer system
    a.   is generally associated with a fast access speed
    b.   usually has a capacity less than that of primary storage
    c.   handles the overflow of data from primary storage
    d.   all the above
    e.   none of the above
5. An offline storage unit
    a.   is not connected to the CPU
    b.   may be controlled from an auxiliary storage unit
    c.   requires supervision by the control unit
    d.   all the above
    e.   none of the above
6. The punched card reader
    a.   reads data directly from a source document
    b.   converts the images read to a machine-readable code
    c.   requires specially prepared inks and printed characters for its use
    d.   is somewhat unreliable when reading data
    e.   none of the above
7. Overlapped processing
    a.   increases the efficiency of the computer system
    b.   eliminates the necessity for the CPU to wait for the I/O devices
    c.   enables the computer to process more data in a given period of
         time
    d.   a and c
    e.   a, b, and c

Discussion questions

1. Discuss briefly the concept of overlapped processing. What are its advantages?
2. Explain briefly how channels are used in overlapped processing.
3. Describe the difference between a magnetic ink character reader and an optical scanner.
4. List the functions of the control unit and the ALU.
5. Name and discuss briefly the two types of registers with respect to their size (in number of bits), uses, and identification numbers.

PROGRAMMING LANGUAGES

CHAPTER 7

Introduction   Before we enter a detailed discussion of programming languages, let us first review the concept of what a program is. A program is a logical series of instructions designed to solve a given problem and which can be executed by a computer. Simply stated, a program is a kind of blueprint which directs a computer to perform some useful work.

Most programs contain the following general types of instructions:

Input   instructions which read data into the computer's memory, usually from an auxiliary storage device such as a card reader, tape, or disk.

Process   instructions which direct the computer to manipulate the stored data or control the sequence in which instructions are executed.

Output   instructions which facilitate the output of results to an appropriate output device such as a printer, tape, or disk.

Before such a program can be executed, it must first be coded in a language which can be understood by the computer, recorded onto a machine-readable medium, and entered into the memory of the computer. The language which is directly understandable by the computer is referred to as a *machine language*.

Machine Language   Despite the belief that computers are super-intelligent copies of man, they are in reality only very fast calculating machines. In fact, most computers have a very limited vocabulary and no ability to think. Computers can execute only a limited set of instructions determined by the engineers who designed them. These instructions are called *machine instructions*. All work performed by the computer is accomplished using combinations of this limited set of instructions.

When stored in the computer's memory, machine instructions consist of a series of bits having the value 0 or 1. The particular combination of bits, or bit pattern, identifies the stored instruction. For the purpose of illustration, let us examine the structure of the machine language used by the IBM 360 and 370 Series computers. Machine language instructions generally consist of two components—an operation code and operands. The *operation code* is always 8 bits long and identifies the instruction to be executed. The *operand* component of the instruction identifies the data or address of the data which will be acted on by the instruction. If the operand contains a data address, it is the address in main storage of the data's location. IBM 360 machine language instructions, for example, are either 16, 32, or 48 bits in length and may contain one, two, or three operands.

When displaying a 360 instruction, the hexadecimal system of nota-

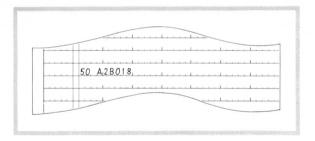

Figure 7-1
Example of a Machine
Language Store
Instruction

tion is used. You may recall from Chapter 5 that in this system each group of 4 bits is represented as a single hexadecimal digit, 0 through F. Since the smallest addressable unit in 360 memory is the byte (8 bits), we can represent each byte as two hexadecimal digits. For example, the byte made up of the following bit string

00111101

can be more easily represented as 3D, its hexadecimal equivalent. With the use of this notation, Figure 7-1 shows a typical 360 machine language instruction.

Symbolic Programming Languages

As you can see from the above example, coding machine language programs can be a tedious and difficult job. Therefore, in order to simplify the coding process, symbolic programming languages were developed.

Unlike machine languages, symbolic languages allow the programmer to code programs using alphabetic names and symbols to represent both the operation codes and the operands of an instruction. It must be remembered, however, that the computer can execute only machine language instructions. Therefore, it is necessary to translate the instructions in any program written in symbolic language to machine language before they can be executed. This process is accomplished by special translating programs which read the symbolic programs (usually in the form of punched cards) and translate them into the equivalent machine language instructions. Such translating programs are generally supplied by the manufacturer of the computer being used.

A characteristic of the translation process with respect to symbolic languages is that, in general, it is "one for one." That is, a single symbolic instruction translates into a single machine language instruction.

An exception to the one-for-one rule of the symbolic language is the use of the *macro*. A macro is a single symbolic statement which translates into several machine language instructions. Macros enable the programmer to code complex operations with simple and easily understood

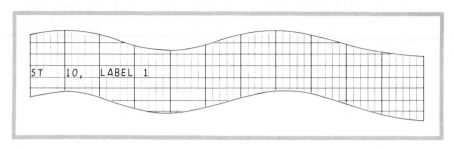

Figure 7-2
Example of Basic
Assembler Language Store
Instruction

statements. An input/output operation, for example, can be coded with a single macro.

A very useful low-level language provided for use on IBM 360 and 370 computers is the Basic Assembler Language (BAL). The process of translating a program written in BAL or any other symbolic language into machine instructions is called *assembling*. In addition to translating the symbolic instructions into machine language, the assembler also checks for coding or *syntax* errors and informs the programmer of any such errors. Figure 7-2 illustrates the symbolic equivalent of the instruction previously shown in Figure 7-1.

Note the use of symbols to describe the instruction code (ST) and an operand (LABEL 1) in Figure 7-2.

In addition to being easier to code in than machine language, symbolic language also makes it easier for someone other than the creator of the program to understand its logic. Figure 7-3 illustrates how a series of symbolic instructions designed to add two numbers and subtract a third might appear in BAL (Basic Assembly Language) for the IBM 360. The two variables to be added are symbolically represented as NUM1 and NUM2, whereas the number to be subtracted is represented by NUM3. The result of these calculations is stored in a variable called RESULT.

Self-study exercise 7-1

1. Most programs contain three general types of instructions: _____, _____, and _____.

◆ ◆ ◆

input
process
output

2. Computers can execute only a limited set of instructions called _____.

◆ ◆ ◆

machine instructions

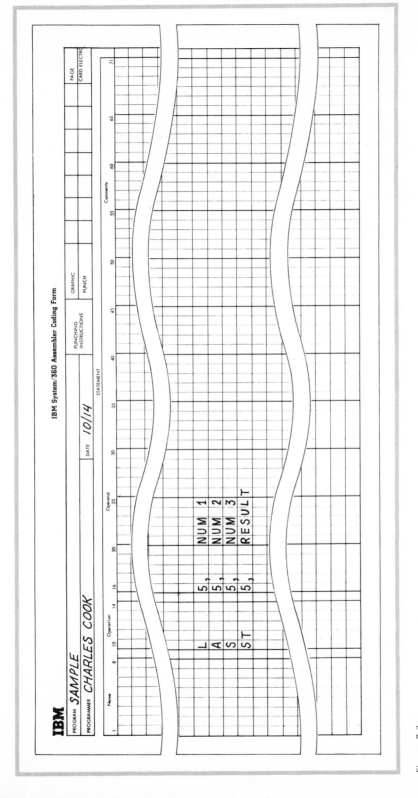

Figure 7-3
A Segment of a BAL
Program

3. The two components of 360 machine language instructions are the _____ and the _____.

◆ ◆ ◆

operation code
operands

4. The IBM 360 machine language instructions are represented using the _____ system of notation.

◆ ◆ ◆

hexadecimal

5. Programming languages which use alphabetic symbols to represent instructions are called _____ languages.

◆ ◆ ◆

symbolic

6. A symbolic instruction which generates more than one machine language instruction is called a(n) _____.

◆ ◆ ◆

macro

High-level Languages   Today, most programs are written in high-level programming languages. This is due in large part to the fact that high-level languages are simpler to learn and use than low-level languages such as machine and assembly programming languages. Two characteristics of high-level language statements are that (1) when translated, they result in several machine language instructions, and (2) these languages are relatively independent of the particular computer system used. In addition, instructions in high-level languages appear more like English statements and mathematical expressions than machine language instructions.

As mentioned earlier, high-level statements must be translated into machine language instructions before they can be executed. A program which performs this translation is called a *compiler* and the translation process, a *compilation*. In addition to performing the translation, compilers also scan the program for syntax errors.

Some of the advantages of high-level languages over low-level languages are:

1. They are easier to use and learn. Since these languages use notations which are more easily learned by the beginning programmer, the format of the language is more easily and quickly mastered.
2. The programmer is not required to know the hardware characteristics of the computer. Since he is not coding in the machine language, the programmer need not be as concerned with the computer's instruction vocabulary.
3. They are standardized languages. There are currently several high-level languages which have been accepted as standard languages in the data processing industry. This allows programs written in these languages to be run on virtually any computer for which a compiler for these languages exists.

The following sections will discuss several of the more common high-level languages found in widespread use today.

FORTRAN.   One of the oldest high-level languages still in wide use today is FORTRAN. FORTRAN was developed by IBM in an effort to create a programming language which could be used by scientific problem solvers —the scientist, mathematician, and engineer. The goal was to create a concise language, making use of mathematical notation which did not require the programmer to have an intimate knowledge of the internal characteristics of the computer. The name *FORTRAN* was derived from FORmula TRANslator, indicating its relationship to mathematical notation.

Procedure-oriented

Figure 7-4 shows an example of a FORTRAN statement which will perform the same calculation previously shown in Figure 7-3.

Note that a single FORTRAN statement can perform the same calculations which would otherwise require several assembler instructions. Note also the use of mathematical notation. Although originally developed by IBM, FORTRAN compilers are currently available from nearly all computer companies serving the scientific data processing industry.

COBOL.   After the introduction of FORTRAN to serve the scientist, the attention of manufacturers was directed to developing a high-level language for business-oriented programming applications. This language was to be a "common" or standard language—a language which would be usable on the various medium- and large-scale computers available at the time with only minor modifications. On May 28, 1959, a meeting was called by the Department of Defense at the request of several computer users for the purpose of examining this possibility. The meeting was called CODASYL (Conference On DAta SYstems Languages). The result of the conference was the formation of a committee composed of six computer manufacturers (Burroughs, IBM, Honeywell, RCA, Remington Rand, and

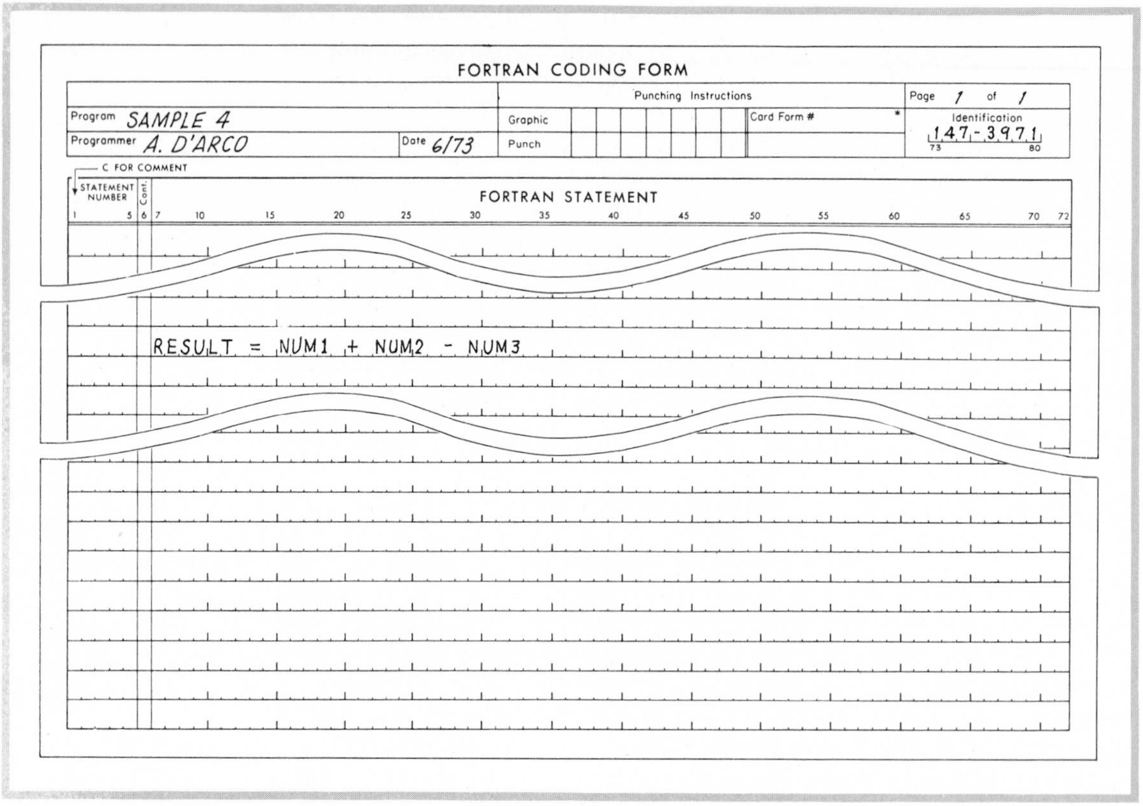

FORTRAN CODING FORM

Program SAMPLE 4
Programmer A. D'ARCO   Date 6/73

Punching Instructions

Page 1 of 1

Identification
1 4 7 - 3 9 7 1

FORTRAN STATEMENT

RESULT = NUM1 + NUM2 - NUM3

Figure 7-4
A Segment of a
FORTRAN Program

Sylvania), two government agencies (the Air Material Command and the Department of the Navy), and a representative of the Bureau of Standards. The primary purpose of the committee was to draw up specifications for a new language. In April of 1960, the first specifications of the language were released. The new language was called COBOL (COmmon Business-Oriented Language).

Unlike FORTRAN, which consists primarily of mathematical notation, COBOL consists of Englishlike statements. The aim was to make the language not only easy to use, but self-documenting as well. This means that a programmer looking at a completed program should be able to determine the program's logic, author, etc., without the need for additional references.

An example of COBOL statements designed to perform the same calculations shown in Figures 7-3 and 7-4 is given in Figure 7-5.

As you can see, COBOL is not as concise a language as FORTRAN. Since COBOL is very near to English in appearance, it tends to be a more "wordy" language than FORTRAN. Although this results in somewhat larger programs, it also results in programs which are more easily read and understood by the nonscientific-oriented programmer or user.

PL/I. Until the introduction of third-generation computer systems in the mid-1960s, most computers and programming applications were designated as being scientific or business-oriented. Computers which handled scientific applications typically ran FORTRAN programs, while business-oriented applications were written in COBOL and run on business computers. Third-generation computers introduced the concept of a single general purpose computer which could handle both business and scientific work equally well.

At the same time, scientific computer users were finding a need for a more sophisticated input/output processing capability not possible through FORTRAN. Business computer users were also becoming more sophisticated and found COBOL lacking in its handling of mathematical operations.

Figure 7-5
A Segment of a COBOL
Program

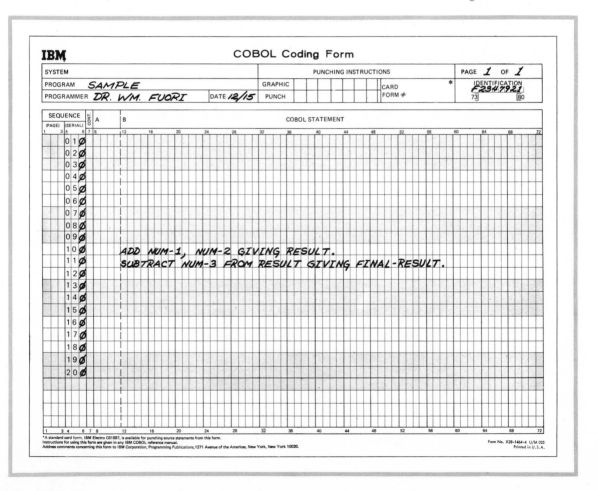

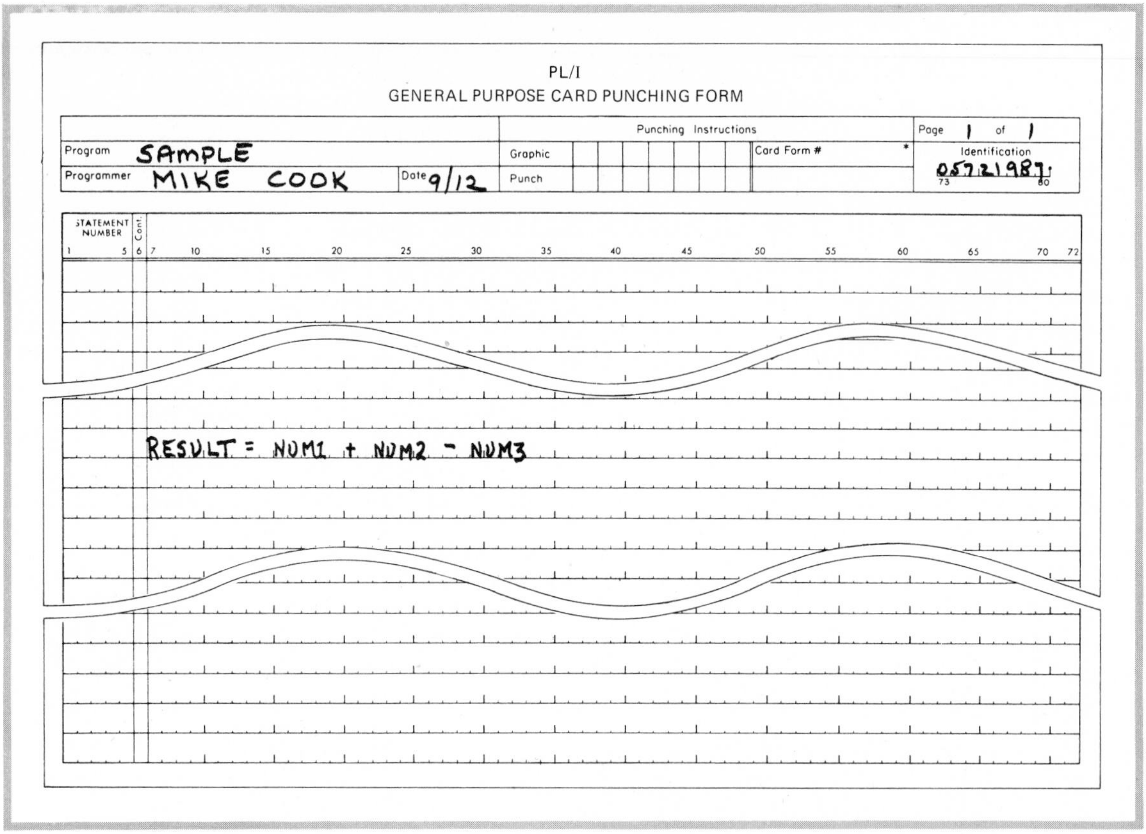

PL/I
GENERAL PURPOSE CARD PUNCHING FORM

| Program | SAMPLE | | Punching Instructions | | | | Page 1 of 1 |
| Programmer | MIKE COOK Date 9/12 | Graphic / Punch | Card Form # | * | Identification 05721987 |

RESULT = NUM1 + NUM2 - NUM3

Figure 7-6
A Segment of a PL/I
Program

The result of these problems was the development of a programming language which could be used equally well by the scientific and business communities. This language, PL/I, incorporated the best features of both COBOL and FORTRAN, while supplying added features to make use of increased third-generation computer capabilities.

Today, many consider PL/I the most advanced and powerful high-level language available thus far. Despite this fact, PL/I is only recently beginning to find wide-scale acceptance. This is attributed to the lack of experienced PL/I programmers and the fact that PL/I is not supported or usable on all makes of computers. An example of PL/I coding is shown in Figure 7-6.

BASIC. The BASIC (Beginner's All-purpose Symbolic Instruction Code) language was originally developed at Dartmouth College. BASIC was intended to be a simple language, useful for teaching programming concepts.

ue to its simplicity and powerful capabilities, however, BASIC became a popular language for use with terminals[1] in a timesharing environment.

In the timesharing environment, terminal users create small- to medium-sized programs and execute these programs directly from the terminal. BASIC, with its easy-to-learn vocabulary and limited input/output capability, was ideally suited for this environment.

In appearance, BASIC is similar to FORTRAN since it also uses a concise mathematical form of notation. The simplicity of the language has prompted many people to declare that BASIC is virtually the easiest programming language to learn. An example of BASIC programming is shown in Figure 7-7.

RPG. RPG (Report Program Generator) was first introduced for use with second-generation computers. RPG was intended for use with small computer systems for the creation of business-oriented reports requiring small to moderate amounts of mathematical calculation. Programs are written in RPG by filling out special RPG specification sheets. These sheets allow the programmer to describe the components of his program in a mechanical fashion requiring very little knowledge of the computer's hardware characteristics. Each component of the program is described on these sheets, one for file description, input processing, calculations to be performed, and output processing.

Problem-oriented

Examples of these specification sheets are shown in Figures 7-8 to 7-13.

Although RPG lacks the flexibility and power of the more sophisticated programming languages such as FORTRAN, COBOL, and PL/I, it does provide a fast and simple technique for producing computer-generated business reports.

Summary

In this chapter, we have seen the concept of the machine language, its logical progression to symbolic languages, and finally its progression to the high-level languages. Although we confined our discussion to the most commonly used languages, there are many languages available which we have not mentioned. These include MAD, JOVIAL, APL, AUTOCODER, NEAT, ALGOL, and QUIKTRAN.

Two programming languages, SNOBOL and COMIT, are especially suited to applications involving the manipulation of arithmetic data strings. These applications deal with the processing of data lists and words rather than numbers and algebraic symbols. Consequently, SNOBOL and COMIT are called *list-processing* languages.

[1]A terminal is an easily used input/output device that will be discussed in detail in Chapter 13.

Figure 7-7
A Segment of a BASIC
Program

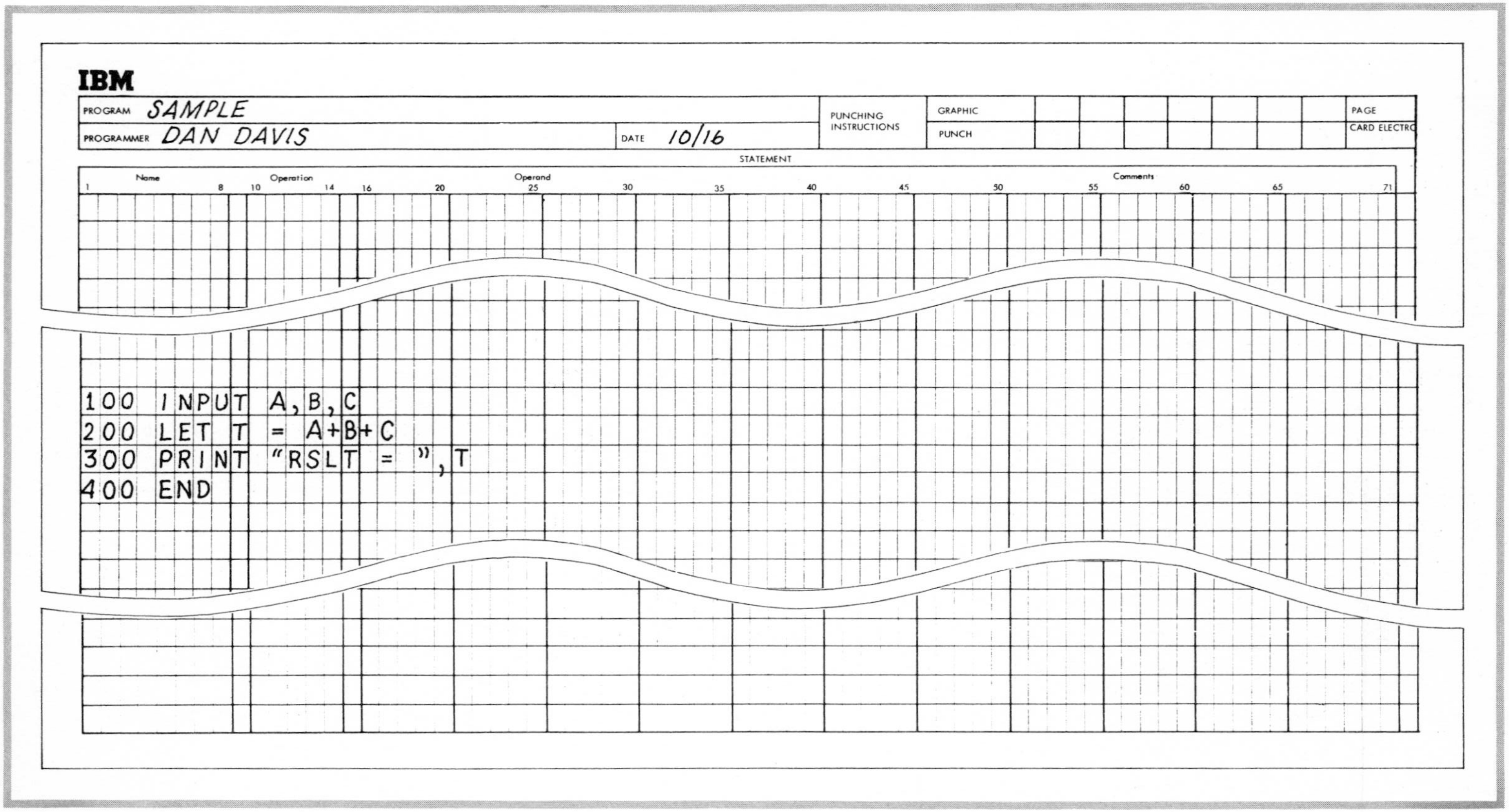
IBM
PROGRAM SAMPLE
PROGRAMMER DAN DAVIS
DATE 10/16
PUNCHING INSTRUCTIONS
GRAPHIC
PUNCH
PAGE
CARD ELECTRO
STATEMENT
Name
Operation
Operand
Comments
100 INPUT A, B, C
200 LET T = A+B+C
300 PRINT "RSLT = ", T
400 END

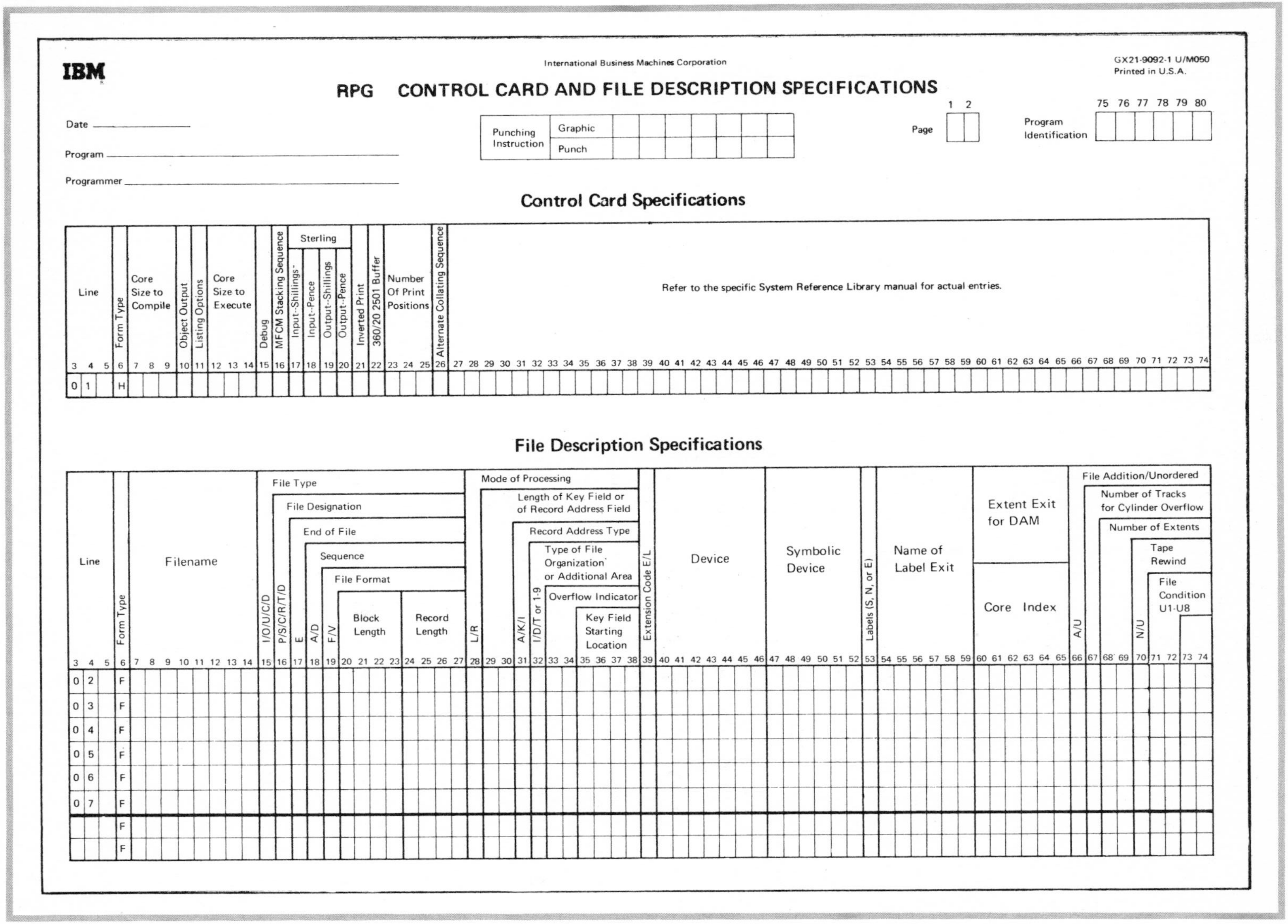

IBM

International Business Machines Corporation

GX21-9092-1 U/M050
Printed in U.S.A.

RPG CONTROL CARD AND FILE DESCRIPTION SPECIFICATIONS

Date

Program

Programmer

Punching Instruction: Graphic / Punch

Page 1 2

Program Identification 75 76 77 78 79 80

Control Card Specifications

Line (3–5)	Form Type (6)	Core Size to Compile (7–9)	Object Output (10)	Listing Options (11)	Core Size to Execute (12–14)	Debug (15)	MFCM Stacking Sequence (16)	Sterling: Input--Shillings (17)	Sterling: Input--Pence (18)	Sterling: Output--Shillings (19)	Sterling: Output--Pence (20)	Inverted Print (21)	360/20 2501 Buffer (22)	Number Of Print Positions (23–25)	Alternate Collating Sequence (26)	27–74
0 1	H															Refer to the specific System Reference Library manual for actual entries.

File Description Specifications

Line (3–5)	Form Type (6)	Filename (7–14)	File Type: I/O/U/C/D (15)	File Designation: P/S/C/R/T/D (16)	End of File: E (17)	Sequence: A/D (18)	File Format: F/V (19)	Block Length (20–23)	Record Length (24–27)	Mode of Processing: L/R (28)	Length of Key Field or of Record Address Field (29–30)	Record Address Type: A/K/I (31)	Type of File Organization or Additional Area: I/D/T or 1-9 (32)	Overflow Indicator (33–34)	Key Field Starting Location (35–38)	Extension Code E/L (39)	Device (40–46)	Symbolic Device (47–52)	Labels (S, N, or E) (53)	Name of Label Exit (54–59)	Extent Exit for DAM / Core Index (60–65)	File Addition/Unordered: A/U (66)	Number of Tracks for Cylinder Overflow (67)	Number of Extents (68–69)	Tape Rewind: N/U (70)	File Condition U1-U8 (71–72)	73–74
0 2	F																										
0 3	F																										
0 4	F																										
0 5	F																										
0 6	F																										
0 7	F																										
	F																										
	F																										

Figure 7-8
RPG Control Card and
File Description
Specification Form

Figure 7-9
RPG Indicator Summary

IBM

International Business Machines Corporation

RPG INDICATOR SUMMARY

GX21-9095-0 UM/025*
Printed in U.S.A.
*No. of forms per pad may vary slightly

Date ________

Program ________

Programmer ________

Punching Instruction	Graphic							
	Punch							

Page 1 2

Program Identification 75 76 77 78 79 80

Circle Indicators Used:

Note: All indicators are not valid with all systems.

01	02	03	04	05	06	07	08	09	10	11	12	13	14	15	16	17	18	19	20
21	22	23	24	25	26	27	28	29	30	31	32	33	34	35	36	37	38	39	40
41	42	43	44	45	46	47	48	49	50	51	52	53	54	55	56	57	58	59	60
61	62	63	64	65	66	67	68	69	70	71	72	73	74	75	76	77	78	79	80
81	82	83	84	85	86	87	88	89	90	91	92	93	94	95	96	97	98	99	
L1	L2	L3	L4	L5	L6	L7	L8	L9		OA	OB	OC	OD	OE	OF	OG	OV		
H1	H2	H3	H4	H5	H6	H7	H8	H9		U1	U2	U3	U4	U5	U6	U7	U8		

Predefined Indicators: IP LO LR MR HO

M–C: M1 M2 M3 M4 M5 M6 M7 M8 M9 C1 C2 C3 C4 C5 C6 C7 C8 C9

Line (3 4 5)	Form Type (6 7)	Indicators: Record Identifying (8 9 10)	Input Field (11 12 13)	Calculation Result (14 15 16)	Matching and Chaining (17 18 19)	Control Level, Overflow, Halt and User (20 21 22)	23 24 25 26 27 28 29 30 31 32 33 34 35 36 37 38 39 40 41 42 43 44 45 46 47 48 49 50 51 52 53 54 55 56 57 58 59 60 61 62 63 64 65 66 67 68 69 70 71 72 73 74
01	F *	ID	F	C	M	L	FUNCTION OF INDICATORS
02	F *						
03	F *						
04	F *						
05	F *						
06	F *						
07	F *						
08	F *						
09	F *						
10	F *						
11	F *						
12	F *						
13	F *						
14	F *						
15	F *						
	F *						
	F *						
	F *						

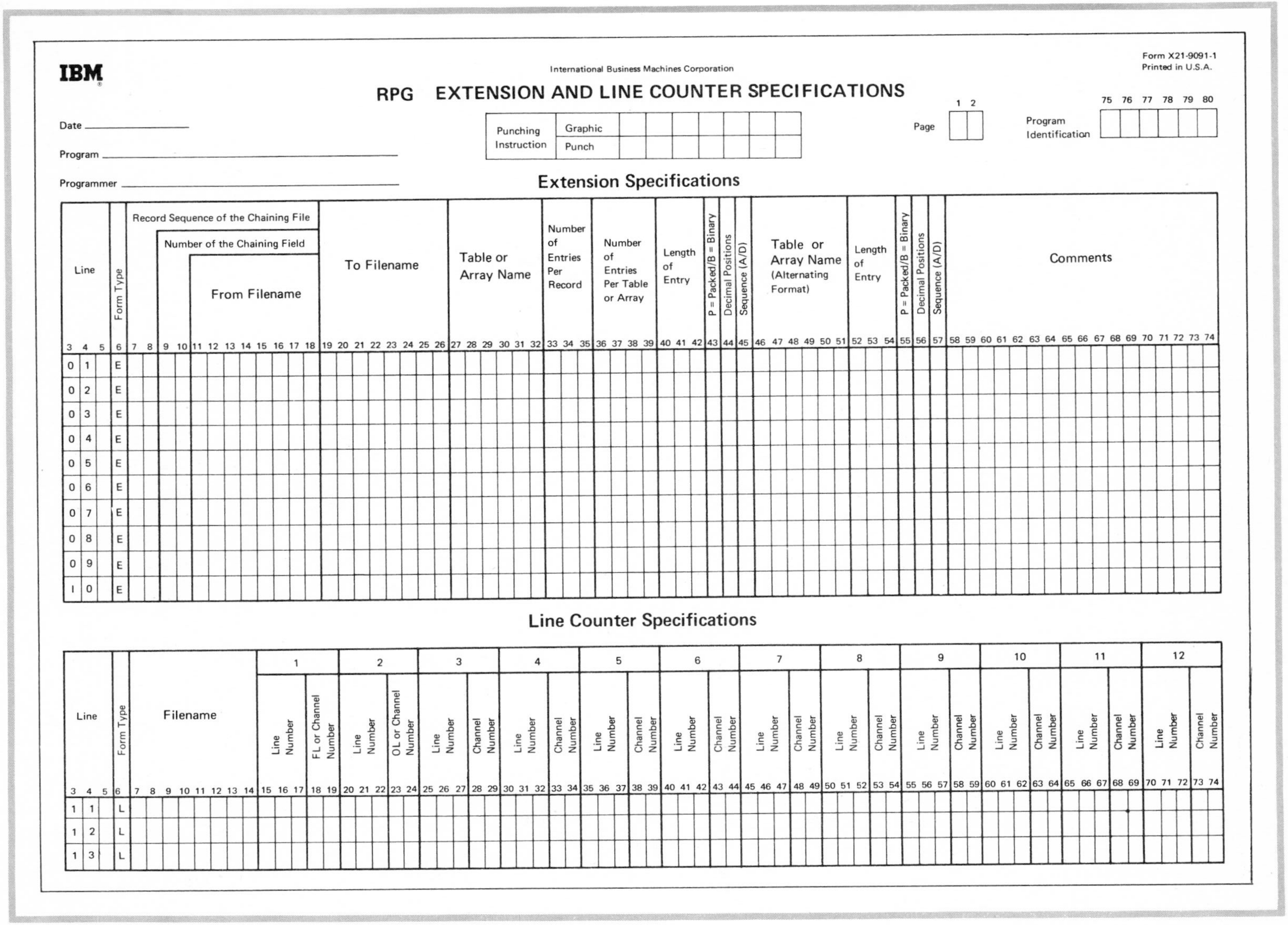

Form X21-9091-1
Printed in U.S.A.

International Business Machines Corporation

RPG EXTENSION AND LINE COUNTER SPECIFICATIONS

IBM

Date

Program

Programmer

Punching Instruction: Graphic / Punch

Page 1 2

Program Identification

75 76 77 78 79 80

Extension Specifications

Comments

Line	Form Type	From Filename (Record Sequence of the Chaining File / Number of the Chaining Field)	To Filename	Table or Array Name	Number of Entries Per Record	Number of Entries Per Table or Array	Length of Entry	P = Packed/B = Binary	Decimal Positions	Sequence (A/D)	Table or Array Name (Alternating Format)	Length of Entry	P = Packed/B = Binary	Decimal Positions	Sequence (A/D)
0 1	E														
0 2	E														
0 3	E														
0 4	E														
0 5	E														
0 6	E														
0 7	E														
0 8	E														
0 9	E														
1 0	E														

Line Counter Specifications

Line	Form Type	Filename	1 (Line Number / FL or Channel Number)	2 (Line Number / OL or Channel Number)	3 (Line Number / Channel Number)	4 (Line Number / Channel Number)	5 (Line Number / Channel Number)	6 (Line Number / Channel Number)	7 (Line Number / Channel Number)	8 (Line Number / Channel Number)	9 (Line Number / Channel Number)	10 (Line Number / Channel Number)	11 (Line Number / Channel Number)	12 (Line Number / Channel Number)
1 1	L													
1 2	L													
1 3	L													

Figure 7-10
RPG Extension and Line
Counter Specification
Form

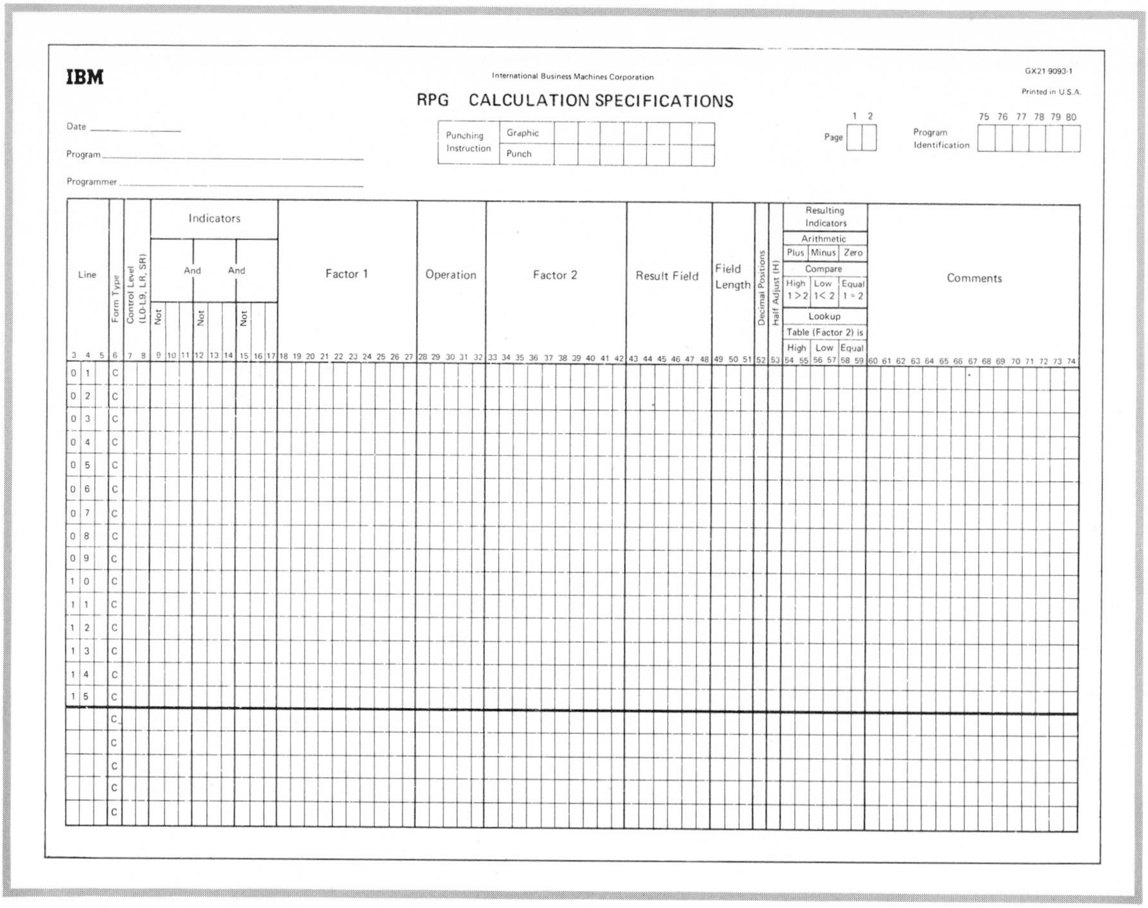

Figure 7-11
RPG Calculation
Specification Form

Self-study exercise 7-2

1. The 360 assembler language (BAL) is an example of a(n) _____ symbolic language.

◆ ◆ ◆

low-level

2. High-level translation programs are called _____.

◆ ◆ ◆

compilers

3. One of the oldest high-level languages originally intended for the scientific programmer is _____ .

◆ ◆ ◆

FORTRAN

4. _____ was the first language developed specifically to serve the business-oriented programming community.

◆ ◆ ◆

COBOL

Figure 7-12
RPG Input Specification
Form

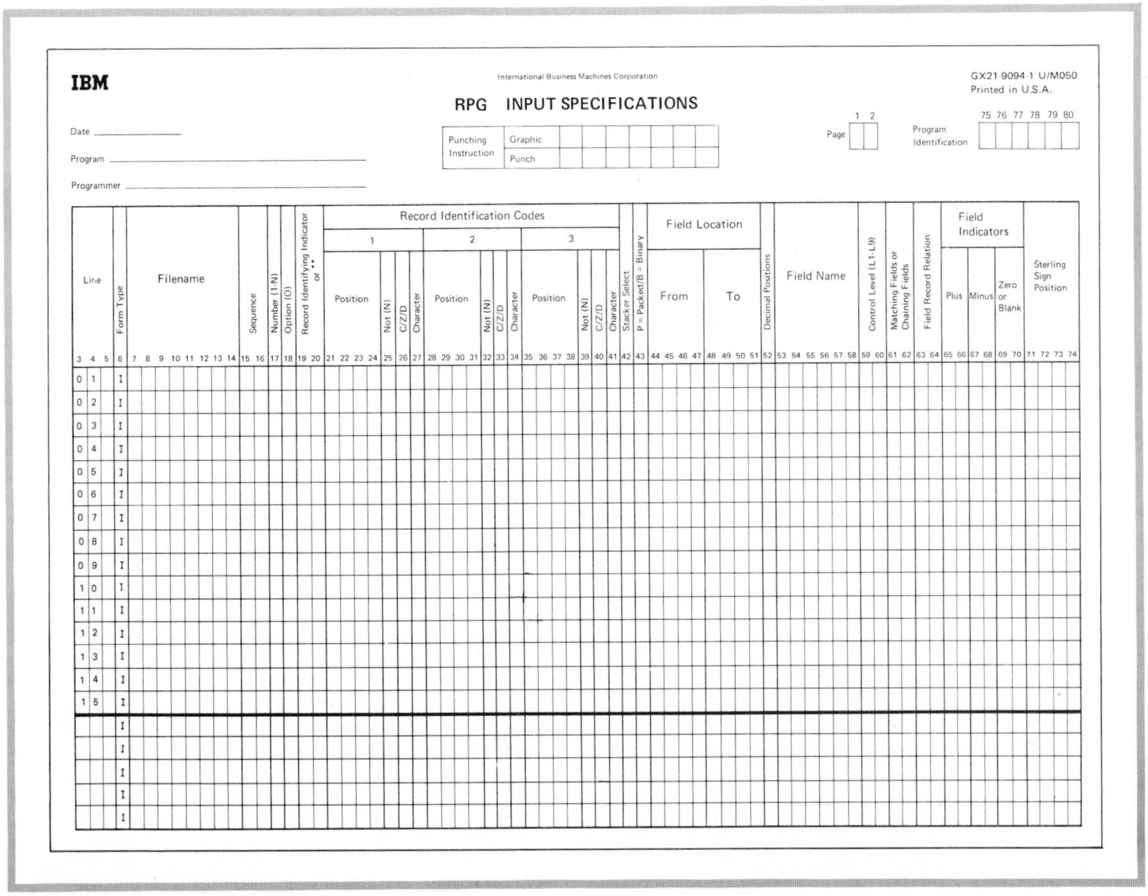

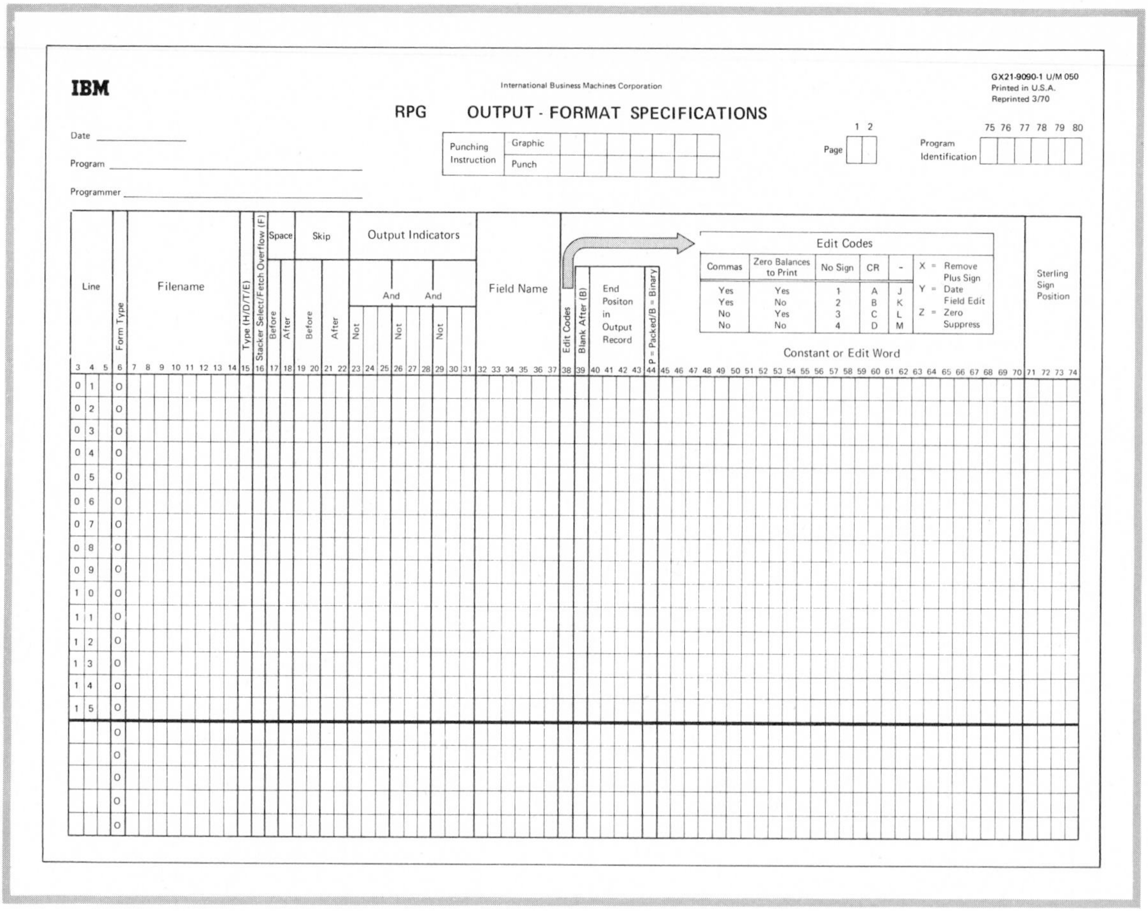

IBM

International Business Machines Corporation

GX21-9090-1 U/M 050
Printed in U.S.A.
Reprinted 3/70

RPG OUTPUT - FORMAT SPECIFICATIONS

Date _____

Program _____

Programmer _____

Punching Instruction: Graphic / Punch

Page

Program Identification

	Edit Codes				
Commas	Zero Balances to Print	No Sign	CR	–	X = Remove Plus Sign
Yes	Yes	1	A	J	Y = Date Field Edit
Yes	No	2	B	K	
No	Yes	3	C	L	Z = Zero Suppress
No	No	4	D	M	

Constant or Edit Word

Line, Form Type, Filename, Type (H/D/T/E), Stacker Select/Fetch Overflow (F), Space (Before/After), Skip (Before/After), Output Indicators (And/And, Not), Field Name, Edit Codes, Blank After (B), End Position in Output Record, Packed/B = Binary, Sterling Sign Position

Figure 7-13
Output Format
Specification Form

5. A language designed for third-generation computer use and incorporating features of both COBOL and FORTRAN is _____.

◆ ◆ ◆

PL/I

6. Originally developed at Dartmouth College as a teaching tool, the _____ language has become one of the most popular timesharing languages in use today.

◆ ◆ ◆

BASIC

True-false exercise

1. Computers are super-intelligent copies of man.
2. When stored in the computer's memory, machine instructions consist of a series of bits having the value 1 or 2.
3. The BCD (Binary Coded Decimal) system of notation is used when displaying an IBM 360 instruction.
4. The bit string 10010011 can be represented hexadecimally as 93.
5. Today, most programs are written in low-level programming languages.
6. A language used by much of the business industry today is FORTRAN.
7. FORTRAN compilers are available only on IBM computers.
8. COBOL stands for Common Business-Oriented Language.
9. PL/I incorporates the best features of both COBOL and FORTRAN.
10. BASIC was created at Harvard for use as a timesharing language.
11. RPG is a more powerful language than either COBOL or FORTRAN.

Multiple-choice exercise

1. The limited set of computer-executable instructions determined by the engineers who designed the computer is called
   a. engineers' language
   b. machine instructions
   c. macro instructions
   d. simple instructions
   e. none of the above
2. IBM 360 machine language instructions are
   a. 16 bits in length
   b. 32 bits in length
   c. 48 bits in length
   d. all the above
   e. none of the above
3. A characteristic of the translation process with respect to symbolic languages is that, in general,
   a. they are easy to code
   b. they are easily understood by all programmers
   c. they are a one-for-one translation
   d. they are understood only by computer engineers
   e. none of the above
4. A single assembler statement which translates into several machine language instructions is called a(n)
   a. macro
   b. compiler instruction
   c. translator word

    d. all the above

    e. none of the above

5. Assembly programming language is an example of a(n)

    a. high-level language

    b. low-level language

    c. engineering language

    d. machine language

    e. none of the above

6. An advantage of high-level languages over low-level languages is

    a. that the programmer is not required to know the hardware characteristics of the computer

    b. that they are standardized languages

    c. that they are easier to use and learn

    d. all the above

    e. none of the above

7. FORTRAN is an example of a

    a. low-level procedure-oriented language

    b. high-level procedure-oriented language

    c. symbolic language

    d. all the above

    e. none of the above

8. COBOL was developed to

    a. serve the scientist

    b. serve the engineer

    c. serve the general business community

    d. take the place of FORTRAN

    e. none of the above

9. The programming language PL/I was developed

    a. so that scientific users could have a more sophisticated input/output processing capability

    b. so that the best features of both COBOL and FORTRAN could be combined in one powerful language

    c. to increase the mathematical capabilities of the business computer users

    d. all the above

    e. none of the above

10. The programming language developed for small computer systems for the creation of business-oriented reports is

    a. PL/I

    b. RPG

    c. COBOL

    d. FORTRAN

    e. none of the above

Discussion questions

1. Discuss the advantages and disadvantages of symbolic programming languages.
2. Explain the development of the COBOL programming language and several of its advantages.
3. Discuss several of the differences between high-level and low-level programming languages.
4. Explain why languages such as PL/I and BASIC were developed.
5. Discuss RPG (Report Program Generator) as a useful tool to the programmer.

PROGRAM EXECUTION

CHAPTER 8

Introduction As you may have concluded from your reading of the previous chapters, the automated processing of data through a computer system is indeed a complex process. The variety of operations, both simple and complex, employed to process data accurately and efficiently is representative of the functions performed daily by data processing (DP) personnel. One of the contributors to the total DP effort is the computer operator. The computer operator represents a major and integral part of any DP complex. It is through his efforts that the tasks associated with the use of a computer are handled efficiently, thereby creating a continuous flow of processing within the DP system.

There is often a tendency for many people to underestimate the importance of the computer operator. We should caution the reader against relegating the computer operator to the status of a mere button pusher or paper handler. As you will discover in subsequent chapters, these types of activities are only a small part of the computer operator's total job. Each of the tasks performed by the operator is directly related to the maintenance of the computer in an active processing state. The operator's reaction to any and all of the various conditions that arise in the course of a day is a measure of his efficiency and fundamental value to the overall computing system. It is for this reason that it is not sufficient for the operator to merely know what buttons to push, but essential that he also have a conceptual understanding of what is occurring within the system corresponding to the pushing of each button, the turning of each dial, and the flipping of each switch.

The purpose of this chapter, then, is to introduce the reader to some of the concepts related to the execution of programs within an IBM System/360 or System/370. In relation to these systems, we shall discuss the following topics:

1. The types of programs that are executable in the system
2. The various states of the CPU during processing
3. Interrupts and their use in the system
4. Program status words

It is felt that the discussion of these topics will greatly enhance the student operator's ability to function within a typical computer environment. In addition, the operator will gain invaluable insights into the operational nature of the computer and what has occurred as a result of his interaction with the system.

In the majority of cases, the operator will concern himself with the processing of computer programs. Therefore, it is appropriate that we discuss, as our next topic, those types of programs that are executable within the computer system.

Self-study exercise 8-1

1. The operator is a(n) _____ part of the data processing complex.

♦ ♦ ♦

integral

2. The importance of the operator, within the data processing cycle, should not be _____ .

♦ ♦ ♦

underestimated

3. All _____ completed by the operator are designed to maintain the computer in an active _____ state.

♦ ♦ ♦

tasks
processing

4. The operator's reaction to the various conditions that arise within the computing system is a(n) _____ of his efficiency.

♦ ♦ ♦

measure

5. To effectively operate _____ the system, the operator must understand what is occurring _____ the computer.

♦ ♦ ♦

on
within

Though it is common to refer to all types of programs simply as computer programs, this designation is not sufficient for the computer operator. He must classify programs into one of two specific categories: *manufacturer-supplied programs* and *user-written programs*.

    A manufacturer-supplied program, as its name implies, is a program supplied by a computer manufacturer which is designed to satisfy a partic-

Programs Executable within the System

Types of programs

ular application. For example, a manufacturer-supplied program could be used to:

1. Carry out a given predescribed process such as producing a company payroll. These programs are often referred to as *packages*.
2. Transfer data from one medium to another (i.e., copy data from a magnetic disk to a magnetic tape, or vice versa). This type of manufacturer-supplied program is generally referred to as a *utility program*.
3. Place data into a desired sequence. The program used for this type of application is referred to as a *sort program* and can be applied to data stored on magnetic tape or disk.

When applicable, by using a manufacturer-supplied program, a company could save the costs incurred by the company's programming staff in writing, testing, and documenting the program. Generally, the computer manufacturer servicing your installation has available a complete listing of these specialty programs, indicating their purposes and areas of application.

For the most part, though, the preponderance of programs processed by the operator will be of the user-written variety. User-written programs are prepared by the various company-employed programmers. Since each company will process data to satisfy its own special needs, each user-written program will be unique in its purpose. Thus, user-written programs will vary markedly in content, thereby affecting the manner in which they are to be processed and thus affecting the role of the computer operator.

In processing most programs, an interaction between manufacturer-supplied and user-written programs is inevitable. A user-written program may be written in any of the various computer languages (i.e., FORTRAN, COBOL, etc.). As we previously learned, in order for this program to be processed, it must first be converted into a language format usable by the computer—machine language. The manufacturer-supplied programs that convert user-written programs to machine language are called *compilers*. When assembly language is used, the required conversion program is referred to as an *assembler*.

The processing of any program, be it a user-written, manufacturer-supplied, compiler, or assembler program, must be accomplished in the CPU. The program undergoing processing within the CPU is designated as the *problem program*. We may define the problem program as a program requiring input, processing, and output which has interacted with the supervisor during its execution. The purpose of the *supervisor program* and the nature of its interaction with the problem program are the next areas we shall discuss.

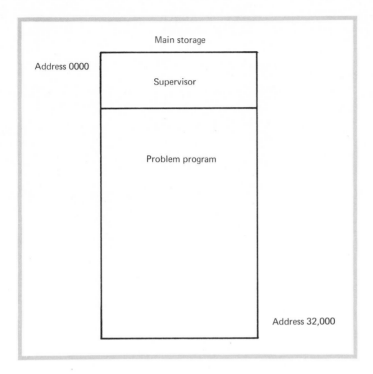

Main storage

Address 0000

Supervisor

Problem program

Address 32,000

Figure 8-1
The Supervisor Program
as It Is Stored in the CPU

Residing in the CPU. The *supervisor program* is a control program stored in the memory of an IBM System/360 or System/370 computer to oversee the performance of input/output and processing operations within the system. The supervisor is part of the complex of routines referred to by most manufacturers as an *operating system*. The supervisor controls and directs the activities of the computer during the processing of all problem programs. To effectively control all aspects of processing, the supervisor must reside in main storage (CPU). As depicted in Figure 8-1, the supervisor occupies the lower-numbered addresses in main storage.

The supervisor program

    To control the processing of any program, the supervisor must be capable of freely interacting with it. Because of this requirement, the most frequently processed user-written or manufacturer-supplied programs (i.e., a FORTRAN compiler, payroll program, etc.) are stored on an auxiliary storage device, such as a magnetic disk unit. Since the supervisor can operate on a program only when it resides within main storage, the problem program must be retrieved from the auxiliary storage unit. The supervisor will control the retrieval of the problem program to main storage, supervise its processing, and return it to auxiliary storage. Figure 8-2 depicts the interaction of the supervisor and various problem programs.

    Pictorially, we may observe that the supervisor calls in the problem program from the magnetic disk and stores it in the higher-numbered

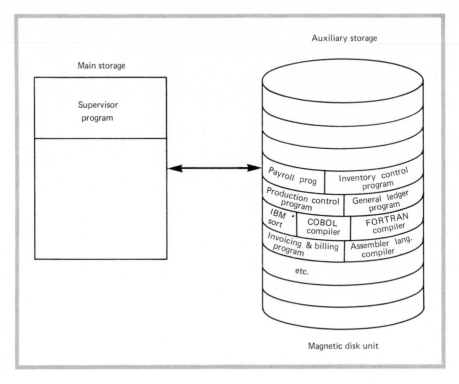

Figure 8-2
The Interaction of the
Supervisor with the
Problem Programs Stored
within Auxiliary Storage

address locations in main storage. Note that the supervisor always maintains its position in the lower-numbered storage addresses.

Specific functions of the supervisor.   At this point, we have discussed the supervisor in rather general terms. That is, we have stated that it is a program which controls all activities that surround the processing of any problem program. To this end, the supervisor must fulfill the following major functions:

1.   Scheduling the execution of problem programs
2.   Control and coordination of all input/output activities
3.   Satisfactorily handle all interrupts

The supervisor will establish the order and manner of execution for all programs processed by the system. This will remain true whether the system is relatively small and processes one job at a time or is quite sophisticated and has an extensive processing capability to handle more than one program at a given time. The supervisor will establish the sequence in which programs are to be executed.

During the processing of most programs, input/output operations will be performed. It is the responsibility of the supervisor to control and direct all required input/output operations. It should be noted, however, that *no input or output operation can be completed without the involvement of the supervisor.* The supervisor will always establish the instructions required to initiate and complete an input/output operation.

The handling of interrupts presents a somewhat different problem for the supervisor. An interrupt represents a stoppage within the flow of processing and results from an exception condition occurring in the CPU. Each type of exception condition must be handled in a particular way. To handle an interrupt satisfactorily, the supervisor must:

1. Notice the interrupt
2. Classify it as to the type of interrupt
3. Provide the specific set of instructions to handle that interrupt

At the completion of the interrupt handling sequence, the supervisor will return to the problem program and continue its processing.

We may readily conclude that the supervisor is a very comprehensive program. It has the capability to handle all the various conditions which may arise during processing.

Self-study exercise 8-2

1. Programs may be classified into two types: _____ and _____.

◆ ◆ ◆

manufacturer-supplied programs
user-written programs

2. Manufacturer-supplied programs are _____ to satisfy particular applications.

◆ ◆ ◆

designed

3. Manufacturer-supplied programs can be used to _____.

◆ ◆ ◆

prepare a payroll, transfer data between storage media, or order a data sequence

4. A manufacturer-supplied program which transfers data from a magnetic tape to disk may be referred to as a(n) _____.

♦ ♦ ♦

utility program

5. A manufacturer-supplied program that sequences data in a predetermined order may also be referred to as a(n) _____.

♦ ♦ ♦

sort program

6. User-written programs are written by _____ programmers.

♦ ♦ ♦

company-employed

7. User-written programs must be converted to _____ before they can be processed.

♦ ♦ ♦

machine language

8. The program that is generally used to convert high-level user-written programs to machine language is called a(n) _____.

♦ ♦ ♦

compiler

9. When assembly language is used, the conversion program is referred to as a(n) _____.

♦ ♦ ♦

assembler

10. The program undergoing processing within the CPU is designated as the _____.

♦ ♦ ♦

problem program

11. The control program which oversees all activities within the system is referred to as the _____.

♦ ♦ ♦

supervisor program

12. The supervisor program occupies the _____ addresses of _____.

♦ ♦ ♦

lower-numbered
main storage

13. The supervisor can operate on a problem program _____ when both reside in main storage.

♦ ♦ ♦

only

14. The major functions of the supervisor are _____.

♦ ♦ ♦

scheduling the execution of problem programs, control and coordination of all input/output operations, and satisfactorily handling all interrupts

15. No input or output operation may be performed without control of the _____.

♦ ♦ ♦

supervisor

16. An interrupt represents a(n) _____ in the flow of processing and results from a(n) _____ occurring in the CPU.

♦ ♦ ♦

stoppage
exception condition

17. The three steps involved in handling an interrupt are _____, _____, and _____.

◆ ◆ ◆

notice the interrupt
classify the type of interrupt
provide those instructions to handle that type of interrupt

Job Control

Job control language (JCL)

Since the supervisor is of primary importance in the processing of all programs, the computer operator must have a means of communicating with the supervisor. This interaction is accomplished through the use of *Job Control Language,* a computer language specifically designed for this purpose. This language is commonly referred to by its initials, JCL. JCL data is made available to the computer through a series of punched cards, referred to as *job cards,* via a card reader input device. Figure 8-3 illustrates the interaction of the system and JCL cards. Through the use of JCL, the operator can indicate those jobs to be run, the desired sequence of program processing, and the peripheral devices to be used, and he can request use of any of the special instruction sets available with the particular supervisor operating within the system.

For example, let us assume that the operator must process a job

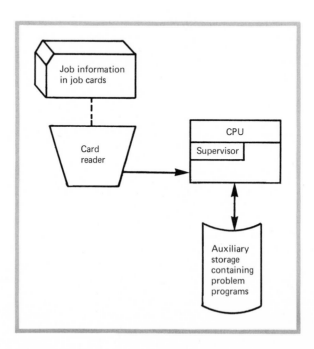

Figure 8-3
JCL Data Being Input to
the System

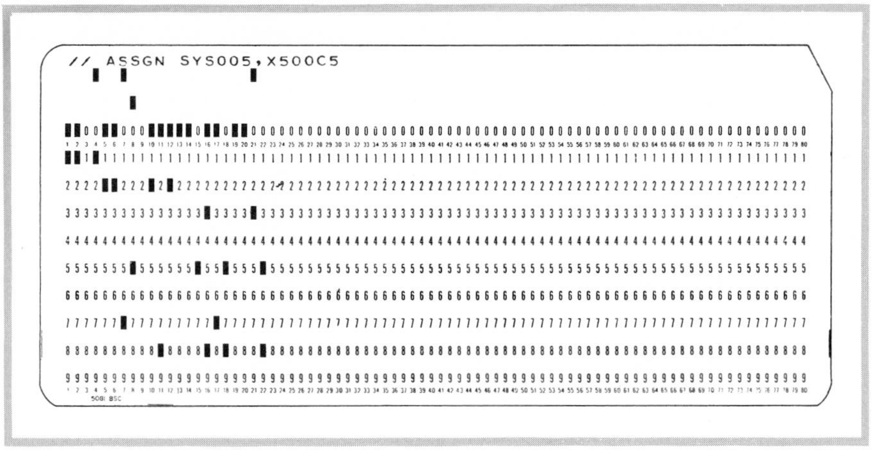

Figure 8-4
A JCL Card Used to
Assign a Particular Tape
Unit to the System

requiring the use of a magnetic tape unit. He must decide which of the available tape units will be used and indicate his selection of that unit to the supervisor. The supervisor, in turn, will establish all the required input/output operations with respect to the specified tape unit. The operator is able to assign the particular magnetic tape unit to the job at hand using only JCL. Figure 8-4 depicts a JCL card which could be used for this purpose.

Those special options available through JCL can be specified with the aid of job cards. These special features vary in purpose and, as a result, are selectively employed by the operator. In the next section we will discuss many of the available job control features.

JCL options

Through JCL, the operator or programmer can indicate to the supervisor the manner in which the problem program is to be processed. Prior to discussing the specific job control options, let us briefly review how a program is processed.

We know that through the use of an assembler or compiler, a source program is converted to a machine language program, or *object program,* which is executable by the computer. An object program is the only form of program that a computer can execute. Thus, when no errors are found to exist after assembly, or compilation, the object program can be executed.

The operator may elect to have the object program punched onto cards, resulting in a deck of cards containing the object program, the *object deck.* This object deck can now be used to process data—the operator need only add data cards. To exercise the control statement for the production of an object deck, the *DECK option* may be specified on a JCL card.

The DECK option represents one of a group of control statements

Table 8-1. Selected JCL Options

JCL Command	Results
LIST	A complete listing of the source program is produced.
EXEC F (*computer language*)	The source language employed by the problem program is indicated to the supervisor.
LINK and EXEC LNKEDT	The supervisor is directed to store the object program on an auxiliary storage device, such as a magnetic disk. This option can be employed only when the DECK instruction is not used—and vice versa.
DUMP	If the program is stopped during processing because of a program error, a printout revealing the contents (in hexadecimal) of every CPU storage position is produced.
EXEC	The supervisor is directed to execute the object program being stored and process the data supplied. This command is followed only if the compiled object program is found to be error-free.
/*	This command indicates that no further source program cards or data cards are provided.
/&	This command notes that the end of the deck of cards representing the entire problem program has been reached.

available to the operator. Table 8-1 lists other selected control statements available through JCL.

Figure 8-5 illustrates how JCL cards containing some of these options might be placed within a program prior to its processing. Since a more detailed discussion of this topic is beyond the scope of this text, we shall not discuss JCL any further.

As we have previously learned, during the processing of a program many activities take place within the CPU. The CPU must continually adapt itself to the various conditions induced by processing. In the next section we will introduce the various CPU states that may evolve in the course of its processing activities.

Self-study exercise 8-3

1. The computer language designed to permit interaction with the supervisor is _____ .

◆ ◆ ◆

Job Control Language (JCL)

2. Punched cards used to input JCL data to the system are referred to as _____ .

◆ ◆ ◆

job cards

Figure 8-5
The Sequence of JCL and Program Cards Which Could Be Used to Process a Job

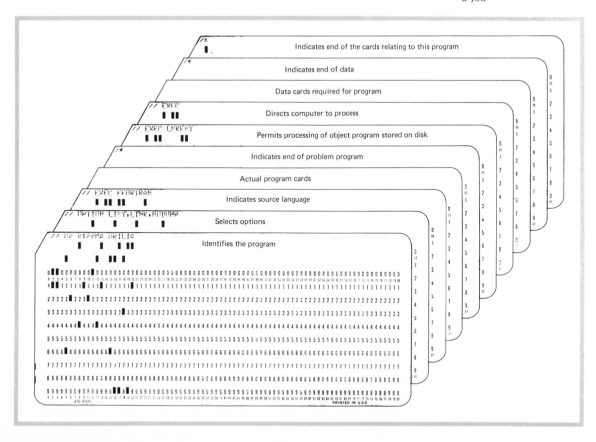

3. Using JCL, the operator can indicate _____.

◆ ◆ ◆

programs to be run, the desired sequence of processing, the peripheral devices to be used, and any special instruction sets that are required

4. The machine language program compiled from a source program may be referred to as a(n) _____.

◆ ◆ ◆

object program

5. The object program is the only form of program that can be _____.

◆ ◆ ◆

executed

6. With the object program punched onto cards, the resulting deck of cards is called a(n) _____.

◆ ◆ ◆

object deck

7. To request the production of an object deck, the _____ option, via JCL, can be used.

◆ ◆ ◆

DECK

8. The _____ option, in JCL, will cause a complete listing of the source program to be produced.

◆ ◆ ◆

LIST

9. The JCL command EXEC FFORTRAN indicates to the supervisor that _____.

◆ ◆ ◆

the source language of the problem program is FORTRAN

10. To direct the supervisor to store the object program on an auxiliary storage device, the JCL commands _____ are used.

♦ ♦ ♦

LINK and EXEC LNKEDT

11. A printout revealing the contents of CPU storage is possible when the JCL option _____ is employed.

♦ ♦ ♦

DUMP

12. The JCL command _____ directs the supervisor to process the object program.

♦ ♦ ♦

EXEC

We should now clearly see that the CPU is the hub of all activities within the computer system. Residing in the CPU is the supervisor, a program controlling the operation of the system. We also now know that to process a given program, both the supervisor and problem programs must reside in main storage. Thus, at any given moment, the CPU may be executing instructions from the supervisor or problem program, depending on which has the attention of the control unit of the CPU. When the CPU is executing instructions from the supervisor, it is said to be in the *supervisor state*. Conversely, if problem program instructions are being executed, the state of the CPU is referred to as the *problem state*.

The status of the CPU, when operating under either of these two states, is unique. That is, instructions executable in the supervisor state are not executable in the problem state, and vice versa. For example, the supervisor controls the execution of all input/output instructions. These instructions can be found only in the supervisor, since they control the manner in which the I/O operation will be completed. Thus, the problem program will indicate that an I/O operation is to be performed, but the supervisor is the only program which can effect its completion. On the other hand, when processing a payroll program, the CPU is said to be in a problem state. The CPU can process only those instructions which relate to the problem program and which are, therefore, not executable by the supervisor.

In either case, we have observed that it is possible for the CPU to exist in two different states. We shall use the term *program state* as a

Status of the CPU

Table 8-2.   Program States

Program State	The CPU Is
Stopped	Incapable of executing any instructions, and no processing whatsoever may occur.
Operating	Fully operational, and all types of instructions are executable. The operator may also interact (communicate) with the computer at any time.
Running	Fetching and executing instructions from both the supervisor and problem programs, as normal processing proceeds.
Waiting	Not processing any instructions since it has completed its activities. The CPU is awaiting further instructions or directions from the computer operator, supervisor program, or problem program.
Supervisor	Processing instructions as directed by the supervisor control program.
Problem	Processing only those instructions found within the problem program.
Masked	Protected against any interruptions in the normal flow of processing, be they operator-initiated or directed by the supervisor control program, until processing is completed.
Interruptible	Capable of having the normal flow of processing interrupted at any time by an operator communication or supervisor intervention.

definition of the status of the CPU at any given time. Both the supervisor and problem states are examples of program states and represent two of the possible eight program states the system may enter. Table 8-2 briefly details the eight possible program states.

Figure 8-6 will assist our discussions of how these program states are related.

Initially, we should notice that the CPU is in either a stopped or an operating state. When it is in a stopped state, no processing is possible within the CPU. With the CPU placed in an operating state, processing may be undertaken since the CPU assumes one of two possible program states, running or waiting. In the running state, the CPU fetches and processes program instructions. Entry of the CPU into the waiting program state indicates that the CPU has temporarily suspended processing, and further instructions are pending from the supervisor program, problem program, or computer operator.

With the entry of the CPU into a running program state, the system selects one of two states: the supervisor or problem state. Entry of the CPU into either of these two states implies that instructions taken from the supervisor or problem program will be executed. We recall, from our discussion in a previous section, that the relationship between these programs is indeed unique in that they are mutually exclusive. The CPU can devote its full attention to only one of these programs at a given time. As we may have observed from Figure 8-6, there is no counterpart to the supervisor or problem program state when the CPU is in a waiting state. This is simply because in a waiting state, no data is being processed, the CPU is not accessed, and no instructions require execution.

At any given time, whether the computer is waiting for instructions or processing data under control of the supervisor or problem program, the computer operator may elect to intervene in these program states. The response of the system to the operator's inquiry depends on whether the CPU is in a masked or an interruptible program state. If the CPU is in an interruptible state, the operator's request to interrupt the existing program state is immediately handled. The masked state is designed to protect the existing program state momentarily. That is, the CPU recognizes the desire of the operator or supervisor to gain the attention of the CPU, but permits the instruction(s) currently being processed to be completed. At the completion of those instructions, the computer acknowledges the operator's request.

The operator's request is an example of an action which will interrupt an existing program state. There are, however, conditions which arise from the program being processed that will cause similar types of program state

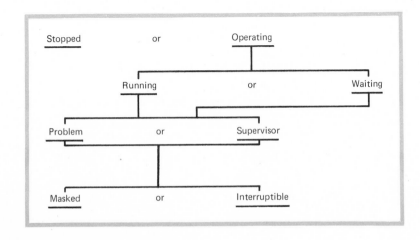

Figure 8-6
The Relationship of the
Various Program States

interruptions. These varied conditions result from the activities involved in the program being processed. Let us therefore turn our attention to a discussion of interrupts and how they are caused.

Self-study exercise 8-4

1. When the CPU is executing instructions from the supervisor, it is in a(n) _____ state.

♦ ♦ ♦

supervisor

2. Conversely, if instructions are executed from the problem program, the CPU is said to be in a(n) _____ state.

♦ ♦ ♦

problem

3. For either of the above states, the status of the CPU is _____.

♦ ♦ ♦

unique

4. The supervisor and problem states represent _____ of the _____ possible CPU states.

♦ ♦ ♦

two
eight

5. In the _____ state, the CPU is incapable of executing any instructions.

♦ ♦ ♦

stopped

6. All types of instructions are executable when the CPU is in a(n) _____ state.

♦ ♦ ♦

operating

7. After entry into an operating state, the CPU may assume a(n) _____ or _____ status.

◆ ◆ ◆

waiting
running

8. In a waiting state, the CPU has _____ its activities and _____ further instructions.

◆ ◆ ◆

completed
is awaiting

9. In a running state, the CPU can _____ and _____ instructions from any program.

◆ ◆ ◆

fetch
execute

10. With entry into the running state, the CPU may assume two states: the _____ or _____.

◆ ◆ ◆

supervisor state
problem state

11. The _____ CPU state protects against interruptions in the normal flow of processing.

◆ ◆ ◆

masked

12. Operator intervention is permitted when the CPU is in a(n) _____ state.

◆ ◆ ◆

interruptible

13. If the request for intervention is delayed, the CPU was in a(n) _____ state.

♦   ♦   ♦

masked

14. The CPU (may/may not) enter the masked or interruptible state from a waiting state.

♦   ♦   ♦

may not

Interrupts

The concept of an interrupt

Normally, a computing system will be in a running program state, executing instructions from either the supervisor or problem program. Occasionally, however, an exception condition will occur somewhere within the computer system, one which will affect the processing being performed. The computer must then determine the nature of this exception condition and its effect upon the system. To call attention to the existence of this special condition, the system is programmed to generate some type of special signal to the CPU. This special signal is defined as an *interrupt*. The interrupt represents a request, on the part of the computer, for a change in the state of the CPU. In essence, the CPU is being requested to switch from its current program state to one in which the newly recognized interrupt can be handled. We will define the switching of the CPU from one program state to another as a *status-switching operation*. At this point, we shall consider an example to assist our discussion.

ILLUSTRATIVE EXAMPLE

Let us consider an input operation in which a magnetic tape is used. When data is read from the magnetic tape, it is possible for an error to occur and data to be read incorrectly. When this condition does occur, the computer senses the error. The CPU issues instructions causing the tape to backspace and that data to be reread. Quite often, this subsequent attempt results in the correct reading of the tape.

In our example, when the supervisor noticed the problem program's request for a tape read operation, an interrupt was issued. The request for a change in the status of the CPU was acknowledged, and the CPU state shifted from a problem to a supervisor state. The supervisor was then able to issue those instructions used to verify the tape reading operation. It is noteworthy that although the input and output operations are part of a problem program, they can be completed only when the computer is functioning under the supervisor control program. *All* input/output operations are controlled by the supervisor. Thus, in order to execute those supervisor instructions which control input/output operations, the CPU must be in the supervisor state.

In the previous example we illustrated one form of interrupt. There are five types of interrupts to which the system will respond and which cause a change in the status of the CPU. The five classes of interrupts are:

Types of interrupts

1. Input/output (I/O)
2. External
3. Program-check
4. Machine-check
5. Supervisor call

We have already discussed the occurrence of an *I/O interrupt* in the previous example. But briefly, an I/O interrupt occurs when an input or output operation is initiated or completed. The status of the CPU changes to, or from, problem and supervisor states. Because this type of interrupt occurs quite regularly within the processing of a problem program, it is considered a separate class of interrupt. It also belongs to the class of supervisor call interrupts discussed below.

An *external interrupt* occurs whenever the operator depresses the INTERRUPT pushbutton on the computer console. Through the use of this key, the operator can intervene in the processing currently occurring in the CPU. The operator may then affect the processing being performed by the system. The INTERRUPT key, as well as the entire computer console, will be discussed at length in Chapter 14.

An interrupt caused by an exception condition *within* the problem program is defined as a *program-check interrupt*. Program-check interrupts may occur as a result of the following conditions:

1. Arithmetic overflow—the results of processing are too large for a given register or their assigned storage location.
2. Data improperly specified—the format of data to be processed was improperly specified within the problem program. For example, data was described using one format, and in reality a different input format was used.
3. Improper use of instructions—within the problem program, computer language instructions were incorrectly written or improperly used.

4. Storage protection violation—an attempt by a problem program to enter a special storage area of the CPU. In certain systems, areas of the CPU are set aside for special data and protected from being accessed. An attempt to enter this reserved area will result in a program-check interrupt.

A *machine-check interrupt* occurs whenever the computer senses a machine malfunction in other than an I/O unit. An example of a machine check is a *parity check*. It is possible to gain or lose a bit while data is being transferred from one location to another. To protect against such a condition going undetected, a parity check is conducted routinely after any operation involving the manipulation of data.

A *supervisor call interrupt* occurs whenever specific instructions, referred to as supervisor call instructions, are executed by a problem program. The CPU will status-switch from the problem to supervisor state. Supervisor call instructions are required when reading and writing data, loading new programs to be executed, canceling a problem program under execution, or under any condition where the supervisor must assume control of the computer. An example of this type of interrupt is the end-of-job condition. When a problem program is finished processing, control of the computer must be turned over to the supervisor. After the supervisor call interrupt is issued, the supervisor locates the next program to be run and brings it into the CPU for processing.

At this point in the chapter, we have discussed those activities which control processing or handle exception conditions and which may arise within the system. We have not discussed the means by which the computer records the CPU state it has achieved. This will be the next topic of discussion.

Self-study exercise 8-5

1. With the CPU in the running state, instructions from either the _____ or the _____ program will be executed.

◆ ◆ ◆

supervisor
problem

2. To indicate the existence of an exception condition, the computer generates a(n) _____.

◆ ◆ ◆

interrupt

3. The interrupt represents a request for a(n) _____ in the state of the CPU.

♦ ♦ ♦

change

4. The switching of the CPU from one program state to another is defined as a(n) _____ .

♦ ♦ ♦

status-switching operation

5. To handle an interrupt condition, the CPU must be in a(n) _____ state.

♦ ♦ ♦

supervisor

6. All input/output operations (will/will not) cause an interrupt.

♦ ♦ ♦

will

7. The five types of interrupts are _____ .

♦ ♦ ♦

input/output, external, program-check, machine-check, and supervisor call

8. An I/O interrupt occurs whenever the problem program requests a(n) _____ .

♦ ♦ ♦

input or output operation

9. Depression of the INTERRUPT key on the console causes a(n) _____ to occur.

♦ ♦ ♦

external interrupt

10. Exception conditions caused by the problem program result in _____ interrupts.

◆ ◆ ◆

program-check

11. A(n) _____ interrupt occurs whenever the computer senses a machine malfunction.

◆ ◆ ◆

machine-check

12. A(n) _____ interrupt is issued whenever the supervisor must assume control of the computer.

◆ ◆ ◆

supervisor call

Program Status Words The computer must have a means of determining its logical status with respect to the program undergoing processing. The term *logical status* refers to those logical conditions that exist in the computer at any time. Such conditions may be the current status of the CPU, the address of the next instruction to be executed, or the relationship of the last data items that were compared. The vehicle employed to record internally the logical status of the CPU is the *program status word*. The program status word is a *doubleword* in length and is referred to by its initials, PSW.

Current, old, and new PSWs As we shall observe, there are several PSWs involved in the operation of a computing system. But at any one time, there is only one PSW in a position to influence the activities of the CPU. It is defined as the *current PSW*. It, as well as the others we will discuss, is kept in a specific location within main storage. In addition to the current PSW, there are two more PSWs of interest, the *old PSW* and the *new PSW*. The purpose of each may be explained as follows.

Current PSW the PSW currently influencing the operation of the system. It provides the address of the instruction currently undergoing processing.

New PSW the PSW which contains the address of the first instruction of the series of supervisor instructions designed to handle the particular interrupt encountered.

Old PSW   the PSW which temporarily stores the current PSW while an interrupt is being handled.

The PSW provides the computer with the ability to maintain a status on the processing being performed within the system. Its function is closely linked with the supervisor's handling of all classes of interrupts. Let us examine this relationship in further detail.

To review, we know that an interrupt is the response of the computer to an exception condition that has arisen within the system. After determining the type of interrupt encountered, the CPU accomplishes a status-switching operation and enters a supervisor state. The supervisor control program will handle the particular class of interrupt and enable the CPU to return to a problem state, so that processing may continue.

The operational handling of interrupts

The PSW plays an important role within the interrupt-handling sequence. Through the use of the PSW, the computer maintains an awareness of the sequence of instructions to be executed. The following sequence of steps will assist our discussion of how a PSW is employed by the computer.

Step 1.   The computer recognizes the existence of an interrupt.

Step 2.   The current PSW, noting the instruction currently being processed, is stored in the old PSW area.

Step 3.   The new PSW, indicating the address of the first instruction for the set of supervisor control instructions specifically designed to handle that type of interrupt, is transferred to become the current PSW.

Step 4.   The supervisor control program enters at the location specified in the current PSW.

Step 5.   With the CPU in the supervisor state, those instructions necessary to satisfy handling of the interrupt are executed.

Step 6.   Upon completion of the interrupt-handling routine, the old PSW is moved to become the current PSW, and the CPU reenters the problem state.

Step 7.   The problem program is reentered at the location specified in the current PSW.

Logically, the student may ask, If the new PSW holds the address of the first supervisor instruction to handle an interrupt, what directs the computer to the next instruction in the problem program? The answer to this question lies with the current PSW. The configuration of the current PSW contains the number of storage positions the computer must increment from its current storage position in order to attain the address of the next sequential instruction of the problem program. Thus, the current PSW provides the problem program instruction to be worked on and the number of storage positions to the next instruction to be processed.

Let us expand our discussion of the sequence of steps employed by the computer in accessing a PSW. We may recall that after an interrupt is completely handled, the old PSW replaces the current PSW. As a result, the CPU returns to a problem state and completes the processing of the statement that originally caused the interrupt. With the completion of that statement, the current PSW is examined, and the supervisor knows the number of storage positions required to move to the next instruction. The computer then moves to the new instruction, and a *new* current PSW is established.

The manner in which the computer operates on, and with, a PSW is quite complex and beyond the scope of this text. Should the student operator desire further information on this topic, he is directed to the computer manufacturers' technical manuals relating to the execution of programs within the CPU.

Self-study exercise 8-6

1. The logical conditions that exist in the computer at any time are referred to by the term _____.

◆　◆　◆

logical status

2. The logical status might describe the _____, _____, or _____.

◆　◆　◆

current status of the CPU
the address of the last instruction executed
the relationship of the last data items compared

3. The _____ is used to record the logical status of the CPU.

◆　◆　◆

program status word (PSW)

4. The PSW is a(n) _____ in length.

◆　◆　◆

doubleword

5. The PSW that will influence the activities of the system is referred to as the _____.

♦ ♦ ♦

current PSW

6. The _____ temporarily stores the current PSW during the handling of an interrupt.

♦ ♦ ♦

old PSW

7. The new PSW contains the address of the _____ instruction of the series of supervisor instructions designed to handle the particular interrupt.

♦ ♦ ♦

first

8. After determining the type of interrupt, the CPU enters a(n) _____.

♦ ♦ ♦

supervisor state

9. With the CPU in the supervisor state, the instructions designated via the _____ are executed to process the interrupt.

♦ ♦ ♦

new PSW

10. To accomplish the handling of the interrupt, the new PSW must become the _____.

♦ ♦ ♦

current PSW

11. With the completion of the interrupt-handling routine, the _____ becomes the current PSW.

♦ ♦ ♦

old PSW

12. The current PSW contains the _____ of storage positions to the next _____ to be processed in the problem program.

♦ ♦ ♦

number
instruction

End-of-chapter Exercises

True-false exercise

1. A manufacturer-supplied program can be used to satisfy only one specific application.
2. An assembler can be used to translate a FORTRAN program to machine language.
3. The supervisor provides partial control over the computing system.
4. I/O operations can be completed only through control of the supervisor.
5. JCL data is input to the system using job cards.
6. Object programs are the only form of program executable by the computer.
7. There are 10 possible CPU states.
8. In the supervisor state, instructions removed from the problem program may be executed in the CPU.
9. Interrupts are discarded and ignored when the CPU is in a masked state.
10. I/O operations will not create an interrupt.
11. Depression of the INTERRUPT key on the console causes an external interrupt to occur.
12. A supervisor call interrupt is issued whenever a status-switching operation is performed.
13. A PSW is a fullword long.
14. The current PSW directs the computer to the next instruction to be processed.

Fill-in exercise

1. Programs are classified into two general types: _____ and _____.
2. A(n) _____ program is a manufacturer-supplied program designed to sequence data contained in a file.
3. The term _____ defines the program currently undergoing processing in the CPU.
4. The operator may interact with the supervisor through use of _____ language.
5. If the object program is punched onto cards, these cards are referred to as a(n) _____.

6. Each CPU state is _____ .
7. When executing instructions from the problem program, the CPU is said to be in the _____ .
8. All types of instructions may be executed when the CPU is in its _____ state.
9. Operator intervention is possible when the CPU is in its _____ state.
10. Alternating between the various CPU states is defined as a(n) _____ operation.
11. A machine malfunction will result in a(n) _____ interrupt.
12. The _____ PSW can influence the activities of the system.
13. Upon the completion of an interrupt-handling routine, the _____ PSW becomes the _____ PSW.
14. To process an interrupt, the CPU must enter a(n) _____ state.

Multiple-choice exercise

1. A manufacturer-supplied program designed to transfer data from one storage medium to another is referred to as a
   a. user program
   b. specially prepared program
   c. utility program
   d. tape program
   e. none of the above
2. The computer program that converts a user-written program to a machine language program is referred to as
   a. a converter
   b. a compiler
   c. a translator
   d. an object program
   e. none of the above
3. For use, the supervisor program must reside in
   a. main storage, low-numbered storage locations
   b. main storage, high-numbered storage locations
   c. auxiliary storage, low-numbered storage locations
   d. auxiliary storage, high-numbered storage locations
   e. anywhere in the entire computer configuration
4. The occurrence of an exception condition within the CPU will result in a condition called
   a. a stoppage
   b. a special
   c. an interrupt
   d. an error state
   e. none of the above

5. Through JCL, the following options may be selected.
   a. DECK, LISTING, LNKEDT, and LINK
   b. DECK, DUMP, EXEC, and LINK
   c. DUMP, LIST, EXEC LNK, and LINK
   d. LISTING, LINK, EXEC, and DUMP
   e. EXEC LNK, EXEC, DUMP, and LIST
6. A sequence of states that the CPU may not pass through is
   a. stopped
   b. operating, running, supervisor, and masked
   c. operating, running, problem, and interruptible
   d. operating, waiting, and interruptible
   e. all the above
7. With the CPU in a running state, instructions from any program are
   a. run and processed
   b. run and executed
   c. fetched and executed
   d. fetched and stored
   e. none of the above
8. An interrupt generated by the problem program is a
   a. machine-check
   b. write check
   c. program-check
   d. console check
   e. none of the above
9. The logical status of the CPU is recorded in the
   a. problem program
   b. problem state
   c. status program state
   d. program status state
   e. none of the above
10. The new PSW contains
    a. the address of the instruction being processed
    b. the address of the problem program instruction to be processed
    c. the address of the supervisor program for that interrupt
    d. the address of the interrupt
    e. none of the above

Discussion questions

1. List and briefly discuss each of the major functions of the supervisor control program.
2. Outline and discuss the three steps required to handle an interrupt.
3. Discuss the uses of job control language (JCL).

4. List and discuss each of the CPU states which the CPU may attain for an IBM Model 360.
5. In outline form, discuss the five types of interrupts. Cite an example of each type.
6. List and describe the three types of program status words (PSWs).
7. Outline and discuss the manner in which an interrupt is handled. Carefully detail the uses, if any, of the PSW in that sequence.

UNIT IV
INPUT/OUTPUT DEVICES

CARD READER/PUNCH CHAPTER 9

Introduction   The card reader/punch is utilized in both the first and last stages in the data processing cycle of input, processing, and output. With few exceptions, data is initially entered into the computer system through the card reader/punch in the form of punched cards. The card reader/punch is composed of two distinct devices housed in a single unit—an input device and an output device. The card reader unit is used to sense information punched into cards and transfer this information, in the form of electric impulses, to the CPU (Central Processing Unit). The card punch unit, under the control of the program being processed, is used to punch output data into cards. Together, these units facilitate both input and output operations with respect to the punched card medium in one device. Thus, we have the derivation of the name the *card reader* and *card punch,* or shortened, the *card reader/punch.*

Since most data processing applications begin with the reading of data stored on punched cards, the computer operator will find a significant proportion of his time taken up directly or indirectly by the card reader/punch. The operator's functions include the placement of cards into the card reader and their removal after they have been read. On the card punch side, the operator must ensure that this unit is provided with a sufficient number of blank cards so that a punching operation can be performed. The operator will respond to error conditions which may require the rereading of one or more cards and the replacement of cards that have become bent or jammed during a reading operation. When a jammed card condition occurs, the operator has to free the cards manually and restart the card reading sequence. The operator's performance of this task, as well as others, will be discussed later in the chapter.

Thus, this chapter will introduce and discuss the purpose of the card reader/punch. In addition, it will provide the student operator with details of many of the operational requirements of the card reader/punch. With this idea in mind, let us begin our discussions.

As in any data processing operation, the value of any computed result depends, to a large extent, on the accuracy of the input data. Despite the great computing power and accuracy of the computer, the results of processing can be worthless if data is misread during the input stage of processing. It is for this reason that the computer operator must be aware of the importance of proper operation of the card reader/punch.

The operation of a card reader/punch depends on the type of device used in the system. We shall discuss the types of card reader/punches currently available in the next section.

Concepts of   As we have previously stated, the card reader/punch is classified as an input
Operation   and output device, since it houses both a card reader and card punch. For ease of understanding, we will introduce each component separately, since
Types of card   each will in actuality function independently.
readers

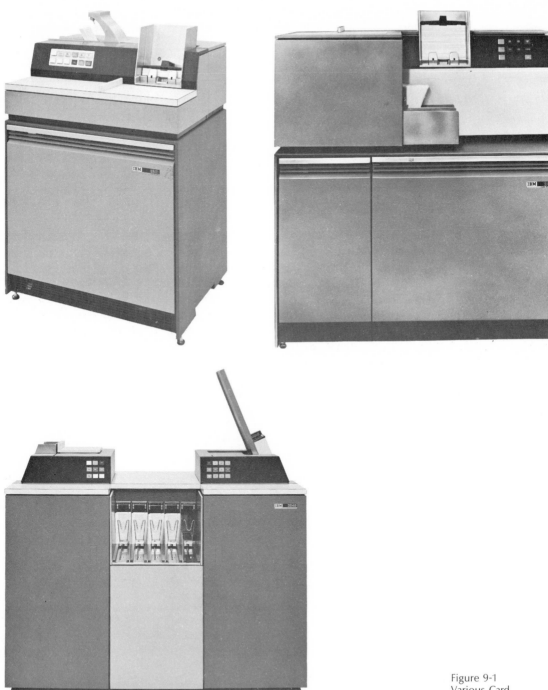

Figure 9-1
Various Card
Reader/Punch Units

Most modern card readers are similar in appearance and principles of operation, but are divided into two types, depending on how they read cards. These are:

1. Brush reader
2. Photoelectric reader

The brush reader type of device uses a series of 80 metal brushes to read data. The card passes under these brushes, and the presence of holes in the card is sensed as the brushes make contact with the metal roller beneath the card. The electric impulses produced are converted by the card reader and temporarily stored as data. These impulses will be compared to a second set of impulses, produced from a second reading of the same card. In general, brush readers contain two sets of brushes which allow a card to be read twice. The results of these two readings can then be compared, thereby providing a check on the validity of the data read. (See Figure 9-2.)

Photoelectric card readers sense punched holes in a different manner. The card passes through a beam of light, and the presence of punched holes is noted as the light penetrates the holes on the card and strikes a series of photoelectric cells located beneath the card. There are 12 photoelectric cells provided—one cell for each row on a card. (See Figure 9-3.)

The configuration of light impulses sensed by the photoelectric cells

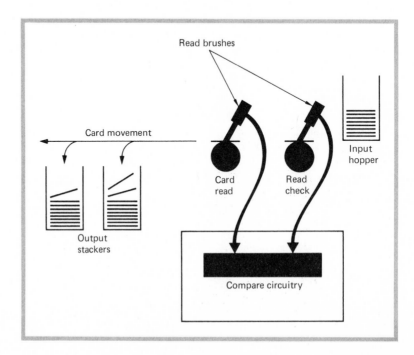

Figure 9-2
Electronic Comparison of Impulses Read at Each Station

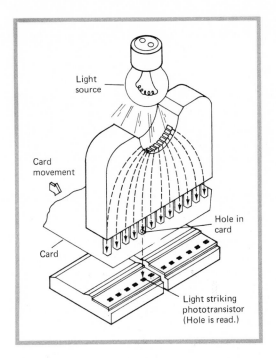

Figure 9-3
Schematic of
Photoelectric Reading
Device

is converted into electric impulses and is temporarily stored. A verification process, similar to that used with the brush reader device, is performed to check data input. Generally, photoelectric card readers are faster than brush readers.

Card readers are also classified as either *parallel* or *serial* card readers. Serial card readers read punched cards column by column, whereas parallel card readers read row by row. This difference is significant since serial card readers need to read only those columns in which data is punched. In this way, the speed of serial card readers may vary depending on the number of card columns used to store data. Parallel card readers, on the other hand, must read every row of each card, regardless of the amount of data punched on the cards.

Card reading speeds can be as high as 2,000 cards per minute depending on the type and model of card reader, with the most common speeds being approximately 800 to 1,000 cards per minute.

Common to all card reader/punches are the following components.

Card reader/punch components

Input hopper. On the card reader side, the input hopper holds those cards to be read, whereas on the punch side, blank cards are stored in the input hopper. A sufficient number of cards should be placed in each input hopper

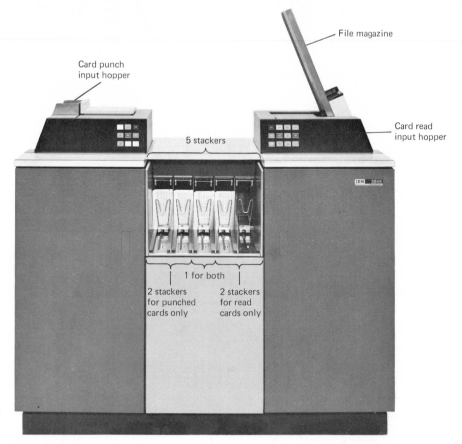

Figure 9-4
IBM 2540 Card Read/
Punch

to minimize the number of times the operator will have to load cards into a hopper. This is particularly important with reference to the card reader hopper, when we consider the vast number of cards that will be read. To increase the capacity of the input read hopper, the attachment of a file magazine, fitting directly over the input hopper, is made. (See Figure 9-4.) Thereby, a large quantity of cards may be stacked at one time.

Output stacker. The output stacker contains those cards that have been read, run out of the machine, or punched. The number of output stackers available on a card reader/punch varies with the manufacturer and the model of the card reader/punch. Examples of two card reader/punch units are shown in Figures 9-4 and 9-5. Note that the unit in Figure 9-4 contains one input hopper for reading, one input hopper for punching, and five output stackers. Two of these stackers are used for cards being punched, two for cards being read, and the fifth, or middle, stacker can be used for cards which have been either punched or read. The unit in Figure 9-5 contains one input hopper and two output stackers. Cards placed in the input hopper are either read or punched, with the processed cards being directed to either of the two output stackers.

Card feed mechanism. The card feed mechanism consists of a series of feed blades and rollers which move the cards from the input hopper, past the read or punch station, and into the output stacker. All card reader/punch units must allow the operator to gain access to the card feed mechanism. This access is essential in cases where card jams occur within the feed mechanism or transport area, thereby preventing further reading or punching operations. When a card jam occurs, it is the operator's responsibility to clear the card feed mechanism and restore the card reader/punch to an operational state.

1 common input hopper for both the reading and punching of cards

2 output stackers capable of receiving punched or read cards

Figure 9-5
IBM 2520 Card Read/
Punch

Read or punch station. Reading or punching takes place at the read or punch station, respectively. The read station may consist of metal brushes or a photoelectric unit, as described earlier, while the punch station consists of a series of punch knives (similar to those on the keypunch) which cause the punching of the desired holes in blank cards. As in the case of card readers, card punches are classified as serial or parallel. Card punching speeds can be as high as 500 cards per minute with the most common speeds being between 200 and 300 cards per minute.

Control panel. The control panel contains the pushbutton keys and indicator lights necessary to monitor and control the operation of the particular unit.

Error checking

An important function of any card reader/punch is its ability to detect possible errors which could occur during the punching or reading of cards. The detection of errors prior to their introduction into the computing system is of considerable value. Two types of error checking performed by most card readers are *validity checking* and *read checking*.

Validity checking ensures that the punches which exist in a punched card constitute a valid character in Hollerith or EBCDIC code. When a validity-check error is found, it is usually the result of a keypunch which is not functioning properly. An example would be the incorrect punching of two characters in the same card column or the *off-punching* of a character (a character improperly punched between card columns).

Read checking, however, is performed to verify that a card has been correctly read by the card reader. This is accomplished by passing the card through two consecutive read stations. Electronically, the two sets of impulses produced by the separate readings of the card are compared. Thus, we are assured that the data read at each station is identical. This technique is shown schematically in Figure 9-2. If either a validity-check or read-check error occurs, the card reader ceases reading cards, and an appropriate indicator light lights. The operator's response will be the examination and correction of the card if a validity check is indicated or simply initiating a rereading of the card if a read error is indicated. If a read-check error occurs due to off-punching, then the cards that are in error must be corrected and then reread. Should no cards be in error, the operator should check the brushes or photoelectric unit for the presence of dust particles.

Some card punches also test for punching errors by passing the card through a read station after it has been punched. The punch unit verifies that the data read at the read station is the same as the data entered at the punch station. If not, a *punch-check error* is signaled by the activation of an indicator light on the control panel (punching side).

Self-study exercise 9-1

1. The card reader/punch represents the _____ stage(s) in the data processing cycle.

◆ ◆ ◆

first and last

2. The two types of card readers are the _____ reader and the _____ reader.

◆ ◆ ◆

brush
photoelectric

3. Generally, _____ card readers are the faster of the two types of card readers.

◆ ◆ ◆

photoelectric

4. Card readers which read cards column by column are referred to as _____ card readers.

◆ ◆ ◆

serial

5. Card readers which read cards row by row are referred to as _____ card readers.

◆ ◆ ◆

parallel

6. The speed of serial card readers depends on _____.

◆ ◆ ◆

the number of columns containing actual data

7. Cards are loaded into the card reader/punch at the _____.

◆ ◆ ◆

input hopper

8. Cards are fed into the _____ after they have been processed.

◆ ◆ ◆

output stackers

9. Two common types of error checking performed by card reader devices are _____ checking and _____ checking.

◆ ◆ ◆

read
validity

10. _____ checking ensures that a proper Hollerith-coded character has been punched into each card column.

◆ ◆ ◆

Validity

11. Read checking ensures that _____.

◆ ◆ ◆

the input data was correctly read

12. A similar check made by the card punch which requires reading the card just punched is called a(n) _____ check.

◆ ◆ ◆

punch-

The IBM 2540
Card Read/Punch

The IBM 2540 Card Read/Punch (Figure 9-4) can be found in many data processing installations because of its ability to handle significant amounts of card reading and punching. Because of its wide-scale use and acceptance, the remainder of this chapter will concentrate on the 2540 when

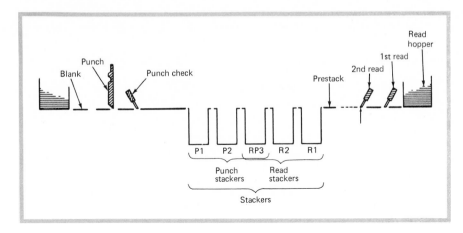

Figure 9-6
Schematic Diagram of
2540 Card Read/Punch

discussing operating procedures. The IBM 2540 can be attached to any computer in the IBM 360 Series from the Model 25 up. It is capable of reading cards at speeds up to 1,000 cards per minute and punching cards at up to 300 cards per minute.

The two input hoppers, located on either end of the 2540, hold the cards to be read or punched. The read input hopper, with magazine, has a capacity of approximately 3,100 cards, whereas the punch input hopper has a capacity of approximately 1,350 cards.

There are five output stackers on the 2540. These are labeled P1, P2, RP3, R2, and R1. The P stackers are used to store punched output, while the R stackers hold the cards which have been read. The RP3 stacker can hold cards processed by either the reader or the punch. This relationship is shown schematically in Figure 9-6. Under normal operation, cards are fed into the P1 and R1 stackers. However, under control of the program being processed, they can be directed into the other stackers.

Each stacker can hold approximately 1,350 cards. Should any one stacker be filled to capacity, the machine will automatically turn itself off and signal the operator by activating the appropriate indicator light.

Read operation

Card reading on the 2540 is accomplished by passing the card through a read station which determines the presence or absence of holes punched in the card. The 2540 is a brush reader, in which the reading operation requires three machine cycles (see Figure 9-6), namely,

1. A card is moved from the input hopper to the first read station.
2. The card is then moved from the first read station to the second read station.
3. The card is finally moved past the second read station to the prestack station.

A read-check operation is performed on all data read by the 2540. If discrepancies are noted, a *read-check* condition is indicated.

Punch operation   Cards are punched as they pass under the punch station. Punching takes place as a result of a punch instruction which is executed as part of a program being processed.

The punch operation requires four machine cycles, namely,

1. A card is moved from the punch input hopper to the blank station (located immediately before the punch station).
2. The card is then moved from the blank station to the punch station.
3. Data is punched into the card as the card moves row by row through the punch station.
4. The card is finally moved from the punch station to the punch-check station. Here the card is read by a series of brushes, and a check is made to verify that the data read is the same as the data punched. If the data is not the same, a *punch-check* condition is indicated. The card is then moved into one of the punch stackers.

Operator controls and indicator lights   Operator controls and indicator lights are divided into three groupings: reader keys and lights, punch keys and lights, and common indicator lights (see Tables 9-1, 9-2, and 9-3). The indicator lights serve to alert the operator to the status of the 2540, whereas the pushbutton keys are employed to effect changes in the operation of the card reader/punch. The common lights, located on the reader side of the 2540, note common operational states which either the punch or reader sides have assumed.

Operating procedures   The operator's duties regarding the 2540 can be subdivided into two categories: those duties which are required for normal operation and those duties required of the operator in response to one of several possible error conditions.

Let us first examine normal operating procedures.

Normal operating procedures.   Normal operating procedures for the 2540 include starting the reader, starting the punch, and responding to normal conditions which will require operator response.

CARD READER START
1. Clear all cards from within the card reader. This is done by performing a nonprocess runout. First, remove all cards from the input hopper, open the joggler gate (Figure 9-10), and depress the START key. The START key should be held depressed until

Table 9-1. Reader Keys and Lights and Their Functions

Keys and Lights	Functions
START Key	Depressing the START key places the card reader in a ready status and begins feeding cards into all reading stations. The contents of the first card read are placed into storage.
END OF FILE Key	The card reader will stop when it senses that the input hopper is empty even though the last card has not passed through to a stacker. Depressing this key and the START key will start the card reader and read the remaining cards in the feed mechanism.
STOP Key	When the STOP key is depressed, all card movement in the read area ceases. The reader END OF FILE light is turned off, and the reader is removed from the ready status.
READY Light	This light indicates that the card reader is in a ready status or that the 2540 is now under control of the CPU.
END OF FILE Light	This light indicates that the END OF FILE key has been pressed. This light will automatically go out when the last card has been read and placed in the output stacker or when the STOP key has been pressed.
VALIDITY CHECK Light	This light indicates that a card containing an invalid character has been read, meaning that the punches received did not compare to list of characters available to the CPU.
READ CHECK Light	This light indicates that the card just read was read incorrectly. The comparison of data read from the first and second readings of the card was not equal.
FEED STOP Light	The FEED STOP light indicates the reader motor has stopped due to a card jam or misfeed. This light can be turned off by initiating a nonprocess runout, described later in this chapter.

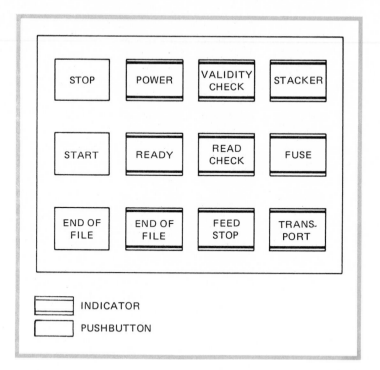

Figure 9-7
Card Reader Keys and
Lights for the IBM 2540

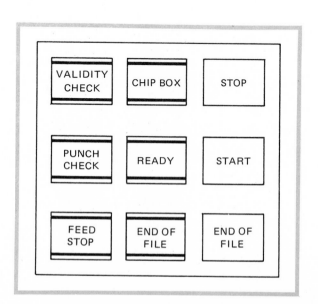

Figure 9-8
Card Punch Keys and
Indicator Lights for the
IBM 2540

all cards have been removed from within the transport area and fed into the output stacker.

2. Load the cards to be read into the input hopper 9 edge first, face down, and close the joggler gate. A metal card weight (Figure 9-10) should be placed on top of the last card loaded to ensure proper feeding.

3. Depress the reader START key.

Table 9-2. Punch Keys and Lights and Their Functions

Keys and Lights	Functions
START Key	Depressing this key places the card punch in the ready status and begins feeding cards into the punching stations.
STOP Key	When the STOP key is depressed, card movement in the punch area is stopped and the card punch is removed from the ready status.
END OF FILE Key	When this key is depressed along with the START key, the punch mechanism is started, and the remainder of the cards are passed into the stackers.
PUNCH CHECK Light	This light goes on when data sensed in the read station of the punch area is not the same as that data entered at the punch station.
FEED STOP Light	When the punch motor is stopped by a card jam or misfeed, the FEED STOP light will be turned on and can be turned off by a non-process runout, which will be described later in this chapter.
CHIP BOX Light	This light will turn on when the chip box is either full or improperly positioned.
READY Light	When lighted, it indicates that the punch is in a ready status. It should be noted that if the punch side is not in a ready status, cards cannot be punched even though instructed to by the computer.
END OF FILE Light	This light indicates that the END OF FILE key has been pressed.

Table 9-3. Common Indicator Lights[1]

Light	Function
POWER	This light indicates that the 2540 is being supplied by dc power.
STACKER	When any one of the output stackers is full (approximately 1,350 cards), this light will go on, and the 2540 will shut off. When the stacker has been emptied, the light will go off, and the machine must be started again.
FUSE	This indicates that a signal fuse in the 2540 has been blown.
TRANSPORT	This light indicates that a card jam has occurred in the feed mechanism (the transport area), or the cover is raised (opened to gain access to the transport area). The light will go off when the obstruction is cleared and cover closed. See Figure 9-9.

[1]See Figure 9-7.

Raised cover

Raised cover

Punch transport area

Read transport area

Figure 9-9
IBM 2540 with Covers
Raised

Card weight

Joggler
gate

Figure 9-10
2540 Card Read/
Punch—End View

CARD PUNCH START
1. Remove the card weight and blank cards from the punch hopper.
2. Depress and hold down the START key to perform a nonprocess runout. Any cards remaining in the unit will feed into stacker P1 (leftmost stacker).
3. The last two cards should be blank. Place these with the blank cards which were removed from the hopper.
4. Reload the blank cards 12 edge first, face down into the punch hopper, replace the card weight on the last card, and depress the START key.

Conditions which may occur during normal operation and require operator response are:

1. **Stacker full.** Indicated by the STACKER light on and READY light off, this condition occurs when one of the output stackers has become filled to its capacity with cards. To recover from this condition, merely remove all or some cards from the filled stacker, and depress the START key.
2. **Input hopper empty.** If the reader or punch is started and the END OF FILE key is not pressed, the unit will stop processing when it senses that the input hopper is empty. To continue

processing, more cards should be loaded in the input hopper and the START key pressed. In order to read the last card, the END OF FILE and START keys should be depressed in the above sequence.

Responding to error conditions. During reading or punching operations, one or more error conditions requiring operator intervention may occur on the 2540. In almost all cases, the operator can easily correct the problem and restart processing.

Table 9-4 describes the procedures to follow in order to restart the 2540 following an error condition. (*Note:* A PFR operation refers to a Punch Feed Read operation, possible only if the 2540 is equipped with the special features discussed below.)

Special features on the 2540

In addition to the capabilities already discussed, special features can be added to the 2540 to meet a variety of special processing needs.

Punch feed read. This feature allows the reading and punching of cards entered at the punch input hopper. The extra read brushes are installed in the blank station of the card punch.

51-column interchangeable read feed. This feature allows the reading of either 51- or 80-column cards. To use this feature, the operator must modify the input hopper and output stackers to accommodate the different card size. This requires the installation of guide rails at each side of the file feed magazine to center the shorter cards. In addition, side plates must be installed in the input hopper.

The output stackers, R1 and R2, are modified by pulling forward the card guides at the rear of the stackers, swinging down the adjustable card pivot levers, and pushing the levers in toward the back of the machine. In 51-column card mode, the reader maximum speed drops from 1,000 to 800 cards per minute. This procedure is reversed when switching from 51- to 80-column cards.

Column binary. The column binary feature is actually installed on the 2821 control unit rather than on the 2540 itself. This feature allows the reading of binary cards and cards with multiple-digit punching in a single column.

Self-study exercise 9-2

1. The 2540 reads at speeds up to _____ cards per minute and punches at up to _____ cards per minute.

◆ ◆ ◆

1,000
300

Table 9-4.

Indications	Restart Procedures
Reader FEED STOP Light (Only)	1. Remove cards from stacker R1.
	2. Open hopper joggler gate, and remove cards from hopper.
	3. Open covers and remove any jammed cards from read feed. Reconstruct any damaged cards.
Note: If read-check or validity-check indications accompany FEED STOP, follow procedure for read check or validity check.	4. If the END OF FILE light is on, press STOP switch to reset end-of-file circuits.
	5. With joggler gate still open, press and hold reader START key to clear feed.
	6. Remove cards just run out into stacker R1, place them and any reconstructed cards in proper sequence ahead of cards removed from hopper, and replace this deck in hopper or ahead of cards in file feed magazine.
	7. Close joggler gate.
	8. Press reader START key.
Reader FEED STOP Light READ CHECK Light	This combination of error indications accompanies a 2540 read clutch failure; there may be cards in stacker R1 that have not been read. Restart the job from the last checkpoint. The CE should be advised when this error occurs.
READ CHECK Light	1. Remove cards from stacker R1. Determine (perhaps with aid from programmed message) which was last card read into processing unit, and correct any off-registration punching in it. Place this corrected card in stacker R1.
(If card is read and stacked with single command)	2. Open joggler gate, and remove cards from hopper.
	3. If END OF FILE light is on, press STOP switch to reset end-of-file circuits.
	4. With joggler gate open, press and hold reader START key to clear read feed.
	5. Remove cards from stacker R1, and place them ahead of cards removed from hopper. Place this deck in hopper or ahead of cards in file feed magazine.
	6. Close joggler gate.
	7. Press reader START key.
READ CHECK Light	1. Remove cards from stacker R1.
	2. Follow steps 2 to 7 of preceding procedure, correcting any off-registration punching in first card run out into stacker R1.
(If stacker selection is delayed)	

Table 9-4. (Cont.)

Indications	Restart Procedures
VALIDITY CHECK Light (If card is read and stacked with single command)	1. Remove cards from stacker R1. Determine (perhaps with aid from programmed message) which was last card read into processing unit (this card may be in another stacker), and correct any errors in this card. Place the corrected card in stacker R1. 2. Open joggler gate, and remove cards from hopper. 3. If END OF FILE light is on, press STOP switch to reset end-of-file circuits. 4. With joggler gate open, press and hold reader START key to clear read feed. 5. Remove cards from stacker R1, and place them ahead of cards removed from hopper. Place this deck in hopper or ahead of cards in file feed magazine. 6. Close joggler gate. 7. Press reader START key.
VALIDITY CHECK Light (If stacker selection is delayed)	1. Remove cards from stacker R1. 2. Open joggler gate, and remove cards from hopper. 3. If END OF FILE light is on, press STOP switch to reset end-of-file circuits. 4. With joggler gate open, press and hold reader START key to clear read feed. 5. Locate and correct invalid character(s) in first card in stacker R1. 6. Place corrected card ahead of cards in stacker R1. Place all cards in stacker R1 ahead of cards removed from hopper. Place this deck in hopper or ahead of cards in file feed magazine. 7. Close joggler gate. 8. Press reader START key.
VALIDITY CHECK Light PUNCH CHECK Light (If 2540 is performing PFR read operation)	1. Remove card from punch hopper. 2. If END OF FILE light is on, press STOP switch to reset end-of-file circuit. 3. Press and hold punch START key to clear punch feed. 4. Remove last three cards from stacker P1. 5. The first of these three cards may have to be reconstructed because it has been read and punched but not punch-checked. 6. The second card caused the validity check. Correct it as necessary. 7. Place these three cards, after any necessary corrections, in front of the cards removed from the hopper. Place this deck in the hopper. 8. Press the punch START key.

Table 9-4. (Cont.)

Indications	Restart Procedures
	9. Reconstruct internal data in the system as necessary to restart at the start I/O instruction that caused the reading of the first card run out of the punch feed in step 3. *Note:* In some programs, reconstruction of internal data may not be provided for. In that case, restart the job from the last checkpoint.
Punch FEED STOP Light (Only) (If the 2540 is not performing PFR operations)	1. Remove cards from stacker P1. 2. Remove cards from hopper. 3. Open covers and remove any jammed cards from punch feed. 4. Press and hold punch START key to clear punch feed. 5. Discard last card punched (2540 will repunch this card automatically). 6. Replace blank cards in hopper, and press punch START key. Last card will be repunched automatically, and 2540 enters ready status.
Punch FEED STOP Light (Only) (If 2540 is performing PFR operation)	1. Remove cards from stacker P1. 2. Remove cards from hopper. 3. If END OF FILE light is on, press STOP switch to reset end-of-file circuits. 4. Open covers and remove any jammed cards from punch feed. Press and hold punch START key to clear feed. 5. Any card removed or run out from between punch station and punch-check brushes should be reconstructed, because it has been punched but not punch-checked. 6. Place reconstructed cards and cards run out into stacker P1 in proper sequence ahead of cards removed from hopper, and place this deck in hopper. 7. Press punch START key. 8. Reconstruct internal data in the system as necessary to restart at the start I/O instruction that caused the first card removed or run out to be read at the PFR station. *Note:* In some programs, reconstruction of internal data may not be provided for. In that case, restart the job from the last checkpoint.
PUNCH CHECK Light	1. Remove cards from hopper. 2. Press and hold punch START key to clear punch feed. 3. Remove last four cards from stacker P1. The last two cards are blank; the first two should be discarded.

Table 9-4. (Cont.)

Indications	Restart Procedures
(If 2540 is not performing PFR operation and is using stacker P1)	4. Replace blank cards and cards removed from hopper in hopper. 5. Reconstruct internal data in the system as necessary to restart at the start I/O instruction that caused the first card removed from stacker P1 to be punched. *Note:* In some programs, reconstruction of internal data may not be provided for. In that case, restart the job from the last checkpoint.
PUNCH CHECK Light (If 2540 is not performing PFR operation and is not using stacker P1)	1. Examine and correct, if necessary, error card, which is last card in stacker P1. (2540 automatically routes error cards to stacker P1.) 2. Place this card in appropriate stacker. 3. Press and hold punch START key to clear feed. 4. The 2540 will force the card following the error card into stacker P1 also. Place this card in the appropriate stacker. *Note:* Because the error card and the card following it are both directed to stacker P1, the program can correct a nonPFR punch-check without operator intervention by repunching both cards and directing them to appropriate stackers. The operator can then discard all cards in stacker P1 at the end of the job.
PUNCH CHECK Light (If 2540 is performing PFR operation)	1. Remove cards from punch hopper. 2. If END OF FILE light is on, press STOP switch to reset end-of-file circuits. 3. Press and hold punch START key to clear feed. 4. Remove last four cards from stacker P1. The last two cards are correct; prepunching in the first two must be reconstructed. 5. Place the two reconstructed cards, the two correct cards, and the cards removed from the hopper, in that sequence, in the hopper. 6. Reconstruct internal data in the system as necessary to restart at the start I/O instruction that caused the first reconstructed card to be read at the PFR station. *Note:* In some programs, reconstruction of internal data may not be provided for. In that case, restart the job from the last checkpoint.
Punch FEED STOP Light PUNCH CHECK Light	This combination of error indications accompanies a 2540 punch clutch failure; there may be cards in stacker P1 that have not been processed. Restart the job from the last checkpoint. The CE should be advised when this error occurs.

2. The card reader input hopper has a capacity of up to _____ cards.

♦ ♦ ♦

    3,100

3. There are _____ output stackers on the 2540, labeled _____.

♦ ♦ ♦

    five
    P1, P2, PR3, R2, R1

4. Only the _____ stacker can contain cards entered from either the reader or the punch input hopper.

♦ ♦ ♦

    PR3

5. Each output stacker can hold up to _____ cards.

♦ ♦ ♦

    1,350

6. The 2540 uses the _____ reading principle.

♦ ♦ ♦

    brush

7. Card reading on the 2540 requires _____ machine cycles while punching requires _____ cycles.

♦ ♦ ♦

    three
    four

8. All card reading ceases at the end of the current operation when the _____ key is pressed.

♦ ♦ ♦

    STOP

9. The card reader is placed in ready status when the _____ key is pressed.

♦ ♦ ♦

START

10. Pressing the END OF FILE key serves to _____.

♦ ♦ ♦

allow the last card to be read without other operator intervention

11. Three indicator lights which indicate the need for operator intervention on the card reader are the _____, _____, and _____ lights.

♦ ♦ ♦

VALIDITY CHECK
READ CHECK
FEED STOP

12. A full or improperly positioned chip box in the card punch is indicated by the lighting of the _____ light.

♦ ♦ ♦

CHIP BOX

13. When the STACKER light is lit, it indicates that _____.

♦ ♦ ♦

one of the five output stackers is full

14. The _____ light indicates that a card jam within the transport area has occurred.

♦ ♦ ♦

TRANSPORT

15. Two conditions which may occur during normal operation and require operator intervention are _____ and _____.

♦ ♦ ♦

stacker full
input hopper empty

16. Before starting the card reader, the operator should perform a(n) _____.

◆ ◆ ◆

nonprocess runout

17. A nonprocess runout is performed by _____.

◆ ◆ ◆

pressing the START key with the joggler gate open

18. The operator may be required to repunch cards which have off-column punches, a condition which is indicated when the _____ light is lit.

◆ ◆ ◆

READ CHECK

19. The combination of the reader _____ light and the _____ light indicates a read clutch failure.

◆ ◆ ◆

FEED STOP
READ CHECK

20. The _____ feature allows both the punching and reading of cards entered from the punch input hopper.

◆ ◆ ◆

punch feed read (PFR)

Other Card Reader/Punch Units

The Honeywell 223 card reader and 214-1 card punch

There are two models of the Honeywell 223 card reader. The 223 reads cards at 800 cards per minute while the 223-2 reads at 1,050 cards per minute. Both card readers can be attached to the Honeywell 8200 computer system. In addition, both card readers use the photoelectric principle of reading and can accept 51- or 80-column cards as input.

Cards are read serially, column by column. The capacities of the input hopper and output stacker for the 223 are 3,000 and 2,500 cards, respectively. Instead of having an auxiliary output stacker, the 223 card reader has the capability to *offset-stack* under program control. Figure 9-12 illustrates a deck of cards that has been read with misread cards being offset. The offsetting of the card alerts the operator that the card has been misread.

Figure 9-11
Honeywell 223 Card
Reader

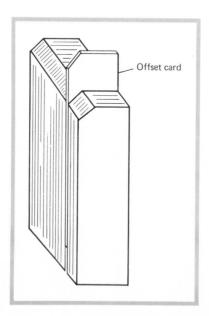

Offset card

Figure 9-12
Offset Stacking

The 214-1 card punch punches 80-column cards at speeds up to 400 cards per minute, depending on the number of columns punched. The input hopper and output stackers have capacities of 1,200 and 1,300 cards, respectively.

The 214-2 card reader/punch combines all the features of the 223 card reader and 214-1 punch into a single unit. Cards entered at the single input hopper can be read, punched, or read and punched. Punching speeds can be as high as 400 cards per minute, depending on the number of columns punched. If the unit is reading only, cards are read at 400 cards per minute. If both reading and punching are to be performed, the unit will generally operate at a somewhat slower speed. The input hopper and output stacker capacities are 1,200 and 1,300 cards, respectively.

The Honeywell 214-2 card reader/punch

The UNIVAC punched card subsystem includes a card reader, capable of reading at speeds up to 900 cards per minute, and a card punch capable of punching up to 300 cards per minute. The card reader (Figure 9-14) uses the photoelectric principle of reading, but unlike the Honeywell reader,

The UNIVAC punched card subsystem

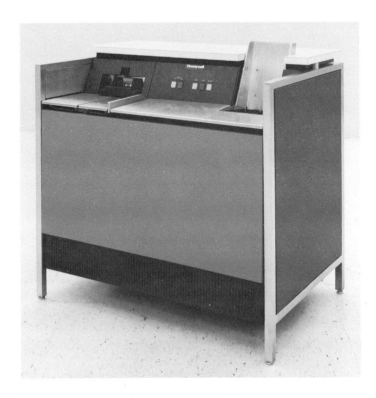

Figure 9-13
Honeywell 214-2

Figure 9-14
UNIVAC Card Reader

this unit reads in parallel, row by row. A single input hopper and two output stackers are provided. When a reading error is sensed, the misread card is automatically fed into the second of the two output stackers, referred to as the reject stacker.

The input hopper has a capacity of up to 3,000 cards, whereas the primary output stacker and the reject stacker have capacities of up to 2,400 and 100 cards, respectively.

The card punch (Figure 9-15) also uses the parallel technique, punching cards row by row. Incorrectly punched cards are automatically sensed and fed into an error stacker. The input hopper and two output stackers of the card punch have capacities of 1,000 and 850 cards, respectively.

Self-study exercise 9-3

1. Data can be punched in Hollerith code or in _____ code.

♦ ♦ ♦

column binary

2. The two models of the Honeywell 223 card reader can read at speeds of _____ and _____ cards per minute.

◆ ◆ ◆

800
1,050

3. The Honeywell 223 card readers employ the _____ principle of reading; thus, cards are read _____, or column by column.

◆ ◆ ◆

photoelectric
serially

4. Instead of a secondary output stacker, error cards are _____ on the Honeywell card readers.

◆ ◆ ◆

offset-stacked

Figure 9-15
UNIVAC Card Punch

5. The Honeywell 214-1 card punch punches at up to _____ cards per minute.

♦ ♦ ♦

400

6. The 214-1 input hopper and output stacker can hold _____ and _____ cards, respectively.

♦ ♦ ♦

1,200
1,300

7. A special feature on the 214-1 punch that increases the speed of the punch operation is its _____.

♦ ♦ ♦

high-speed column skipping

8. The Honeywell _____ combines the card reader and punch units into a single card read/punch unit.

♦ ♦ ♦

214-2

9. The UNIVAC card reader can read at speeds up to _____ cards per minute, while the card punch can punch at speeds up to _____ cards per minute.

♦ ♦ ♦

900
300

10. The UNIVAC card reader reads in a(n) _____ manner, row by row.

♦ ♦ ♦

parallel

True-false exercise

1. The card reader unit is used to sense information that is punched into data cards.
2. When a jammed card condition occurs, the operator must simply restart the machine to correct the condition.
3. The operator need not intervene if data are misread.
4. There are two types of card readers.
5. Card readers combine both metallic brushes and photoelectric sensors to read cards.
6. Serial card readers read punched cards row by row.
7. Access to the card feed mechanism is essential to the removal of jammed cards.
8. Card punches can be classified only as serial.
9. Card readers read each card twice to perform an operation called validity checking.
10. A punch-check is performed in much the same manner as a read-check.
11. The IBM 2540 Card Read/Punch is capable of reading up to 2,000 cards per minute.
12. The IBM 2540 Card Read/Punch can punch up to 300 cards per minute.
13. The machine will not stop reading or punching cards if an output stacker fills up.
14. The 2540 performs three machine cycles in reading one card.
15. In order to read the last card, the END OF FILE and START keys should be depressed.
16. All card readers read in parallel (row by row).

Multiple-choice exercise

1. Which of the following is true for the IBM 2540 Card Read/Punch?
   a. It is a serial photoelectric reader.
   b. It is a serial brush reader.
   c. It is a parallel photoelectric reader.
   d. It is a parallel brush reader.
   e. None of the above.
2. The photoelectric card reader senses data on a card by
   a. interpreting the characters printed on the top of the card with special laser lights
   b. passing the card between a beam of light and special photoelectric sensors located beneath the card
   c. using a combination of lights and brushes to read the card
   d. two of the above
   e. none of the above

3. Which of the following is not a function of a card reader?
   a. Validity checking
   b. Punch checking
   c. Read checking
   d. Sequence checking
   e. Two of the above
4. The IBM 2540 Card Read/Punch has
   a. one read stacker
   b. two read stackers
   c. three read stackers
   d. four read stackers
   e. five read stackers
5. What happens when an output stacker is full?
   a. The machine stops, and an indicator light goes on.
   b. An indicator light goes on, but the machine does not stop.
   c. Nothing happens; the operator must be alert.
   d. The cards will jam in the machine.
   e. None of the above.
6. To clear all cards from within the card reader, the operator must do which of the following?
   a. Perform a nonprocess runout
   b. Physically remove all cards from the card reader
   c. Press the NONPROCESS RUNOUT key
   d. Press the START key
   e. None of the above
7. The IBM 2540
   a. comes with all available options at no extra cost
   b. has no extra options available
   c. can be ordered with special options
   d. is available only in the standard model
   e. none of the above
8. The Honeywell card reader
   a. reads serially, row by row
   b. uses brushes to read cards
   c. is a photoelectric, parallel machine
   d. is a duplicate of the GE card reader
   e. none of the above
9. The UNIVAC card subsystem
   a. reads in parallel
   b. reads up to 900 cards per minute
   c. punches up to 300 cards per minute
   d. all of the above
   e. none of the above

Discussion questions

1. Card readers are divided into two basic groups. Discuss the differences between them.
2. Discuss some of the features common to all card reader/punches.
3. Explain the purpose of the three machine cycles in the reading operation of the IBM 2540 Card Read/Punch.
4. Discuss four of the reader punch keys and lights and their functions.
5. Discuss the characteristics of two of the card reader/punches of manufacturers other than IBM.

PRINTER

CHAPTER 10

Introduction

Types of Printers

> Impact printers

> Nonimpact printers

IBM 1403 Model N1 Printer

> Major components

> Operating procedures

* Other Printers

> Burroughs line printers

> XDS model 7450 buffered line printer

> Honeywell 222 printer

End-of-chapter Exercises

Introduction　The printer is utilized in the last stage of the data processing cycle of input, processing, and output. It provides the user with a visual record of the data output from the computer. Without the documentation that the printer provides, the thousands of calculations accomplished by the CPU could not be displayed in an easily readable form.

In a commercially oriented business system, the printer is one of the most important and commonly used pieces of peripheral equipment. It provides the computer system with the capability of producing reports, data, etc., in an easily readable format. These reports can be produced in various formats and quantities. Thus, the printer is a fundamental and essential piece of peripheral equipment in any computer system. It is therefore essential that the operator be familiar with the operating characteristics of the printer. An operator who is not well versed on each piece of peripheral equipment can drastically reduce the overall efficiency of the entire computer system. That is, a computer system is only as efficient as the level of operating efficiency of each component.

Types of Printers　When a report is to be prepared, after the CPU has completed the processing operation, the computed results are sent to the system's printing unit. This data is received by the printer in the form of electric impulses. Once in the printer, these impulses are converted into corresponding character representations which are then printed on a paper form.

Printers can print on ordinary paper or on specially prepared forms such as invoices, labels, and other special purpose forms used in the operations of a business, as shown in Figure 10-2.

Printers, such as the IBM 1404 and the RCA 8248 Bill Feed Printer (Figure 10-3), even fulfill the needs of business for accuracy and speed in printing on card documents such as checks, earning statements, premium notices, and bills.

Printers can be subdivided into two broad categories—nonimpact and impact—with impact printers being the most common.

Impact printers　An impact printer is one in which printing occurs as a result of the impact of a metal character form striking against an inked ribbon which in turn causes the ribbon to press an image of the character onto paper. This can be accomplished one character at a time or one line at a time, depending on the particular printing device being used. Four major types of impact printing devices are:

1. Print wheel
2. Wire matrix
3. Ball typewriter
4. Chain or drum

IBM 1443

IBM 1445

IBM 1404

IBM 1403

Figure 10-1
Various Printers

Let us discuss each type of impact printer and its mode of operation.

Print wheel printer. The print wheel printer consists of several rotary print wheels, one for each print position on a line.

Each print wheel contains a complete set of characters, including numerals, letters of the alphabet, and special characters (period, comma,

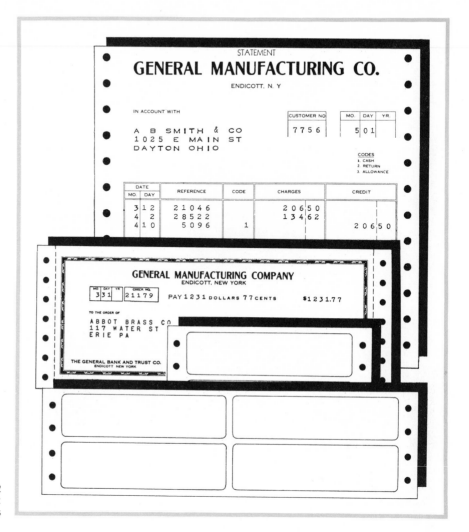

Figure 10-2
Sample Computer Output
Forms

plus sign, etc.). At the time of printing, all the print wheels are correctly positioned to represent the data to be printed, as shown in Figure 10-4. All print wheels are printed simultaneously, thus producing one complete line of print. Average printing speed for print wheel printers is approximately 150 lines per minute.

Wire matrix printer. In the wire matrix printer, each character is printed as a pattern of dots formed by the ends of small wires arranged in a rectangular array. By extending selected wires, the patterns may be arranged in the shape of the desired characters as depicted in Figure 10-5.

Printing is accomplished when the selected wires are pressed against an inked fabric ribbon. Printing speeds range from 500 to 1,000 lines per minute, depending on the model of the printer.

Ball typewriter. The ball typewriter, used as a computer output device and shown in Figure 10-6, is similar to the electric typewriters used by secretaries.

The major difference is that control of the ball typewriter printer and its printing is accomplished automatically by the computer, instead of by manually striking keys. The ball typewriter printer can print at speeds up to about 600 characters per minute. Line spacing and carriage return are automatic.

Chain or drum printer. The chain or drum printer is the device most commonly used in medium- to large-scale computer systems. This is principally due to its fast printing speeds and good print quality. These devices consist

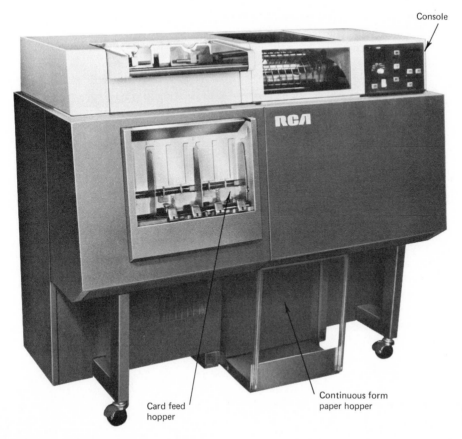

Console

Card feed hopper

Continuous form paper hopper

Figure 10-3
RCA 8248 Bill Feed Printer

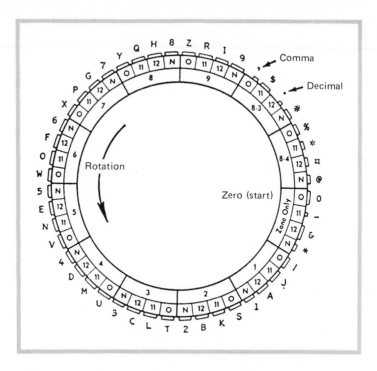

Figure 10-4
The Print Wheel

of a rotating chain or drum on which are stored the various characters, consisting of alphabetic, numeric, and special characters.

As the chain rotates, and as each character moves into its desired print position, a magnetically activated hammer is engaged, causing the paper to be pressed against the desired character. In some models, the chain is replaced by a rotating drum employing the same operating principal as the chain printer.

Print speeds for chain printers can exceed 1,200 lines per minute. The print chain in these printers can be easily changed to provide a choice of print style or character arrangement.

Let us now examine, in detail, the operational characteristics of a typical printer. For this purpose, we have chosen the IBM 1403 Printer since it is one of the most commonly used printers and since it is similar in operation to most other commonly used printers.

Nonimpact printers Nonimpact printers, xerographic or electronic, are the fastest of all printers, with top speeds of approximately 64,000 lines per minute. Printers of this type are not heavily used for several reasons:

1. Special and more expensive paper is required.
2. Printed output is not as sharp or clear as with impact printers.

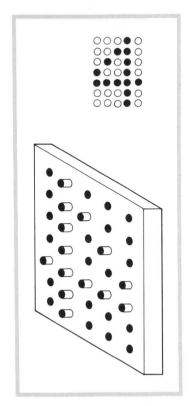

Figure 10-5
Arrangement of a Wire
Matrix Dot Pattern for
the Digit 4

Figure 10-6
The IBM Ball Typewriter
and Element

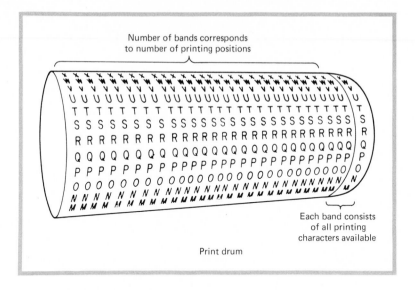

Number of bands corresponds
to number of printing positions

Each band consists
of all printing
characters available

Print drum

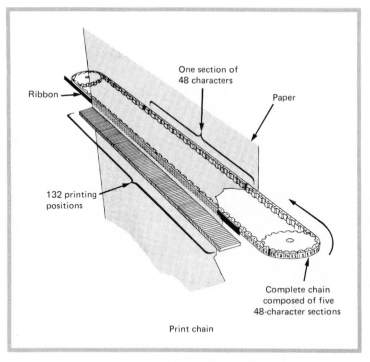

Ribbon

One section of
48 characters

Paper

132 printing
positions

Complete chain
composed of five
48-character sections

Print chain

Figure 10-7
The Print Drum and Chain

3. Only one copy can be printed at a time.
4. Output cannot easily and satisfactorily be copied on office copiers.

Due to the limited use of nonimpact printers, we shall not discuss them in any greater depth.

Self-study exercise 10-1

1. Within the data processing cycle, the printer is utilized in the _____ stage.

◆ ◆ ◆

final

2. The printer enables us to produce _____, in an easily _____ format.

◆ ◆ ◆

reports
readable

3. Printers are separated into two broad categories, _____ and _____, with _____ printers being the most common.

◆ ◆ ◆

nonimpact
impact
impact

4. Of the two types of printers, the _____ type of printer is the fastest.

◆ ◆ ◆

nonimpact

5. Impact printers are composed of _____ major types, which are _____.

◆ ◆ ◆

four
print wheel, wire matrix, ball typewriter, and chain or drum

6. Impact printers require that a(n) _____ strike an inked ribbon against the paper form.

◆ ◆ ◆

metal character

7. On a print wheel printer, each wheel contains _____.

◆ ◆ ◆

a complete set of characters

8. The _____ used in a computer system is similar in appearance and operation to an office typewriter.

◆ ◆ ◆

ball typewriter

9. The print unit houses the rotating _____.

◆ ◆ ◆

print chain

IBM 1403 Model N1 Printer

There are eight different models in the IBM 1403 Printer Series, varying in the number of possible print positions as well as in the maximum printing speeds. The Model N1, besides being one of the most powerful printers in the series, is extremely versatile in that it can be attached to any system in the IBM 360 Series computers. The 1403 prints at a maximum speed of 1,100 lines per minute and has 132 available print positions on each line. Paper forms used on the 1403 include fanfold paper, continuous forms, preprinted forms, and adding machine paper.

The 1403 N1 is a chain printer with a character set of 48 characters. The character set is composed of 26 alphabetic, 10 numeric, and 12 special characters. All these characters, called *print slugs,* are assembled in a train. This train is restrained in a track and driven at high speed by a series of internal gears. The entire print train is called an *interchangeable cartridge*. It can be removed and replaced with another cartridge to allow for different printing styles and arrangements.

This printer is significant for its ability to print at high speeds. The next section of this chapter will discuss the major components of the 1403 which allow control of the device during its operation.

Major components

You are probably asking yourself, for example, how the 1403 is capable of such high-speed printing, what control indexes the paper one line at a time during normal printing, how the correct number of lines is indicated, and what operator controls, indicator lights, and console pushbuttons are available. Let us now discuss the answers to these and other questions by examining the inner workings of the IBM 1403 Printer.

Carriage control unit. Every printer must have a means by which the line-by-line movement of the paper is controlled. In the 1403, as with most other printers, the movement of the paper within the printer is controlled by the carriage control unit. This unit it composed of two fundamental parts:

1. Tape-controlled carriage
2. Carriage control tape

TAPE-CONTROLLED CARRIAGE

The *tape-controlled carriage* is the means by which the printer controls the indexing of paper—line by line. The term used to describe the indexing of a paper form is *spacing*. Therefore, the carriage unit controls the vertical print spacing of the output form. The tape-controlled carriage and its position on the machine are shown in Figure 10-8.

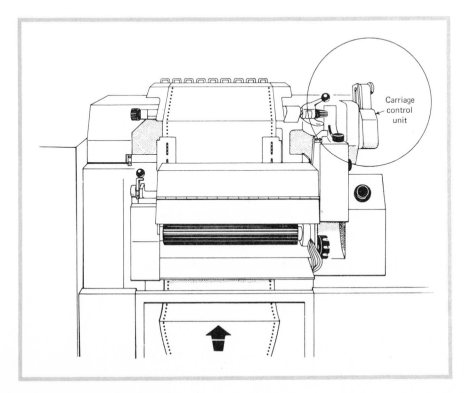

Figure 10-8
Position of the Carriage
Control Unit in the Printer

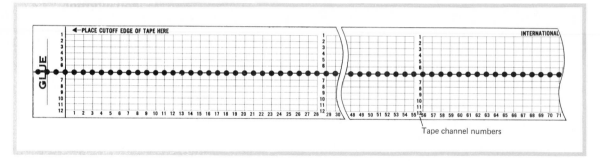

Figure 10-9
Typical Carriage Control
Tape

CARRIAGE CONTROL TAPE

The carriage control unit is constructed in a pulley-type arrangement. A paper tape fits completely around this pulley arrangement. This paper tape is called a *carriage control tape*. This control tape contains information, in the form of coded punched holes, which controls the vertical spacing to be used in the printing of a given report. As the coded tape passes around the tape-controlled carriage, the holes are sensed, and the document being printed is spaced accordingly. Thus, by preparing an appropriate carriage control tape, the operator can control the vertical spacing of any size form used in the printer.

The carriage control tape is a paper strip, as shown in Figure 10-9. When in use within the printer, the control tape must be used as a *continuous* paper strip. Thus, before it can be used, both ends must be glued together.

Since the tape is used to control any size form, the number of lines available for printing must be indicated. A series of whole numbers, beginning with 1, exists in the lefthand margin of the tape, as shown in Figure 10-9. Each number corresponds to a line which can be used on the chosen form. The relation of the carriage control tape and the form used for printing is illustrated in Figure 10-10. Depicted is a portion of a printer spacing chart, a form used by a programmer to lay out the actual physical appearance of the form to be printed. Note that there are 38 lines available for printing on the proposed form, and the carriage control tape has 38 positions available to control that printing.

Further examination of the control tape reveals a series of circular holes, uniformly spaced down the center of the tape. This series of holes allows for the automatic spacing of a form—exactly one line at a time. When seated on the tape-controlled carriage, these holes fit directly on series of prongs on the pin-feed drive wheel, as shown in Figure 10-12. As the tape rides around on top of the carriage, the holes are sensed, and the form being printed is spaced one line at a time.

Not all jobs assigned to the printer are of a line-by-line variety. Many printing formats require the printing of one line of data, a space of two or more unprinted lines, and then additional printed lines. *Channels,* available on the carriage control tape, are used to accomplish this type of printing. There is a total of 12 channels available on the carriage control tape. These channels are indicated at the top of the control tape, as in Figure 10-9, and can be used throughout the entire length of the control tape. Thus, by using the 12 channels provided, the form undergoing printing may be spaced and stopped at 12 different predetermined positions.

A punched control tape is shown in Figure 10-13. Note that a rectangular punch appears in channel 2, at line 16, and another at channel 3, at line 20. The printer sensing the first punch, upon the completion of printing line 16, moves directly to line 20 and readies itself for printing on that line.

Channel 1 is always used to indicate that line on a form where printing is to begin. With the use of this technique, printing begins on the same line of every form. Channel 12 is always used to denote the last available printed line for every form. Upon sensing the punch in that

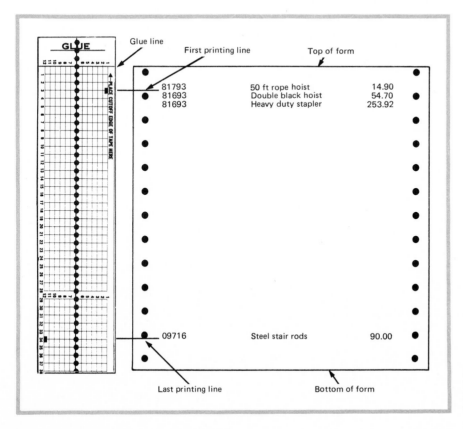

Figure 10-10
The Relationship between the Carriage Tape and the Form to Be Printed

Figure 10-11
Printer Spacing Chart

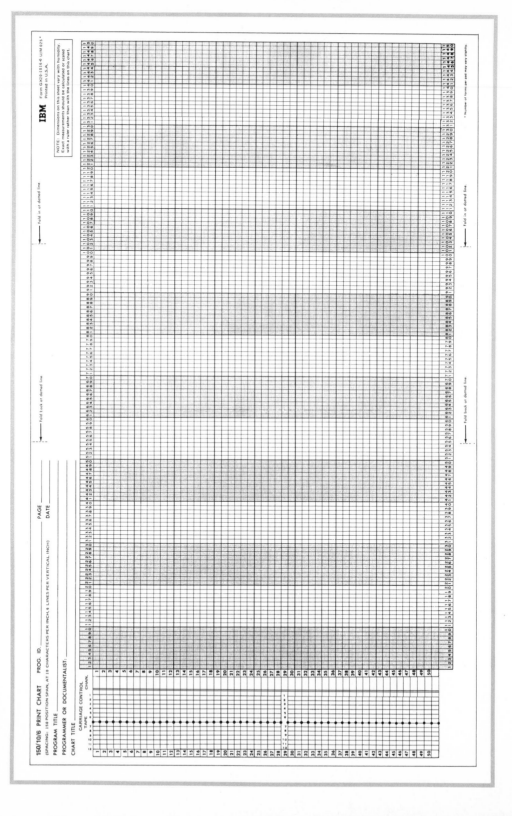

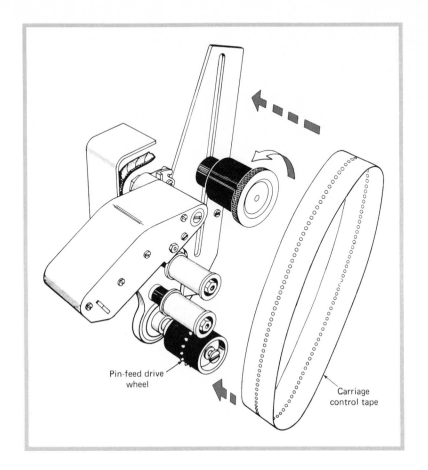

Pin-feed drive
wheel

Carriage
control tape

Figure 10-12
A Detailed View of the
Carriage Control Tape
Unit

channel, the printer completes the printing of that last line and indexes
to the top of the next form on which printing must occur.

For our example in Figure 10-13, the printer senses the punch in
channel 12, at line 50. It prints the data required for line 50 and automatically indexes to the top of the next form. The printer senses the punch

Figure 10-13
An Example of a Punched
Carriage Control Tape

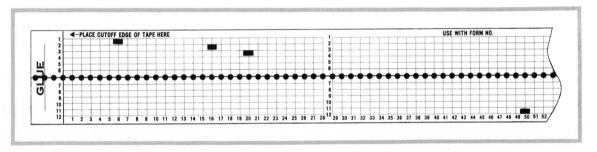

in channel 1, at line 6, and stops the movement of paper. The printing of data then commences again.

CARRIAGE TAPE BRUSHES

The sensing of holes punched on the carriage control tape is performed by the *carriage tape brushes.* The punches in the tape are sensed by these brushes, and impulses are transmitted to the printer carriage, which controls the movement of forms being printed. The carriage tape brushes consist of two sets of brushes housed in the brush holder, illustrated in Figure 10-14.

Manual controls. Jobs performed on the printer are quite diverse, ranging from a line-by-line listing to the preparation of three-copy customer invoices.

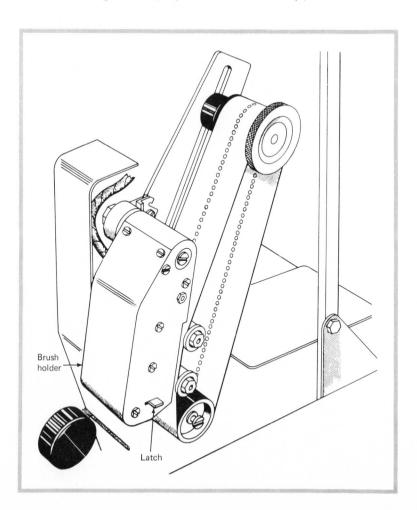

Brush holder

Latch

Figure 10-14
Carriage Control Tape
with Brush Holder and
Latch

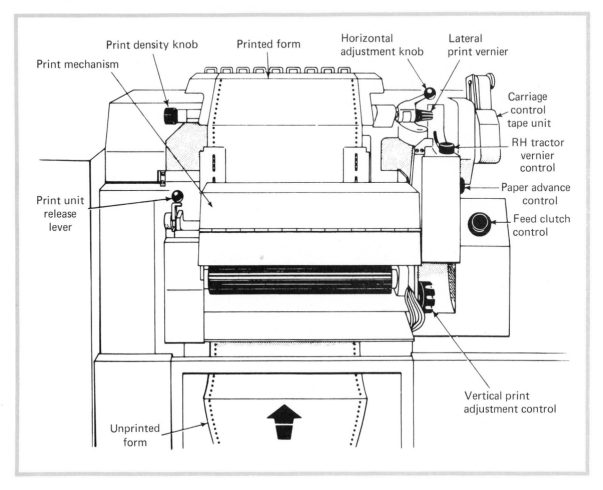

Figure 10-15
A Schematic of the
Printer Showing the
Manual Controls

To facilitate this usage, the operator is required to change the type of paper form, or document, used in the printer. With the placement of each type of form, he is required to make adjustments on the printer. A series of manual controls are provided to accomplish these required adjustments. Table 10-1 lists the manual controls available and their purposes.

Display lights. The operator is required to monitor the entire computer system during its operation. Included in his surveillance are the pieces of peripheral equipment. On the printer, there are five display lights which denote its operational state. These lights appear within the printer's control panel, as shown in Figure 10-18. Table 10-2 discusses the display lights and their functions.

Table 10-1. IBM 1403 Model N1 Printer Manual Controls

Control	Figure	Function
Horizontal Adjustment Knob	10-15	It enables the operator to move the entire printing unit horizontally.
Righthand Tractor Vernier	10-15	It allows the operator to correctly seat the form for printing. This dial permits fine adjustments up to $\frac{1}{2}$ in. which will smooth out the paper surface, remove ripples, and permit the paper to pass flatly over the print unit. This dial is used only after the paper has been initially seated in the printer and with the feed clutch in its NEUTRAL position.
Print Density Control	10-15	It controls the force with which the print slugs strike the paper. Density should be increased from normal when printing on multiple-copy forms or when the printing ribbon becomes worn. This permits printing to appear on all copies of a form and the printed character to be of a good quality and easily readable nature.
Feed Clutch	10-16	It engages the operation of the tape control carriage. With the feed clutch in its NEUTRAL position, forms cannot be fed through the printer. The feed clutch permits the operator to select either a 6 or an 8 lines-per-inch spacing format.
Paper Advance Knob	10-16	It permits the operator to vertically position the paper form. The feed clutch must be in the NEUTRAL position to use the paper advance knob.
Print Line Indicator and Ribbon Shield	10-17	It aligns the first print position of the printer with the form being used. A marker indicates the lower edge of the first character that can be printed.
Tractor Slide Bars	10-17	These bars are clamplike devices which are used to guide paper forms through the printer. The form to be used is initially seated within the tractor slide bars. Forms varying in size from $3\frac{1}{2}$ to $18\frac{3}{4}$ in. can be seated for printing.

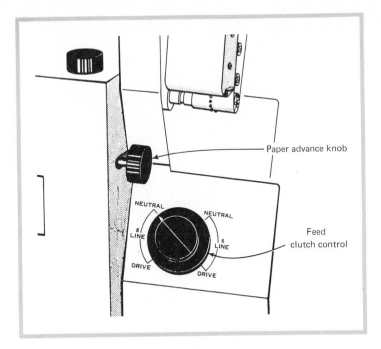

Figure 10-16
Paper Advance Knob and
Feed Clutch Control

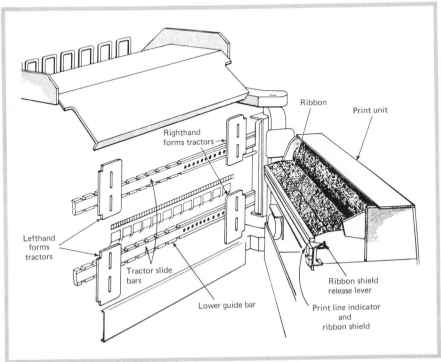

Figure 10-17
Tractor Slide Bars, Print
Line Indicator, and
Ribbon Shield

Figure 10-18
The Printer's Pushbuttons
and Display Lights

Table 10-2. IBM 1403 Model N1 Printer Display Lights

Display Light	Function
PRINT CHECK	It indicates a malfunction within the internal printer circuits.
FORM CHECK	It indicates that the paper form is not feeding properly or that the printer was incorrectly set up to handle form feeding (i.e., feed clutch in NEUTRAL, control tape improperly installed, or sensing control tape brushes not lowered).
END OF FORM	It indicates that the end of paper or printing medium has been reached.
PRINT READY	It indicates that the printer is ready to accept data from the computer. Unless this light is lit, nothing can be printed.
SYNC CHECK	It indicates that the printer chain within the printer is not correctly synchronized. Depressing the CHECK RESET pushbutton will correct the printer's internal timing. Hitting the START pushbutton permits the printing to resume.

Pushbuttons. The pushbuttons on the printer's console enable the operator to exercise control over the operation of the printer. The status of the printer, at any given time, is indicated by its display lights. Changes and corrections on the IBM 1403 can then be made via the printer console pushbuttons (see previous discussion of the SYNC CHECK light). The pushbuttons are shown in Figure 10-18. Table 10-3 discusses the pushbuttons and their uses.

The printer is housed in a soundproof metal container with a power-operated cover. To raise or lower this cover, the COVER RAISE or COVER LOWER pushbutton is used, respectively. Under normal operating conditions, the printer cover is raised to change or adjust forms. The cover automatically rises when a stoppage occurs in the normal printing cycle. The operator should ensure that no objects are placed on the printer cover. The print unit must be completely engaged to permit the cover to be lowered. A safety device ensures that the cover will not be lowered while the operator is working on the printer.

Indicator lights. In addition to the display lights, several indicator lights are located within the printer and must be monitored by the operator. These indicator lights denote the existence of one or more specific error states. They are located below the feed clutch lever, in the lower righthand corner of the printer, as shown in Figure 10-19. Table 10-4 notes the use of these lights which are of concern to the computer operator.

Self-study exercise 10-2

1. The 1403 N1 printer is a(n) _____-type printer, with a character set of _____ .

♦ ♦ ♦

chain
48 characters

2. The print chain is called a(n) _____ .

♦ ♦ ♦

interchangeable cartridge

3. The movement of paper through the printer is controlled by the _____ .

♦ ♦ ♦

tape-controlled carriage

Table 10-3. IBM 1403 Model N1 Printer Pushbuttons

Key	Pressing This Pushbutton
START	Readies the printer to begin printing data. A duplicate key is located in the rear of the printer.
STOP	Places the printer in a nonprinting state. The last line undergoing printing will be completed, though. A duplicate key is located in the rear of the printer.
CHECK RESET	Resets the printer to an operating state, resetting all controls and checks within the printer. The START key must be pressed after hitting the CHECK RESET key to begin printing.
SINGLE CYCLE	Causes the printer to print one line each time this key is hit. This key is used under special circumstances, such as when an end-of-form condition exists. Hitting the START key returns the printer to a normal operating state.
SPACE	Spaces the form undergoing printing one line each time this key is hit. This pushbutton is used with the printer in a normal operating state and after the STOP key is hit. Depressing the START key will resume normal printing. *No* printing occurs when the SPACE key is used.
CARRIAGE RESTORE	Will cause the form undergoing printing to automatically index to the top of the next page. The STOP key must be hit before the key can be used in this manner. To continue normal operation, the CHECK RESET and START keys, respectively, are depressed on the printer console. The CARRIAGE RESTORE key may be used to automatically match the first position of the control tape with the first printing position of a new form being positioned. Prior to this usage, the STOP pushbutton is hit, and the feed clutch placed in a NEUTRAL position. To resume printing, reengage the feed clutch, and depress the CHECK RESET and START keys.
CARRIAGE STOP	Prohibits use of the control carriage. This key is used when some type of form alignment must be accomplished.

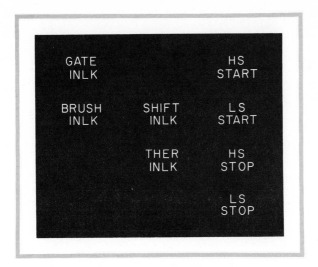

Figure 10-19
The Printer's Indicator
Panel

4. Use of the _____ enables the printer to control paper movement.

◆ ◆ ◆

carriage control tape

5. The carriage control tape must be used as a(n) _____ strip. Therefore, both ends of the tape must be _____.

◆ ◆ ◆

continuous paper
glued together

Table 10-4. IBM 1403 Model N1 Printer Indicator Lights

Indicator Light	Becomes Lit When—
GATE INLK (Interlock)	The printing unit is not correctly locked in position.
BRUSH INLK	The carriage control tape brushes are not seated in their proper position directly above the control tape.
SHIFT INLK	The feed clutch is placed in its NEUTRAL position.
THER INLK	A fuse has burned out within the printer's electrical system.

6. As holes punched in the various _____ contained on the carriage control tape are sensed, forms may be advanced and stopped at desired positions.

♦   ♦   ♦

channels

7. There are _____ display lights on the printer's console face, namely, _____ .

♦   ♦   ♦

five
PRINT CHECK, FORM CHECK, END OF FORM, PRINT READY, and SYNC CHECK

8. The pushbuttons on the console of the IBM 1403 are utilized by the operator to _____ .

♦   ♦   ♦

control the operation of the printer

9. The _____ indicator lights available on the printer inform the operator of _____ .

♦   ♦   ♦

four
any error conditions

10. To permit printing to occur, the _____ must not be in its NEUTRAL position.

♦   ♦   ♦

feed clutch

Operating procedures   The printer, during normal operation, requires little operator intervention. Nevertheless, the operator is responsible for carrying out several procedures, when required. These include:

1. Punching a new carriage control tape
2. Carriage control tape insertion
3. Forms insertion

4. Forms stacking
5. Ribbon changing
6. Cartridge changing

Operator intervention may also be required following certain error conditions, such as a SYNC CHECK, PRINT CHECK, etc. In most cases, pressing the CHECK RESET key followed by the START key returns the printer to normal operation. If adjustments are required when new forms are inserted into the printer, they will be required only once, and should last until the forms are changed again. However, it is good operating procedure to periodically check that the printer is maintaining its proper settings.

Procedures are provided later in this chapter to assist the operator in the performance of the above-listed functions.

Punching a new carriage control tape. A new carriage control tape may be required when the old tape becomes damaged or when a program requires a non-standard control tape for special form spacing. A new control tape is created by punching the appropriate holes in the new tape and then gluing the ends together to form a belt. A small compact punch, as shown in Figure 10-20, is provided for punching the tape.

The following steps should be followed when punching a new control tape:

1. Lay the tape flat beside the left edge of the form it is to control, with the top line even with the top edge of the form.

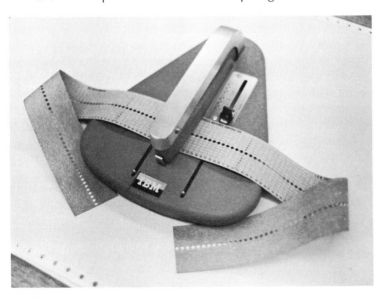

Figure 10-20
The Paper Tape Punch
Used on the Carriage
Control Tape

2. Place a mark in the channel-12 position of the tape corresponding to the last print line of the form.
3. Place marks in the tape corresponding to any other desired stopping positions. The corresponding positions on the form represent the print lines which one may skip while under program control.
4. Place the tape in the punch so that the round center holes of the tape fit over the pins projecting from the base of the punch.
5. Match up the desired line to be punched with the guideline on the base of the punch. The indicator slide is then moved until the arrow points to the number of the channel to be punched.
6. Press on the top back portion of the punch to cut a rectangular hole at the intersection of the desired line and channel.
7. Repeat the procedure for each mark on the tape. Only *one* channel should be punched on any line.

Carriage control tape insertion. The following procedure should be followed when inserting a new carriage control tape.

1. Raise the printer cover.
2. Turn the feed clutch to NEUTRAL.
3. Move the latch on the side of the brush holder to the left, and raise the assembly (see Figure 10-12).
4. With the printing on the outside of the loop, place the loop 12 edge first over the pin-feed drive wheel so that the pins engage the holes down the center of the tape. Place the other end of the loop around the adjustable carriage control tape idler.
5. Adjust the idler by loosening the locking knob and moving it in its track until the carriage control tape is tightened to hold approximately 2 lb of pressure. Since it is difficult to gauge this pressure, a visual check used frequently is a $\frac{1}{4}$-in. deflection of the tape.
6. Lower the brush assembly. A click can be heard when the latch engages.
7. Press the carriage RESTORE key. If the carriage control tape has been improperly installed, the carriage will not function properly. After the tape has returned to the starting position (channel 1) and the proper forms have been aligned, engage the feed clutch.
8. Close the printer cover. (*Note:* The proper forms should always be checked for printing position alignment before the cover is closed, since it obstructs a good view of the printed form.)

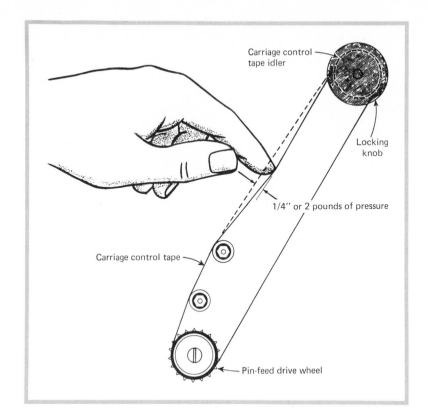

Carriage control
tape idler

Locking
knob

1/4″ or 2 pounds of pressure

Carriage control tape

Pin-feed drive wheel

Figure 10-21
Testing the Tension on a
Mounted Carriage
Control Tape

Forms insertion. The following procedure should be followed when inserting new forms in the 1403 N1 printer.

1. Raise the front cover of the printer to allow access to the print unit and forms area.
2. Turn the feed clutch to NEUTRAL.
3. Unlock and swing back the print unit by pulling the print unit release lever toward you (Figure 10-22).
4. Set both of the lefthand forms tractors slightly to the left of the first printing position. Pull the tractor until it latches in the appropriate notch.
5. Open the lefthand tractor covers, and place the forms over the pins (see Figure 10-23). Close the covers.
6. Open both of the righthand tractor covers.
7. Move the righthand tractors to the right side of the forms. Pull out the tractor pin latch, and slide the tractor until the pin snaps into the appropriate position (see Figure 10-23).

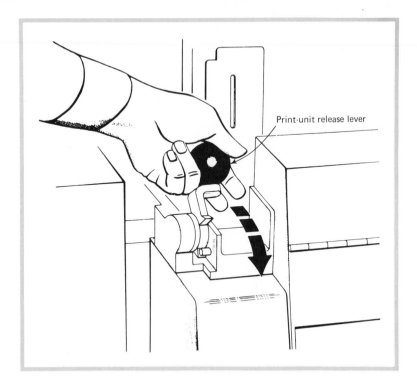

Figure 10-22
The Print Unit Release
Lever

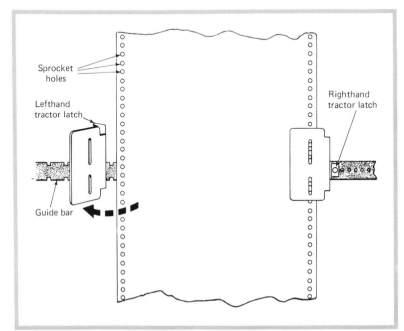

Figure 10-23
The Printer's Upper
Tractors Showing the
Lefthand Tractor Open

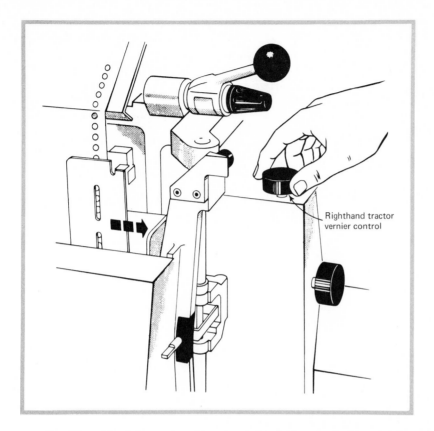

Figure 10-24
Final Adjustment of the
Righthand Tractors

8. Place the forms over the tractor feed pins, and close the tractor covers.
9. Tighten the tension on the forms, using the righthand tractor vernier. The tension should be set at approximately $\frac{1}{2}$ lb of pressure to allow enough give in the paper for proper printing.
10. To position the form, turn the paper advance knob until the block, line, or area on which the first line of print occurs is just visible above the ribbon guide bar. Align the desired hammer position to the form with the horizontal adjustment knob and lateral print vernier control (Figure 10-25). Observe the relationship of the markings on the ribbon guide bar to the form. Now, turn the paper advance knob *counterclockwise,* three line spaces if in 6 LINE NEUTRAL, or four line spaces if in 8 LINE NEUTRAL. The form is now properly positioned and ready for use.
11. Close and lock the print unit.
12. Be sure to push the print unit release lever as far back as it will go.

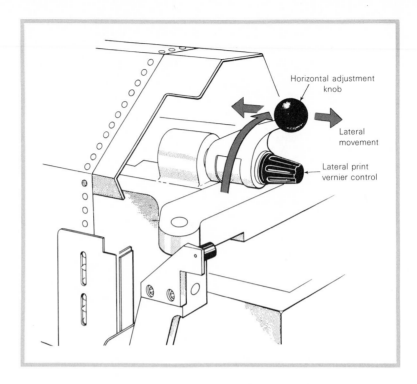

Figure 10-25
Lateral Alignment of the
Print Mechanism

13. Restore the carriage tape to the first printing position by pressing the CARRIAGE RESTORE button.
14. Set the feed clutch to DRIVE. Set it for a spacing of either 6 or 8 lines per inch, depending on the form to be printed.
15. Close the cover of the printer.
16. Position the paper supply on the input-paper cart so that the forms feed straight up into the machine.

Forms stacking. There are three major parts to the stacking mechanism:

1. A set of stacker tension rollers
2. Inner guide gate
3. Outer guide gate

After the forms have been printed, they continue over the top of the printer into the stacker area in the rear of the machine. As they enter this area, they pass beneath the powered tension rollers and down the inner guide gate. Satisfactory stacking requires initial care in positioning the first forms in the stacking area.

Self-study exercise 10-3

1. During use of the printer, the operator may be required to perform numerous operations, some of which are _____.

♦ ♦ ♦

changing forms, changing the print ribbon, replacing the print cartridge, punching a new carriage control tape, and changing carriage control tapes

2. A new carriage control tape is required when _____.

♦ ♦ ♦

the old tape becomes worn and when a program requires special spacing of the form

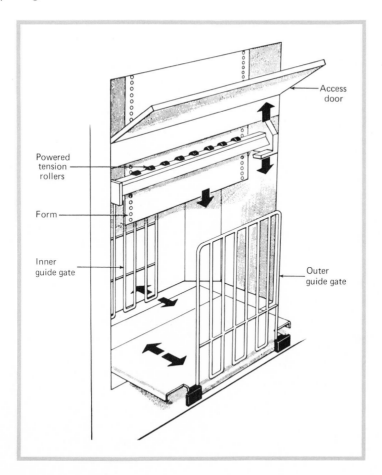

Figure 10-26
Path of Forms into Stacker

3. The last line to be printed on a form is noted by a punch in _____ of the control tape.

◆ ◆ ◆

channel 12

4. Only _____ per line is permitted on the carriage control tape.

◆ ◆ ◆

one control punch

5. Lines on the control tape _____ to the lines that will be printed on the form.

◆ ◆ ◆

correspond

6. Channels enable the printer to _____ and _____ at desired locations within the form.

◆ ◆ ◆

advance
stop

7. During control tape insertion, the tape must be securely seated over the _____. This is to ensure that _____.

◆ ◆ ◆

pin-feed drive wheel
the pins are correctly engaged with the holes running down the center of the control tape

8. The carriage control tape idler, within the carriage control unit, is utilized to remove _____ from the control tape after it has been seated.

◆ ◆ ◆

slack

9. Upon completion of the control tape insertion, the _____ must be lowered into a position above tape.

◆ ◆ ◆

carriage control tape brush holder

10. To replace forms within the printer, after the cover is raised, the _____ must be unlocked and swung open.

◆ ◆ ◆

print unit

11. The first position to be printed on the form is aligned with _____.

◆ ◆ ◆

the print line indicator and ribbon shield

12. When the print unit is locked into its printing position, the _____ must be pushed back to its furthest position.

◆ ◆ ◆

print unit release lever

13. While forms are inserted, the first line of print desired should be just visible above the _____.

◆ ◆ ◆

ribbon guide bar

14. With the form position set for the first line of print, the feed clutch in NEUTRAL, and the print unit engaged, the _____ key is depressed, thereby aligning the channel-1 position on the control tape with the first line of printing on the form.

◆ ◆ ◆

CARRIAGE RESTORE

*Ribbon changing. After a period of time, it may be necessary to replace the printer ribbon to maintain printing quality. If the printer output is to be used as input to an Optical Character Reading (OCR) device, high print quality must be achieved. The procedure for changing the ribbon on the IBM 1403 N1 Printer is:

1. Raise the printer cover.
2. Pull back and unlock the print unit release lever. Swing the print unit out.
3. Open the top ribbon cover (see Figure 10-27).
4. Unlatch the print line indicator ribbon shield, and swing it against the form (see Figure 10-17).
5. Slide the top ribbon roll to the right (hinged side) of the print unit, lift out the left end of the ribbon roll, and remove the roll from the driven end of the mechanism.
6. Slip the ribbon from under the ribbon correction roller (Figure 10-28).
7. To remove the bottom roll, slide the ribbon roll to the right, lower the left end of the ribbon roll, and remove it from the mechanism.
8. When replacing the ribbon in the machine, hand-tighten the ribbon to remove slack from the front of the printing mechanism.

Ribbons are available in an 11-in. width in addition to the standard 14-in. width. The ribbon width lever can adjust the ribbon feed mechanism to accommodate the above ribbon widths.

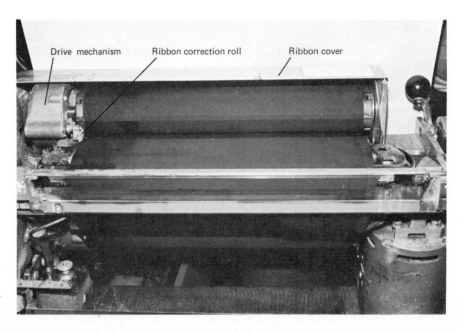

Drive mechanism   Ribbon correction roll   Ribbon cover

Figure 10-27
Ribbon Mechanism

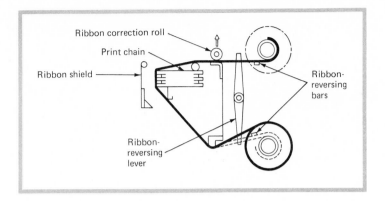

Figure 10-28
Schematic of Ribbon Path

*Cartridge changing.   The IBM 1403 N1 Printer permits the operator to choose from a variety of interchangeable cartridges. To change the cartridge:

1. Raise the printer cover.
2. Pull back and unlock the print unit release lever. Swing the print unit out.
3. Open the top ribbon cover.
4. Unlatch the print line indicator, and swing it against the form.
5. Remove the top ribbon spool as described above in the section called Ribbon Changing, and place it on the tray at the bottom of the print unit.
6. Pivot the two handles on top of the cartridge to their vertical position. The cartridge is now unlocked and may be lifted free of the print unit by its handles (see Figure 10-29).
7. Using the special tool attached to the printer, turn the notched driver on the right side of the print unit until a screw is visible in the nearby open hole in the faceplate (see Figure 10-30). If any further adjustment is required to align the notch in the driver with the notch in the casting, complete the alignment. This final adjustment is minor if the screw is properly positioned.
8. With the same tool, turn the driver gear in the new cartridge until the appropriate character, on the specially marked slug, is in line with the arrow engraved on the cartridge base.
9. Lock the cartridge in place by pivoting the handles down to their horizontal (original) position.
10. Replace the ribbon spool.
11. Close and lock the print unit.
12. Lower the cover.

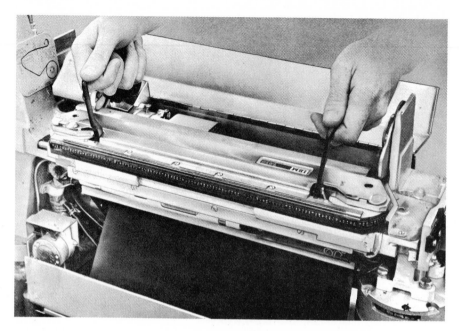

Figure 10-29
Interchanging the Print
Chain Cartridge

Self-study exercise 10-4

1. Ribbon changing occurs when the printer ribbon has become _____, and thus a high _____ quality cannot be maintained.

◆ ◆ ◆

worn
printing

Figure 10-30
Tool for Cartridge
Changing

2. Changing the ribbon on a printer is _____ to the same operation on a typewriter.

◆ ◆ ◆

similar

3. After replacement of the ribbon, hand-tighten the ribbon to remove _____.

◆ ◆ ◆

slack

4. By changing the print cartridge, the operator may select _____.

◆ ◆ ◆

different character sets and a variety of printing styles

5. The entire cartridge is replaced as a(n) _____ unit.

◆ ◆ ◆

complete

6. After seating the cartridge, the _____ must be aligned, with an arrow on the printer's baseplate using a specially marked slug.

◆ ◆ ◆

new cartridge

*Other Printers

In addition to the IBM 1403 Printer, the following printers are commonly found in data processing installations.

Burroughs line printers

Burroughs line printers, designed for use with the Burroughs B2500 and B3500 computer systems, include several models ranging from the B9240 to the B9245-1 printer. Each of these printers accepts continuous forms and utilizes a special unit to control paper skipping and spacing. Each is capable of printing a line of 120 to 132 characters, with each character being a letter, a digit, or one of 28 special characters. And each of these printers provides for a vertical spacing of either 6 or 8 lines per inch.

Figure 10-31
Burroughs Line Printer

Burroughs printers, like the IBM 1403, employ a carriage control tape to control the feeding and spacing of forms. However, in place of a print train or cartridge, the Burroughs printers use a print drum which houses the print characters. Therefore, in order to obtain the maximum printing speed, the characters in the drum are arranged in order of frequency of use.

**XDS model 7450
buffered line printer**

The 7450 printer, designed for use on XDS (Xerox Data Systems) Sigma computers, consists of a line printer device and a control unit to interface[1] the printer unit and the computer. This printer, as shown in Figure 10-32, is capable of printing up to 128 characters per line with a character set consisting of 64 characters.

In this printer, the speed depends on the number of different characters actually printed. That is, the greater the number of different characters printed, the slower the printing speed attained. For example, a printing speed of 225 lines per minute can be maintained if all 64 characters are

---

[1]*Interface* is the linking of two devices by means of a third hardware device.

printed. However, higher speeds are possible if a somewhat reduced character set is used.

Communications between this printer/control unit and the computer occur in a unique way. Instead of communicating with the printer a line at a time, as is the case with most other printers, the computer must communicate with this printer/control unit in bursts of a half-line at a time—first the odd-numbered characters from a given line, then the even-numbered characters from that line. Thus, the computer must send two half-lines of print to the printer/control unit for each complete line of print to be printed.

Once the printer receives the characters to be printed, printing begins. This is accomplished by a series of hammers which strike the paper against a cylindrical drum, on which the print characters are engraved. This drum rotates at a speed of 450 rps, and printing occurs when the desired character reaches the correct position on the print line.

Vertical form spacing in the XDS 7450 is controlled by a carriage control tape as in the case of the IBM 1403 and the Burroughs Model B9240 and B9245-1 printers.

The Honeywell 222 printer has four models with speeds ranging from 450 to 1,100 lines per minute and with 96 to 132 available print positions, as **Honeywell 222 printer**

Figure 10-32
Xerox Data Systems
Model 7450 Buffered Line
Printer

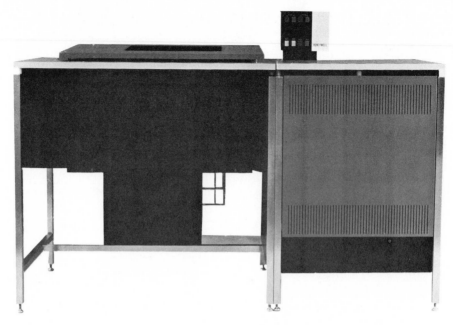

Figure 10-33
Honeywell 222 Printer

shown in Figure 10-33. As with H9240, H9245-1, and XDS 7450, the Honeywell 222 Printer utilizes a rotating drum which contains 63 available characters consisting of 26 alphabetic characters, 10 numeric characters, and 26 special characters. If faster speeds are desirable, they may be obtained by using a high-speed drum containing fewer special characters.

A special feature of the Honeywell 222 printer series is a bar code drum which produces a print directly readable by a Honeywell optical character reading (OCR) device.

Self-study exercise 10-5

1. As with the IBM 1403 Printer, Burroughs printers are controlled by a(n) _____.

◆ ◆ ◆

carriage control tape

2. The Burroughs print unit is composed of a(n) _____ housing the character set.

◆ ◆ ◆

print drum

3. The 7450 printer, used with Xerox Data Systems (XDS) Sigma computers, uses a(n) _____ in the printing of forms.

◆ ◆ ◆

rotating, cylindrical print drum

4. Replacement of the normal _____ on the Honeywell 222 printer will give higher printing speeds.

◆ ◆ ◆

print drum

5. The _____ , an option with the Honeywell 222 printer, produces printing directly readable by an OCR device.

◆ ◆ ◆

bar code drum

End-of-chapter Exercises

True-false exercise

1. The printer is used in the last stage in the data processing cycle.
2. Printers are restricted in the type of printed reports they can produce.
3. Printers can be subdivided into two broad categories—impact and nonimpact.
4. Nonimpact printers are the most economical to use.
5. Impact printers are faster than nonimpact printers.
6. Four major types of impact printing devices are print wheel, wire matrix, ball typewriter, and chain or drum.
7. Average printing speed for a print wheel printer is approximately 150 lines per minute.
8. The IBM 1403 Printer prints at a maximum speed of approximately 1,100 lines per minute.
9. The 1403 is a wire matrix printer.
10. The carriage control unit controls the movement of paper line by line.
11. Punches in channels on a carriage control tape control the skipping of lines.
12. The pushbuttons on the printer console enable the operator to exercise control over the operation of the printer.
13. The printer's indicator lights are used to denote the existence of one or more specific error states.
14. No operator intervention is required during forms stacking.

15. Deflection of ½ in. is optimum during carriage control tape mounting.
16. The print density control knob controls the force with which the print slugs strike the paper.
17. The PRINT CHECK display light, when lit, indicates the printer is accepting information from the CPU.
18. The END OF FORM light indicates that the end of the paper or of forms in the printer has been reached.
19. The CHECK RESET key is used to reset the printer to an operating state.
20. The IBM 1403 N1 Printer is limited to one set of characters for printing.
21. Burroughs printers employ a print drum.
22. The XDS Model 7450 Printer communicates with the computer on a line-by-line basis.

Fill-in exercise

1. The IBM 1403 Model N1 is a(n) _____ type of printer.
2. The 1403 printer console's READY display light is not lit when a(n) _____, _____, _____, or _____ is indicated.
3. If forms undergoing printing are not feeding properly through the IBM 1403 Printer, the _____ display light lights.
4. The CARRIAGE RESTORE pushbutton automatically aligns _____ with the _____ to be printed on the form.
5. The indicator panel lights on the 1403 are located _____.
6. In general, when any adjustments on the IBM 1403 Printer are performed, the _____ should be placed in NEUTRAL.
7. The wire matrix printer uses a(n) _____ of selected _____ to print its characters.
8. The four major types of impact printers are _____, _____, _____, and _____.
9. When forms are inserted into the printer, the _____ is used to align the form.
10. The character set on the 1403 N1 consists of _____ characters.
11. A _____ sensing channel 12 on the control tape causes the printer to index the form to the _____ of the _____ page.
12. The _____ pushbutton ceases all printing operations on the printer.
13. Indicator lights alert the operator to _____.

Problems

1. Discuss the difference between nonimpact and impact printers.
2. Discuss the conditions indicated by the display lights.
3. Discuss the preparation and mounting of a carriage control tape.
4. Discuss the steps required for forms insertion.
5. Discuss steps required in cartridge changing.

MAGNETIC TAPE MEDIUM AND UNIT

CHAPTER 11

Introduction Magnetic tape is one of the principal recording media in use with computers today. Its areas of application within a computer system are many and diverse.

For example, it can serve as an alternate medium to the punched card for initially recording either application program instructions or source data. Both can be accomplished utilizing a key-to-tape device, such as the IBM 050 Data Inscriber illustrated in Figure 11-2. As the operator depresses a particular key on the keyboard of the inscriber, the corresponding character is magnetically recorded on tape.

Magnetic tape may also be utilized for the temporary storage of intermediate results during the execution of an application program. These intermediate results can then be read back into the computer when they are needed. In this way, the limited capacity of primary storage can be utilized to store data which will be more frequently referenced.

Still another important use of magnetic tape is as an efficient auxiliary or external secondary storage medium. For example, one reel of magnetic tape can store an amount of data equivalent to that contained on more than 400,000 punched cards. This advantage of magnetic tape over the punched card medium is further enhanced by the fact that current magnetic tape units are capable of reading or writing in excess of 300,000 characters per second compared to the punched card medium's maximum speeds of approximately 1,500 characters per second.

Magnetic tape, like the punched card, is principally a *sequential* storage medium. That is, data recorded on magnetic tape may be read only in the order in which it was written. The third data record, for example, can be accessed only after the first and second data records have been read. For some applications, this fact will offer no particular problems. But for other applications it is essential that a capability exist for directly accessing any given data record. In these cases, a more appropriate storage medium would be the magnetic disk or magnetic drum. These *direct access* storage devices will be discussed in detail in the next chapter.

Magnetic Tape Medium The variety of magnetic tape used with computers is very similar in constitution to the tape used in home tape recorders, but it is of a substantially higher quality. It consists of a plastic base, approximately $\frac{1}{2}$ in. wide, coated on the side with a compound containing microscopic iron particles (Figures 11-3 and 11-4). By passing this tape over a read/write mechanism, the iron particles can be rearranged into magnetized patterns or bits. These bits occur in groups of seven or nine across the tape, thus forming either seven or nine parallel *tracks* along the tape.

Data recorded on seven-track tape is recorded in BCD (Binary Coded Decimal), the 6-bit code which is also utilized with the IBM System/3 card. The additional bit, referred to as a *parity* or *check bit*, is generated by the

2803 Model 1 or 2

2415 Model 1 or 4

2420 Model 7

2401 Model 2, 3, 5, 6 or 8

2401 Model 1 or 4

Figure 11-1
Various Magnetic Tape
Units

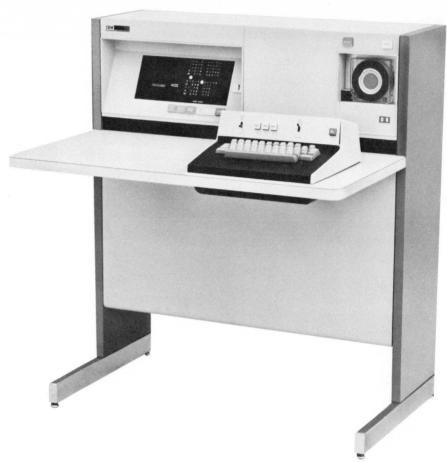

Figure 11-2
IBM 050 Data Inscriber

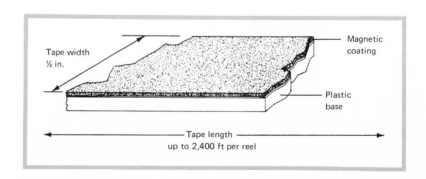

Figure 11-3
Composition of Magnetic
Tape

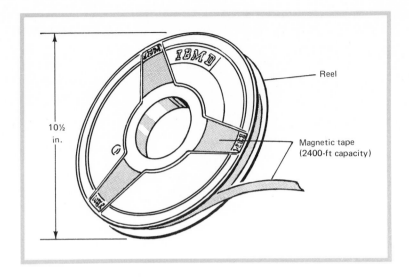

Figure 11-4
Reel of Magnetic Tape

computer for internal checking of character validity. This concept will be discussed in greater depth in the next section.

On the other hand, data recorded on nine-track tape utilizes the Extended Binary Coded Decimal Interchange Code (EBCDIC), the 8-bit code which is also employed when storing data (zoned decimal format) in primary storage. As with seven-track tapes, the additional (ninth) bit serves as a parity bit for detecting possible errors.

Error checking

Although unlikely, it is nevertheless possible that the computer could introduce a coding discrepancy while attempting to read, write, or process a character. The purpose of the parity bit is to detect such an error, should it occur. The system employed in determining whether the parity bit is a

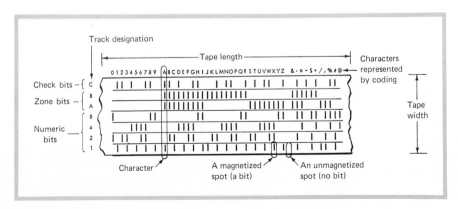

Figure 11-5
Characters Recorded on a Section of Seven-track Magnetic Tape

1 or 0 bit is quite simple. The total number of 1s in each character must be either odd (odd-parity machine) or even (even-parity machine). For discussion's sake, let us assume an odd-parity machine utilizing the BCD coding scheme. In this case, if we were to examine the bit configuration for the digit 6, we would see that it consists of an even number of 1s.

Bit names	C[1]	B	A	8	4	2	1
BCD code	?	0	0	0	1	1	0

Thus, for the total number of 1s to be odd, the check bit C would have to be a 1. That is, the bit configuration for the character 6 would be 1000110.[2]

Should an error now occur in the reading or processing of this character, such that 1 of the 7 bits is changed (from a 1 to a 0, or vice versa), the parity would no longer be odd, but even, revealing an error. The probability of 2 or more of the 7 bits being misread or miswritten is so minute that no test for these possibilities is included.

In addition to checking parity across the tape, character by character, a horizontal parity check is also made at the end of every tape record. That is, an additional parity bit is placed at the end of each record in each track. These parity bits will serve to further identify an error, should it occur.

Other methods of detecting errors are possible and in use; however, they are beyond the scope of this text.

Tape format   Magnetic tape must be moving at a constant speed when data is being read from or written onto it. As a result, a blank space, or *interblock gap* (*IBG*), is automatically recorded after each record of data written. This IBG serves to signal the end of one or more records during the reading of the tape. At the same time, it acts as a space in which the tape can accelerate to a required speed before a reading or writing operation and decelerate to rest after the operation is completed.

These gaps range in size from 0.6 to 0.75 in., a space which could otherwise record up to 1,200 characters. Therefore, to make the best possible use of a reel of tape, the number of IBGs must be minimized. This is accomplished by utilizing blocked records.

Blocked records.   Data processing applications are often concerned with the processing of data *files* maintained on magnetic tape. These files consist of a number of *logical records* (a complete record concerning one item or transaction).

[1]C is the parity bit.
[2]See Figure 2-9 for the BCD bit configurations of other characters.

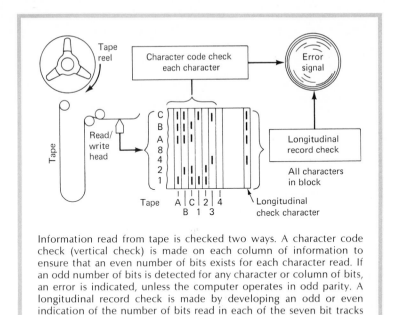

Information read from tape is checked two ways. A character code check (vertical check) is made on each column of information to ensure that an even number of bits exists for each character read. If an odd number of bits is detected for any character or column of bits, an error is indicated, unless the computer operates in odd parity. A longitudinal record check is made by developing an odd or even indication of the number of bits read in each of the seven bit tracks of the record, including the bits of the check character. If any bit track of the record block indicates an odd number of bits after it is read, an error is indicated, unless odd parity is required by system design.

Figure 11-6
Seven-track Validity Checks, BCD Mode Even Parity

The efficiency of processing such a file is generally enhanced if during the creation of the file, logical records are recorded in groups, or blocks, of a fixed number of records. In this case, each *physical record* (group, or block, of logical records) is separated from the next by an IBG, and the file is said to be *blocked* (consisting of blocked records).

The *blocking factor* is a term which refers to the number of logical records recorded in one physical record. For example, a tape with a blocking factor of 4 would contain 4 logical records in each physical record on the tape. An example of a tape file containing 4 logical records per physical record is shown in Figure 11-7.

There are two principal advantages to blocking data on tape:

1. More efficient use of the tape. The higher the blocking factor, the fewer the IBGs. Thus, more data can be stored on the same amount of tape.
2. Faster access speed. A single read command initiates the reading of an entire tape record. This may be a logical record or, if the tape file is blocked, a physical record. Thus, if the tape is blocked, fewer read commands will be required to read the same data than if the tape file were unblocked. This then results in fewer starts and stops of the tape.

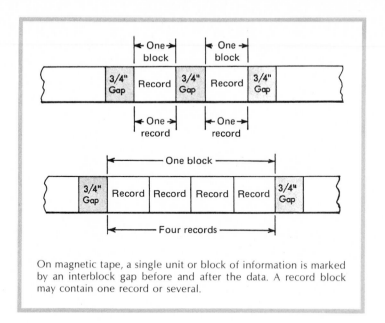

On magnetic tape, a single unit or block of information is marked by an interblock gap before and after the data. A record block may contain one record or several.

Figure 11-7
Blocked Data Records

There is, however, a question as to what is the most appropriate blocking factor to use with a given tape file. The answer to this question is controlled to a great extent by the availability of primary storage. As we have previously stated, data may only be processed from primary storage. Hence, the physical record must first be read into primary storage before it can be processed. There are also other considerations which play a vital role in determining the most appropriate blocking factor for a given tape file. However, these considerations are of concern only to the programmer, and they are beyond the scope of this text.

Tape indicators. In addition to the IBG, which indicates the end of a physical record, there are several indicators which have special significance when the magnetic tape medium is utilized. Some of these are:

Tapemark a special character (represented as hexadecimal 7F on IBM tape units) used to denote the end of a tape file. When a file is *created* (initially recorded on tape), an end-of-file tapemark is recorded on the tape at the physical end of the file. If several files are recorded on a single reel of tape, each file must be separated from the next by a tapemark.

Load Point Marker a small metallic strip, also called a *reflective strip,* which is attached to the edge of the tape on the side opposite the recording surface. It is used to indicate the load point, or start, of data on the tape. When a tape is mounted and made ready, the tape unit will position the tape at its load point. At least 10 ft should separate the beginning of a tape and its load point to allow for threading the tape onto the machine reel.

End-of-tape Mark a second reflective strip, placed after the last IBG on that tape and approximately 14 ft from the end of the tape, used to denote the physical end of the usable portion of the tape. This space allows for 10 ft of leader plus 4 ft on which is recorded an additional data record—a tape label.

Tape labels. At the time a data file is created, two special purpose data records are generally added. These records are referred to as tape labels and typically contain descriptive information relative to the records and files contained on a tape reel. One of these labels serves as a header label and precedes the file, while the other is a trailer label and follows the file. Header labels usually identify the file and its format, while trailer labels mark the end of the file and usually contain a count of the total number of records

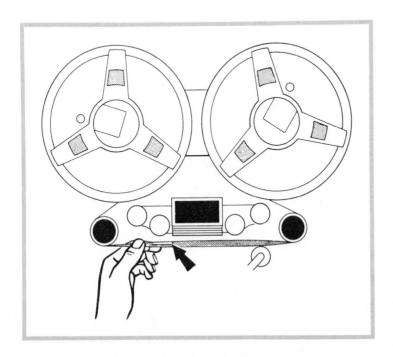

Figure 11-8
End-of-tape Marker

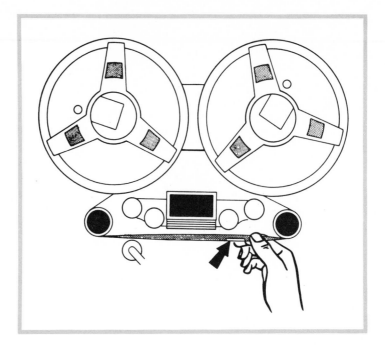

Figure 11-9
Load Point Marker

in the file. Although not required, tape labels are essential to maintaining efficient control over large tape libraries. Most computer systems are equipped with manufacturer-supplied programs, or software, for automatically creating and maintaining tape labels of a standard format. The programmer can, however, create or read labels of a nonstandard format. It is also a common practice to place an external label on the tape reel similar to the one indicated in Figure 11-10, after the tape file has been created.

Tape handling   Precautions must be taken to prevent the magnetic tape medium from getting dusty, dirty, or damaged. This can best be accomplished by following some very simple procedures for its handling. Some of the more important are:

1.   Never handle tape with dirty or greasy hands.
2.   Always store tapes which are not being used in their protective covers.
3.   Verify that the tape cover is free from dust or other foreign particles before enclosing the actual tape.
4.   Be certain not to crease or wrinkle the tape when handling it.
5.   Keep the tape library or storage area free from dust. When cleaning the tape library, never use a broom, which will stir the dust.

6. Periodically clean the tape units, particularly the read/write mechanism. A cleaning is also a good idea before any extensive tape operations. The read/write mechanism should be cleaned with a lint-free cloth dabbed in a special tape cleaning solution.

Self-study exercise 11-1

1. The magnetic tape unit can be used as an extension to main storage or as a(n) _____ storage device.

◆ ◆ ◆

auxiliary

2. A full reel of tape can hold more data than _____ fully punched cards.

◆ ◆ ◆

400,000

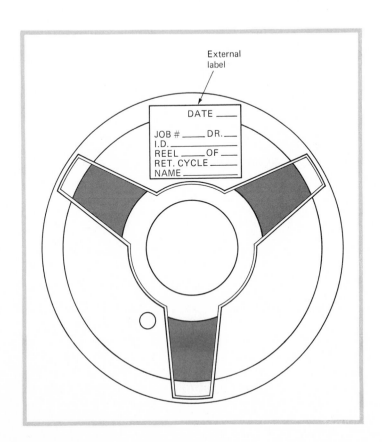

Figure 11-10
External Tape Label

3. A device used to record data directly on magnetic tape is called a(n) _____ .

♦ ♦ ♦

key-to-tape device

4. Magnetic tape is primarily a(n) _____ storage medium.

♦ ♦ ♦

sequential

5. The most common tapes used in magnetic tape units are _____ in. wide and _____ ft long.

♦ ♦ ♦

1/2
2,400

6. Tapes are recorded at either _____ or _____ track.

♦ ♦ ♦

seven
nine

7. A common technique for detecting error conditions on tape is the use of the _____ bit in each character.

♦ ♦ ♦

parity

8. The space of blank tape between each record is called the _____ .

♦ ♦ ♦

interblock gap (IBG)

9. A term which refers to the number of logical records recorded in each physical tape record is _____ .

♦ ♦ ♦

blocking factor

10. A(n) _____ is a special character which denotes the end of a data file on tape.

♦ ♦ ♦

tapemark

11. A reflective strip at the beginning of a tape reel is called the _____.

♦ ♦ ♦

load point marker

12. Tape labels are useful in identifying the different _____ on the tape.

♦ ♦ ♦

files

Tape Operations

Functionally, the tape unit is composed of two tape reels. The first, called the file reel, holds the tape being accessed, while the second, called the machine reel, is used to take up the tape which has already passed through the read/write mechanism. Typically, the file reel is located on the left side of the unit while the machine reel is located on the right side (see Figure 11-11). Thus, the direction of tape movement during a forward reading or writing operation is from left to right.

The read/write mechanism, located in the center of the tape drive unit, is bounded on each side by a vertical vacuum column. These columns hold a fixed amount of tape and act as a buffer to protect the tape from damage resulting from the abrupt starting and stopping of the tape as it is being read or written. Located at the top of the tape drive unit is a group of manual keys and indicator lights which gives the computer operator control over the operation of the tape drive and which also indicate the status of the tape unit at any given time.

Mounting tape reels

Before a tape can be read or written, it must be mounted on a tape drive and the tape drive made ready for operation. This involves mounting the tape on the file reel of the drive unit and threading the tape through the tape transport mechanism onto the machine reel (see Figure 11-11). In anticipation of this operation, the read/write mechanism should be raised when not in use. The operator then depresses the appropriate buttons, causing the read/write mechanism to drop to its ready position over the tape and the tape to advance until it is positioned at its load point. At this time, both the tape and drive units are ready to commence reading

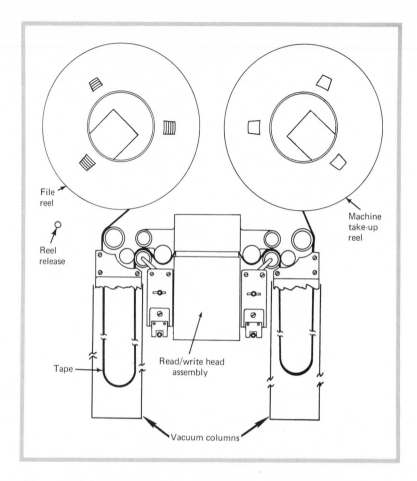

Figure 11-11
Schematic of Model 2401
Magnetic Tape Drive

or writing operations. During these operations, the tape advances from the file reel down into the left vertical vacuum column and up again to pass over the read/write mechanism. From the read/write mechanism, the tape advances down into the right vacuum column and up again until it is finally drawn onto the machine reel which serves as a take-up reel.

In most drive units, both the machine and file reels operate independently. This independent operation is controlled by a *magnetic drive clutch* for each reel. This clutch is engaged or disengaged by a vacuum-activated switch located in each of the vertical vacuum columns. As the loop of tape in the left vacuum column reaches a predetermined minimum level, tape is automatically drawn off the file reel. Similarly, when the loop of tape in the right vertical column reaches a predetermined maximum level, tape is drawn up by the machine reel.

Once a tape has been completely read or written, it must be rewound to its load point. This rewind operation is initiated by the operator or program being processed. If initiated by the operator, it can be accomplished in one of two ways.

In the first way, referred to as a *normal rewind,* the tape is backspaced one record at a time until the reflective spot or load point is reached. During a backspacing operation, the tape may be read but generally not written on.

The second method of rewinding a tape, referred to as a *high-speed rewind,* causes the file reel to pull the tape off the machine reel at a constant, but rapid, rate. To facilitate this operation, the tape is drawn up from the vacuum columns and commences the high-speed rewind which is now monitored by a photoelectric cell and light beam mounted on the tape drive. As this monitoring device senses that the tape is nearing the load point, the rewind operation is switched from a high-speed rewind to a normal rewind, thus preventing the tape from being damaged by being torn off the machine reel.

The self-loading, or automatic threading, tape drive eliminates the need for manually threading the tape onto the machine reel. Instead, the mounting operation simply entails placing the reel of tape on the file reel, while allowing a small strip of tape to extend from the reel. The subsequent depression of the START button then causes the tape to be automatically threaded through the transport area and onto the machine reel. To ensure that the tape loads properly, the operator should visually verify that the beginning of the tape is smooth and free of wrinkles. Should the operator detect any wrinkles, cuts, or other flaws in the tape leader (approximately the first 10 in. of the tape), he should then cut off the damaged piece of tape. If this cutting would not leave an adequate leader, the file(s) contained on the tape would have to be recreated on a new tape.

Self-loading tapes

A tape cartridge consists of a reel of tape and a take-up reel enclosed in a case which protects the tape from contamination by dirt and damage through mishandling. These cartridges are easily and directly mounted on the tape drive and automatically loaded. Thus, there is no need to ever remove the tape reels from the tape cartridge or to physically handle the actual tape. By simply depressing the START button after having mounted the tape cartridge, we automatically open the tape cartridge, thread it onto the machine reel, and advance it to the load point. Once the tape has been completely read or written and rewound, the tape cartridge is automatically closed. It can then be dismounted.

Tape cartridge

Once a data file has been created, it must be protected from accidental destruction. Such destruction could happen in various ways, the most common of which is the accidental mounting of the tape reel containing the data file and writing over or destroying the data file. To protect a tape

File protection

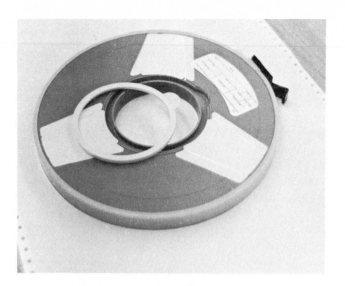

Figure 11-12
Tape Reel Showing File
Protection Method "No
Ring, No Write."

file against such accidental destruction, it may be file-protected. This is accomplished by removing a small plastic *file protection ring* from the back of the reel on which the tape is wound. Figure 11-12 illustrates this plastic ring and the tape reel with the ring removed. By removing this plastic ring, a small pin located on the tape drive can pop up into the groove vacated by the ring. With this pin in the UP position, no writing can take place. A phrase used to remind operators of the use of the ring is *No Ring, No Write*. Thus, once data has been recorded on a tape, it can be protected against accidental destruction by simply removing the plastic file protection ring from the back of the reel.

Speed of operation　The speed of operation of a magnetic tape unit, as with all input/output devices, directly affects the overall processing speed of a computer system. In the case of magnetic tape, its speed of operation is a function of three things: load time, rewind time, and the data transfer rate.

Load Time　the time required to mount a tape reel on a tape drive and make the tape ready. Load time depends to a large extent on the skill of the operator and the type of tape unit being used. Those tape units described as self-loading are typically faster and easier to load than non-self-loading units.

Rewind Time　the time required to rewind a tape. Rewind time is extremely important, especially when processing is halted while a program waits for a tape to be rewound, dismounted, and another tape mounted in its place. The high-speed rewind feature is especially advantageous for tapes requiring lengthy rewinds.

Data Transfer Rate   a measure of the speed at which data is transferred to the CPU. The data transfer rate is dependent on two factors: the speed with which the tape moves past the read/write mechanism and the density at which characters are recorded on the tape. Measured in characters per second, the transfer rate is calculated by multiplying the transport speed (inches per second) by the tape density (characters per inch). Tape densities are generally 200, 556, 800, or 1,600 characters per inch. Data transfer rates may be as high as 320,000 characters per second. Although this speed seems quite high, it must be remembered that each time a tape record is read or written, the tape comes to a stop within the IBG.

Self-study exercise 11-2

1. The two reels on a magnetic tape unit are called the _____ reel and the _____ reel.

◆ ◆ ◆

file
machine

2. The vacuum columns are used to protect the tape from sudden _____.

◆ ◆ ◆

stops and starts

3. Once a tape has been completely read or written, it must be rewound to its _____.

◆ ◆ ◆

load point

4. Two types of magnetic tape device that eliminate threading are _____.

◆ ◆ ◆

self-loading tapes and tape cartridges

5. The file-protect facility makes it impossible to write on a tape unless
_____ .

♦ ♦ ♦

the plastic ring is in the tape reel

6. The phrase to remind operators of this facility is _____ .

♦ ♦ ♦

No Ring, No Write

7. Speed of operation of a magnetic tape unit is a function of three things:
_____ .

♦ ♦ ♦

load time, rewind time, and data transfer rate

8. The data transfer rate for tape operations depends on the tape _____
and transport speed.

♦ ♦ ♦

density

IBM 2401 Magnetic Tape Unit   The IBM 2401 Magnetic Tape Unit is a member of the IBM 2400 Series of tape units and is available in six models. Each of the six models of the 2401 tape unit is similar in operation and appearance and is compatible with the IBM 360 Series computers.

Depending on the model and features ordered, a 2401 tape unit can have various characteristics. Some of these are given below in Table 11-1.

In addition to these features, seven- and nine-track compatibility can be ordered to allow a single 2401 tape unit to read and write both seven- and nine-track tapes.

Physical components   The keys and lights associated with the operation of the IBM 2401 tape unit are illustrated in Figure 11-13.

Operator lights.   Through the use of the operator lights on the control panel of the IBM 2401 tape unit, the operator may observe the status of the tape unit—that is, whether the tape has been correctly mounted and whether the tape unit is otherwise ready for operation. Table 11-2 discusses the various operator lights used in processing magnetic tapes.

Table 11-1. Characteristics of Various 2401 Model Tape Units

Characteristics	2401 Tape Units					
	Model 1 / Model 4	Model 1	Model 2 / Model 5	Model 2	Model 3 / Model 6	Model 3
Number of Tracks	Nine-track	Seven-track	Nine-track	Seven-track	Nine-track	Seven-track
Density (Bytes Per Inch)	800 / 1,600	a. 800 b. 556 c. 200	800 / 1,600	a. 800 b. 556 c. 200	800 / 1,600	a. 800 b. 556 c. 200
Data Rate (Bytes Per Second)	30,000 / 60,000	a. 30,000 b. 20,850 c. 7,500	60,000 / 120,000	a. 60,000 b. 41,700 c. 15,000	90,000 / 180,000	a. 90,000 b. 62,500 c. 22,500
Tape Speed (In./Sec.)	37.5	37.5	75.0	75.0	112.5	112.5
Interblock Gap (In.)	0.6	0.75	0.6	0.75	0.6	0.75

Operator keys. To effect direct control over the tape unit, keys within the 2401's control panel are utilized. The tape unit will respond directly to the depression of any of these keys, since their use directly controls the reading and writing of data in tape.

Let us discuss these lights and keys as they would be utilized by an operator while processing a job whose purpose is to create a master tape file.

Operator functions

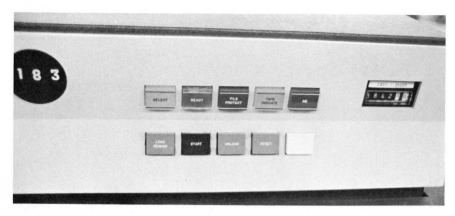

Figure 11-13
2401 Tape Unit Control Panel

Table 11-2. Operator Lights and Their Functions

Light	Function
SELECT	When the computer addresses the tape unit, the SELECT light is turned on. If the operator has mounted the tape reel and threaded it onto the machine or take-up reel, depressing the LOAD REWIND key will cause the tape to be drawn down into the left and right vertical vacuum columns in addition to causing the read/write head to descend to its operational position. If, on the other hand, the tape has already been loaded and read or written to the extent that the machine reel contains more than $\frac{1}{2}$ in. of read or written tape, depressing the LOAD REWIND key will initiate a high-speed rewind. This will continue until there is less than $\frac{1}{8}$ in. of tape remaining on the machine reel, at which time the tape will drop back into the vacuum columns, commencing a low-speed rewind which continues until the load point marker is detected. During this operation, the reel access door must be kept closed to avoid damaging or breaking the tape. However, neither of these operations can take place while the READY light is on. That is, when the READY light is on, the LOAD REWIND key is inoperative.
READY	The READY light is turned on when the tape is properly loaded and can be accessed by the computer. This light is turned on by pressing the START button after the tape is mounted and after the LOAD REWIND key has been pressed.
FILE PROTECT	The FILE PROTECT light is turned on to indicate that no writing or erasing can take place on the mounted tape. The FILE PROTECT light will be lit when the loaded tape is file-protected (no ring), the file reel is missing, a load rewind operation is in progress, or an unload operation is in progress. When a non-file-protected tape is mounted and made ready, the light goes off.
CB	This light is lit when a circuit breaker is tripped. The tape unit cannot be used until the circuit breaker is reset by a customer engineer.

Table 11-2. (Cont.)

Light	Function
TAPE INDICATE	The TAPE INDICATE light is turned on when the end-of-tape marker is sensed during a forward operation. This light can be turned off by executing a backward tape operation, by pressing the UNLOAD key, by opening the reel door, or when the tape unit receives a REWIND UNLOAD command.

Tape load procedure. In preparation for this program, the operator mounts a blank or scratch tape, containing a file protection ring, on the appropriate drive unit in the following manner:

Step 1. The reel door is opened and the file *reel hub latch* pulled forward (Figure 11-14). The reel is then firmly pressed against the stop on the back of the file *reel mounting hub* and the latch closed.

Step 2. While depressing the REEL RELEASE button with his left hand, the operator unwinds approximately 4 ft of tape from the file reel with his right hand (Figure 11-15).

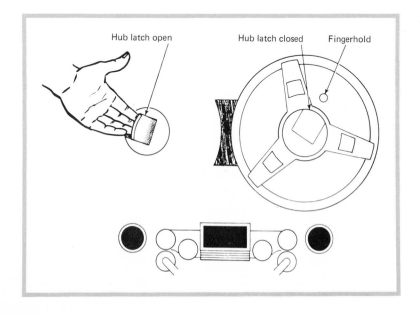

Figure 11-14
Tape Reel Hub Latch

Table 11-3. Operator Keys and Their Functions

Key	Function
START	This key is used to place the tape unit in a ready status. When the START key is depressed following a load rewind operation (which positions the tape at the load point), the tape will be ready for reading or writing, and the READY light will go on.
UNLOAD	The key is used to unload the tape. That is, when depressed, it causes the read/write head to raise up from the tape and the tape to be withdrawn from the vacuum columns. This key is only operative, however, when the tape is in the vacuum columns and the READY light is off. Thus, to remove a tape reel, the operator need only depress first the LOAD REWIND key to rewind the tape and then the UNLOAD key.
RESET	The RESET key is used to remove a tape from ready status and return it to manual control. When the RESET key is pressed, the READY light goes off, and all tape operations, with the exception of an unload operation, are terminated. If a high-speed rewind is in progress and the RESET key is pressed, the tape is lowered into the vacuum columns, and a low-speed rewind is initiated. If the RESET key is again depressed, the rewind stops.
REEL RELEASE	The REEL RELEASE button is located on the tape drive to the left of the file reel. Pressing this button allows the reels to be turned manually. Threading the tape from the file reel to the machine reel requires that the REEL RELEASE button be depressed.
REEL DOOR INTERLOCK	When the reel door is open, an interlock prevents any normal tape operation from occurring. The reel door should never be opened when a load rewind operation is in progress or when the READY light is on.
LOAD REWIND	The depressing of this key initiates one of two operations—the loading of a tape or the rewinding of a tape.

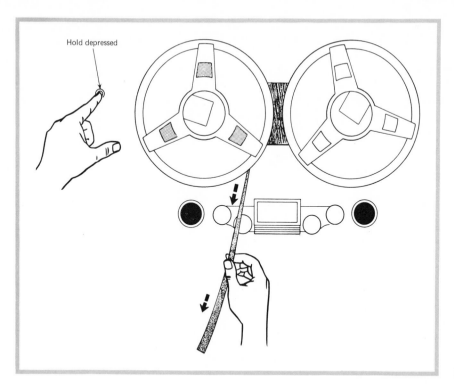

Hold depressed

Figure 11-15
Stripping Off Tape Leader

Step 3.   The tape is then passed around the *left rewind idler,* through the read/write mechanism, and around the *right rewind idler.* If the machine reel or take-up reel is equipped with a cutout in the front flange of the reel, the operator then places the tape on the hub of the reel using his right index finger inserted through the cutout. While the REEL RELEASE button is held down, the tape can be wound onto the machine reel by rotating the machine reel clockwise. An indentation or finger hole on the machine reel is now used to turn the reel until the load point marker or reflective spot has moved *past* the read/write mechanism (see Figures 11-16 and 11-17). The reel door is now closed.

Step 4.   The LOAD REWIND key is depressed, lowering the read/write head, drawing the tape down into the left and right vacuum columns, and positioning the tape *at* its load point.

Step 5.   The START key is depressed, causing the READY light to go on and making the tape accessible to the computer.

The application program can now begin the actual operation of creating the tape file. When the computer addresses the drive unit in

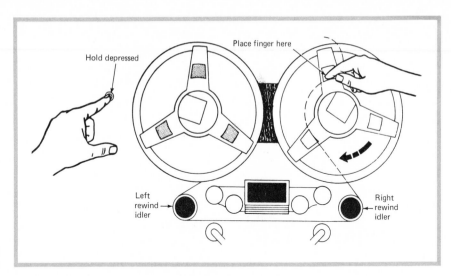

Figure 11-16
Threading Tape

question, the SELECT light on that unit goes on. When the tape file has
been created, it is generally rewound automatically by instructions contained within the program used to create the file. If this is not done by
the program, it must be completed by the operator. The procedure followed
by the operator to accomplish both this rewinding operation and the
unloading of the tape is given below.

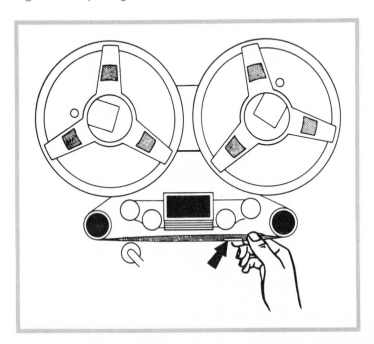

Figure 11-17
Position of Load Point
Marker After Tape Has
Been Threaded

Tape unload procedure.

Step 1. If the READY light is on, the operator must return the tape unit to manual control by depressing the RESET key. The READY light should now go out.

Step 2. The LOAD REWIND key is then depressed, effecting the rewinding of the tape to its initial load point.

Step 3. When the rewind operation has been completed, the UNLOAD key is depressed, drawing the tape out of the vacuum columns and raising the read/write mechanism. The reel door may now be opened.

Step 4. The operator now need only depress the REEL RELEASE button and manually rewind the file reel counterclockwise, utilizing the finger hole previously discussed. When the tape has been completely rewound onto the file reel, the hub latch is opened and the reel removed.

Step 5. The plastic file protection ring may then be removed to prevent the file from being accidentally destroyed.

Self-study exercise 11-3

1. The 2401 tape unit can support data rates of _____ to _____ characters per second.

♦ ♦ ♦

30,000
180,000

2. The _____ key is used to position a tape at its load point.

♦ ♦ ♦

LOAD REWIND

3. The _____ light is turned on when the end-of-tape marker is sensed during a forward operation.

♦ ♦ ♦

TAPE INDICATE

4. The _____ key turns on the READY light and places the tape unit in a ready status.

♦ ♦ ♦

START

5. The _____ key is pressed just prior to removing the tape reel from the tape unit.

◆　◆　◆

UNLOAD

6. A tape is removed from ready status and returned to manual control when the _____ key is pressed.

◆　◆　◆

RESET

7. The file reel cannot be manually turned unless the _____ button is depressed.

◆　◆　◆

REEL RELEASE

8. The _____ is activated whenever the tape reel door is opened.

◆　◆　◆

REEL DOOR INTERLOCK

9. Whenever the computer addresses the tape unit, the _____ light is turned on.

◆　◆　◆

SELECT

10. The _____ light is lit when no writing or erasing of data can take place.

◆　◆　◆

FILE PROTECT

11. When a tape reel is mounted, tape should be wound onto the machine reel until the _____ is moved past the read/write head.

◆　◆　◆

load point marker

12. After tape is properly threaded, the tape is made ready by pressing the
_____ and _____ keys in sequence.

◆ ◆ ◆

LOAD REWIND
START

Other Magnetic Tape Units

The IBM 2420 Magnetic Tape Unit is available in two models, Model 5 and Model 7. Both models record data at 1,600 bytes per inch, but they differ in their data transfer rates. Model 5 transfers data to the CPU at 160,000 bytes per second and Model 7 at 320,000 bytes per second.

The IBM 2420 tape drive offers several capabilities not available on any of the IBM 2401 models. Some of these are:

1. Automatic threading
2. Tape cartridge input
3. More sophisticated tape transport system
4. Correction of single-track errors while the tape is in motion

The IBM 2420, however, accommodates only nine-track tape as opposed to the seven- or nine-track capability of the IBM 2401. Error checking is similar to the IBM 2401, employing both longitudinal and vertical parity checks. Other characteristics of the 2420 tape unit are:

Characteristic	Model 5	Model 7
Tape speed (inches per second)	100	200
Interblock gap (inches)	0.6	0.6
Rewind time (minutes)	1.2	1.0
Autothreading operation (seconds)	10.0	7.0

UNIVAC uniservo 16 magnetic tape subsystem

The Uniservo 16 tape system is designed for use with UNIVAC computer systems. Similar in operation to the IBM 2401 tape unit, the Uniservo 16 can record data at either 200, 556, or 800 characters per inch. Data can be recorded on seven- or nine-track tapes. The Uniservo 16, however, is not available with an automatic threading capability. Other characteristics of the Uniservo 16 include:

Tape speed (inches per second)	120
Transfer rate (characters per second)	24,000, 66,720, and 96,000
Interblock gap (inches)	0.75 (seven-track) 0.60 (nine-track)

2420 Model 7

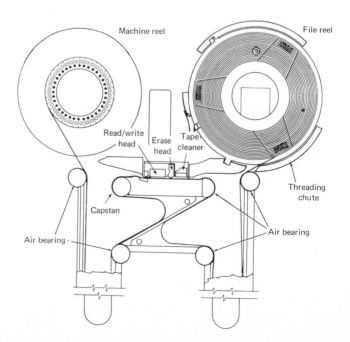

Figure 11-18
IBM 2420 Tape Transport
Mechanism and Drive
Unit

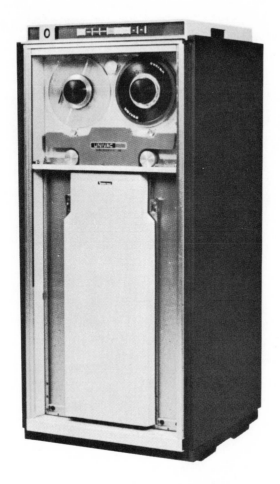

Figure 11-19
UNIVAC Uniservo 16

The Honeywell 204 Series of magnetic tape units consists of three complete families of tape units, each compatible with the Honeywell Model 8200 computer system. The three families are divided into:

Honeywell 204 series magnetic tape unit

1. Units that process $\frac{1}{2}$-in. tape recorded on seven tracks
2. Units that process $\frac{3}{4}$-in. tape
3. Units that process $\frac{1}{2}$-in., 9-track tape at 800 and 1,600 characters per inch

Within these three families of tape units, there are several submodels which differ in speed of operation and density of data storage. Data transfer speeds range from 7,200 to 224,000 characters per second for units processing $\frac{1}{2}$-in. tape and from 32,000 to 88,000 characters per second for $\frac{3}{4}$-in. units. A unique feature of the Honeywell 204 Series tapes is the use of the

Figure 11-20
Honeywell 204 Series
Magnetic Tape Units

interblock gap (IBG). When processing these tapes, it is not essential that the tape stop within an IBG. If a read or write command is issued while the tape is decelerating within an IBG, the tape will accelerate, complete the gap, and continue to read or write the next record.

All Honeywell tapes incorporate the vacuum-column technique to protect the tape from sudden starts and stops. Like the IBM 2420 tape unit, in the Honeywell 204 unit the tape makes contact with only the read/write mechanism. Unlike the 2420, however, automatic threading is not supported, and the tape being loaded is placed on the right side of the drive unit with forward tape movement being from right to left. Error checking on $\frac{1}{2}$-in. tapes is accomplished with vertical and longitudinal data bits. On $\frac{3}{4}$-in. tapes, a more sophisticated error detection system provides the ability to regenerate any track on the tape on the basis of the parity established by the other tracks and the vertical parity bits. This error detection and correction system is called *orthotronic control.*

Self-study exercise 11-4

1. The IBM 2420 tape unit has the special feature called _____.

♦ ♦ ♦

automatic threading

2. The 2420 Model 5 has a data rate of _____, while the Model 7 has a data rate of _____ bytes per second.

♦ ♦ ♦

160,000
320,000

3. The 2420 records data at a single density of _____ bytes per inch.

♦ ♦ ♦

1,600

4. The only contact made with tape on the 2420 is at the _____.

♦ ♦ ♦

read/write mechanism

5. Data is recorded on the 2420 using only the _____ tape.

♦ ♦ ♦

nine-track

6. The Uniservo 16 tape unit can record data at densities _____, _____, or _____ characters per inch.

♦ ♦ ♦

200
556
800

7. Transfer rates on the Uniservo 16 vary from _____ to _____ characters per second.

◆ ◆ ◆

24,000
96,000

8. The Honeywell 204 Series consists of _____ families of tape units.

◆ ◆ ◆

three

9. In addition to ½-in. tape, the Honeywell 204 tape units can process _____-in. magnetic tape.

◆ ◆ ◆

¾

10. Data transfer speeds on the Honeywell 204 Series range from _____ to _____ characters per second.

◆ ◆ ◆

7,200
224,000

11. Honeywell 204 Series tapes have the unique feature of not having to stop within the _____.

◆ ◆ ◆

IBG (interblock gap)

12. A sophisticated error checking and correction system used on ¾-in. Honeywell tape units is the _____ system.

◆ ◆ ◆

orthotronic control

End-of-chapter Exercises

True-false exercise

1. Blocking is the combining of several logical records into a physical record.
2. Nine-track tape utilizes the BCD code principle.

3. A trailer label is a special purpose data record at the end of the tape containing information such as record count.
4. Magnetic tape is used as both a secondary storage and an input medium.
5. The density of data recorded on magnetic tape refers to the number of recorded characters per inch of tape.
6. IBG is the gap between fields on a tape.
7. High-speed rewind takes place when the loop point marker is sensed by a photoelectric cell.
8. Pressing the REEL RELEASE button automatically rewinds tape to the load point marker.
9. The file protection ring should never be removed.
10. Unload procedure cannot take place until the READY light goes out and the drive returns to manual control.

Multiple-choice exercise

1. Magnetic tape is not generally considered to be
   a. external storage
   b. internal storage
   c. secondary storage
   d. all the above
   e. none of the above
2. A parity check is used to
   a. compare totals
   b. aid in ensuring the accuracy of information stored in a computer
   c. inform the computer when end-of-file has been reached
   d. light up when load point marker is read
   e. none of the above
3. The REEL RELEASE button allows
   a. tape to come off the spindle
   b. automatic rewinding of the file reel
   c. manual rewind of the file reel
   d. all the above
   e. none of the above
4. Information can be placed on magnetic tape by
   a. the use of a IBM 050 Data Inscriber
   b. the use of a card reader and the computer
   c. the use of a disk drive and the computer
   d. all the above
   e. none of the above
5. Magnetic tape can store information
   a. randomly
   b. sequentially

  c. by direct access
  d. all the above
  e. none of the above

6. The IBG allows the machine to
  a. accelerate to a rated speed
  b. indicate the end of one or more records
  c. decelerate to rest
  d. all the above
  e. none of the above

7. The blocking factor equals the number of
  a. physical records in one logical record
  b. logical records in one physical record
  c. files in one block
  d. all the above
  e. none of the above

8. Information on tape labels includes
  a. end-of-tape mark
  b. load point mark
  c. descriptive information relative to the records
  d. all the above
  e. none of the above

9. Tape unit is composed of two tape reels—
  a. a file reel on the left and a machine reel on the right
  b. a machine reel on the left and a file reel on the right
  c. a file reel on the right and a tape reel on the left
  d. a tape reel on the right and a file reel on the left
  e. none of the above

10. The IBM 2401 may mount tapes in
  a. cartridge form
  b. self-loading form
  c. reel form
  d. all the above
  e. none of the above

Discussion questions

1. Discuss the advantages and disadvantages of magnetic tape as an initial recording medium. What do you predict for the future of key-to-tape devices?
2. Discuss the tape loading procedures on the IBM 2401 magnetic tape drive.
3. Discuss reasons for blocking records.

DISK AND DRUM PROCESSING

CHAPTER 12

Introduction

Disk Storage Devices

Removable disk devices

Nonremovable disk devices

Direct access storage facility

Disk Concepts

The disk track

The disk cylinder

Accessing data records on disk

Data access speed

Effective disk storage capacity

Magnetic Drum

File Organization

Sequential files

Direct files

Indexed sequential files

IBM 2311 Disk Storage Unit

Operating procedures

Disk pack handling procedures

Mounting and dismounting disk packs

Other Direct Access Devices

IBM 2305 disk storage unit

IBM 2314 direct access storage facility

UNIVAC fastrand 11 mass storage unit

IBM 2321 data cell drive

End-of-chapter Exercises

In our previous discussions, we noted that the primary storage capacity available with most computer systems is insufficient; hence the computer system must rely on auxiliary storage media and devices to complement this limitation. One such auxiliary storage device previously discussed was the magnetic tape drive. We learned that for those applications where data was to be accessed in a particular order or sequentially, magnetic tape proved to be an inexpensive and efficient storage medium. However, for those applications which do not lend themselves to the sequential processing of data, the use of the magnetic tape can be most inefficient. Thus, in these cases, other auxiliary media and devices must be employed. Most notable among these are the magnetic disk and the magnetic drum. These devices are similar in that both provide the capability for either sequential or random access of data.

Because of this facility for random or direct access, the disk and drum are called Direct Access Storage Devices (DASDs). The number and scope of computer applications employing DASDs are ever increasing. Some of the more spectacular examples include hotel and airline reservation systems, inventory systems, management information systems, etc. The majority of applications, however, are concerned with the processing of routine, everyday production jobs.

In order to avoid the confusion that could result from discussing the characteristics and operational aspects of the drum and disk concurrently, we shall initially examine the disk and later examine the drum in contrast to the disk.

Introduction

The magnetic disk device is the most common of today's random access auxiliary storage devices. Although there are differences among the various types of available disk storage devices, their principle of operation is basically the same. Each device consists of thin metal circular plates (disks) on which data can be recorded. Each side of these disks is coated with a magnetic recording material. One or more of these disks are stacked on a vertical shaft, each separated from the others by a small space. The disks revolve about this shaft at a very high, but constant, speed. As these disks are revolving about the shaft, *read/write access arms* are free to move in and out within the space between the disks (see Figure 12-1). In general, data can be recorded on the upper and lower surfaces of each disk except for the top and bottom disks. As a precaution against loss of data due to possible mishandling, the outer surfaces of the top and bottom disks are not used to store data.

At the end of the read/write access arms are the *read/write heads*. These heads are capable of sensing, or recording, patterns of magnetic spots which represent characters of information—numbers, letters, or special

**Disk Storage
Devices**

Read/write heads & access arms

Magnetic disks

Figure 12-1
IBM 2311 Disk Storage
Drive Showing Mounted
Disk Pack and Access
Arm

characters. The movement of these access arms is controlled by the Central Processing Unit (CPU) of the computer system.

Disk storage devices are currently available in three forms:

1. Devices with removable disks
2. Devices with nonremovable disks
3. Direct access storage facility

Removable disk devices   A disk pack device is composed of two components referred to as the *disk drive* and the *disk pack*. The disk drive contains the read/write mechanism and the motorized unit which controls the rotation of the disks. The disk pack is a removable unit generally containing either 6 or 11 disks (14 in. in diameter) on which data is recorded. A typical disk pack and disk drive are illustrated in Figure 12-2.

Just as magnetic tape must be mounted on a tape drive unit before it can be processed, so must the disk pack be mounted on the disk drive prior to processing. When a disk pack containing a data file is not being used, it should be dismounted and stored in a protective cover. These covers protect the disks from dust and other extraneous particles which may damage the disks. In addition, these covers are used when mounting and dismounting the disk pack from the disk drive.

Disk packs vary in size and storage capacity. Examples of two common disk packs and a disk cartridge are illustrated in Figure 12-3.

Nonremovable disk devices   Nonremovable disk devices are available in two models. One model contains a single module consisting of 25 slightly oversized (20 in. in diameter) disks, while the other model contains two such modules. Each module is capable of storing over 113 million characters on its 48 usable surfaces. Figure 12-4 illustrates a nonremovable disk device.

Depending on the particular model, a direct access storage facility consists of either five or nine distinct disk drives. In the smaller model, all five drives may be online (tied directly to and under the control of the CPU) at the same time, while in the case of the larger unit, eight of the nine available disk drives may be online at one time. The remaining disk drive is held in reserve in the event that one of the other eight in use should require service.

Direct access storage facility

    Regardless of the model, each disk pack consists of 11 disks, or a total of 20 recording surfaces. Thus, the five- and nine-disk drive models have a maximum storage capacity of 146 and 233 million characters, respectively. Figure 12-5 illustrates a nine-disk drive direct access storage facility.

Figure 12-2
Disk Storage Unit

2311 Disk storage drive   1316 Disk pack

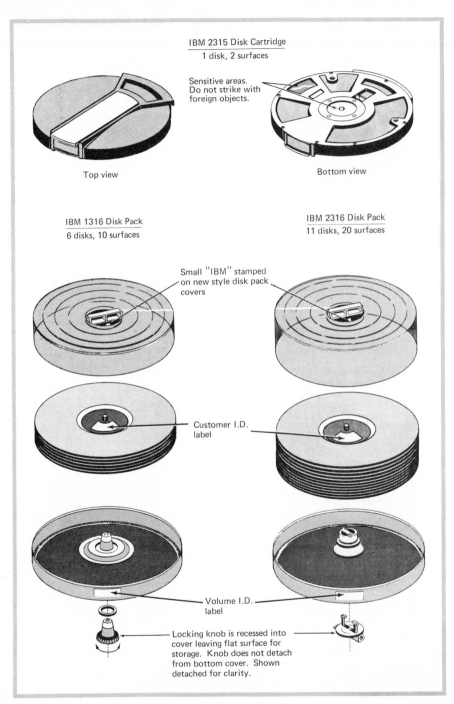

IBM 2315 Disk Cartridge
1 disk, 2 surfaces

Sensitive areas.
Do not strike with
foreign objects.

Top view

Bottom view

IBM 1316 Disk Pack
6 disks, 10 surfaces

IBM 2316 Disk Pack
11 disks, 20 surfaces

Small "IBM" stamped
on new style disk pack
covers

Customer I.D.
label

Volume I.D.
label

Locking knob is recessed into
cover leaving flat surface for
storage. Knob does not detach
from bottom cover. Shown
detached for clarity.

Figure 12-3
Disk Pack and Disk
Cartridge Assembly

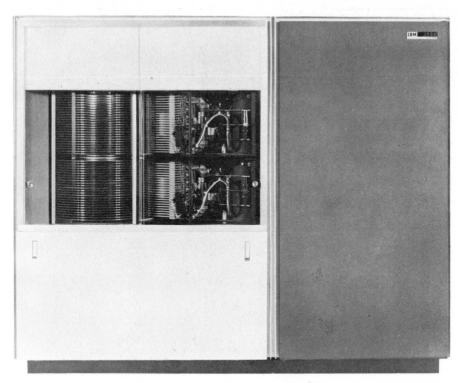

Figure 12-4
IBM 2302 Nonremovable
Disk Device

Self-study exercise 12-1

1. The disk and drum are _____ storage devices which complement
   _____ storage in a computer system.

◆   ◆   ◆

auxiliary
primary

Figure 12-5
A Direct Access Storage
Facility

2. DASD stands for _____.

◆ ◆ ◆

direct access storage device

3. A DASD can provide either _____ or _____ access of data.

◆ ◆ ◆

sequential
random

4. In general, data can be recorded on both the _____ and _____ surfaces of a disk, but not _____.

◆ ◆ ◆

top
bottom
on the outer surfaces of the top and bottom disks

5. Data may be accessed by _____ heads.

◆ ◆ ◆

read/write

6. Read/write access arms are controlled by the _____ of the computer system.

◆ ◆ ◆

CPU

7. Three types of disk storage device are: _____, _____, and _____.

◆ ◆ ◆

devices with removable disks
devices with nonremovable disks
direct access storage facilities

8. The disk pack device is composed of two components, namely, _____ and _____ .

♦ ♦ ♦

disk drive
disk pack

9. The disk drive unit contains the _____ mechanism and a motorized unit which controls the disk rotation.

♦ ♦ ♦

read/write

10. The disk pack contains _____ disks.

♦ ♦ ♦

6 or 11

11. Disk packs that are not in use should be _____ in their protective covers.

♦ ♦ ♦

stored

12. Protective covers are used in _____ and _____ disk packs from disk drives.

♦ ♦ ♦

mounting
dismounting

13. A nonremovable disk module generally contains _____ disks.

♦ ♦ ♦

25

14. The direct access storage facility contains _____ distinct disk drives.

♦ ♦ ♦

five or nine

15. Direct access storage facility contains _____ disks per pack.

◆ ◆ ◆

11

Disk Concepts

The disk track

Data is recorded on the surface of a disk by creating patterns of magnetized spots in the iron oxide coating of the disk. The recording surfaces of each disk are subdivided into concentric areas called *tracks* similar in structure to the concentric circles on a rifle or archery target. In a single rotation of the disk, the entire contents of a track can be read or written.

Data is recorded serially around a track with multiple data records being separated by blank spaces or interblock gaps (IBGs). In order to be able to uniquely identify and access any given record, each record is preceded by a *disk address record.* This record indicates the unique position of the data record on the disk pack (shown in Figure 12-6) and is automatically created each time a new data record is recorded on the disk.

Each track on the disk has the same total storage capacity. On tracks nearer the center of the disk, which are shorter than those near the outer

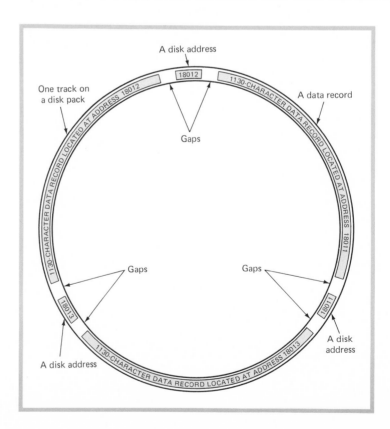

Figure 12-6
Typical Storage of Data
Records on a Disk Track

edge of the disk, the *density* of the data is greater. That is, the closer the track is to the center, the greater the number of bits recorded per inch of track.

The question arises, How would a file be recorded on disk if it consisted of more data than could be stored on a single track? That is, when a track is used to capacity and there is still more data to be recorded, where does the additional data go? Clearly, another track must be selected—but which one? To answer this question, we must determine which track can be reached most quickly by the read/write heads from their present position. Realizing that there is a read/write head for each usable disk surface and that these heads move together, one could reason that several other tracks are immediately accessible, without any movement of the access arms containing the read/write heads. These tracks would be those located directly above or below the existing, completely used, track. Each of these tracks would already have a read/write head positioned above it and hence be equally appropriate. It is common practice, however, to choose the same track on the next surface below the one just recorded. By repeating this process, all the tracks which line up vertically can be filled with data before the read/write access arms must be moved. Such a set of vertical tracks is referred to as a *disk cylinder.* Thus, a disk pack would contain as many cylinders as there are concentric tracks on a disk surface. This relationship is illustrated in Figure 12-7 with a typical disk pack consisting of 6 disks and 203 cylinders (tracks per disk).

The disk cylinder

A quick calculation reveals that, excluding the outer surfaces of the top and bottom disks, each cylinder contains ten tracks of disk storage, one per recording surface.

Now that we have determined the meaning of the terms *disk track* and *disk cylinder,* we can discuss how a given data record can be accessed.

In order to access a given data record from a disk, the address of the data record (the cylinder and track within the cylinder) must be known. Once this address is known, the read/write access arms can be moved to the proper cylinder, and the appropriate read/write head activated. Although all the read/write heads are capable of reading or writing data, only one can be in use at a time.

Accessing data records on disk

A common addressing scheme assigns the number 0 to the outermost cylinder, 1 to the adjacent inner cylinder, etc., for all cylinders on the disk. Similarly, each track within a cylinder is assigned a number, beginning with 0 for the uppermost usable track and increasing by 1s for each lower track (refer to Figure 12-7).

In some disk devices, the track is even further subdivided into smaller segments called *sectors.* In these cases, a data address would consist of a cylinder number, a track number, and a sector number.

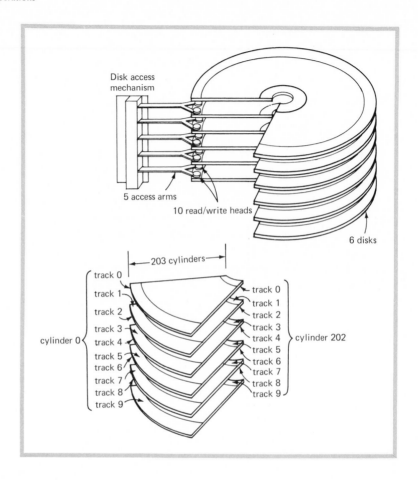

Figure 12-7
Typical Disk Pack and
Disk Access Mechanism
(IBM 2311 DASD Device
and 1316 Disk Pack)

Data access speed   As mentioned earlier, the speed at which data can be accessed from a storage device is of critical importance in a computer operation. Many programs are able to run only as fast as the speed at which data can be read or written from an auxiliary storage device. For this reason, it is important to understand what factors determine the access speed associated with a particular disk or drum.

The data access time for a direct access device is measured in four stages:

Seek Time   the time required to position the read/write heads over the cylinder containing the data to be accessed. This process is called a *seek operation*. On drums which have nonmovable read/write heads, no seek time exists. Seek time depends largely on the distance the read/write arms must travel. An average seek time for an IBM 2311 disk drive unit, for example, is about 75 milliseconds, with faster drive units being available. In the case of an IBM 2305, seek time is nonexistent since the read/write heads are fixed.

Head Selection the time required to electronically select the read/write head which will read or write the data. The head selected is the head which is positioned over the correct recording surface. This time is negligible in compairson with seek time.

Rotational Delay the time spent waiting for the desired data record to revolve around to a position directly beneath the read/write head. In the case of the IBM 2311, average rotational delay is 12.5 milliseconds. On the other hand, for the IBM 2305 the average rotational delay is less than 3 milliseconds.

Data Transfer the time required to transfer data from the disk to core storage at a relatively rapid (data transfer) speed. This speed depends on the density of the stored data bits and the rotational speed of the disk. Data transfer speeds for an IBM 2311 can be as high as 156,000 bytes of data per second, while for the IBM 2305 data transfer speeds can be as high as 3 million bytes per second.

The effective storage capacity of a disk unit is generally somewhat less than the total capacity of the unit or disk pack. For example, in the IBM 1316 disk pack illustrated in Figure 12-7, only 200 of the 203 usable cylinders are accessible at any one time. The remaining 3 cylinders are used as alternate tracks should trouble develop in any of the other 200 tracks. Therefore, in this case, the maximum usable capacity of the disk unit is over 7 million bytes (3,625 bytes per track × 10 tracks per cylinder × 200 cylinders).

Effective disk storage capacity

The large number of computer systems utilizing the magnetic disk for auxiliary storage is easily justified when one considers that, with respect to the above examples, any record on the disk can be accessed in from slightly over 90 milliseconds (average access time for an IBM 2311) to less than 3 milliseconds (average access time for an IBM 2305-1) and that data can be transferred to and from the disk and the CPU at up to 3 million bytes per second.

Self-study exercise 12-2

1. Data is recorded on the surface of a disk by creating patterns of _____.

◆ ◆ ◆

magnetized spots

2. The recording surfaces of each disk are subdivided into areas called _____.

◆ ◆ ◆

tracks

3. The entire contents of one disk track may be read or written in _____ rotation(s) of the disk.

◆ ◆ ◆

a single

4. Data is recorded _____ within a track.

◆ ◆ ◆

serially

5. Data records contained on the same disk track are separated by _____.

◆ ◆ ◆

blank spaces or IBGs

6. Each record stored on a disk is preceded by a(n) _____.

◆ ◆ ◆

disk address record

7. The storage capacity of each track on a disk is _____.

◆ ◆ ◆

the same

8. _____ is a term which refers to the number of bits recorded per inch around the disk.

◆ ◆ ◆

Density

9. Data recorded on tracks closer to the center of the disk are recorded with a(n) _____ density of data than those tracks closer to the outer edge of the disk.

◆ ◆ ◆

greater

10. When a track has been filled with data and there is still more data to be recorded, the additional data is generally placed on a track _____ in line with the one just completed.

◆ ◆ ◆

vertically

11. A set of vertical tracks constitutes a(n) _____ .

◆ ◆ ◆

disk cylinder

12. The most commonly used disk pack contains _____ disks and _____ cylinders.

◆ ◆ ◆

6
203

13. In order to address a record on disk, the _____ and _____ in which the record is located must be known.

◆ ◆ ◆

cylinder
track

14. Occasionally, a disk is subdivided beyond tracks and cylinders into
_____.

♦ ♦ ♦

sectors

15. Many programs process data as rapidly as the data can be _____ from
an auxiliary storage device.

♦ ♦ ♦

read

16. The access speed for data stored on disk depends on _____ factors,
namely, _____.

♦ ♦ ♦

four
seek, head selection, rotational delay, and data transfer time

17. In IBM 1316 disk packs, there are _____ usable cylinders.

♦ ♦ ♦

200

Magnetic Drum The magnetic drum represents another direct access storage device. It
consists of a nonremovable hollow metal cylinder coated with a magnetic
material similar to that which coats the surface of a disk. This drum rotates
at a constant speed of 3,000 to 12,500 rpm, depending on the particular
drum used. Data is read and written on the drum exactly as it is on disk.
That is, data is recorded serially on tracks which circle the drum as illustrated in Figure 12-8.

The disk and drum differ, however, in the fact that on a drum the
read/write heads are fixed in place, one head over each track. That is, in
the case of the disk unit, both the disk and the read/write heads physically
move to access a given data record, while in the case of the drum, only
the drum moves. Thus, the access time associated with a drum is generally
less than that associated with a disk. In addition, the storage capacity of
the drum is also less than that of the disk. Currently available magnetic
drum devices have access times ranging from 4 to over 90 milliseconds and
storage capacities of from 125,000 to 12 million bytes. Drum data transfer
speeds reach as high as 1 million bytes per second.

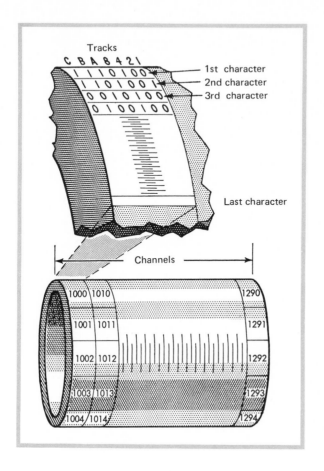

Figure 12-8
Schematic of Drum
Storage

Thus, the drum is utilized for those applications requiring rapid and direct access to relatively limited amounts of data. Since the capacity of the drum is limited and since the drum is not removable, it is sometimes necessary to dump all or part of the contents of the drum onto magnetic tape in order to make room for data required in a current application. When this data is needed at a subsequent date, it may be recorded back on the drum after other inactive data has been dumped onto magnetic tape.

Self-study exercise 12-3

1. The magnetic drum can be classified as a(n) _____ access storage device.

♦   ♦   ♦

direct

2. The magnetic drum consists of a(n) _____ hollow metal cylinder.

♦ ♦ ♦

nonremovable

3. Data records are recorded serially on _____ which circle the drum.

♦ ♦ ♦

tracks

4. The disk and drum differ in that read/write heads on a drum are _____, one head over each _____.

♦ ♦ ♦

fixed in place
track

5. The storage capacity of a drum is generally _____ that available with disk.

♦ ♦ ♦

less than

6. The drum is utilized for those applications requiring _____ access to relatively limited amounts of data.

♦ ♦ ♦

rapid and direct

File Organization   The type of applications which will be processed by a given computer system plays a vital role in determining (1) whether or not there is a need for auxiliary storage to complement the computer's primary storage capacity and (2) if there is such a need, whether it should consist of magnetic tape, magnetic disk, magnetic drum, or a combination of these and other auxiliary storage devices. The nature of a particular application is also a significant factor in determining the manner in which data is organized on the tape disk, drum, etc. That is, depending on how this data is organized and can be accessed, a data file is categorized as either sequential, direct, or indexed sequential.

Sequential files can be utilized with both sequential access and direct access devices. However, even when utilized with a direct access device, a sequential file would be processed sequentially, not randomly.

Sequential files

Direct files, on the other hand, can be stored only on a direct access device such as the drum or disk, facilitating random processing but not lending themselves to sequential processing.

Direct files

An indexed sequential file is utilized with a direct access storage device. Data records in an indexed sequential file may be processed randomly or sequentially, depending upon the nature of the application at hand. An indexed sequential file used in a banking application might be processed sequentially to produce a listing of the status of all account balances, while also being processed randomly when recording a deposit or withdrawal to a specific account.

Indexed sequential files

Self-study exercise 12-4

1. The type of application that will be processed by a given computer system plays a vital role in determining _____ .

♦ ♦ ♦

first, whether or not there is a need for auxiliary storage to complement the computer's primary storage capacity and second, if there is such a need, whether it should consist of magnetic tape, magnetic disk, magnetic drum, or a combination of these and other auxiliary storage devices

2. The type of application is also significant in determining the type of _____ to be utilized.

♦ ♦ ♦

file organization

3. A data file is categorized as either _____ , _____ , or _____ .

♦ ♦ ♦

sequential
direct
indexed sequential

4. Sequential files can be used with _____ access devices.

◆ ◆ ◆

both sequential and direct

5. Direct files can only be stored on a(n) _____ such as _____.

◆ ◆ ◆

direct access device
a magnetic disk or drum

6. Indexed sequential files utilize a(n) _____ storage device.

◆ ◆ ◆

direct access

7. Indexed sequential files may be processed _____.

◆ ◆ ◆

randomly or sequentially

IBM 2311
Disk Storage Unit   We shall now concern ourselves with some of the operational aspects of disk storage units. In order for this discussion to be as meaningful and practical as possible, we shall begin by again focusing our attention on the IBM 2311 disk storage unit, a very commonly used unit and one which is representative of both larger and smaller disk storage units.

The IBM 2311 disk storage unit is made up of the disk drive and the 1316 disk pack discussed earlier. (See Figure 12-2.)

Operating procedures   As shown in Figure 12-9, the 2311 contains very few manual controls. Consequently, the operator has relatively few functions regarding the operation of this unit.

In normal operation, the computer operator is generally called upon to mount and dismount disk packs. As many computer operating systems (disk operating systems) are stored on disk, they must be mounted and made ready before the system can be started up. At other times, the operator will generally mount a given disk pack only in response to a specific request by a processing program.

General. Before attempting to use a disk pack, the operator should examine it to make certain that it is the desired disk pack and that it is conditioned

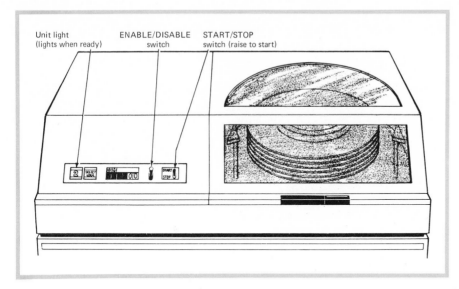

Unit light (lights when ready) ENABLE/DISABLE switch START/STOP switch (raise to start)

Figure 12-9
Manual Controls IBM
2311

to the temperature of the computer room. A disk pack is usually identified by paper labels located in two places on the disk. These labels are used to identify such items as the file recorded on the disk, the volume, the creator of the file, and occasionally the date created. An example of these labels and their location is shown in Figures 12-10 and 12-11. After the disk pack label is checked, the operator must make certain that the disk pack is properly temperature-conditioned. Two hours in the computer room is generally considered a sufficient period of time to condition a disk pack. In this way, costly reading and writing errors can be eliminated. It is generally recommended that room temperature be between 60 and 90°F and that the relative humidity be between 10 and 80 percent.

Because disk packs are removable units, they are frequently handled by operators. As with any precision instrument, care must be taken when handling and storing the disk pack. The following precautions should be taken to ensure error-free operation and long disk pack life:

Disk pack handling procedures

1. Always attach the bottom cover to the plastic disk pack cover. Even if there is no pack within the cover, this will protect the cover from accumulating dust.
2. Clean the protective cover frequently with a soft, lint-free cloth or paper to remove any accumulated dust.
3. If a cover becomes cracked or damaged, it should be replaced.
4. Never touch the actual disk surfaces or lay objects on the disks.
5. Do not stop the disks from turning on the disk drive. Even if

Place in trim cover only
Remove old label

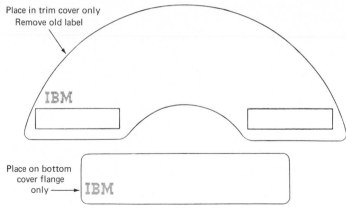

Place on bottom
cover flange
only ——→

Volume and Customer ID Labels

Volume ID Label

Figure 12-10
Sample Labels

Customer ID Label

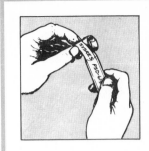

Figure 12-11
Disk Pack Identifier

the disk is coming to a stop, do not attempt to slow it down by touching the disk.

6. Keep all foreign objects such as tobacco and ashes away from the disk storage area.

7. Air filters located within the pack should be replaced as needed. Replacement should take place when the filter darkens to a grayish color.

8. The machine room should be vacuumed or wet-mopped daily to prevent accumulation of dust. *Do not* use a broom which may raise the dust into the air.

The following procedure should be followed when dismounting and mounting disk packs.

Mounting and dismounting disk packs

Dismounting.

1. Move the START/STOP switch on the disk drive to STOP, and wait until the rotating disk has come to a complete stop.

2. Take the disk pack cover and separate the cover from the bottom plate.

Figure 12-12
Disk Pack Protective Cover

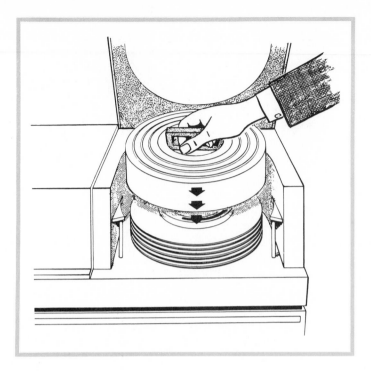

Figure 12-13
Placing Cover Over Disk
Pack

3. Carefully raise the cover of the disk drive by pressing down on the release lever located in the front of the unit. Then lower the disk pack cover over the disk pack (see Figures 12-12 and 12-13), being careful not to strike it against the disk.

4. With the disk pack cover resting securely on the disk pack, rotate it counterclockwise at least two full revolutions (shown in Figure 12-14). This will fasten the cover to the pack and also free the pack from the drive spindle.

5. Lift the disk pack cover containing the disk pack from the spindle.

6. Now replace the base of the cover by placing it against the bottom of the disk pack and turning the plastic knob on the base clockwise until secure.

The disk pack can now be stored away and, if necessary, a new pack mounted on the disk drive.

Mounting.

1. Hold the disk pack from the top, and remove the cover base by turning the bottom knob counterclockwise.

2. After the disk drive is opened and with the spindle at rest, place the pack on the spindle as shown in Figure 12-15.

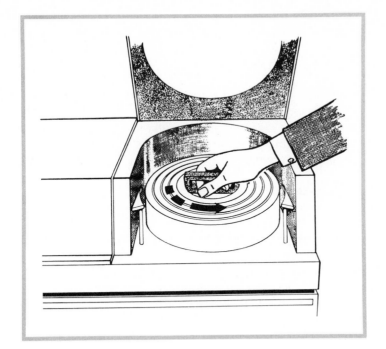

Figure 12-14
Turning Disk Pack Off
Spindle

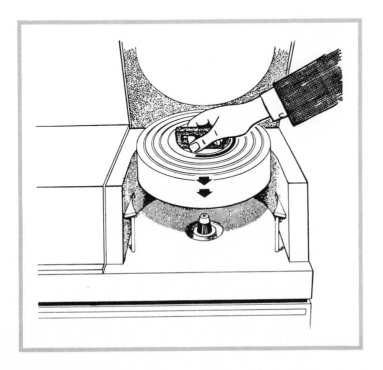

Figure 12-15
Lowering Disk Pack Onto
Spindle

3. Rotate the cover in a clockwise direction until firm resistance is met. The disk pack should now be secure on the spindle and released from the cover. Carefully lift the cover from the pack and store with its base.

4. Raise the START/STOP switch to START. This will start the disk rotating. After a few seconds when the proper speed is reached, the disk surfaces will be cleaned of dust and extraneous particles by a moving cleaning arm. Finally, the read/write access arms will move into position, and the disk is ready for use. This is noted by the green UNIT light, on the left, being lit.

The time period from when the disk drive is started until the UNIT light turns on is about 1 minute. If the light does not come on, the disk cannot be accessed by the computer.

Should the operator want to prevent access to a disk while the disk is mounted, he can turn the ENABLE/DISABLE switch to DISABLE. This will prevent access to the disk without his having to first stop the disk.

The SELECT LOCK indicator lights only when an error condition or hardware failure is sensed. If this light comes on, the operator should disable the disk drive unit and inform his immediate superior or call a repairman.

Self-study exercise 12-5

1. The IBM 2311 disk storage unit consists of the _____ and the 1316 _____.

♦ ♦ ♦

disk drive unit
disk pack

2. Operator controls on the 2311 include _____ switches, namely, _____.

♦ ♦ ♦

2
a START/STOP switch and an ENABLE/DISABLE switch

3. Before a disk pack is used, _____.

♦ ♦ ♦

its labels should be checked, and if the disk pack is the one desired, it should then be temperature-conditioned

4. Recommended operating condition for a disk pack is a temperature between _____ and a relative humidity between _____ .

◆ ◆ ◆

60 and 90° F
10 and 80 percent

5. The paper label attached to the disk pack and its cover is used to identify the _____ .

◆ ◆ ◆

file recorded on the disk, the volume, the creator of the file, and occasionally the date created

6. The disk drive cover should be opened only after the disk has _____ .

◆ ◆ ◆

stopped rotating

7. The fact that a disk pack is ready for use is indicated by _____ .

◆ ◆ ◆

the lighting of the UNIT light

8. A malfunction of the disk drive unit is noted by _____ .

◆ ◆ ◆

the lighting of the SELECT LOCK light

Other Direct Access Devices

IBM 2305 disk storage unit

The IBM 2305 disk storage device was designed for use with the IBM 370 Series computers. Each module of this unit consists of 6 permanent disks (10 recording surfaces) of 72 tracks each (64 accessible tracks and 8 alternate tracks). Data is read or written by one of 64 read/write heads contained in four access mechanisms which are permanently positioned around the disk (see Figure 12-16).

Each access mechanism contains two sets of read/write heads (eight usable and one spare head in each set).

IBM 2314 direct access storage facility

The IBM 2314 Direct Access Storage Facility is very similar to, although larger than, the 2311 disk drive unit. The disk pack, called an IBM 2316, contains

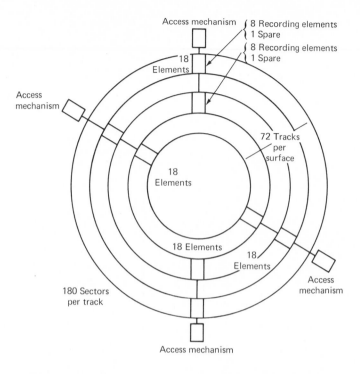

Figure 12-16
IBM 2305 Fixed Head
Storage and 2855 Storage
Control

11 metal disks with a total of 20 surfaces available for data storage. The disks are identical in size and function to the IBM 1316 disk pack used on the IBM 2311 disk drive unit and contain 200 cylinders of 20 tracks each (see Figures 12-3 and 12-5).

The storage capacity of the IBM 2316 disk pack is 38 million bytes of data, or over 5 times the storage capacity of the IBM 1316. The additional capacity is gained from the fact that the data is stored on the 2316 with twice the density used on the 1316, in addition to the fact that the number of tracks per cylinder on the 2316 doubled. The data transfer rate of the IBM 2314 disk drive unit is 312,000 bytes per second, double that of the 2311 disk drive unit.

A single 2314 storage facility can contain from two to eight disk drives, depending on the features ordered. Because of its great storage capacity and rapid data transfer speed, the IBM 2314 is frequently used in large-scale computer systems requiring a substantial online storage capability.

The Fastrand 11 mass storage unit by UNIVAC is a direct access device combining some of the general features of both drum and disk.

UNIVAC fastrand 11 mass storage unit

Data is stored on one of two drums. The total storage capacity exceeds 130 million characters of data. However, unlike a conventional drum, the read/write heads on the Fastrand 11 are not fixed. Instead, 24 read/write heads, attached to a common arm, must be moved into position over the desired track as the drum rotates at 870 rpms. The average access for the Fastrand 11 is 35 milliseconds. If one unit does not provide a sufficient auxiliary storage capacity, up to seven additional units can be added. The total storage capacity available with eight Fastrand 11 storage units exceeds 1 billion characters.

Another direct access storage unit which differs slightly from the disk and drum is the IBM 2321 Data Cell Drive. Designed to hold very large amounts of data, the IBM 2321 Data Cell Drive is capable of storing up to 400 million bytes of data.

IBM 2321 data cell drive

Instead of using a rotating disk or drum, the 2321 uses ten removable data cells as shown in Figure 12-19. Each data cell contains 200 magnetic strips which serve as the recording medium. Data is read or recorded by selecting the proper data cell, selecting the desired magnetic strip, and then

Figure 12-17
UNIVAC Fastrand II Mass Storage Unit

Table 12-1. Characteristics of Fastrand 11

Storage Capacity (Per Unit)	22,020,096 Words or 132,120,576 Alphanumeric Characters
Average Access Time	92 milliseconds
Recording Density	1,000 bits per inch
Tracks per Inch	106
Drum Speed	870 rpm
Moveable Read/Write Heads	64
Character Transfer Rate	153,540 characters per second
Word Transfer Rate	25,590 words per second
Fastbands (Fixed Read/Write Heads)	24
Fastband Average Access Time	35 milliseconds
Fastband Storage Capacity (per Unit)	258,048 characters
Write Lockout Protection	Yes
I/O Channels	1 or 2 per subsystem
No. of Units per Subsystem	8 (1,056,964,608 characters per subsystem)

Figure 12-18
IBM 2321 Data Cell Drive

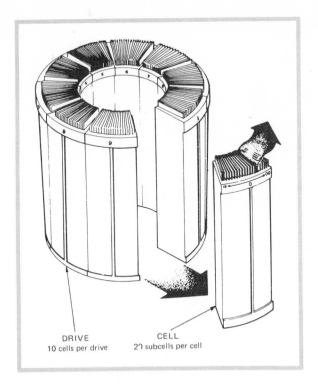

DRIVE
10 cells per drive

CELL
20 subcells per cell

Figure 12-19
Removable Data Cells

wrapping it on a rotating drum. Once the strip is mounted on the drum, data can be read from it or recorded onto it using a cylinder/track concept with movable read/write heads.

Although capable of great storage capacity, the 2321 has a relatively slow data access time. The time needed to access a given data item can be from 175 to 600 milliseconds. Average time to access another cylinder on the same magnetic strip is 95 milliseconds. The average rotational delay, once a strip is mounted on the drum, is 25 milliseconds with a data transfer rate of 55,000 bytes per second.

The IBM 2321 Data Cell Drive is used in applications demanding exceptionally large amounts of online direct access storage.

Self-study exercise 12-6

1. The IBM 2314 Direct Access Storage Facility is operationally similar to, but larger than, the _____.

◆ ◆ ◆

IBM 2311 disk drive unit

2. The IBM 2316 disk pack has over _____ times the total storage capacity of the IBM 1316.

♦ ♦ ♦

5

3. The IBM 2316 disk pack consists of _____ cylinders with _____ tracks per cylinder.

♦ ♦ ♦

200
20

4. The IBM 2314 Direct Access Storage Facility has twice the data transfer rate of the IBM 2311 because of the greater _____.

♦ ♦ ♦

density at which data is recorded

5. The UNIVAC Fastrand 11 system combines features commonly found on _____.

♦ ♦ ♦

disks and drums

6. The UNIVAC Fastrand 11 contains _____ movable read/write heads.

♦ ♦ ♦

24

7. The IBM 2321 Data Cell Drive is characterized by its great _____.

♦ ♦ ♦

storage capacity

8. The IBM 2321 Data Cell Drive consists of _____ cells, each containing 200 _____.

♦ ♦ ♦

10
magnetic strips

9. Data access time on the 2321 is relatively slow because of the time required to access and mount the _____ on the _____.

♦   ♦   ♦

magnetic strip
rotating drum

True-false exercise

1. Disk and drum are considered to be auxiliary storage devices.
2. The disk can be used as both a sequential and a direct access storage device.
3. The disk is primarily a sequential-type device.
4. Disk pack drives use fixed read/write heads.
5. Disk packs should always be stored within their protective covers.
6. Disk packs generally have the same storage capacities.
7. Nonremovable disks contain at least 50 disks.
8. The recording surface of each disk is divided into cylinders.
9. Each track on the recording surface of a given disk has the same total storage capacity.
10. A set of vertical tracks is referred to as a cylinder.
11. The address of a given data item stored on disk is its cylinder number.
12. Seek time is that time required to seek data from the disk and transfer it to the CPU.
13. A drum generally has a larger storage capacity than a disk.
14. The read/write heads on the disk and drum are operationally the same.
15. Drum access times are generally less than disk access times.
16. Disk packs should be conditioned to the temperature of the computer room before they are mounted on the disk drive.
17. The ENABLE/DISABLE switch is used to stop the rotation of the disk.
18. When mounting a disk pack on the spindle, the protective cover is rotated clockwise.
19. The SELECT LOCK indicator lights when the computer is retrieving information from the disk.
20. The UNIVAC Fastrand 11 combines features generally found on both the drum and disk.
21. Data cells are used when it is necessary to store extremely large amounts of data to be accessed directly.

Fill-in exercise

1. The disk and drum units are capable of both _____ and _____ accessing data.
2. The disk and drum are classified as _____ devices.
3. The disks revolve at a very high but _____ rate.
4. Data can be recorded on the _____ and _____ surfaces of most disks within a disk pack.

5. Read/write heads sense magnetic patterns on the surface of a drum or disk which represent _____.
6. The magnetic disk is the most common of today's _____ devices.
7. Disk packs vary in _____ and _____ capacity.
8. Two of the most common disk packs are _____ and _____.
9. DASD stands for _____.
10. The IBM 1316 disk pack contains _____ usable recording surfaces.
11. When data is recorded on a disk surface, each record is preceded by a(n) _____.
12. The number of bits or bytes recorded per inch on a given medium is referred to as _____.
13. A disk pack contains as many _____ as there are concentric tracks on any usable disk surface.
14. A disk pack with six disks would generally contain _____ usable recording surfaces.
15. The data access speed for a DASD is a combination of four factors, namely, _____, _____, _____, and _____.
16. The 2311 storage unit is comprised of a(n) _____ and a(n) _____.
17. In many computer systems the _____ system is contained on disk.
18. To be properly temperature-conditioned, a disk should be placed in the room for approximately _____ hours.
19. When the _____ light on an IBM 2311 disk drive unit lights, a malfunction or error is indicated.
20. When the disk drive unit is ready for use, the _____ light goes on.

Problems

1. Discuss the advantages and disadvantages of a direct access storage facility over a single disk drive unit.
2. Compare the capabilities of magnetic tape with those of magnetic disk and drum.
3. Compare the similarities and differences of the three forms of disk storage device currently available.
4. Define each of the following:
   - a. Track
   - b. Cylinder
   - c. Sector
   - d. Direct access
   - e. Access time
   - f. Data transfer speed
5. Define and give examples of the following:
   - a. Sequential access files
   - b. Direct access files
   - c. Indexed sequential files
6. Discuss the mounting and dismounting procedures for the removable disk packs.
7. State, in detail, those disk handling procedures discussed in this chapter.

TERMINALS

CHAPTER 13

Introduction The terminal is a relatively recent addition to the data processing (DP) family of input/output devices. Generally speaking, a terminal is an input/output device which facilitates two-way communication with a Central Processing Unit (CPU) or another terminal over great distances. In simpler terms, the terminal extends the power of the computer to a user who might not be located at the computer site.

The importance of the terminal can be seen in its use in the following areas:

1. Message Switching—routing messages entered at one terminal to one or more terminals at different remote locations. An example of a message-switching application is the use of terminals in large brokerage houses. These terminals receive stock transactions which are actually messages sent from the computer.

2. Remote Job Processing—sending computer jobs prepared at remote DP locations via a terminal to a CPU where these jobs are scheduled and processed. The results of the processing can then be sent back to the remote terminal from which the job originated or to one or more other remote terminals.

3. Inquiry or Transaction Processing—request for information from one of several remote terminals to a computer. The requested information can then be accessed from the central data files maintained at the computer site and sent back to the terminal. If the computer is requested to process data by executing a stored program, the operation is called *transaction processing*. An example of an inquiry and transaction processing application is an airline reservation system.

   This system allows a reservation clerk to determine if a given flight has a vacancy and, thus, whether he can book a passenger on that flight. The function of determining whether a flight has a vacancy is the inquiry portion of the application. Updating the data files to indicate a new or changed reservation requires processing a transaction program. This and other transaction programs are stored at the computer site and are activated by the reservation clerk at the terminal.

4. Data Collection—collection of data from one or more terminals to store for later processing. The value of a data collection system is its ability to enter data directly from source documents into data files on disk or magnetic tape. This process eliminates the need for keypunching the data onto cards and then reading them into the computer.

Terminals can take various shapes and forms, depending on the application and technique used for entering and displaying data. Some representative terminals are shown in Figure 13-1.

Telespeed tape-to-tape system

Teletypewriter

Telephone

TT Teledata tape transmitter/receiver

Data transmission combining telephone, transmitting subset, and transmitting terminal

Figure 13-1
Various Terminal
Equipment

Figure 13-2
Visual Display

The visual display terminal (Figure 13-2) is especially suited for inquiry-oriented applications, such as reservation systems. This type of terminal contains a keyboard on which inquiries can be quickly entered and a display screen on which information is easily viewed. The display screen, a cathode ray tube, is similar to a commercial television tube. These terminals are sometimes referred to as *CRT* terminals. Unlike a typewriterlike terminal which produces a permanent hard-copy record, visual display terminals erase old data continuously to display new information. The advantage of this terminal is its ability to display large amounts of information quickly.

With the rise of data processing applications using terminals, a new term for data processing has evolved. This is *teleprocessing*. Teleprocessing, a term formed from the words telecommunications and data processing, is used to describe data processing which includes the use of terminals.

Self-study exercise 13-1

1. The terminal extends the power of the CPU to _____ .

◆ ◆ ◆

a user who might not be located at the computer site

2. Four types of data processing applications which depend on terminals are _____ .

◆ ◆ ◆

message switching, remote job processing, inquiry or transaction processing, and data collection

3. Information entered at one terminal that is automatically routed to one or more terminals at different remote locations is an example of _____ .

◆ ◆ ◆

message switching

4. _____ is when computer jobs are prepared at remote DP locations and sent via terminals to a CPU where the jobs are scheduled and processed.

◆ ◆ ◆

Remote job processing

5. The type of data processing common to airline reservations is called _____ .

◆ ◆ ◆

inquiry or transaction processing

6. The term *teleprocessing* is formed from the words _____ and _____ .

◆ ◆ ◆

telecommunications
data processing

Concepts of Terminal Operation Despite the many variations in types of terminals and communications systems, teleprocessing systems generally consist of the following components:

Terminal the input/output device used to input data and capable of capturing and/or displaying data.

Modem data set which converts the data into a form suitable for transmission over a data communi-

Figure 13-3
Examples of
Communication Lines

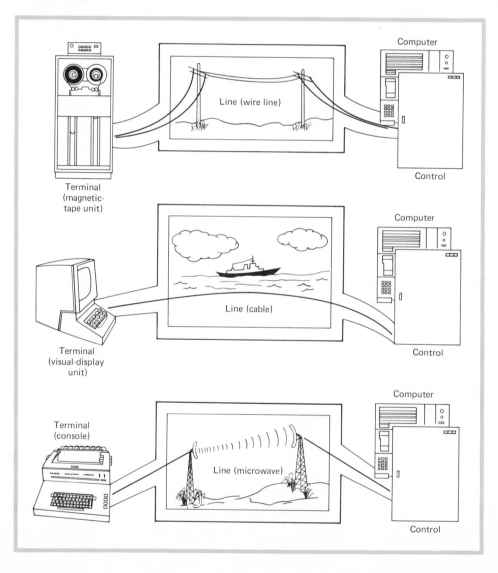

cation line. At the other end of the communication line, a second modem converts the data back into a readable format. These functions, called *modulation* and *demodulation,* respectively, will be discussed in more detail later in the chapter.

Communication Line connects the terminal to its receiving destination. Communication lines (also called *transmission lines*) can take the form of telephone or telegraph wires, cables, or even microwave transmission (see Figure 13-3).

Transmission Control Unit before data sent from a terminal can be entered into the CPU, it must pass through a transmission control unit. This device serves many functions, including the examination of special line control characters inserted in the transmitted data, the testing for errors which occur during data transmission, and separating the data received from several terminals into separate data elements. Finally, the data is sent from the transmission control unit to the CPU over a *multiplexer channel.* The multiplexer channel, a standard device on most computers, allows the attachment of several low-speed input/output devices to the CPU. These devices include card readers, card punch devices, printers, and transmission control units. The channel derives its name from the fact that several input/output devices can be sending data through a single multiplexer channel at the same time. This operation, called *multiplexing,* is achieved by dividing the channel path into several subchannels, one for each low-speed device.

A schematic of the relation between the above basic teleprocessing components is shown on the next page.

Modes of transmission. As mentioned earlier, the techniques and equipment used for transmitting data can vary widely depending on the terminal and its operating environment. Two of the most common types of transmission techniques are *asynchronous* and *synchronous.* Terminals which use asynchronous transmission surround each character of data transmitted by a pair of start and stop data bits (see Figure 13-4). These bits are used to separate characters and to synchronize the receiving station with the

Data transmission

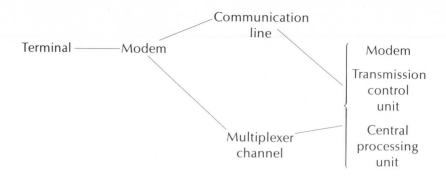

sending station. In asynchronous transmissions, each character is transmitted as a series of bits, one behind the other. For this reason, asynchronous transmission is also called *serial start/stop transmission*.

Synchronous transmission does not use start/stop bits. Instead, synchronous transmission relies on more complex hardware which can detect the transmission rate and automatically synchronize the receiving and transmitting stations. Since there is no need to insert start/stop bits into each character of data, transmission speeds are typically higher with the synchronous technique. In fact, most low-speed terminals utilize the

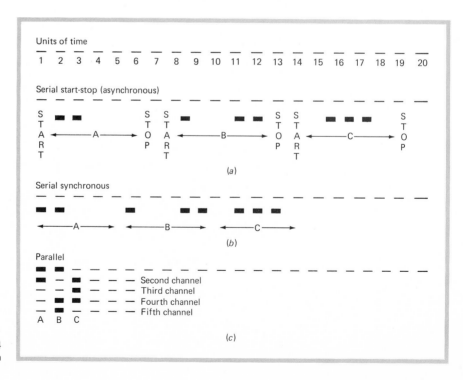

Figure 13-4
Modes of Transmission

asynchronous technique, while high-speed terminals use the synchronous technique.

A third method of data transmission is *parallel transmission* (Figure 13-4) and is used primarily for very high speed transmission. In this method, all the bits composing a single character are transmitted together, in parallel. This is accomplished by using a channel with several paths. As you can see from Figure 13-4, this technique is similar to the concept employed in a multiplexer channel.

Transmission codes. The data bit pattern used to represent a character or numeric value is based on a particular coding system. When data is transmitted over communication lines, the coding system, or transmission code, is usually determined by the type of terminal and line being used. Listed below are four common types of transmission codes.

Baudot Code	code using only 5 bits to represent each character. This permits a maximum of 32 possible combinations. Since 32 possible combinations are not sufficient to uniquely identify 26 alphabetical characters, 10 digits, and some required special characters, a *shift bit* was added to the code.
	A typewriter has a SHIFT key giving uppercase and lowercase characters. The Baudot system operates in the same manner. However, the shift is one of two characters placed in front of a particular field, either alphabetic or numeric (see Figure 13-5).
Four-of-eight Code	unique code representing each character as a combination of 8 bits consisting of exactly four 1 bits and four 0 bits. Since each character consists of a unique combination of the same number of 1 and 0 bits, errors can be easily detected.
Binary Coded Decimal (BCD)	an extension of the Hollerith code. The code is structured by converting the punched card designations into a binary pattern. The 12, 11, and 0 (zero) zones become 2-bit combinations and the digits 4-bit patterns. When this 6-bit code is expanded to 8 bits, it becomes the EBCDIC (Extended Binary Coded Decimal Interchange Code) code (shown in Figure 13-6).
ASCII Code	a code developed in an attempt to standardize communication codes. It stands for American Standard Code for Information Interchange. This

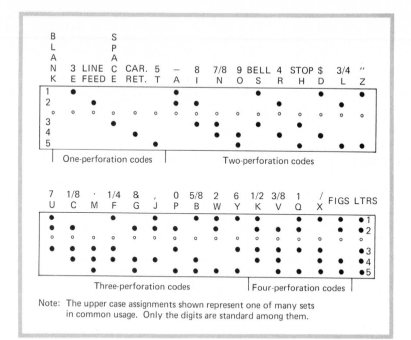

Figure 13-5
Example of Baudot Code

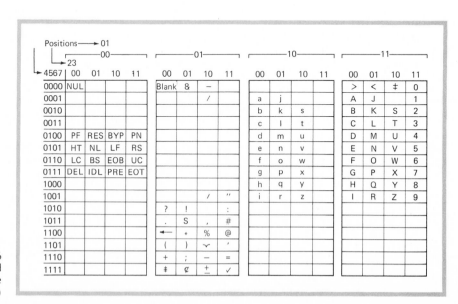

Figure 13-6
Extended Binary Coded
Decimal Interchange
Code (EBCDIC)

b_4 b_3 b_2 b_1	Column / Row	$^0{}_0{}_0$ = 0	$^0{}_0{}_1$ = 1	$^0{}_1{}_0$ = 2	$^0{}_1{}_1$ = 3	$^1{}_0{}_0$ = 4	$^1{}_0{}_1$ = 5	$^1{}_1{}_0$ = 6	$^1{}_1{}_1$ = 7
0 0 0 0	0	NUL	DLE	SP	0		P	@	p
0 0 0 1	1	SOH	DC1	!	1	A	Q	a	q
0 0 1 0	2	STX	DC2	''	2	B	R	b	r
0 0 1 1	3	ETX	DC3	#	3	C	S	c	s
0 1 0 0	4	EOT	DC4	$	4	D	T	d	t
0 1 0 1	5	ENQ	NAK	%	5	E	U	e	u
0 1 1 0	6	ACK	SYN	&	6	F	V	f	v
0 1 1 1	7	BEL	ETB	'	7	G	W	g	w
1 0 0 0	8	BS	CAN	(	8	H	X	h	x
1 0 0 1	9	HT	EM	)	9	I	Y	i	y
1 0 1 0	10	LF	SS	*	:	J	Z	j	z
1 0 1 1	11	VT	ESC	+	;	K	[	k	{
1 1 0 0	12	FF	FS	,	<	L	~	l	¬
1 1 0 1	13	CR	GS	−	=	M	]	m	}
1 1 1 0	14	SO	RS	.	>	N	^	n	I
1 1 1 1	15	SI	US	/	?	O	−	o	DEL

Figure 13-7
American Standard Code
(ASCII)

code represents each character as 7 bits plus 1 parity bit. Figure 13-7 shows the complete ASCII code. A version of this code used by Teletype Corporation is called the *data interchange code* and is illustrated in Figure 13-8.

Modulation and demodulation. As mentioned earlier, a modem or data set is required to translate the data into a form in which it can be transmitted across a communication line. This is necessary because the communication line transmits data as a continuous electric signal or wave form. Data entered at the terminal in the form of digital 1 and 0 bits must first be converted into a continuous signal by the modem before it can be transmitted. This action, called *modulation,* is repeated in reverse at the receiving terminal by a second modem. The process of converting the electronic signal, or wave, back into digital form is called *demodulation.* There are various methods of modulating electronic signals; however, three of the most commonly used methods are *amplitude modulation, frequency modulation,* and *phase modulation.*

AMPLITUDE MODULATION
In amplitude modulation (AM), the amplitude of the signal is varied according to the presence of a 1 or 0 bit. An example of amplitude modulation is shown in Figure 13-9.

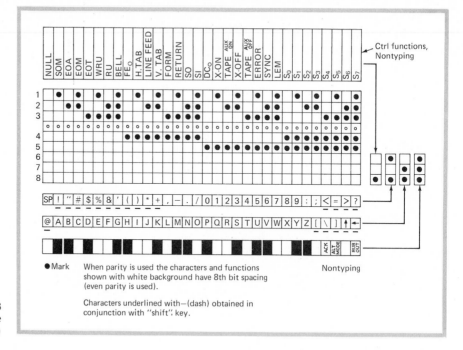

Figure 13-8
Data Interchange Code
(DIC)

FREQUENCY MODULATION

In frequency modulation (FM), the frequency of the signal is varied while the amplitude remains constant. The change in frequency matches the change from a 1 bit to a 0 bit of the digital signal (shown in Figure 13-9).

PHASE MODULATION

The third technique of modulation, phase modulation, denotes changes in bit value by altering the direction or phase of the signal wave. Since phase modulation can show only two directions of phase, this system is especially suited for binary representation.

A comparison of five of these techniques is shown in Figure 13-9.

Modes of operation. In every data communication facility there are three possible modes of operation. These are:

Simplex a mode of operation in which communication can take place in one direction only. For example, communications travel either from the terminal to the CPU or from the CPU to a remote device. A device using a simplex line can be used only as either input or output and cannot be interchanged.

Half Duplex   a mode in which communications can take place in both directions, but only one way at a time. If an input/output terminal utilizing a half-duplex line is used, the computer cannot print out a message while input is being fed in.

Full Duplex   a mode in which communication can take place in both directions at the same time. This is the most expensive type of the three, but it can decrease processing time up to 50 percent. Output is displayed while input is being transmitted.

Line speeds. The speed with which data can be transmitted varies, depending on the communication line. A measure of transmission speed is the *baud*. A baud can be loosely defined as one bit per second, although on some communication facilities this definition is not completely accurate. Most facilities are divided into one of four grades, depending on transmission speed. These are:

Telegraph Grade   the lowest-speed facilities. These channels were designed to handle a maximum of 75 bits per second as used on teleprinter service.

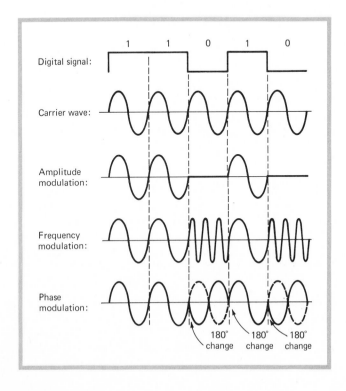

Figure 13-9
Modulation Techniques

Subvoice Grade channels lying between telegraph and voice grade (telephone channels) and falling in the range of 100 to 180 bits per second. Two common subvoice grade facilities support 150 and 180 bits per second.

Voice Grade channels deriving their name from their use as telephone facilities. Maximum data speeds on these channels are up to 2,400 bits per second, although some higher speeds can be obtained and lower speeds are frequently used.

Broad Band channels used for data communications requiring extremely high data transfer rates. These facilities allow transfer rates of 4,800 to 9,600 bits per second, and occasionally higher.

Communication line offerings. There are two distinct types of communication facilities offered by the common carriers (telegraph and telephone companies). These are *switched facilities* and *leased facilities*. Switched facilities are communication lines which make use of the telephone network. Before communication can take place between the terminal and receiving station, the transmission line must be established by dialing the correct telephone number. A leased line facility, also called a *private facility,* consists of a permanent line between two stations (point to point) or several lines connecting several stations (multipoint). Although a switched line requires the user to reestablish the connection each time he wishes to begin a terminal session, it may be cheaper than a leased line which is charged for on a rental or leased basis. A leased line, on the other hand, is always connected and available for data transmission.

Some communication services marketed by common carriers include the following:

Data-Phone a service, offered by Bell System companies, which allows the user to use the switched telephone system. A modem provided by the telephone company combines the functions of a telephone and a modulator/demodulator into a single unit. Special features can be ordered to allow for automatic dialing and answering.

Wide-area Telephone Service (WATS) a system allowing a user of the Bell switched network system to place an unlimited number of calls at a flat monthly charge or fixed hourly rate. The restrictions are that all calls be confined to a specified geographical area.

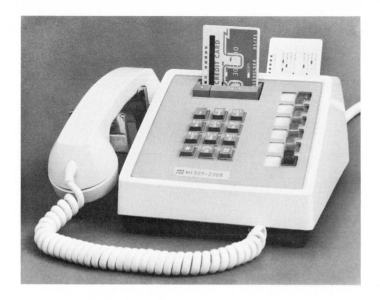

Figure 13-10
Data-Phone

Teletypewriter Exchange Service (TWX) the teletypewriter service offered in the United States by the Bell System and other telephone companies. Each subscriber has an individual line which is assigned a TWX number and listed in a nationwide directory. Each station is equipped with a dial, and numbers are dialed in the normal manner. The terminal provided is a teletypewriter with keyboard and printer. Line speeds of approximately 45 and 110 bits per second are available. Line charges are based on the length of the call and time used with established minimums.

Telex a worldwide exchange offered domestically by Western Union. This system is similar to TWX, using a teleprinter (equivalent to the teletypewriter) as a terminal. Unlike with TWX, however, calls can be placed by dialing no more than seven digits. Another difference is that charges for Telex do not include a minimum time period, as in the TWX system.

Self-study exercise 13-2

1. The modem is sometimes called a(n) _____.

◆　◆　◆

data set

2. The _____ method of transmission surrounds each character of data by start/stop bits.

♦ ♦ ♦

asynchronous

3. Most low-speed terminals use the _____ transmission method.

♦ ♦ ♦

asynchronous

4. A transmission method which transmits all the bits representing a character simultaneously is called _____ transmission.

♦ ♦ ♦

parallel

5. Three kinds of wave modulation are _____.

♦ ♦ ♦

amplitude, frequency, and phase

6. A facility in which communication can take place in only one direction is called _____.

♦ ♦ ♦

simplex

7. Communication in two directions, but not at the same time, is called _____.

♦ ♦ ♦

half duplex

8. A _____ facility permits communication in both directions at the same time.

♦ ♦ ♦

full duplex

9. The slowest kind of communication line is called _____ grade.

◆ ◆ ◆

telegraph

10. Communication lines which use the telephone system are called _____ grade.

◆ ◆ ◆

voice

The IBM 2741 Communications Terminal consists of an IBM Selectric typewriter, modified to permit transmission over communications lines. The 2741 is mounted on a typewriter stand (see Figure 13-11) which contains the operator controls necessary for communication.

IBM 2741 Communications Terminal

Terminal mode switch

Terminal power switch

Figure 13-11
IBM 2741
Communications Terminal

The 2741 transmits data using the asynchronous transmission method. This means that each character is transmitted with a pair of start/stop bits automatically inserted. Depending on how the terminal is ordered, either the BCD or EBCDIC transmission code will be supported. The 2741 is a nonbuffered terminal. This means that each character is transmitted as the key is pressed. A buffered terminal would allow the operator to key in a complete line or more before transmitting a single character. When the operator is satisfied that the entered data is correct, he can press a single key and automatically transmit the entire contents of the buffer to the receiving station.

The IBM 2741 keyboard   The keyboard on the 2741 (shown in Figure 13-12) is nearly identical to that used on the IBM Selectric typewriter. The only difference is the addition of a special terminal control key, the attention key (labeled ATTN) located on the right side of the keyboard.

When using the 2741, the keyboard will be in either an *opened state* or a *locked state*. When in an open state, keys can be pressed in the normal way. Each time a key is depressed, the character will print out on the paper form inserted in the terminal, and the character will be transmitted over the communication line. When the keyboard is locked, the operator will not be able to depress any keys with the exception of the ATTN key. These two keyboard states reflect the fact that the terminal is in either sending or receiving mode. When the terminal is in sending mode, the keyboard is open, and characters may be entered. When it is in receiving mode, the keyboard is locked, and the terminal can only receive data. The passing from receive to send mode is accomplished by sending or receiving special line control characters which are recognized by the terminal hardware.

Figure 13-12
IBM 2741 Keyboard and
Controls

Pressing the RETURN key when the terminal is in send mode will cause the following events to take place:

1. A carrier return (returns the type ball to leftmost position)
2. A single line of paper is fed
3. Insertion of an end-of-transmission line control character

The end-of-transmission character not only signifies the end of transmitted data but also causes the keyboard to lock and puts the terminal into receive mode. A message sent to the terminal will also end with a line control character. This character changes the terminal status back to send mode and reopens the keyboard. As you can see, all messages entered on the 2741 keyboard should end with the operator's pressing the RETURN key. These control characters are not visible to the terminal user (since they are not printed) and are automatically inserted and deleted by hardware.

As mentioned earlier, the ATTN key is the only key which may be pressed when the keyboard is locked. Pressing this key allows the operator to stop the printing of an unwanted message on the terminal and changes the terminal from receive to send mode. This is an especially important capability when a message of considerable length is being sent to the terminal and the operator decides it is not needed. Without depressing this key the keyboard would remain locked until the entire message had been received.

The use of the other special keys such as the TAB and BACKSPACE keys is dependent on the program which is communicating with the terminal.

For example, the BACKSPACE key will physically cause the type ball to backspace one position. But it is the responsibility of the program communicating with the terminal to recognize the backspace character and logically backspace the transmitted message.

A terminal MODE switch, located on the left side of the terminal stand, must be set to COM for communication to take place. When the switch is set at LCL, or local, the 2741 can be used as an ordinary electric typewriter (see Figure 13-11).

The technique for establishing a communication line and initiating transmission depends on the type of line being used. If a leased or private line is used, the line remains open at all times. When a switched line is used, the operator must establish the connection by dialing the appropriate number on a special device called a Data-Phone (shown in Figure 13-10). The Data-Phone is available from the telephone company and combines the functions of a data set with a telephone.

Initiating transmission

The procedure for initiating transmission when a leased line is used is:

1. With the ON/OFF switch set to OFF, set the terminal MODE switch to COM (see Figure 13-12).
2. Now turn the ON/OFF switch to ON. This will open the keyboard and place the terminal in a send status. Communications can now take place.

When a switched line is being used, the following procedure should be followed to initiate communications:

1. Set the terminal MODE switch to COM and the ON/OFF switch to ON.
2. Using the Data-Phone, press down the button labeled TALK. Lift the receiver, and dial the appropriate number.
3. Following one or more "rings," a sustained high-pitched tone will be heard. When the tone is heard, press the button on the Data-Phone labeled DATA, and replace the receiver in its cradle. The line is now established, and the keyboard is open.

Self-study exercise 13-3

1. The 2741 is almost identical to the IBM _____ .

◆ ◆ ◆

Selectric typewriter

2. The 2741 uses the _____ method for data communications.

◆ ◆ ◆

asynchronous

3. Either the _____ or _____ coding system can be used by the 2741.

◆ ◆ ◆

BCD
EBCDIC

4. The major difference between the 2741 and Selectric typewriter keyboard is the _____ key.

◆ ◆ ◆

ATTN

5. The 2741 keyboard alternates between a(n) _____ and a(n) _____ state.

♦ ♦ ♦

open
closed

6. These states correspond to whether the terminal is _____ or _____ data.

♦ ♦ ♦

sending
receiving

7. The keyboard is locked whenever the _____ key is pressed.

♦ ♦ ♦

RETURN

8. The _____ key is used to interrupt printing on the terminal and place the keyboard in a _____ mode.

♦ ♦ ♦

ATTN
sending

9. A terminal MODE switch can be set to either _____ or _____.

♦ ♦ ♦

COM
LCL

10. When in _____ mode, the 2741 can be used individually as a Selectric typewriter.

♦ ♦ ♦

LCL

11. Data transmission is initiated over a switched line by dialing the appropriate number on a(n) _____ .

♦ ♦ ♦

Data-Phone

12. When a number is dialed on a Data-Phone, the _____ button should be depressed.

♦ ♦ ♦

TALK

13. After the line has been established, the _____ button should be depressed.

♦ ♦ ♦

DATA

Other Terminals

Burroughs TU 100 series data collection and inquiry system

The Burroughs TU 100 Series terminal (shown in Figure 13-13) is specially designed for use in applications involving data collection and inquiry. Unlike the IBM 2741 which uses the common electric typewriter as an input/output device, the TU 100 employs a specially designed input/output station.

Input is entered in several ways. Four function keys located on the terminal keyboard allow the operator to identify the type of message which is following. The message may be a request for information, a transaction, or a file update. In addition to the function keys, there is a set of 10 numeric keys. An unlimited amount of numeric data can be entered through these keys.

The TU 100 also includes a card reader, badge reader, and credit card reader. In all three cases, data is entered onto the cards in the form of punched holes, using the Hollerith code. Punched cards of 20 to 80 columns can be read.

The ADDS consul CRT terminals

The ADDS Consul Series of CRT (cathode ray tube) terminals are examples of visual display terminals. All output is displayed visually as a light source on a rectangular screen (see Figure 13-14).

The Consul terminals can operate in three modes. In the *conversational mode,* data entered on the keyboard is transmitted one character at a time, as it is entered. In *page mode,* the complete screen can be filled with data and edited. When sufficient data has been entered, a single key

Input

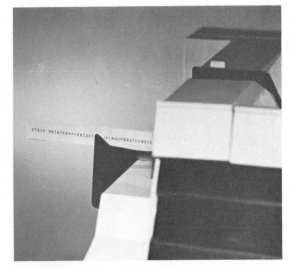

Printer output

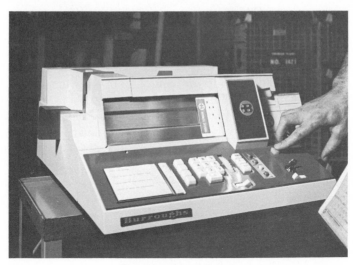

Document printer output

Figure 13-13
Burroughs TU 100
Terminal

can be pressed which will transmit all the data at one time. In this mode, the terminal "buffers" the input data. Finally, the terminal can operate in *message mode,* which transmits data one line at a time.

One of the advantages of this CRT terminal is its ability to edit data quickly and easily before transmission. Special keys located on the Consul keyboard allow the operator to insert or delete characters displayed anywhere on the screen without changing any other characters.

Figure 13-14
ADDS CRT Consul 880

In addition to alphanumeric data, the Consul terminals can also display graphics, which are especially useful for scientific and engineering applications. Standard alphanumeric characters can be displayed simultaneously with graphics for easy annotation.

If a hard copy (printed copy) of the data displayed on the screen is desired, an attachment feature allows the connection of a thermal page printer or a standard teletype (Model 33 or 35). Printing of the contents on the display screen takes place by simply pressing the appropriate control key.

Like the Burroughs terminal, the Consul terminals can be connected over a hard wire, leased, or switched communications line.

The Burroughs TC 500 The Burroughs TC 500 is an example of a terminal which is in fact a minicomputer. Containing memory and programmable logic circuitry, the TC 500 is sometimes referred to as an "intelligent terminal." Combining the features of a terminal and small computer, this device offers several operating capabilities not possible with the standard terminal. These are:

1. Data can be compacted and edited at the terminal before being transmitted to the CPU.
2. The CPU is relieved of many of its housekeeping activites.

3. Full buffering allows faster transmission of data between the terminal and the CPU.

The input unit on the TC 500 consists of a typewriterlike keyboard, a set of numeric keys, and 16 program select keys. The program select keys allow the operator to identify a transaction or inquiry request which is about to be entered. Above the keyboard is a series of operator/system communication lights. These lights, under program control, guide the operator in the entering of data and also indicate the current status of the device.

The TC 500 printer prints at 20 characters per second, but under program control it can skip blank spaces at 200 characters per second.

In addition to keyboard entry and printed output, the TC 500 supports the attachment of an 80-column card reader/card punch and paper-tape reader and punch.

Self-study exercise 13-4

1. Input can be entered on the Burroughs TU Series terminals through the _____ keys.

◆ ◆ ◆

four function

Figure 13-15
Burroughs TC 500

2. The Burroughs TU terminal also serves as a(n) _____ , _____ , and _____ reader.

◆ ◆ ◆

card
badge
credit card

3. Cards input to the TU 100 must be punched using the _____ code.

◆ ◆ ◆

Hollerith

4. Output can be produced on the TU 100 on a(n) _____ printer or a(n) _____ printer.

◆ ◆ ◆

strip
unit document

5. The ADDS CRT terminal is an example of a(n) _____ terminal.

◆ ◆ ◆

visual display

6. The three operating modes of the ADDS terminal are _____ , _____ , and _____ .

◆ ◆ ◆

conversational
page
message

7. In addition to alphanumeric data, these terminals can display _____ .

◆ ◆ ◆

graphics

8. The Burroughs TC 500 terminal has the unique feature of being _____ .

♦ ♦ ♦

programmable

9. A terminal with a programmable feature is called a(n) _____ terminal.

♦ ♦ ♦

intelligent

10. In addition to the typewriter keyboard and numeric keys, the TC 500 includes 16 _____ keys.

♦ ♦ ♦

program select

11. A series of _____ located above the keyboard on the TC 500 are used to guide the operator through his activity.

♦ ♦ ♦

operator/system communication lights

End-of-chapter Exercises

True-false exercise

1. Terminals may be used only if they are in close proximity to the CPU.
2. The use of terminals in data processing is called teleprocessing.
3. The terms *modem* and *data set* are synonymous.
4. Multiplexing is achieved when several subchannels are combined into one channel path.
5. One of the most common types of transmission techniques is *synchronous.*
6. Parallel transmission is a type of data transmission.
7. The four-of-eight code is a common type of transmission code.
8. The process of converting the electric signal, or wave, back into digital form is called modulation.
9. Simplex, half duplex, and full duplex are three examples of modes of operation for a data communication facility.
10. The keyboard on the IBM 2741 terminal is identical to that of the IBM Selectric typewriter.
11. The IBM 2741 terminal may be used only on leased lines.

12. The Burroughs TU 100 terminal was designed to be similar in function to the IBM 2741.
13. The ADDS Consul is capable of operating in three different modes.
14. A disadvantage of the ADDS Consul terminal is that no hard copy of the displayed data is available on the terminal.
15. The Burroughs TC 500 terminal is an example of an "intelligent terminal."

Fill-in exercise

1. The modem performs the functions of _____ and _____.
2. Two common types of data transmission are _____ and _____.
3. The _____ transmission code represents each character with 5 bits.
4. Speeds of 4,800 to 9,600 bits per second and higher are possible on _____ channels.
5. Communication lines which are leased and permanently connected are called _____ lines.
6. The two types of coding systems used by the IBM 2741 terminal are _____ and _____.
7. There are _____ function keys on the Burroughs TU Series terminals.
8. An example of a visual display terminal is the _____.
9. There are _____ operating modes on the ADDS Consul Series terminal.
10. A special feature that displays characters useful for scientific and engineering applications is called the _____ feature.
11. An example of an intelligent terminal is the _____.

Multiple-choice exercise

1. An input/output device which facilitates two-way communication with a CPU is a
   a. card reader
   b. line printer
   c. terminal
   d. all the above
   e. none of the above
2. The process of gathering data from one or more terminals and storing it for later processing is known as
   a. collective processing
   b. data collection
   c. terminal usage
   d. all the above
   e. none of the above

3. Visual display terminals are sometimes referred to as
   a. CRT terminals
   b. TV terminals
   c. tube terminals
   d. all the above
   e. none of the above
4. The device which converts data into a form in which it can be transmitted over a data communication line is called
   a. a modem
   b. a data converter
   c. a communications adapter
   d. all the above
   e. none of the above
5. Serial start/stop transmission is also known as
   a. synchronous transmission
   b. asynchronous transmission
   c. serial transmission
   d. all the above
   e. none of the above
6. When 2 additional bits are added to the binary coded decimal (BCD) code, the expanded version is known as
   a. binary coded decimal
   b. expanded binary coded decimal
   c. extended binary coded decimal interchange code (EBCDIC)
   d. all the above
   e. none of the above
7. Most line transmission facilities are divided into several grades; one is
   a. telegraph grade
   b. subvoice grade
   c. broad band
   d. all the above
   e. none of the above
8. The only difference between the IBM Selectric typewriter keyboard and the IBM 2741 terminal keyboard is
   a. the RETURN key
   b. the BACKSPACE key
   c. the SHIFT key
   d. all the above
   e. none of the above
9. An example of a terminal designed for use in applications involving data collection and inquiries is the
   a. Burroughs TU 100 Series terminal

    b. ADDS Consul Series
    c. Burroughs TC 500 Series
    d. all the above
    e. none of the above

10. An example of a CRT-type display terminal is the
    a. Burroughs TU 100 Series terminal
    b. ADDS Consul Series terminal
    c. IBM 2741 terminal
    d. all the above
    e. none of the above

Discussion questions

1. Discuss several of the components of a teleprocessing system.
2. There are many techniques used for transmitting data called modes of transmission. Discuss two types of transmission techniques.
3. Discuss several transmission codes that might be used in teleprocessing.
4. The speed with which data can be transmitted is dependent upon the type of communication line. Most facilities are divided into four grades depending upon transmission speed. Discuss three of the possible grades.
5. Discuss the major features of the IBM 2741 terminal, the Burroughs TU 100 terminal, and the ADDS Consul terminal.

UNIT V

THE CONSOLE AND CONSOLE TYPEWRITER

THE CONSOLE CHAPTER 14

Introduction   The computer operator must have some means of communication with the computer system he is controlling. This communication link is accomplished with the aid of the computer's System Control Panel, commonly referred to as "the console." By monitoring the System Control Panel, the operator can determine the status of any job running within the computer. Should any type of intervention be required, the operator would generally be alerted via the console. More often than not, these communications would generally be accomplished through the console typewriter—the topic covered in Chapter 15. However, our major concern at this point is familiarizing the operator with the console.

The console affords the operator direct control over the entire computer configuration. When a condition requiring intervention is noted, direct action is taken by the operator through the computer's console. That is, the operator, through the console, controls normal program processing throughout the entire computer system.

In this chapter, you will be introduced to the console of an IBM 360/30—its purpose and physical configuration. The components and features of the console will be described and discussed in detail. Basic operator procedures, performed via the console, will be outlined and illustrated.

Throughout our discussions of the console, we will refrain from merely listing facts or notes. Rather, we will present material only as it relates to the topic under discussion, thus reducing the confusion which arises when too many disjointed facts are presented in rapid succession. Therefore, if a particular feature on the console is not discussed immediately, it will be subsequently.

Self-study exercise 14-1

1. The purpose of the System Control Panel is to _____.

◆ ◆ ◆

facilitate communication between the operator and the computer system

2. The System Control Panel is generally referred to as _____.

◆ ◆ ◆

the console

3. The operator, through the console, controls _____ throughout the entire computer system.

◆ ◆ ◆

normal program processing

Figure 14-1
An IBM System/360
Model 30 with Printer
Keyboard

IBM System/360 Model 30 Console

The vehicle for our discussions of the computer console (System Control Panel) will be an IBM System/360 Model 30. The Model 30 is compatible with other models within the System/360 Series. Thus, this type of console is representative of models ranging upward from the Model 30 (i.e., Model 40, Model 50, etc.). The basic principles discussed with reference to the Model 30 console are applicable and transferable to other manufacturers' computer systems.

The System Control Panel

The IBM System/360 Model 30 is a solid state, high-speed data processing system. Figure 14-1 depicts the Model 30 excluding the usual complement of peripheral equipment. The printer keyboard, a typewriterlike device, is added to the system so that communication between the operator and the system can be documented. Our discussions will be based on a system with an average complement of peripheral equipment.

The operator controls needed for normal processing are contained on the IBM 2030 System Control Panel (console). This console configuration is illustrated in Figure 14-2.

Using this console, the operator can control the performance of the normal computer tasks of turning power on and off, loading programs for processing, resetting the system after a stoppage has occurred, displaying

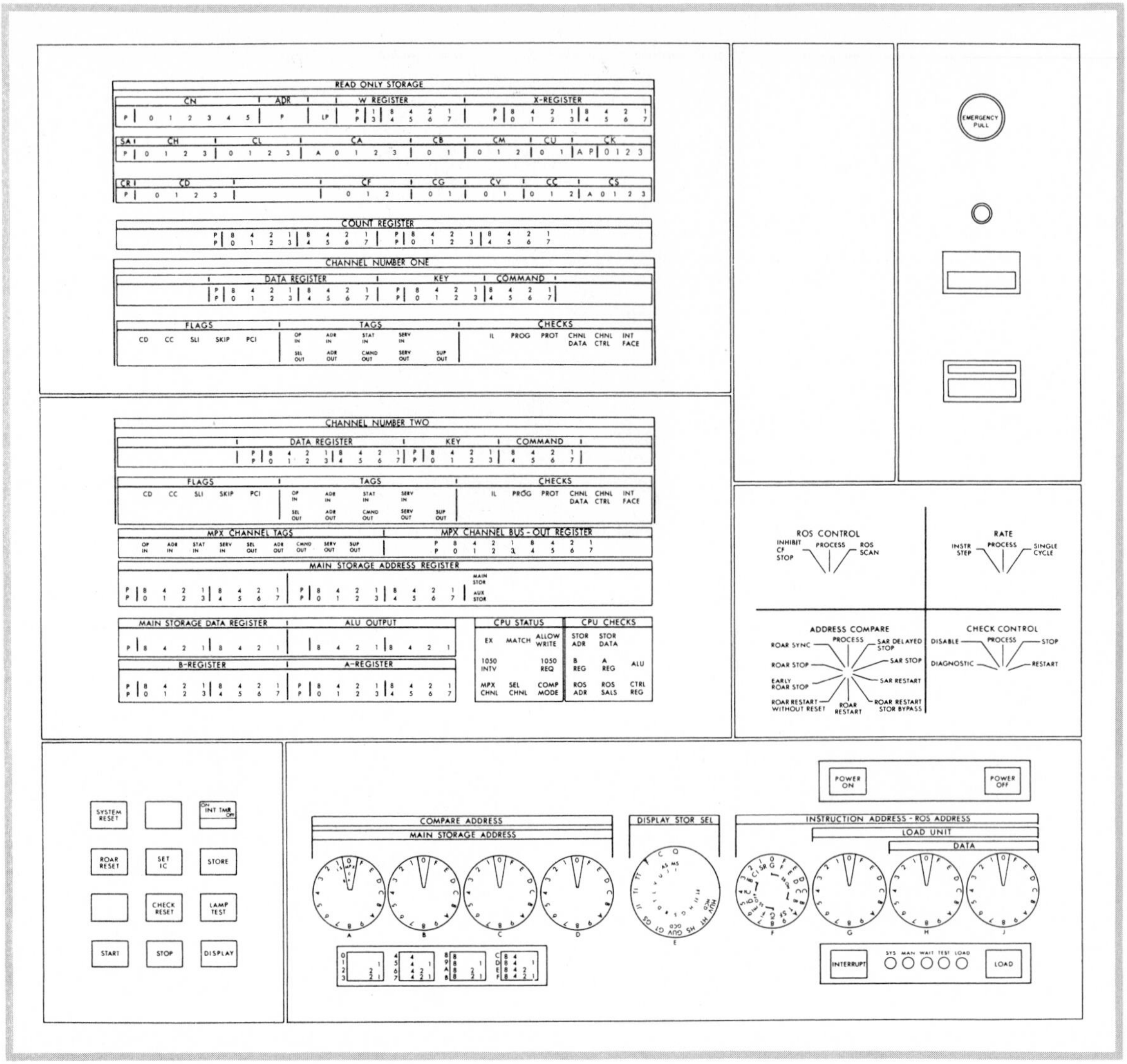

Figure 14-2
IBM 2030 System Control
Panel (Console)

and storing data, and initiating program processing. All these tasks are controlled through the use of the various switches and dials on the console face. To facilitate usage of the console, it has been divided into three major components. They are:

1. Operator Control Panel (OCP)
2. Operator Intervention Section (OIS)
3. Customer Engineer Section (CES)

Purpose. The OCP is located in the lower righthand corner of the console. The lined portion of the console face in Figure 14-3 represents the OCP. A blow-up of the lower portion of the panel is illustrated in Figure 14-4.

    The OCP contains those controls required when the CPU is operating under full control of the supervisor or controlling program. Thus, a minimum of direct manual intervention is required. The computer operator continuously monitors the OCP and intervenes only when alerted. As the panel's name indicates, it provides the means by which the operator can

Operator control panel (OCP)

Figure 14-3
IBM 2030 System Control Panel (Console)

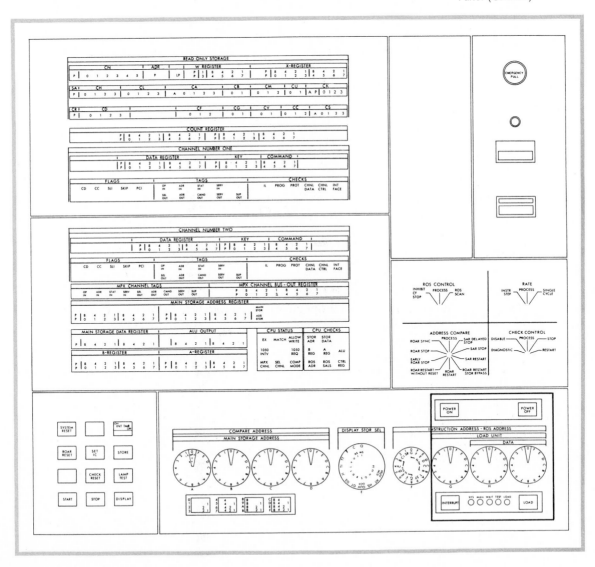

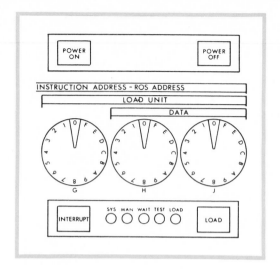

Figure 14-4
Blow-up of Lower Portion
of IBM 2030 System
Control Panel

exercise control over the entire computing system. Through the use of the OCP, the operator can

1. Determine and control the distribution of power
2. Denote the status of the computer system
3. Communicate with the computer
4. Perform Initial Program Loading (IPL)

The OCP indicates the distribution of power throughout the computer system. Should insufficient electric power be supplied, the computer would be rendered inoperative and subject to severe equipment malfunctions and damage. Through use of the OCP, control over the power supplied to the computer system is exercised.

By means of a series of lights on the console face, the status of the computer system is shown. The operator monitors these lights and ascertains the existing status of the system. In this manner, one is aware of whether the computer is in a state awaiting data, processing a program in the CPU, or under manual control of the operator.

Whatever conditions may be noted, the operator must have a means of communication with the machine. The OCP enables the operator to issue necessary commands to the computer system. In addition, data can be directly transmitted into the CPU by the operator via the OCP on the console.

Prior to the processing of any programs, the computer system must be prepared to accept data. This procedure is noted as IPL or Initial Program Loading. Through the IPL sequence, a program is placed into the computer.

This special program will prepare the computer for processing and permit processing to commence.

Having discussed the purpose of the OCP, let us now examine those components with which the operator will work. It is suggested that the student continually refer to the illustrations provided to avoid confusion and ensure component identification. The discussion of components of the OCP will be divided into four units. These units are:

1. EMERGENCY PULL switch and USE meters
2. Pushbutton keys
3. Display lights
4. Rotary switches

EMERGENCY PULL switch and USE meters.   The EMERGENCY PULL switch and USE meters are situated in the upper righthand corner of the console face. The USE meters are found directly beneath the pull switch, as shown in Figure 14-5. As the name implies, the EMERGENCY PULL switch is only used in an emergency. It is designed to be used in case of fire, serious machine malfunction or the existence of severe electric power fluctuations. Extraction of the red-colored emergency switch to its outermost position will sever all internal electric connections and prevent power from entering the

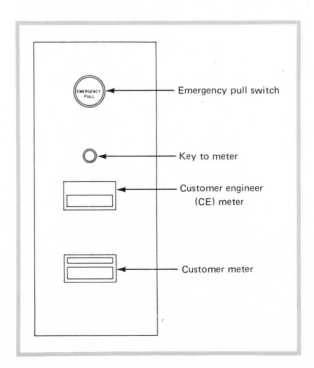

Figure 14-5
USE Meters, EMERGENCY
PULL Switch, and Meter
Key

computer and attached peripheral units. When this condition exists, the console's POWER ON pushbutton is rendered ineffective.

To restore the computer system to a normal operating status, the computer manufacturer must be called. *Only* authorized company maintenance personnel are permitted to perform this service and return the computer to its normal operating state.

With the computer operating within its normal state, one of the console's USE meters is running. The console has two direct-reading meters. Whenever the CPU is in use, one of the two meters is operational. The topmost meter is the *customer engineer (CE) meter,* with the other referred to as the *customer meter.*

Through the use of the key switch, located directly above the CE meter, control is exercised over which meter is running. The manufacturer's Customer Engineer (CE) holds the key for this switch. Under normal processing, the switch is positioned such that the customer meter is used. Whenever the CE is required to perform maintenance on the CPU, he will key the switch to a position that will stop the customer meter and cause the CE meter to run. Thus, whenever the CPU is in use, one of the two meters is recording the time used.

Pushbutton keys. The pushbuttons located on the console face are rectangular in shape. The markings on each pushbutton identify and are indicative of the pushbutton's purpose. Figure 14-6 illustrates the location of the pushbuttons. Table 14-1 notes the pushbuttons contained within the OCP and the effects of their use.

Display lights. The series of display lights is designed to indicate the state of the computer system. The display lights associated with the OCP are

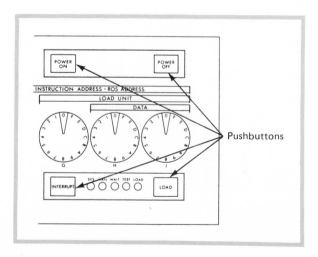

Figure 14-6
Pushbuttons Contained
within the Operator
Control Panel

Table 14-1. Pushbutton Keys on the OCP

Pushbutton	Depressing This Key
POWER ON	initiates the flow of power throughout the system, including all online units. This key is backlighted and will develop a pink glow when initially pressed. Upon completion of the POWER ON sequence when the CPU is ready to begin processing, the key will appear white in color.
POWER OFF	initiates the POWER OFF sequence within the total computing system, thereby removing electric power from each of the online units.
INTERRUPT	requests an external interruption causing the processing to stop. The system recognizes this type of interruption only if it was originally programmed to do so.
LOAD	permits IPL to begin.

situated between the INTERRUPT and LOAD keys, as shown in Figure 14-7. These display lights are described in Table 14-2.

Rotary switches. The last group of components of the OCP is the LOAD UNIT switches. This group of three rotary switches is located directly above the previously discussed display lights, as shown in Figure 14-8. The three switches are bracketed by the label *LOAD UNIT*. This nomenclature is

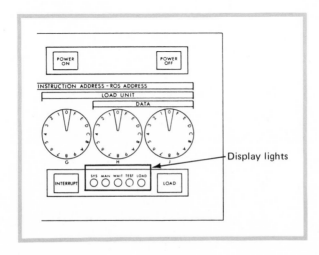

Figure 14-7
Display Lights within the
Operator Control Panel

Table 14-2. Display Lights on the OCP

Display Light	This Light Becomes Lit When
SYS (System)	either the CE or the customer meter is running.
MAN (Manual)	the CPU enters a stopped state and no processing is being performed.
WAIT	the CPU is in a wait state, with no instruction processing occurring and awaiting the input of data.
LOAD	the LOAD pushbutton is depressed. Upon completion of IPL, the light will turn off.
TEST	any of the console's four rotary control switches—ROS CONTROL, RATE, ADDRESS COMPARE, and CHECK CONTROL,—is set to a position other than the PROCESS setting.

printed directly above the switches. The switches may also be identified by the letters G, H, and J (read left to right), located underneath the individual switches.

The dial face of each switch has the 16 settings available marked in hexadecimal (0 to 9, A to F). When referring to this group of three switches, the term *LOAD UNIT switches* is used.

The purpose of the LOAD UNIT switches is to assign the address of the input/output unit that will read the IPL program. This address is

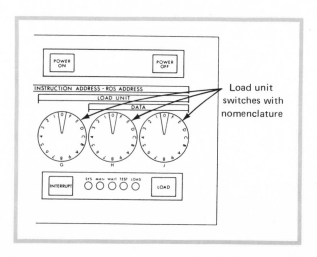

Figure 14-8
Rotary Switches G, H, and J—the Load Unit Switches, within the Operator Control Panel

registered by the actual settings on switches G, H, and J and can be entered into the computer by depressing the LOAD pushbutton.

The OCP enables normal program processing to occur with a minimum of operator intervention. When processing is interrupted, the operator must intervene to reset the computer to its normal state. This intervention is accomplished using another section of the console. This division of the console is designated as the *Operator Intervention Section (OIS)*.

Self-study exercise 14-2

1. The printer keyboard allows for documentation of communications between the _____ and the _____.

♦ ♦ ♦

operator
computer system

2. Some of the tasks that the operator can perform using the console are _____.

♦ ♦ ♦

turning power on and off, loading programs for processing, resetting the system after a stoppage, displaying and storing data, and initiating program-processing

3. The three major components of the console are the: _____, _____, and _____.

♦ ♦ ♦

OCP (Operator Control Panel)
OIS (Operator Intervention Section)
CES (Customer Engineer Section)

4. The operator, through the OCP, can _____, _____, _____, and _____.

♦ ♦ ♦

determine and control the distribution of power
denote the status of the computer system
enable the operator to communicate with the computer
perform IPL

5. The OCP is subdivided into _____ units which are: _____.

◆ ◆ ◆

four
EMERGENCY PULL switch and USE meters, pushbutton keys, display lights, and rotary switches

6. The EMERGENCY PULL switch is used in the event of a serious _____.

◆ ◆ ◆

machine or electrical malfunction

7. Once used, the EMERGENCY PULL switch can only be reset by a(n) _____.

◆ ◆ ◆

authorized manufacturer's representative

8. The console is equipped with two USE meters which are known as the _____ and _____ meters.

◆ ◆ ◆

customer engineer (CE)
customer

9. During normal operations, the _____ meter is operating, and when maintenance is being performed, the _____ meter is operating.

◆ ◆ ◆

customer
CE

10. The particular meter running at any given time is controlled by the position of the _____.

◆ ◆ ◆

key switch

11. The four pushbuttons available on the OCP are: _____ , _____ , _____ , and _____ .

◆ ◆ ◆

POWER ON
POWER OFF
INTERRUPT
LOAD

12. Depressing the INTERRUPT key causes _____ .

◆ ◆ ◆

normal processing to be interrupted

13. The MAN (manual) display light goes on when _____ .

◆ ◆ ◆

the CPU is stopped and no processing is taking place

14. When the CPU is idling and awaiting an instruction, the _____ light comes on.

◆ ◆ ◆

WAIT

15. The LOAD light becomes lit during _____ .

◆ ◆ ◆

IPL

16. When any of the console's four rotary control switches is set to other than PROCESS, the _____ light comes on.

◆ ◆ ◆

TEST

17. The console is equipped with _____ LOAD UNIT switches.

◆ ◆ ◆

three

18. The purpose of these LOAD UNIT switches is to _____.

♦ ♦ ♦

assign the address of the input/output unit that will read the IPL program

Operator intervention section (OIS)

Purpose. This section of the console provides those controls necessary for operator intervention in normal program processing. The controls which comprise the OIS are not found in any one area of the console, but are situated throughout the face of the console. Through the OIS, the operator directs the computing system to

1. Initiate system operation in any of several modes
2. Perform store and display functions
3. Provide a system reset capability

The IBM 360/30 is a third-generation computer. The normal mode of operation would be consistent with third-generation languages. There may arise, upon occasion, the necessity of operating in a mode other than third generation. For example, one may desire to program in a language used on an IBM 1400 Series system (a second-generation computer). Through the OIS, the operator could direct the Model 30 to react as if it were an IBM 1400 Series computer. The computer would then operate under the constraints of the second-generation device.

The OIS enables the operator to perform storage and display functions. Data contained at specific storage locations within the computer can be retrieved and displayed on the console face. Similarly, data may be placed into storage locations within the computer. The addresses of the selected storage locations must be assigned by the operator via the console.

When any type of stoppage occurs within processing or following the completion of an operator intervention, the computer system must be reset prior to the resumption of normal operation. This system reset capability is accomplished through the OIS. In performing this function, the computer reestablishes all internal controls and check circuits, clears registers, and ensures communication is complete to online peripheral equipment. The system is now ready to recommence processing data.

The OIS has a configuration similar to that of the OCP. The OIS is composed of rotary switches and pushbuttons. The paragraphs which follow will discuss the controls within the OIS.

Data and address entry switches. In our discussion of the OCP, we were introduced to three rotary switches. These represent three of the nine rotary

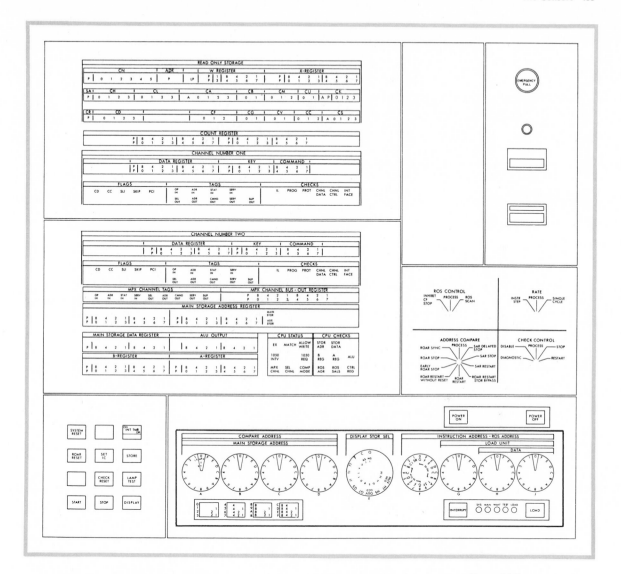

Figure 14-9
All Nine Rotary Switches
Contained on the
Console Face

switches provided for the operator's use. The nine rotary switches, situated at the bottom of the console, are illustrated in Figure 14-9.

Each rotary switch is identified by an alphabetic character—A, B, C, D, E, F, G, H, and J. Every switch has 16 possible settings. Each setting represents one hexadecimal character.

We have already discussed the group of switches G, H, and J—the LOAD UNIT switches. Those groupings of switches utilized with the OIS will be discussed within their functional groups.

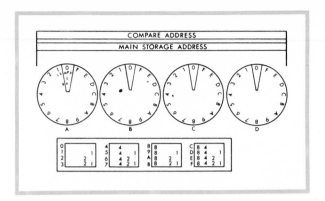

Figure 14-10
Rotary Switches A, B, C,
and D

Figure 14-10
Rotary Switches A, B, C,
and D

ROTARY SWITCHES A, B, C, AND D

This group of four switches is used to manually enter the addresses of storage locations into main storage. Figure 14-10 illustrates this grouping of switches. Note, that there are two labels above this group of switches. They are:

1. MAIN STORAGE ADDRESS
2. COMPARE ADDRESS

These switches are utilized to enter both compare and main storage addresses.

When this switch grouping is designated to imply a MAIN STORAGE ADDRESS, the switches are used to access a specific storage location within the CPU. The address of the chosen storage location is assigned by dialing it through the settings on switches A, B, C, and D. The operator has the option of displaying the contents stored at that address or putting new data into that storage location.

Under the COMPARE ADDRESS designation, switches A, B, C, and D are used to perform a comparison check. The operator completes this checking procedure to ensure that a specific, correct address exists. The selected address is stored within a register within the CPU—the Main Storage Data Register (MSDR) or the Read Only Storage (ROS) address register. The address dialed on switches A, B, C, and D is then compared with the address stored in either of the above registers. Should this comparison reveal that the desired address does not exist, the program being processed would be terminated.

ROTARY SWITCHES H AND J

In our previous discussion, we remarked about the capability of placing new data into a storage location via the console. The question arises as

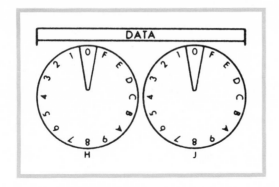

Figure 14-11
Switches H and J, with
Nomenclature DATA

to how the data will be transmitted through the console. Two rotary switches, H and J, are provided for this purpose.

We note that both of these switches help compose the LOAD UNIT grouping—switches G, H, and J. When utilized to represent an item of data, *only* switches H and J are used. Each specific grouping of switches is designed to accomplish a particular task.

Directly above switches H and J is the nomenclature DATA, as shown in Figure 14-11. Using both switches, we can create an 8-bit byte of data. Each switch setting represents one hexadecimal digit or 4 bits. Combining both hexadecimal digits, we have 8 bits or a full byte. Thus, 1 byte of data, for an IBM 360 Series system, can be created.

ROTARY SWITCHES F, G, H, AND J

This grouping of switches represents the last operational group on the console face and is depicted in Figure 14-12. The label above the switches F, G, H, and J reads INSTRUCTION ADDRESS-ROS ADDRESS. It also denotes that the switches must be used together.

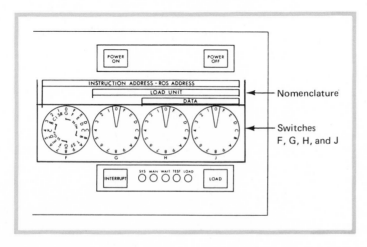

Figure 14-12
Rotary Switches F, G, H,
and J—with Nomenclature
INSTRUCTION ADDRESS-
ROS ADDRESS

Switches F, G, H, and J are utilized to construct addresses of storage locations. Within these storage locations are computer instructions which, when read, will initiate some type of processing.

DISPLAY STORAGE SELECTION SWITCH

To adequately carry out his responsibilities, the computer operator must have access to all storage areas within the system and the knowledge of how to control them. He must have the means to select the correct operational procedure required, the desired storage area, and the storage location to be addressed. The DISPLAY STOR SEL switch enables the operator to control his activities.

The display storage select switch carries the nomenclature DISPLAY STOR SEL, but is more commonly referred to as switch E. It is found amid the other rotary switches (see Figure 14-9) and appears as shown in Figure 14-13.

Utilizing switch E, the operator selects the type of operation to be performed. The operator may elect to:

1. Display data at addressable storage locations within main or auxiliary storage or the CPU registers
2. Store data at addressable storage locations within main or auxiliary storage or CPU registers
3. Select the particular storage area to be addressed

Two settings are most often used to complete the above tasks. They are:

1. The Main Storage or MS position
2. The Auxiliary Storage or AS position

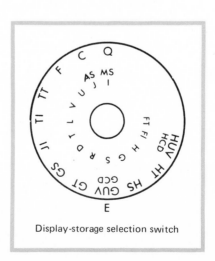

Display-storage selection switch

Figure 14-13
Switch E—the Display
Storage Selection Switch

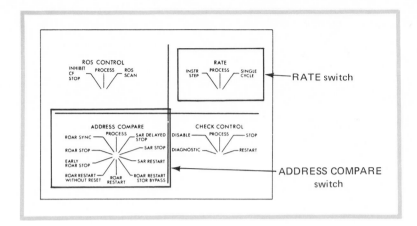

Figure 14-14
The Four Rotary
Operation Control
Switches

Each setting is dialed into position in front of a tricolored background of red, gray, and white (reading down). When the letters MS or AS are seated directly in front of the center, gray-colored strip, switch E is properly positioned.

Using the MS or AS settings, main storage or auxiliary storage may be accessed. Thus, with switch E set at the MS position, the storage or display of data contained within main storage may be performed. Should the operator desire to access any portion of auxiliary storage, the AS setting would be used. The MS position represents switch E's normal setting.

All the previously discussed switches are completely accessible and under constant control of the console operator. There are specific rotary control switches normally used by only the CE, but whose functions are occasionally useful to the operator in processing data. These switches will be discussed in the next section of this chapter.

Operation control switches. The operation control switches are four rotary switches normally used by the CE. All four of these switches are shown in Figure 14-14. The control switches are provided to permit the computer to function in any of several ways. Though there are four operation control switches, only two are considered to be part of the OIS. They are the:

1. RATE switch
2. ADDRESS COMPARE switch

The RATE switch has three operational settings from which the computer operator may select, as illustrated in Figure 14-15. The settings are:

1. PROCESS position
2. SINGLE CYCLE position
3. INSN STEP (Instruction Step) position

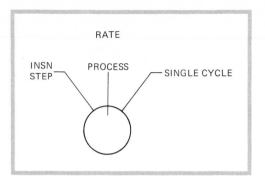

Figure 14-15
The RATE Switch, with
the Three Possible
Settings

For normal program processing, the RATE switch is set into the PROCESS position. Programs will be run with no intervention required. This is the normal operational setting.

When the display of data at specific storage locations is required, the RATE switch is moved to the SINGLE CYCLE position. The system will complete only *one* display cycle at a time. That is, the contents of only one storage location are revealed at a time. This cycle is initiated by pressing the START pushbutton (located in the lower lefthand corner of the console face).

The INSN STEP instruction step setting allows for a similar one-cycle-type control. In this setting, the computer will process *one* complete program instruction and then stop. In this stopped state, the CPU is not processing any data; it is awaiting some type of control intervention by the operator. This state is identical to that condition produced when the STOP pushbutton is used.

To process the next instruction, the START pushbutton must be pressed. The computer will again process only one program instruction and then enter a stopped state. When program instructions are processed in this manner, the term applied to this process is *chaining*.

An important note to the operator: the RATE switch settings should not be changed unless the STOP key has been pressed. The CPU must be in a stopped, nonprocessing state. Failure to do this will cause the computer to react in an unpredictable manner, with the responses given being equally as unpredictable.

The ADDRESS COMPARE switch is used to control the internal, electric circuit wiring used when a comparison of the contents of storage addresses is to be made. It ensures that contents of the selected CPU registers are correctly compared and, subsequent to the comparison, dictates the system's response to the results of that comparison.

Each setting of the ADDRESS COMPARE switch provides for a specific circuit match-up and response from the computer system. There are

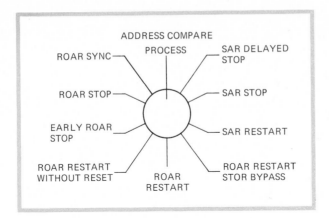

Figure 14-16
The ADDRESS COMPARE
Switch

10 settings available, as shown in Figure 14-16. With the switch set in the PROCESS position, normal program processing will occur.

The two operation control switches we have not previously discussed are the CHECK CONTROL and ROS (Read Only Storage) CONTROL switches. They are not included within the OIS of the console. In all cases, though, to permit normal processing, *all* four of the operation control switches must be set in their PROCESS positions. When not so set, the TEST display light will light.

Pushbuttons. Several pushbutton keys have been provided within the OIS to assist in the manual operation of the console. Table 14-3 describes the five keys within the OIS and their functions. Each of the five pushbuttons is located in the lower lefthand portion of the console and appears as shown in Figure 14-17.

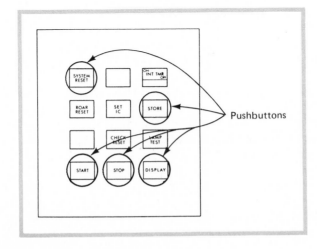

Figure 14-17
The Five Pushbuttons
Found within the OIS

Table 14-3.   Pushbutton Keys on the OIS

Pushbutton	Depressing This Key
SYSTEM RESET	causes the entire computer system to reset. That is, all registers are cleared; all internal checks, limits, and controls are set to their zero values; all initial conditions for processing data are reestablished; and the computer is ready to receive a set of instructions to begin processing. *Note:* none of the offline peripheral devices will be affected by the reset procedure.
STOP	places the CPU in a stopped state. The system is not processing any data or completing an instruction sequence. The system is awaiting directive action by the operator. Upon entering the stopped state, the MAN (manual) display light will become lit.
START	directs the execution of instructions in a manner defined by the RATE switch.
STORE	causes the byte of data, specified by rotary switches H and J, to be entered into the selected storage location. This storage area is designated by switch E, the DISPLAY STOR SEL switch. The storage address is designated by rotary switches A, B, C, and D. Data may be entered into a CPU register or an address within main or auxiliary storage. For the STORE operation to occur, the CPU must be in a stopped state.
DISPLAY	causes the contents of a selected storage location to be displayed on the console face. The storage area is specified by switch E. The storage address is set on switches A, B, C, and D. The CPU must be in a stopped state for this pushbutton to be effective.

This concludes our discussion of the OIS. The components discussed within the OIS and the OCP provide the operator with ability to control, and intervene within, normal program processing. The remaining portion of the SCP—the customer engineer section (CES)—is reserved for use by the manufacturer.

Customer engineer section (CES)   The Customer Engineer Section (CES) of the console is intended for use *only* by the Customer Engineer (CE), the manufacturer's representative. The controls provided within the CES are used during the repair or testing of the computer system. The components of the console not discussed within the OIS and OCP are contained within the CES. These components should not be tampered with or altered by the computer operator.

Self-study exercise 14-3

1. The _____ Section of the SCP provides for operator intervention in normal processing.

◆ ◆ ◆

Operator Intervention

2. With the aid of the OIS, the operator directs the system to _____.

◆ ◆ ◆

initiate system operation, perform store and display functions, and provide a system reset capability

3. Normal operation of the IBM 360/30 is in _____-generation mode. However, through the OIS, the operator can cause the IBM 360/30 to act as a _____-generation computer.

◆ ◆ ◆

third
second

4. If the operator wants to place data directly into a particular storage location, he must _____.

◆ ◆ ◆

assign the specific storage location via the console

5. When the computer system is reset after an interruption in processing, the computer _____.

◆ ◆ ◆

reestablishes all internal controls and check circuits, clears registers, and ensures that communication is complete to online peripheral equipment

6. Rotary switches identified as A, B, C, and D are used to _____.

◆ ◆ ◆

      manually enter the addresses of storage locations into main storage

7. The group of switches A, B, C, and D can be used to designate a(n) _____ ADDRESS or a(n) _____ ADDRESS.

◆ ◆ ◆

MAIN STORAGE
COMPARE

8. Rotary switches, identified by the letters H and J, are used when _____.

◆ ◆ ◆

     new data is to be placed into a storage location

9. The INSTRUCTION ADDRESS-ROS ADDRESS group of switches consists of _____ switches identified by the letters _____. These switches are used to construct addresses of storage locations which contain _____.

◆ ◆ ◆

four
F, G, H, and J
computer instructions

10. Switch E is also labeled _____.

◆ ◆ ◆

DISPLAY STOR SEL

11. Utilizing the DISPLAY STOR SEL switch, the operator can _____.

◆ ◆ ◆

     display data at addressable storage locations within main or auxiliary storage or the CPU registers, store data at addressable storage locations, and select the particular storage area to be addressed

12. Operation control switches are normally used by the _____.

◆ ◆ ◆

customer engineer (CE)

13. The two operation control switches which are generally considered to be part of the OIS are the _____ and _____ switches.

◆ ◆ ◆

RATE
ADDRESS COMPARE

14. During normal operations, the RATE switch is set to the _____ position.

◆ ◆ ◆

PROCESS

15. When it is necessary to display the contents of a specific storage location, the RATE switch is set to the _____ position.

◆ ◆ ◆

SINGLE CYCLE

16. If the RATE switch is set to the INSN STEP position, the computer will process _____ and then _____.

◆ ◆ ◆

only one program instruction
stop

17. The _____ switch is used when a comparison of the contents of storage addresses is to be made.

◆ ◆ ◆

ADDRESS COMPARE

18. Within the OIS, _____ pushbutton keys are provided. They are _____

◆ ◆ ◆

five
SYSTEM RESET, STOP, START, STORE, and DISPLAY

19. Depressing the DISPLAY key, in conjunction with the setting of switches _____, causes _____.

A, B, C, and D
the contents of the selected storage location to be displayed on the console face

20. The STORE key, when depressed, causes _____.

the byte of data specified by rotary switches H and J to be entered into the selected storage location

Basic Console Operations

With the conclusion of our discussion of the console, the reader should now be familiar with the console—its configuration, concepts of operation, and available controls. Our next step is the implementation of the concepts learned in performing some fundamental computer operations. These console procedures represent the simplest tasks for which a console operator might be responsible. The console operations discussed are:

1. POWER ON
2. LAMP TEST
3. POWER OFF

POWER ON

The POWER ON sequence supplies power to the CPU and all online I/O units. A system reset occurs for the CPU and all online I/O units during this sequence. The POWER ON sequence bypasses all offline devices.

The POWER ON sequence for the CPU is:

1. Press the POWER ON key.
2. Wait for the white POWER ON light to become lit. The time required for the POWER ON light to become lit is dependent upon the number of online I/O units. The I/O units are sequenced ON one by one. If power cannot be adequately supplied to a unit, further POWER ON sequencing is interrupted, and the POWER ON light will remain off. When corrective action has been taken and power has been supplied to all units, the POWER ON light becomes lit. The system is now ready to perform as directed.

During the POWER ON sequence, the operator should monitor the console face. In particular, he should ensure that the LP (low pressure)

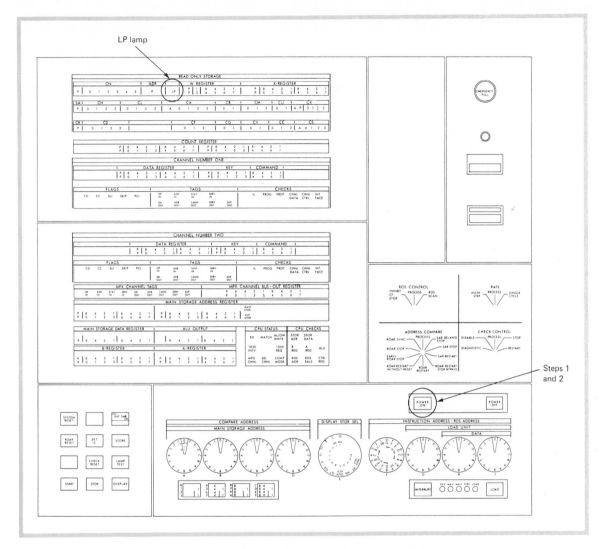

LP lamp

Steps 1 and 2

display light has not become lit. If this light becomes lit, the POWER ON sequence will be interrupted and not completed. A lit LP lamp indicates that the temperature within main storage (CPU) has not reached the required operating level and that air pressure within the computing system is insufficient for computer operation.

The following procedure must be used when applying or removing electric power to online I/O devices:

1. Press the STOP key on the computer console face, and wait for the MAN (manual) display light to come on.

Figure 14-18
POWER ON Operation for the System

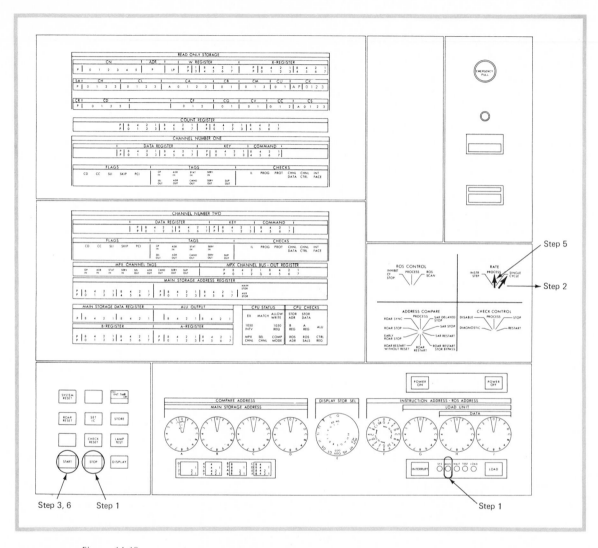

Figure 14-19
POWER ON Sequence
for online I/O Devices

2. Set the RATE switch to the SINGLE CYCLE position (righthand setting).
3. Press the START key on the computer console.
4. Turn the power to ON or OFF on the I/O device.
5. Set the RATE switch to the PROCESS position.
6. Press the computer console START key to resume operation.

This procedure ensures that the system is not processing data to or from storage. Thus, any power surge resulting from the removal or application of power to an I/O unit would not affect the contents of storage.

Once the POWER ON sequence is completed, the system is ready to begin processing. Prior to actually processing data, a check is performed to ensure that no lights on the console have burned out. The LAMP TEST button causes all indicator lights on the console to turn on and become visible. The operator visually checks the console face and determines if all lights are functioning properly.

LAMP TEST

The procedure used in the lamp test is as follows:

1. Press the STOP pushbutton.
2. Press and hold the LAMP TEST pushbutton.

Figure 14-20
LAMP TEST Operation

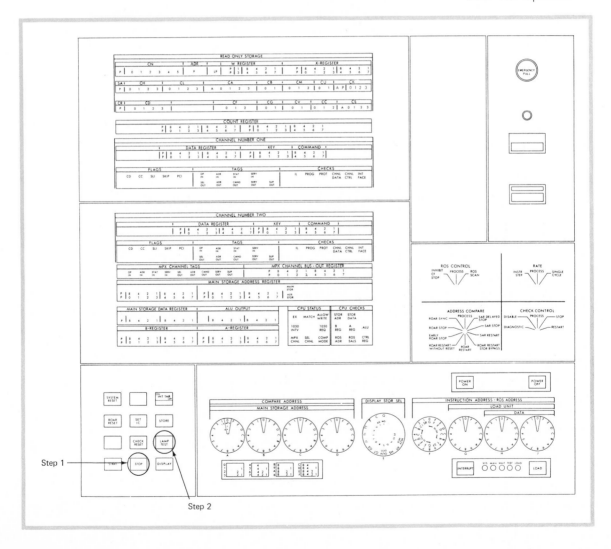

Depressing this key will cause the console lights to become lit. Holding the key down keeps the indicator lights lit. The console lamps will be slightly dimmer than during normal operation. The operator, upon noting a defective light, should note its position and contact the CE. The operator should not attempt to repair the light. It is recommended that the operator have available copies of an illustration of the console face. The operator noting a lamp deficiency could quickly mark its position on the form. Identification will then be exact, and erroneous data won't be given to other shift control operators or the CE.

POWER OFF The POWER OFF sequence removes power from the CPU and all online I/O units. The contents of main storage are not altered during a POWER OFF operation. Input or output interrupt conditions are reset when the POWER OFF key is used. Any pending I/O interruptions are lost during a POWER OFF operation.

The POWER OFF key takes precedence over the POWER ON key. The recommended POWER OFF sequence is:

1. Press the STOP key on the console. This will cause the CPU to enter a stopped state. (*Note:* Depressing the STOP key on an offline I/O unit *does not* cause the computer system to enter a stopped state.)
2. Wait for MAN display light to turn on. This indicates the CPU is in a stopped state and ensures that all pending interruption requests are serviced.
3. Press the POWER OFF key.

Self-study exercise 14-4

1. The three steps required in order to turn off power are: _____ , _____ , and _____ , in that order.

◆ ◆ ◆

press the STOP key
wait for the MAN display light to go on
press the POWER OFF key

2. The POWER ON sequence involves two steps, namely, _____ and _____ .

◆ ◆ ◆

press the POWER ON key
wait for the POWER ON light to come on

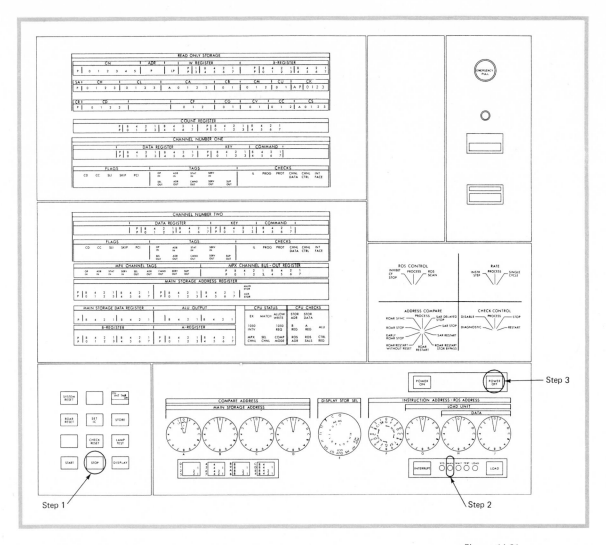

Figure 14-21
POWER OFF Operation

3. The POWER ON sequence _____ all offline devices.

♦ ♦ ♦

bypasses

4. The POWER ON sequence will be automatically interrupted should the _____ light go on.

♦ ♦ ♦

LP (low pressure)

5. When applying or removing power from online I/O devices, the sequence of steps which must be performed is: _____ .

♦ ♦ ♦

press STOP key and wait for MAN light to come on
set the RATE switch to SINGLE CYCLE
press the START key
turn power to ON or OFF on the I/O device
set the RATE switch to the PROCESS position
press the computer console START key to resume operation

6. Following the above procedure will ensure that any resulting power surge will not _____ .

♦ ♦ ♦

affect the contents of storage

7. The purpose of the lamp test is to _____ .

♦ ♦ ♦

cause all indicator lights on the console to turn on so that any light failures can be easily determined

8. The steps involved in making a lamp test are: _____ .

♦ ♦ ♦

press the STOP pushbutton; press and hold the LAMP TEST pushbutton

* The IBM System/370 Console   Within the chapter, the reader was introduced to some of the operational aspects of the IBM System/360 Model 30 console. Since the operational aspects of the IBM System/370 computers are similar to those of the IBM 360 Series computers, and since the IBM System/370 represents both the most recent and the most sophisticated of IBM's computers, we shall now discuss this computer series.

The IBM System/370 (see Figure 14-22) is a high-performance data processing system that provides reliability and convenience to its users. It includes the advantages, characteristics, and functions pioneered by the IBM System/360 series. Some of the attributes of the IBM System/360 that are improved on the IBM 370 Series include:

1. Overlapping, processing and input/output operations
2. High-speed buffer storage
3. Overall internal performance
4. Channel capabilities

In general, most IBM System/360 input/output units, user programs, and programming systems can be used in the IBM System/370 without change. The console is also utilized in a similar manner in each of these computer series. There is, however, a marked difference between the configuration of the IBM 370 console and its counterpart for the IBM 360. This is readily seen by a comparison of the IBM 370's console in Figure 14-23 and the IBM 360's console, previously shown in Figure 14-2. The entire composition of the IBM 370's console is severely altered: the USE meters have been moved, and only eight rotary switches exist; the LOAD UNIT switches remain fixed in their position on the console; and the control switches (i.e., RATE switch, etc.) have been realigned.

Added to the IBM 370's SCP (System Control Panel) are a series of lever switches and a new group of pushbutton keys with their associated display lights (immediately above the control switches and three rows wide

Figure 14-22
An IBM System/370
Model 155 Computing
Configuration

Figure 14-23
The Console from a
System 370 Model 155
Computer

across the face of the console). These levers and keys, indicative of the additional operating dimensions of the IBM System/370, are provided for greater operator control and convenience. It is suggested that the operator thoroughly acquaint himself with IBM 370's technical publications before working with the system.

End-of-chapter Exercises

True-false exercise

1. The SYS display light when lit denotes that the CPU is processing data.
2. The IBM Model 30 console is not compatible with any other console in the IBM 360 Series.
3. IPL is only accomplished in the morning.
4. When data is dialed onto the console's rotary switches, it is in a hexa-decimal format.
5. The configuration of an 8-bit byte of data is established on dials H and J, for placement into storage.
6. The Model 30 is incapable of operating in more than one mode.
7. The CES is to be used by only the manufacturers representatives.
8. When the CPU enters the stopped state, the MAN display light is turned off.
9. In the POWER ON sequence, all offline devices are activated.
10. The POWER OFF key has precedence over the POWER ON key.

Multiple-choice exercise

1. The operator control panel enables the operator to
    a. control all offline devices
    b. denote the status of the system
    c. display data within the CPU
    d. alter the contents of a storage location
    e. all the above
2. The OIS permits the operator to
    a. initiate system operation in any mode
    b. perform store and display operations
    c. system reset
    d. all the above
    e. none of the above
3. Rotary switches G, H, and J are used to assign the
    a. operating mode
    b. LOAD UNIT address
    c. level of control for the program to be run
    d. desired offline auxiliary storage unit
    e. one byte of data required to activate the online storage unit
4. Rotary switches F, G, H, and J assign addresses for
    a. an instruction to set up processing
    b. the comparison of data in registers
    c. main storage processing
    d. the channel through which data is to be transferred
    e. none of the above
5. The correct nomenclature for switch E is
    a. DISPLAY switch
    b. STORAGE SELECT switch
    c. DISPLAY STORAGE switch
    d. DISPLAY STORAGE SEL switch
    e. none of the above
6. If the four operation control switches are not set to the PROCESS position,
    a. the SYS light will turn on
    b. the CPU will continue to process wrong data
    c. the TEST light will be lit
    d. the CHECK RESET key should be hit
    e. none of the above
7. The ADDRESS COMPARE switch is used for control when
    a. an address error is found
    b. the ROAR and SAR addresses match
    c. the ROAR or SAR address matches dials F, G, H, and J
    d. incorrect storage addresses are compared, found, and changed
    e. none of the above

8. To place the CPU in a stopped state, depress the
   a. OFF key
   b. TEST key
   c. STOP key
   d. WAIT key
   e. RESET key
9. For the storage operation to be accomplished, the CPU must be
   a. processing normal data
   b. waiting for new data
   c. in a stopped state
   d. in a single-instruction cycle
   e. in a test mode
10. Upon noting a defective light during a lamp test, the operator should
   a. mark the light on the console face
   b. note its position and replace it later
   c. note its position and call the CE
   d. shut the computer down and replace the light
   e. leave it alone

Fill-in exercise

1. The Model 30 SCP is composed of three major sections: _____ , _____ , and _____ .
2. With the CPU active, the _____ light is lit.
3. To assign an address for the manual storage of data, the location is the address on dials _____ , _____ , _____ , and _____ .
4. The operation control switch which controls the mode of processing is the _____ .
5. On the RATE switch, the INSN STEP setting causes the computer to _____ .
6. To accomplish storage of data after the data byte is selected on dials H and J, the _____ is depressed.
7. During the POWER OFF sequence, the contents of main storage remain _____ .
8. The POWER ON key light becomes lit only after _____ .
9. To check the display lights on the console face, the operator performs a(n) _____ .
10. The SCP, thus, affords the console operator _____ .

Discussion questions

1. Outline the procedure for the application of power (POWER ON) to an online I/O device.

2. Describe the series of steps you would complete upon noticing a bad lamp on the console face.
3. Outline the components (i.e., rotary switches, display lights, push-buttons) that compose the OCP and OIS console sections.
4. Discuss briefly the purpose of the following switches:
   a. Rotary switches A, B, C, and D
   b. Rotary switches F, G, H, and J
   c. Rotary switches G, H, and J
   d. Rotary switches H and J
5. Outline the steps employed by the operator to POWER ON and POWER OFF the CPU.
6. Discuss the relationship between the use of the console and the computer operator's function.

THE CONSOLE TYPEWRITER

CHAPTER 15

Introduction   In previous chapters, we learned that the CPU is the nerve center of the entire computer system. It is through the CPU that communications between the system and the operator must pass. We also learned that the console functions as a window which allows the operator to monitor the internal operations of the CPU and in addition provides him with a control panel to direct the operations of the computer system.

Certain operations, however, are both time-consuming and cumbersome to execute utilizing only the console. Therefore, in order to simplify the operator's function and at the same time provide printed documentation of operator communications with the CPU, a console typewriter may be added to the computer system. With the aid of this console typewriter, the operator can more easily interact with and control the operations of the computer. It must be noted, however, that this device in no way eliminates the need for or the uses of the console; it merely complements the console.

Since its inception, the console typewriter has grown in the number and complexity of its uses. In recent years, this device has been deemed so essential to the efficient operation of a computer system that sophisticated computer software is being designed that requires this device.

Therefore, we shall devote this chapter to the nature, uses, and operational aspects of the console typewriter. In order to make this discussion as practical and universally applicable as possible, we shall focus our attention on the IBM 1052 Printer Keyboard.

We have chosen this particular make and model console typewriter because of its wide use and operating similarities to other currently used devices.

Self-study exercise 15-1

1. The console typewriter facilitates _____ between the computer operator and the _____ .

◆   ◆   ◆

communication
CPU

2. The console typewriter _____ the computer console; it _____ the console.

◆   ◆   ◆

does not replace
complements

3. While simplifying the task of the operator, the console typewriter also provides _____ documentation of communications between the operator and the CPU.

◆ ◆ ◆

printed

4. Today's computer operator relies heavily upon the _____ to interact with the computer.

◆ ◆ ◆

console typewriter

5. The IBM _____ is an appropriate console typewriter to study because of its _____ and _____ to other currently used console typewriters.

◆ ◆ ◆

1052 Printer Keyboard
wide use
operating similarities

The IBM 1052 Printer Keyboard is the basic console typewriter in use with the IBM 360 Model 30 computer system. It is but one of several IBM 1050 Series console devices currently available and contributing to the flexibility of IBM computer systems. The IBM 1052, as well as each of the other IBM 1050 Series console typewriters, is connected directly (*online*) to and under the control of the CPU. Thus, the principal purpose of the IBM 1052 Printer Keyboard is to facilitate communication between the computer operator and the CPU (IBM 2030 processing unit) of the IBM 360 Model 30. In addition, the IBM 1052 provides written documentation of operator-initiated commands, system-generated error messages, and system-generated responses to the operator's intervention or inquiry. Thus, a permanent written record is immediately available for the operator's subsequent review and analysis.

The IBM 1052 Model 7 Printer Keyboard

The IBM 1052 Model 7 Printer Keyboard is illustrated in Figure 15-1. Some of the standard features available with this model console typewriter are:

1. A pin-fed carriage capable of handling continuous-form paper up to $13\frac{1}{8}$ inches in width
2. Up to 120 characters per line

Figure 15-1
IBM 1052 Model 7 Printer
Keyboard

3.   6 lines per inch of printed line spacing
4.   10 character per inch character spacing

The operation of the Model 7, in much the same manner as the keypunch, is controlled by a keyboard and switch panel. However, in the case of the console typewriter, the switches are combined with a series of lights into an *indicator panel*. Let us now examine, in detail, the purpose and functions of the console typewriter keyboard.

Keyboard and switches   The keyboard and indicator panel available with the Model 7 are shown in Figure 15-2. The two switches depicted on the indicator panel are:

1.   The ONLINE switch
2.   The CONTIN WRITE switch

The ONLINE switch, when placed in its downward (ON) position, provides power to the 1052 and connects it *online* to the IBM 2030 processing unit. Until this connection has been made, communications between the console keyboard and the CPU are impossible.

The alternate or up position of the ONLINE switch is labeled CE MODE. This setting is only to be used by the manufacturer's representative (customer engineer) while maintaining or testing the system. In order to avoid possibly serious and unpredictable results, the operator should refrain from using this setting.

The CONTIN WRITE switch is a rarely used switch which makes possible a special control option. Since this switch is generally disconnected and rendered inoperative, we shall not discuss it any further.

You will notice from Figure 15-2 that there are many similarities between the IBM 1052 Printer Keyboard and the keyboard of an electric typewriter. Some of these similarities are:

1. Both are capable of printing uppercase and lowercase characters.
2. Both include numeric characters or digits on the upper rows of the keys.
3. Both contain a SHIFT key which must be depressed when printing upper case characters.
4. Both contain a LOCK key which is used to lock the SHIFT key in a depressed position.

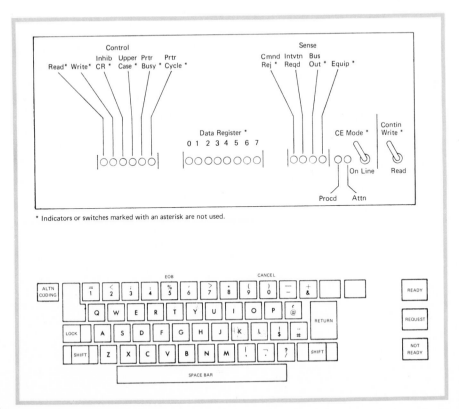

Figure 15-2
Schematic of IBM 1052
Model 7 Keyboard and
Indicator Panel

5. Both contain a space bar to advance the printing position one space.

6. Both contain a RETURN key to advance the printing to the first position of the next line.

7. Both contain a pointer and scale indicating the position of the next character to be printed. In the case of the 1052, this pointer is called the *print element carrier pointer*. This red-tipped pointer rides beneath a marked scale which denotes the printing position. The carriage positions are individually noted and numbered in groups of five each (i.e., 0, 5, 10, . . ., 120).

Keys and indicator lights

Again referring to the keyboard illustrated in Figure 15-2, we note three rectangular keys at the right of the keyboard. From top to bottom, they are labeled:

1. READY
2. REQUEST
3. NOT READY

The READY key serves to activate the keyboard of the 1052 after it has been connected online to the CPU. Thus, after the ONLINE switch is turned to ON (downward) and the READY key is depressed, the console typewriter is capable of transmitting data to the CPU. The subsequent depressing of the NOT READY key will render the 1052 inoperative. Though the power will remain on, no communications between the console typewriter and the CPU are possible. The console typewriter can be returned to a ready state by simply again depressing the READY key.

When the operator is ready to transmit a message to the CPU, he must first gain the attention of the CPU. This can be accomplished by depressing the REQUEST key. Once this request has been received, at the discretion of the CPU, a communications channel will be opened as soon as one is available. During this time, the CPU is said to be in an *attention state*. To indicate to the operator that this communication channel is now available and that he may commence transmitting, the proceed light (labeled PROCD) will go on. Corresponding to the operator's subsequent transmission, this light will be extinguished.

The PROCD light is but one of a group of indicator lights contained within the indicator panel. These display lights serve to keep the operator aware of the state of communications between the console typewriter and the CPU, as well as alerting him to a possible malfunction.

A list of some of the more important indicator lights, together with a description of their functions, is given in Table 15-1.

Alternate code keys

We can see from Figure 15-2 that the console typewriter contains most keys normally found on a typewriter. There are, however, keys on the console

Table 15-1. Indicator Lights on the IBM 1052

Indicator Light	The Indicator Is Lit . . .
INTVTN REQD (Intervention Required)	when the NOT READY key is depressed or when the printer is out of paper. The 1052 enters a not-ready state when an end-of-forms condition exists. Reloading paper and depressing the READY key return the 1052 to a ready state.
ATTN (Attention)	when the REQUEST key is used to create an attention state at the CPU. As soon as the request has been accepted and the operator may begin transmitting, the ATTN light is turned off, and the PROCD light turns on.
PROCD (Proceed)	as a signal to the operator that the keying-in of data may start.
READ	while data is being entered into the system via the console typewriter.

typewriter having no counterpart on an ordinary typewriter. Such a key is the ALTN CODING (Alternate Coding) key. This key is used in conjunction with other keys to increase the number of functions which these keys can initiate.

To illustrate the effect of this key, we shall examine its use in conjunction with the 0 key. Normally, depressing the 0 key would cause the printing of the lowercase character 0 (zero), and simultaneously depressing this key and the SHIFT key would cause the printing of the uppercase character) (close parenthesis). However, striking this key while holding the ALTN CODING down will cause the 0 key to initiate a third operation—the cancel operation. This cancel operation causes an interruption in the transmission of data from the keyboard to the CPU. Thus, if the computer operator should find it necessary to abort or cancel a transmission, he need only depress the CANCEL (0) key while holding down the ALTN CODING key, effecting an immediate interruption in the transmission. To remind the operator of this key's third function, the label *CANCEL* is printed directly above this 0 key.

Referring again to the IBM 1052 Printer Keyboard (Figure 15-2), you will note that the 5 key also has a label (EOB) printed above it, indicating a three-function capability. When this key is depressed while holding down the ALTN CODING key, an EOB (End-of-Block) character is generated. This character is used to indicate that the keyboard transmission has been completed.

The effect of transmitting the EOB character to the computer parallels the effect of a period in an English sentence. That is, as the period indicates the end of an English sentence, the EOB character signifies an end to a single line of transmission to the computer. Once the EOB has been received, the computer may turn its attention from the console typewriter to the task of implementing the previously transmitted instruction and either proceed with normal processing or transmit an appropriate reply to the operator via the console typewriter. A typical computer reply might be to indicate the existence of an error condition or simply to indicate the need for additional information.

The CANCEL and EOB keys are standard features with the IBM 1052 Printer Keyboard. When depressed, they induce the identical response from any IBM computer system. It should be carefully noted, however, that these characters (CANCEL and EOB) are control characters, not characters of data. Hence, when transmitted, they are acted upon by the computer, but are not read into storage.

Other nonstandard control characters are available on the 1052. One such nonstandard optional control character is EOT (End Of Transmission). This control character may be used to perform the same function as EOB. When available, it is generally located on the 6 key. Since the EOT control character is nonstandard, the computer system must be specially programmed for its use.

Several other optional control characters are available on the 1052. Should any of these optional control characters be ordered with the 1052, their names would be printed just above the top row on the keyboard. The operator should, therefore, make himself aware of those options present on the system's console typewriter. Details concerning the number and function of the optional control characters available with a particular computer system can generally be found in the system's technical or operations manuals.

Now that we have a fundamental understanding of the indicator panel and keyboard, let us turn our attention to how they might be used by the computer operator under normal operating procedures.

Self-study exercise 15-2

1. The basic console typewriter for an IBM 360 Series system is the _____ .

◆　◆　◆

IBM 1052 Printer Keyboard

2. The 1052 represents one of a variety of IBM _____ console devices.

♦ ♦ ♦

1050

3. The 1052 is directly connected to the _____.

♦ ♦ ♦

2030 processing unit

4. The console typewriter permits communication _____ the operator and the computer in addition to providing a means of _____ all messages to and from the computer.

♦ ♦ ♦

between
documenting

5. On the 1052 Model 7, the pin-fed carriage permits one to use paper up to _____ wide.

♦ ♦ ♦

13⅛ in.

6. In its ON position, the ONLINE switch _____ the 1052 _____ to the IBM 2030 processing unit.

♦ ♦ ♦

connects
online

7. No commands may be issued from the 1052 when the ONLINE switch is _____.

♦ ♦ ♦

not ON

8. The alternate setting for the ONLINE switch is _____, the up position and used by the CE.

♦ ♦ ♦

CE MODE

9. The CE MODE setting is _____ used by the computer operator.

◆ ◆ ◆

never

10. The 1052's CONTIN WRITE switch is _____ on most panels.

◆ ◆ ◆

a special option and inoperative

11. The 1052's keyboard is constructed _____ to an electric typewriter.

◆ ◆ ◆

similar

12. The print element carrier pointer is a red-tipped pointer which indicates _____ .

◆ ◆ ◆

the carriage position to be printed

13. Use of the ALTN CODING key provides some keyboard keys with a _____ functional use.

◆ ◆ ◆

third

14. The 0 (zero) key may be used to define a(n) _____ operation.

◆ ◆ ◆

cancel

15. To permit this use, the zero key is depressed while the _____ key is held down.

◆ ◆ ◆

ALTN CODING

16. If both the zero and ALTN CODING keys are held down, any transmission from the 1052's keyboard may be _____.

♦ ♦ ♦

aborted or stopped

17. The 5 key may also be used to represent the _____ operation.

♦ ♦ ♦

EOB (End-of-Block)

18. The EOB key, in order to be used, is depressed simultaneously with the _____ key.

♦ ♦ ♦

ALTN CODING

19. The EOB key is used to signify the _____ of a keyboard transmission.

♦ ♦ ♦

end

20. The EOB character is similar to a(n) _____ used at the end of a sentence of words.

♦ ♦ ♦

period

21. When available on the 1052, the EOT (end of transmission) key is defined by the _____ key.

♦ ♦ ♦

6

22. The EOB and CANCEL code keys are _____ on the 1052.

♦ ♦ ♦

standard

23. The three pushbutton keys on the 1052 are the _____, _____, and _____ keys.

♦ ♦ ♦

READY
REQUEST
NOT READY

24. Data cannot be entered through the 1052 keyboard until the _____ pushbutton is depressed.

♦ ♦ ♦

READY

25. The READY pushbutton is depressed at the end of the CPU's _____ sequence, placing the 1052's keyboard in a(n) _____ state.

♦ ♦ ♦

POWER ON
active

26. To render the keyboard inoperative, the _____ pushbutton is depressed.

♦ ♦ ♦

NOT READY

27. The REQUEST key is used to gain the _____ of the CPU.

♦ ♦ ♦

attention

28. The creation of the attention state at the CPU is signaled by the activation of the _____ light.

♦ ♦ ♦

ATTN (attention)

29. When the _____ light is lit, signifying that the transmission of data (via the keyboard) may start, the _____ light is turned off.

◆ ◆ ◆

PROCD (proceed)
ATTN

30. While data is being keyed in, the _____ light is on.

◆ ◆ ◆

READ

31. Depression of the NOT READY key will activate the _____ light. This light is also lit by the existence of a(n) _____ condition on the 1052.

◆ ◆ ◆

INTVTN REQD (intervention required)
end-of-form

Operating Procedures

Early in his career, the computer operator learns the importance and necessity of adhering to established and proved operating procedures. With respect to the console typewriter, these operating procedures can be classified into two general types: those concerned with readying the console typewriter for transmission and those concerned with the actual transmission of information.

Readying the IBM 1052 printer keyboard for transmission

As we have previously stated, the console typewriter must be in a ready state before it can be used. In readying the 1052 for transmission, the operator should observe the following general procedures:

1. Ensure that the paper forms are correctly loaded on the carriage of the console typewriter and that sufficient paper remains. If only a few sheets remain, a new stock of continuous-form paper should be installed.
2. Place the ONLINE switch in its downward or ON position. This will supply power to the 1052 and connect it online to the CPU. The INTVTN REQD light should now be on.
3. Depress the READY key. The INTVTN REQD light should go out. At this point, the console typewriter is ready to commence transmission. It is only necessary for the operator to request the attention of the CPU when the operator is ready to transmit. At such time, an additional, or fourth, step must be performed.

4. Depress the REQUEST key. This should cause the PROCD light to come on immediately or cause the ATTN light to come on, followed shortly by the lighting of the PROCD light and the extinguishing of the ATTN light.

After completing the above four steps, the operator can immediately commence transmission.

Data transmitting   The entry of data, operational codes, and inquiries can now be initiated from the keyboard. In addition, the operator is now able to react quickly and effectively to the demands of the system. In this manner, he can fulfill his major purpose of creating a steady job stream of work to the computer, thereby allowing the computer to operate at maximum efficiency. With the aid of the console typewriter, the operator can maintain the smooth and uninterrupted flow of jobs through the system.

Let us now review the operations performed by the operator to input actual data from the console typewriter. These operations are as follows:

1. Key in the desired message or data, character by character. Each character is printed as its respective key is depressed. The READ indicator light should be on during this keying process.
2. Upon completion of the entry, the operator must simultaneously depress the ALTN CODING and EOB keys, signaling the end of the entry.
3. If and when all entries have been completed and accepted by the CPU, the READ and PROCD lights will turn off, indicating the resumption of normal processing by the CPU.

Should the operator realize that he has made an error and miskeyed one or more characters of a given entry, he would undoubtedly wish to cancel that entry. To do this, he must perform the following operations:

1. Simultaneously depress the ALTN CODING and CANCEL keys, causing the cancellation of the entry being transmitted. The PROCD light will now be momentarily extinguished and relight when transmission is resumed.
2. Reenter the entire message. It is not necessary to depress the REQUEST key since the channel between the CPU and console typewriter is still open.
3. Normal transmission may now be resumed.

The procedures which we have discussed relative to the readying of the 1052 for transmission and relative to actual data transmission have been long established as standard procedures and should be explicitly followed in order to achieve the best results.

Self-study exercise 15-3

1. When operating in a computer-oriented environment, we must adhere to a(n) _____ of procedures.

◆ ◆ ◆

established set

2. For use, the 1052 must be in a(n) _____ state.

◆ ◆ ◆

READY

3. A not-ready condition will be noted by a lit _____ light.

◆ ◆ ◆

INTVTN REQD

4. The operator ensures that sufficient paper forms are _____ prior to its use.

◆ ◆ ◆

placed onto the carriage of the 1052

5. Depression of the READY key will _____.

◆ ◆ ◆

render the 1052 ready for operation

6. The operator attempts to establish a steady _____, thereby permitting a continuous flow of programs to be _____ by the computer.

◆ ◆ ◆

job stream
processed

7. The operator, by maintaining _____ through the console typewriter, may attain a continuous flow of processing.

◆ ◆ ◆

control of the system

8. After an error is made in a transmission, the operator will generally _____ that message.

◆ ◆ ◆

cancel

9. To cancel a keyboard transmission, the _____ and _____ keys must be held down together.

◆ ◆ ◆

5 or EOB
ALTN CODING

10. A new message may be _____ in after cancelling an incorrect transmission.

◆ ◆ ◆

keyed

Initial Program Loading (IPL)   We must now turn our attention to one of the most essential functions performed by the console typewriter, that of *initial program loading* (IPL).

Concepts   Through the POWER ON sequence, we initially supply electric power to the IBM 2030 processing unit and its online peripheral devices (the 1052 included). Although the CPU is "powered up," absolutely no processing may commence. This is simply because the computer is awaiting the input of a control program. This control program, called the *supervisor program,* oversees the processing of all application programs, directs the flow of data throughout the system, facilitates error recognition and handling, and, in general, prepares the system for any type of processing. However, before the supervisor program can be utilized, it must be loaded into primary storage. The procedure which facilitates the loading of the supervisor program into the CPU is referred to as the IPL procedure.

Should the supervisor program be stored on a disk pack, for example, the operator must make certain that the disk pack containing the supervisor program is mounted and operational prior to commencing the IPL procedure.

Since it is common for the supervisor program to be stored on disk, for the remainder of our discussion we shall assume that this is the case.

After making certain that the supervisor program has been mounted online to the CPU, the operator may begin the IPL sequence. Initially, he must indicate to the computer the storage location of the supervisor program referred to as the *IPL storage address.*

The operator specifies the storage location of the supervisor program with the aid of the LOAD UNIT switches. You may recall that these rotary switches were previously introduced in our discussion of the console's OCP and designated by the letters G, H, and J. The address represented on these switches refers to the *first* byte of the supervisor program. In essence, then, we are directing that the CPU reference the specified address within the appropriate disk device and begin transferring the supervisor to primary storage. Depressing the LOAD button on the console will initiate this operation. Upon completion of this operation the LOAD indicator light will go out, indicating that the entire supervisor program has been loaded into the CPU. The extinguishing of this light also indicates to the operator that he may now input additional required data such as the time and date at which the IPL sequence was begun. Upon receipt of this data by the CPU, the IPL procedure is complete, and the computer system is ready to accept data for processing.

For the IBM 360 Series computer, the IPL operation is standard. The IPL sequence of operations is easily completed with the aid of the console typewriter and computer console.

Prior to reviewing this IPL sequence in a detailed, step-by-step manner, we shall elaborate on the input data required for the system. The operator must have knowledge of the date, time of day, and storage address of the IPL command. This data must be input in a particular format, as required by the IPL program.

The date format is

XX/XX/XX
(month/day/year)

Two digits are required for each entry and must be separated by slashes. Thus, March 8, 1972, would appear as

03/08/72

The clock format, to input the time of day, is constructed similarly. The basic format is

XX/XX/XX
hour/minute/second)

Once again, two digits are always required and must be separated by slashes. Table 15-2 illustrates various times of day with their formats.

Table 15-2. Data Formats for Various Times of Day

Time of Day	Data Entry Format
3:20 A.M.	03/20/00
12:00 P.M.	12/00/00
4:37 P.M.	16/37/00
10:30 P.M.	22/30/00

Note that the time must be represented as it would appear on a 24-hour clock and that the seconds setting is always recorded as 00.

The storage address of the IPL command is represented in hexadecimal notation. The format of this address is

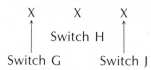

As each of these X's represents a hexadecimal digit, it may be directly represented on the LOAD UNIT switches G, H, and J, respectively. The actual IPL storage address is particular to each computing configuration, and once this storage address has been created, it will remain unchanged. The operator should make it a point to verify the correctness of the IPL storage address prior to representing this address on the LOAD UNIT switches.

Let us now review the various IPL operations in terms of the accepted and standard step-by-step procedures employed in this process.

The role of the console and console typewriter in the IPL procedure

It is commonplace for the console typewriter to be utilized during the IPL procedure. For example, for an IBM 360 Model 30 computer system consisting of an IBM 2030 processing unit and a 1052 Model 7 console typewriter, the IPL procedure would be as follows:

1. Depress the console's CHECK RESET pushbutton.
2. Set the required IPL storage address on the LOAD UNIT switches.
3. Depress the LOAD pushbutton.
4. The console typewriter will print the statement

GIVE IPL COMMAND

and move to the next line in carriage position 1. The console's MAN indicator light will light.

5. Depress the 1052's REQUEST pushbutton, and wait for the PROCD light to turn on. Then, key in consecutively from position 1

SET DATE=XX/XX/XX, CLOCK=XX/XX/XX

To complete this entry, depress the EOB key while holding the ALTN CODING key down. (Note the manditory space between SET and DATE.)

6. Upon completion of the IPL sequence, the 1052 will type out the following statement:

DOS IPL COMPLETE READY FOR COMMUNICATIONS

The console's MAN indicator light will become lit after these statements are typed, indicating that the system is now ready to receive and process data.

Let us use an illustrative example to reinforce this knowledge of the IPL procedure and to further explain the use of the console and console typewriter.

ILLUSTRATIVE EXAMPLE

The operator has the responsibility to IPL the IBM 360 Model 30. The time of day is 2:37 P.M., on September 30, 1972, and the IPL storage address is 190 (in hexadecimal).
The operator's sequence of tasks is:

1. Depress the console's CHECK RESET pushbutton.
2. Set the LOAD UNIT switches—1 on switch G, 9 on switch H, and 0 on switch J.
3. Depress the LOAD pushbutton.
4. Await the system's GIVE IPL COMMAND reply and the MAN light to light.
5. Depress the 1052's REQUEST pushbutton, and wait for the PROCD light to activate. Then key in

SET DATE=09/30/72,CLOCK=14/37/00

Depress the EOB and ALTN CODING keys simultaneously.
6. Wait for the console's MAN light to activate.

Figure 15-3 illustrates the printout produced by the console typewriter as a result of this IPL sequence.

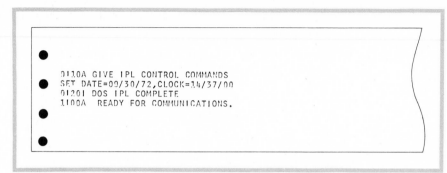

```
0110A GIVE IPL CONTROL COMMANDS
SET DATE=09/30/72,CLOCK=14/37/00
01201 DOS IPL COMPLETE
1100A   READY FOR COMMUNICATIONS.
```

Figure 15-3
Console Typewriter
Printout from IPL
Sequence

The IPL operation may be performed on a computer system at any time; however, an IPL sequence must be executed each time the system has power applied to it.

Also, whenever the communication link between the CPU and the magnetic disk on which the supervisor resides is broken, the system must undergo an IPL operation. This breakdown may result from the removal of this disk pack from its assigned drive, the faulty supply of power to the disk drive, or from the accidental shutting down of the disk drive. Whatever the cause, the operator would be required to again complete the IPL sequence executed previously.

Upon completion of any IPL operation, the system is ready to begin processing. The operator may then begin to feed information into the system. Thus, through use of the console and console typewriter, the computer will alert the operator to its operating status, as well as permit operator interaction with the system.

Self-study exercise 15-4

1. The POWER ON sequence will supply power to the CPU, but no _____ will occur in the CPU.

◆ ◆ ◆

processing

2. The purpose of the IPL operation is to _____ the supervisor control program into the _____ .

◆ ◆ ◆

load
CPU

3. The supervisor is usually stored on a magnetic disk, an _____ storage device.

◆ ◆ ◆

online

4. The LOAD UNIT switches are labeled _____.

◆ ◆ ◆

G, H, and J

5. The address entered through the LOAD UNIT switches represents the storage location of the _____ byte of data of the supervisor.

◆ ◆ ◆

first

6. To initiate the retrieval of the supervisor, depress the _____ pushbutton after setting the _____ switches.

◆ ◆ ◆

LOAD
LOAD UNIT

7. The _____ indicator light will become lit when the loading of the supervisor is completed and after the system has transmitted the _____ message.

◆ ◆ ◆

MAN
GIVE IPL COMMAND

8. After using the REQUEST key, the operator will key in the _____ entry.

◆ ◆ ◆

SET DATE

9. The date entry and clock formats are _____ and _____, respectively.

◆ ◆ ◆

XX/XX/XX representing month/day/year
XX/XX/XX representing hour/minute/second

10. In the SET DATE entry, the _____ in SET DATE is mandatory.

◆ ◆ ◆

blank space

11. Upon completion of the IPL sequence, the system is ready to begin _____ data.

◆ ◆ ◆

processing

12. For an IPL operation at 7:35 P.M., on January 7, 1972, the date and clock settings would be _____ and _____ .

◆ ◆ ◆

date = 01/07/72
clock = 19/35/00

13. The IPL operation may be performed at _____ time of day.

◆ ◆ ◆

any

14. If communication is broken between the disk drive storing the supervisor and the CPU, the operator must _____ again.

◆ ◆ ◆

IPL

15. Normally, though, the IPL sequence is completed after the system is _____ .

◆ ◆ ◆

powered up

End-of-chapter Exercises

True-false exercise

1. The console typewriter completely replaces the computer's SCP.
2. Much of today's computer software is designed with the console typewriter in mind.

3. The basic console typewriter for an IBM 360 Series system is the IBM 1052 Printer Keyboard.
4. The 1052's carriage permits usage of paper sizes up to $12\frac{1}{2}$ in.
5. The CE MODE setting for the ONLINE switch is used only by the CE.
6. The ALTN CODING key is not used during any keyboard transmissions.
7. The EOT key is represented by the 5 key.
8. The EOT key is normally found on most keyboards.
9. Data may be keyed onto the 1052 at any time.
10. The REQUEST key is used to gain the attention of the CPU.
11. The LOAD UNIT switches are G, H, and J.
12. The address entered on the LOAD UNIT switches represents the storage location of the first byte of the supervisor program.
13. The date entry format is XX/XX/XX.

Multiple-choice exercise

1. Using the console typewriter, the operator may communicate with
   a. the entire computer system directly
   b. the CPU, disk packs, and printer only
   c. the CPU only
   d. all online units
   e. none of the above
2. The ONLINE switch in an ON position makes the 1052
   a. powered down
   b. connected online to the processing unit
   c. online to all units in the total system
   d. available for immediate use by the operator
   e. all the above
3. The CONTIN WRITE switch is
   a. a special option
   b. not found on most systems
   c. usually rendered inoperative
   d. all the above
   e. none of the above
4. Depression of the ALTN CODING and CANCEL keys simultaneously will
   a. cause the *last* character transmitted to be erased
   b. cancel *all* previously transmitted messages
   c. cancel *only* the message currently being transmitted
   d. remove the *last* complete word transmitted
   e. none of the above
5. The EOB key is used to
   a. signify the completion of a single keyboard transmission
   b. signify the end of all keyboard messages only

   c. key in numeric data only

   d. begin the entry keyboard messages

   e. none of the above

  6. The ALTN CODING key, to be properly used, must be simultaneously depressed with the

   a. 5 key

   b. 6 key

   c. 0 key

   d. any one of the above

   e. none of the above

  7. Depressing the 1052's READY key will

   a. activate the keyboard only

   b. only create an attention state at the CPU

   c. a and b, together

   d. activate the proceed light immediately

   e. none of the above

  8. Data can be keyed via the 1052

   a. only after the READY key is hit

   b. only after both the READY and REQUEST keys are depressed

   c. after the PROCD light has become lit

   d. after the ATTN light is lit

   e. none of the above

  9. The IPL sequence

   a. supplies power to the CPU

   b. loads the IPL program onto the disk

   c. loads the supervisor into the CPU

   d. prepares the keyboard for processing data

   e. none of the above

 10. To initiate retrieval of the supervisor, depress the console's

   a. CHECK RESET key

   b. LOAD key

   c. IC key

   d. INTERRUPT key

   e. LOAD RESET key

Fill-in exercise

1. The console typewriter provides _____ of all communication between the CPU and the operator.
2. The 1052 is _____ used in computer configurations.
3. The 1052 represents one of a variety of IBM _____ console devices.
4. With the ONLINE switch off, _____ commands may be issued from the 1052.

5. The operator keeps track of the printer position for which data is to be keyed into through the use of the _____.
6. The 0 key may be used to define the _____ operation.
7. Through use of the 0 key, transmissions from 1052's keyboard can be _____.
8. The three pushbutton keys on the 1052 are: _____, _____, and _____.
9. When the attention state is recognized by the CPU, the _____ light is lit.
10. A not-ready condition on the 1052 will activate the _____ light.
11. The supervisor control program is usually stored on _____.
12. The clock setting and date setting, used at 2:45 P.M., on April 12, 1972, would be _____ and _____, respectively.

Discussion questions

1. Outline those steps required of the operator in the completion of the IPL sequence. Assume that you are operating within a Model 30 environment on November 16, 1972.
2. Outline and discuss those steps required in readying the 1052 for message transmission.
3. Discuss the purpose of the ALTN CODING key and its use with the CANCEL and EOB keys.
4. Outline and discuss the operations required to input data from the console terminal.

SELECTED CONSOLE OPERATIONS

CHAPTER 16

Introduction   As a result of our discussions in the previous two chapters, we are aware of those procedures that are utilized to power up an IBM 360/30 computer system—via the console and printer keyboard. In addition, to permit efficient interaction with the computer, we have discussed those procedures required when communication must take place between the operator and the system. Communications such as the above, necessitated by the operator's desire to initiate a required activity within the system, direct the computer toward the completion of a specific task. The operator may initiate these required activities at any time—when a program is undergoing processing or when processing of any type has temporarily ceased. In essence, the operator is provided with the capability to interrupt the normal flow of processing in the computer system. As a result, this type of operator-initiated activity is generally referred to as *operator intervention*.

Both the IBM System/360 and the IBM System/370 are specifically designed to minimize the necessity for operator intervention. That is, these computers are designed to handle automatically most of the troublesome tasks that the system may encounter without the direct assistance or intervention of the operator. There are, however, certain required system tasks over which the operator must exercise direct control. These tasks could include, for example, the storage of data into main storage, the display of data contained in main storage and CPU registers, and the processing of a computer program one instruction at a time.

For the most part, these types of activities are not undertaken during the normal processing of programs. These tasks are generally performed while assisting the customer engineer (CE) during the servicing of the computer or while assisting a programmer in attempting to run a program in which errors have been found. In either case, the operator is an integral part of these activities exercising direct control over the computer system.

This chapter will introduce storage and display operations, as well as the single-instruction operation of the computer. In addition, this chapter will further familiarize the student with other components and displays contained within the console.

Self-study exercise 16-1

1. Through use of the console and console typewriter, the operator may
_____ any activity required by the system.

♦ ♦ ♦

initiate

2. The operator may initiate a required system activity at _____.

♦ ♦ ♦

any time

3. Those actions taken by the operator that interrupt the normal flow of processing within the system are defined as _____ .

◆ ◆ ◆

operator intervention

4. The IBM System/360 and System/370 are designed to _____ the necessity for operator intervention.

◆ ◆ ◆

minimize

5. Operator-initiated activities within the IBM System/360 may include _____ .

◆ ◆ ◆

storage operations, display operations, and processing program instructions one at a time

6. In addition to the previously mentioned activities, the operator may provide valuable _____ to the CE during his servicing of the computer.

◆ ◆ ◆

assistance

7. To complete operator-initiated activities successfully, the computer operator must _____ the computer console.

◆ ◆ ◆

monitor

From our study of Chapter 6, we may recall that data is stored in a computer using small, addressable storage units referred to as bytes. Each byte of storage is identified by a unique storage address. Thus, it is possible to directly access any storage location by its storage address. The term *access* will be defined as the ability of the computer to go to a specific storage location and make available the data contained in that location.

    The performance of *storage* and *display operations* depends on the ability of the computer to access data directly. The display operation requires that the computer go to a specified storage location, access the

Storage and Display Operations

contents of that storage location, and display the data stored there on the face of the console. In essence, through the display operation, the computer operator is provided with a picture window to every storage location in the computer. If desired, every byte of storage may be displayed while leaving the contents of that storage location unaltered.

The storage operation has a somewhat different purpose—it is designed to alter the contents of a specified storage location. With the storage operation, the computer is directed to a desired storage location and a predetermined byte of data, entered via the console, is stored at that location. The original contents of that storage area are destroyed and replaced by the new byte of data.

The storage operation, as well as the display operation, is controlled via the computer console. It is the operator's responsibility to monitor the console during the performance of these tasks. As previously noted, data resulting from either operation is represented on the face of the console. Two display areas on the console are of invaluable assistance to the computer operator when he is performing storage and display opeations. These two display areas are located on the console, as illustrated in Figure 16-1. They are:

1. The Main Storage Data Register (MSDR) display
2. The Main Storage Address Register (MSAR) display

Through use of these displays, the operator may note the data stored at a specific location or the storage address to which the computer was directed. Let us discuss the manner in which each display is utilized by the operator.

Main storage data register (MSDR) display

The purpose of the MSDR display is the representation of data either transferred to or contained within a desired storage location. For the display operation, the MSDR displays the contents of a selected storage location. For the storage operation, the MSDR displays the byte of data stored in the desired storage location. It is possible to display only *one* byte of data in the MSDR.

The byte of data displayed in the MSDR is represented using hexadecimal characters. Because of the configuration of the console, these characters cannot be represented in EBCDIC format. Instead, they must be represented using a 4-bit binary or hexadecimal code, which appears within the 4-bit display areas set aside in the MSDR. An enlargement of the MSDR shows that it is divided into two 4-bit segments (see Figure 16-2). Each 4-bit configuration is capable of representing one-half of a byte of storage (4 binary bits), or one hexadecimal digit. Thus, both halves make possible the representation of one complete byte of data. An example will assist in the explanation of how data is displayed and translated by the operator.

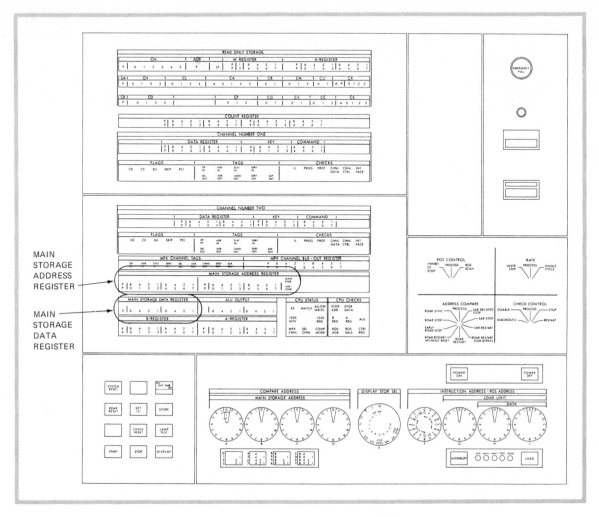

Figure 16-1
The Location of the
MSAR and MSDR
Displays on the Console

MAIN
STORAGE
ADDRESS
REGISTER

MAIN
STORAGE
DATA
REGISTER

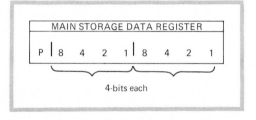

Figure 16-2
A Blow-up of the MSDR
Display Which Notes Its
Two 4-bit Components

Figure 16-3
A Representation of Data
Displayed in the MSDR.
The Circled Numbers
Note Those Bit Lights
That Are Lit

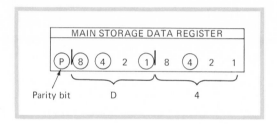

The operator, at the completion of a display operation, scans the MSDR display and finds the display lights lit, as shown in Figure 16-3.

The operator must determine what character was represented by that configuration of lights in the MSDR. To accomplish this, the operator will divide the MSDR into its two 4-bit displays. Beginning with the rightmost half of the display, he totals the values of the bits lit within that display. For this half of the display, the 4 bit was the only bit lit. Therefore, the total of the rightmost half of the display is 4. This amount is converted to its hexadecimal representation, which is also 4.

Turning his attention to the leftmost display half, he finds that the display lights lit are the 8, 4, and 1 bits. Adding these values and converting this total to hexadecimal, the operator obtains the number 13, or hexadecimal character D.

Combining the digits D and 4, the operator has the EBCDIC representation of 1 byte of storage. Either from scanning the EBCDIC conversion table or from memorization, the operator can convert the hexadecimal representation D4 to the alphabetic character M. This character is then recorded and made available to the programmer.

If the operator also desires to record the parity bit associated with this data byte, the P display light in the MSDR is used. For the above example, the P display light is lit, indicating that a parity bit of 1 was added. To verify this fact, the operator may count the number of display lights lit. Excluding the P display lamp, the total lights activated is 4. Assuming that the computer is odd-parity oriented and each active display light represents an internal binary bit of 1, the computer adds an additional 1 bit to the data byte to create an odd parity. The activation of the P lamp notes the addition of the required parity bit and that the number of 1 bits in that byte of data is 5—thereby maintaining odd parity.

Through this illustrative example, we have attempted to introduce a technique used to interpret data as it is revealed via console displays such as the MSDR. Though this technique may be initially awkward, as you familiarize yourself with use of the console, your ability to read the console face and convert character representations will improve. To further explain the conversion of data from its display format, Table 16-1 is provided.

Table 16-1. Converting MSDR Data Displays

MSDR Display[1]		Hexadecimal Representation	Character
P (8)(4) 2 1 8 4 (2) 1		C2	B
(P) (8)(4) 2 (1) 8 (4)(2)(1)		D7	P
(P) (8)(4)(2) 1 (8) 4 2 1		E8	Y
P (8)(4)(2)(1) 8 (4) 2 1		F4	4

[1]The circled number indicates that the display light represented by that number is lit.

Display representations of the MSAR display are converted by a method similar to that used with the MSDR, but the purpose of the MSAR display is quite different. Whereas the MSDR denotes the contents of a byte of storage, the MSAR indicates the address of the byte of storage just read. For this reason, the configuration of the MSAR display is constructed differently, as shown in Figure 16-4. From this illustration, we may note the following points:

1. The MSAR is 2 bytes long.
2. Each byte is divided in half, with each 4-bit grouping identified by the letter A, B, C, or D. These identifying letters will prove to be valuable in our discussion of storage and display operations. We will observe a relationship between the lettered 4-bit grouping—A, B, C, and D—and the rotary switches—A, B, C, and D—used in assigning storage addresses. The representation of the hexadecimal number set with rotary switch A will appear in the 4-bit grouping identified by the letter A. The same applies for rotary switches B, C, and D in their relation to MSAR groupings B, C, and D, respectively.

Main storage address register (MSAR) display

Figure 16-4
An Enlargement of the MSAR Display

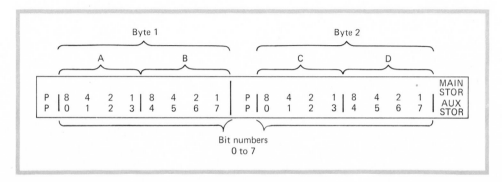

3. Binary bits within each byte are individually identified by the numbers 0 to 7.
4. Two indicators are employed to indicate whether main or auxiliary storage is being accessed. The indicator representing the area being accessed will activate during the storage or display operation.

As previously stated, the purpose of the MSAR is to display a representation of the address of the storage byte just accessed. The operator employs the MSAR display as a cross-reference against the address specified with rotary switches A, B, C, and D.

Let us assume that during a storage operation the operator removes the reading from the MSAR display, as shown in Figure 16-5. From the operator's conversion of readings displayed on the MSAR, we have

Groupings A = 0
Groupings B = 1
Groupings C = 6
Groupings D = 3

Also, the parity bit lamp required for the second byte is lit, signifying its inclusion into that storage byte; and the MAIN STOR display is lit (we note that the storage location accessed was in main storage).

To cross-reference the fact that the correct storage area was accessed, the operator compares the readings removed from the MSAR display, 0163, against the storage address set with rotary switches A, B, C, and D; they are found to be equal. Also, the MAIN STOR display lamp is lit, verifying the fact that the DISPLAY STOR SEL switch, switch E, is set in its MS (main storage) position.

To the computer operator, the completion of these tasks is a series of computer operations which will require his utmost attention and which must be performed in an error-free manner. The ability of the computer to access a specific storage location is also of value to the programmer who is attempting to correct a program while it is being processed by the CPU.

Figure 16-5
A Representation of Data
Displayed in the MSAR.
The Circled Numbers
Note Those Display
Lights That Are Lit

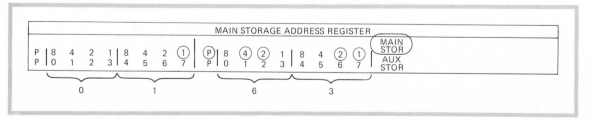

It must be pointed out, however, that storage and display operations are performed infrequently in most computer installations and are usually scheduled apart from the normal workload. Thus, when these tasks are undertaken, the operator must be alert to the responses of the system. With these general thoughts in mind, let us embark on a discussion of those procedures utilized in the performance of storage and display operations. We will discuss these tasks in relation to main storage, general registers, and internal CPU registers.

Self-study exercise 16-2

1. Data is stored in the computer using small, addressable storage units, referred to as _____.

◆ ◆ ◆

bytes

2. Each byte of storage has a unique _____.

◆ ◆ ◆

storage address

3. The term *access* defines the ability of the computer to go to a(n) _____ location and make _____ the data contained in that location.

◆ ◆ ◆

specific storage
available

4. The ability of the computer to access specified storage locations makes possible the performance of _____ operations.

◆ ◆ ◆

storage and display

5. The display operation requires that the computer _____.

◆ ◆ ◆

go to a specified storage location, access the contents of that location, and display the data stored at the location on the face of the console

6. The display operation leaves the contents of the specified storage location _____.

◆   ◆   ◆

unaltered

7. The operator-initiated activity designed to alter the contents of a storage location is defined as a(n) _____ operation.

◆   ◆   ◆

storage

8. During the storage operation, the computer is _____ to a storage location, and 1 _____ of data is entered into that location.

◆   ◆   ◆

directed
byte

9. Both storage and display operations are controlled by the operator, via the _____.

◆   ◆   ◆

console

10. During the performance of storage and display operations, the _____ and _____ display areas are of invaluable assistance to the operator.

◆   ◆   ◆

MSDR
MSAR

11. Through use of the MSDR, _____ byte of data either _____ to or _____ within a storage location may be displayed.

◆   ◆   ◆

1
transferred
contained

12. The MSDR uses _____ 4-bit display areas, representing two _____ digits, to display 1 byte of data.

◆ ◆ ◆

two
hexadecimal

13. Within the MSDR, the display lights lit in the leftmost and rightmost 4-bit segments are 8 and 4, and 4, 2, and 1, respectively. The character represented in the display was _____.

◆ ◆ ◆

G

14. Assuming odd parity for the computer displaying the data in question 13, a parity bit (was/was not) required.

◆ ◆ ◆

was not

15. The MSAR displays a representation of the _____ of the byte of data just read.

◆ ◆ ◆

address

16. The MSAR is _____ in length and subdivided into _____ 4-bit groupings.

◆ ◆ ◆

2 bytes
four

17. The four 4-bit groupings are identified by the letters _____.

◆ ◆ ◆

A, B, C, and D

18. A display indicator situated to the right of the MSAR indicates whether _____ or _____ storage has been accessed.

◆ ◆ ◆

main
auxiliary

19. The operator ensures that the correct storage area was accessed by _____ the address set with rotary switches _____ against the converted readings displayed in the _____ .

◆ ◆ ◆

comparing
A, B, C, and D
MSAR

Operations within
Main Storage

The display of data

The display operation enables the operator to direct the computer to a specific storage location and display a representation of the contents of that storage location on the face of the console. Thus, via the console, any byte of data stored within main storage is accessible to the operator. It is important to remember that on the IBM Model 30, data may be displayed only one byte at a time.

The following procedure outlines those steps which would be employed to display one byte of data stored within main storage. The student should consult Figure 16-6, while reading through this procedure.

1. Press the STOP pushbutton. The MAN indicator light, located on the lower righthand corner of the console, will turn on.
2. Place switch E, the DISPLAY STOR SEL switch, in its MS (main storage) setting. When switch E is correctly set in position, the letters MS will be silhouetted against a red background strip.
3. Set the address of the desired MS location, from which data is to be displayed, on rotary switches A, B, C, and D, respectively.
4. Depress the DISPLAY pushbutton.
5. Record the representation of the data displayed in the MSDR display.
6. Record the representation of the address displayed in the MSAR.

The data representation displayed in the MSDR, when converted from the hexadecimal format, will reveal the contents of the storage location accessed. The address revealed through the MSAR should correspond to the storage address set on rotary switches A, B, C, and D. The contents of a storage location will remain unaltered by the display operation.

The storage operation is designed to alter the contents of a storage location. When the need arises to place a byte of data in main storage, the storage operation is utilized. As with the display operation, only 1 byte of data may be processed with the storage operation. The following sequence of steps is employed by the operator to complete the storage operation (see Figure 16-7):

The storage of data

1. Depress the STOP pushbutton. The MAN indicator will become lit.
2. Place switch E in its MS setting.

Figure 16-6
The Sequence of Steps
Employed during a
Display Operation

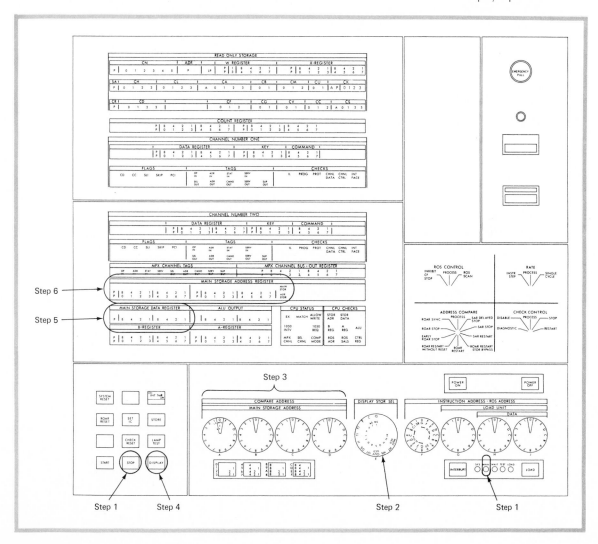

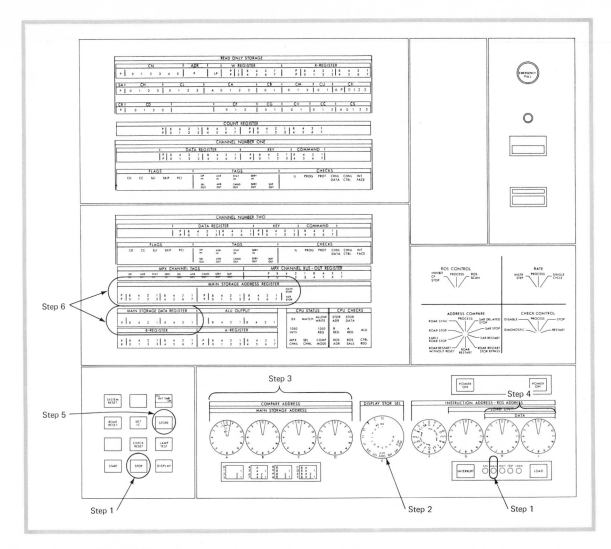

Figure 16-7
The Sequence of Steps
Employed during a
Storage Operation

3. Set the address of the storage location in which data will be stored on rotary switches A, B, C, and D.

4. Set the two-digit hexadecimal representation of the byte of data to be stored on rotary switches H and J.

5. Depress the STORE pushbutton.

6. Record the data representations displayed in the MSDR and MSAR. The data just stored and the address of the storage location in which the data was stored should be displayed, respectively.

An illustrative example will be helpful in further explaining the procedures employed in completing the display and storage operations.

ILLUSTRATIVE EXAMPLE

Let us assume that the operator has been directed to assist the programmer in his debugging efforts and that the programmer wishes to display the contents of the main storage location 02A4. To complete the display sequence, the operator will perform the following steps:

1. Depress the STOP pushbutton, causing the MAN indicator light to activate.
2. Place switch E in its MS setting.
3. Set the storage address to be accessed on rotary switches A, B, C, and D, as follows:
    Switch A: Set to 0
    Switch B: Set to 2
    Switch C: Set to A
    Switch D: Set to 4
4. Press the DISPLAY pushbutton.

As a result of the preceding steps, the following occurred:

1. The MSDR display revealed the contents of that storage location to be 1F.
2. The MSAR displayed the representation of the address of the selected storage location—02A4.

Upon observing these results, the programmer directed the operator to store the decimal number 10, in storage location 016B. To perform the storage operation, the following steps were required:

1. Depress the STOP pushbutton, and await the activation of the MAN indicator light.
2. Set switch E to its MS setting.
3. Set the desired storage address on to rotary switches A, B, C, and D, as follows:
    Switch A: Set to 0
    Switch B: Set to 1
    Switch C: Set to 6
    Switch D: Set to B

4. Convert the decimal number 10 to its hexadecimal equivalent A. Set this number on switches H and J, as follows:
   Switch H: Set to 0
   Switch J: Set to A
5. Press the STORE pushbutton.

As a result of the preceding steps, the following was observed:

1. The MSDR display revealed the hexadecimal representation for A.
2. The MSAR display, after conversion, revealed the selected storage address, 016B.

The operator informed the programmer of these results and resumed the execution of the program.

Self-study exercise 16-3

1. In the display operation, the computer is directed to display the _____ of a specified storage location.

♦ ♦ ♦

contents

2. Data may be displayed only _____ byte at a time.

♦ ♦ ♦

1

3. At the start of storage and display operations, the _____ pushbutton is depressed.

♦ ♦ ♦

STOP

4. The use of switch E, in both the storage and display operations, directs the computer to either _____ or _____ storage.

♦ ♦ ♦

main
auxiliary

5. In the storage and display operations, the address of the storage location to be accessed is set on rotary switches _____.

◆ ◆ ◆

A, B, C, and D

6. Depression of the _____ pushbutton will cause data to be displayed in the MSDR.

◆ ◆ ◆

DISPLAY

7. For storage operations, the two-digit hexadecimal representation of the byte of data to be stored is set on rotary switches _____.

◆ ◆ ◆

H and J

8. To store the byte of data designated by rotary switches H and J, the _____ pushbutton is depressed.

◆ ◆ ◆

STORE

9. In a storage operation, the _____ will display a representation of the data just stored, while the _____ will indicate the address of the storage location.

◆ ◆ ◆

MSDR
MSAR

As introduced in Chapter 6, there are 16 general registers in an IBM Model 30 system. The general registers are identified by the numbers 0 to 9 and A to F (hexadecimal digits) and are located in an area of the computer designated as Auxiliary Storage (AS). Each general register is one fullword of storage. That is, it is composed of 4 bytes, a total of 32 bits. The 4 bytes which compose a general register are numbered 0, 1, 2, and 3, with the 0 byte being designated as the high-order (first) byte (see Figure 16-8). It

Operations within General Registers

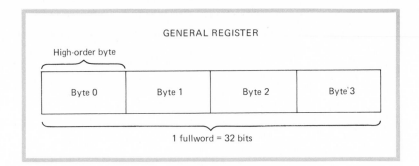

GENERAL REGISTER

High-order byte

| Byte 0 | Byte 1 | Byte 2 | Byte 3 |

1 fullword = 32 bits

16-8
The Configuration of a
General Register

is not possible to display the entire contents of a general register at one time, since only 1 byte of data may be accessed at a time. Thus, to display the entire contents of a general register, four display operations must be performed—accessing the 4 bytes within the general register one at a time.

The display and
storage of data

The following procedure is utilized to display 1 byte of data that is contained within a general register. Figure 16-9 assists in detailing these steps.

1. Depress the STOP pushbutton. The MAN indicator light will light.
2. Set switch E to its auxiliary storage (AS) setting.
3. Set rotary switch A to its LS setting.
4. Set rotary switch B to 0.
5. Set rotary switch C to the hexadecimal digit representing the general register to be accessed. The settings will range from 0 to 9 and A to F.
6. Set rotary switch D to the number of the byte to be operated upon from general register. The possible settings are 0, 1, 2, and 3.
7. Depress the DISPLAY pushbutton.
8. Examine the MSDR and MSAR.

The data contained within the selected byte of the general register is displayed in the MSDR. Only the rightmost byte (byte 2) of the MSAR display is of use to the operator. The first four bits (group C) of the MSAR display represent the number of the general register accessed, whereas the last four bits (group D) of the MSAR display represent the number of the byte entered into the general register.

Should the operator desire to perform a storage operation with a general register, the previous display procedure may be employed until reaching step 6. The procedure should be continued as follows:

7. Set the hexadecimal representation of the byte of data to be entered into the selected general register on rotary switches H and J.

8. Depress the STORE pushbutton.
9. Examine the MSDR and MSAR displays. The data byte entered will appear in the MSDR. The number of the selected general register will appear in the first 4 bits of the second byte of the MSAR, while the byte selected in that general register will appear in the last 4 bits.

An illustrative example of the storage operation will be useful in explaining both the storage and display operations employed with a general register.

Figure 16-9
The Sequence of Steps Employed during the Display of Data Contained in a General Register

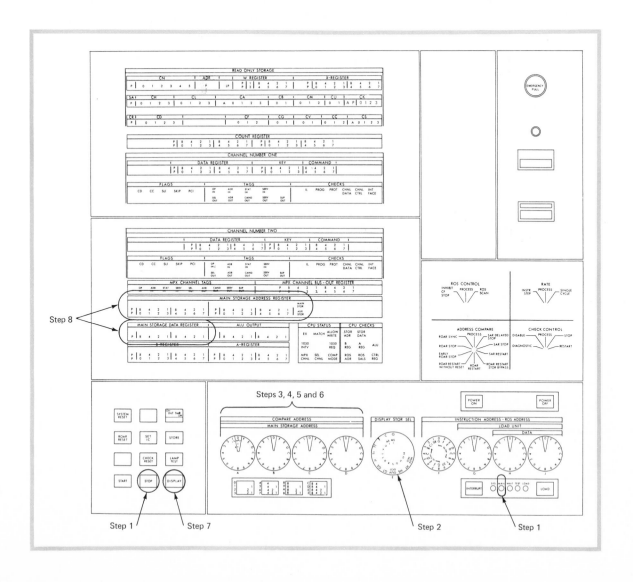

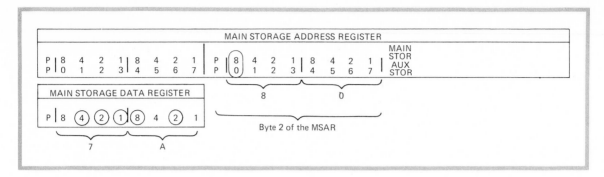

Figure 16-10
A Representation of Data
Displayed in the MSDR
and MSAR Displays. The
Circled Numbers Note
Those Bit Lights That
Are Lit

ILLUSTRATIVE EXAMPLE

Let us assume that the operator is instructed to enter the characters 7A (in hexadecimal) into the first byte of general register 8. Controlling the Model 30 via the console, the operator will perform the following steps:

1. Depress the STOP pushbutton. The MAN indicator light will light.
2. Place switch E in its AS setting.
3. Set switch A in its LS setting.
4. Set switch B to 0.
5. Set switch C to 8.
6. Set switch D to 0. (The first byte of a general register is identified by the number 0.)
7. Set switch H to 7 and switch J to A, respectively.
8. Depress the STORE pushbutton.

As a result of the above steps, the character representation, in hexadecimal, of 7A would appear in the MSDR. Also, the first 4 bits of the second byte of the MSAR would display the number of the general register selected, namely 8. The last 4 bits of that byte would note the number of the general register byte operated on, 0. Figure 16-10 illustrates the MSDR and MSAR displays involved in the above example.

Self-study exercise 16-4

1. In an IBM Model 30 system, there are _____ general registers available for use in processing data.

◆ ◆ ◆

2. Each general register is located in _____ and may be identified by hexadecimal digits _____ .

♦ ♦ ♦

auxiliary storage
0 to 9 and A to F

3. A general register is _____ fullword of storage in length, or _____ bits.

♦ ♦ ♦

one
32

4. Since only 1 byte of data may be accessed at a time, it (is/is not) possible to display the entire contents of a general register.

♦ ♦ ♦

is not

5. The four bytes which compose a general register are numbered _____ .

♦ ♦ ♦

0, 1, 2, and 3

6. The 0 byte is designated as the _____ byte.

♦ ♦ ♦

high-order or leftmost

7. To initiate a storage or display operation for a general register, the _____ pushbutton is depressed.

♦ ♦ ♦

STOP

8. With switch E in its _____ setting, the computer will access auxiliary storage.

♦ ♦ ♦

AS

9. For storing or displaying data in a general register, rotary switches A and B are given settings of _____ and _____, respectively.

◆ ◆ ◆

LS
0

10. For general register storage and display operations, the setting on rotary switch C designates the _____.

◆ ◆ ◆

general register to be accessed

11. Switch _____ is utilized to select that byte of data from the general register to be operated upon when storing or displaying data.

◆ ◆ ◆

D

12. For the storage of data into a general register, rotary switches _____ are employed to enter the specified byte of data.

◆ ◆ ◆

H and J

13. For general register operations, depression of the DISPLAY pushbutton will cause the MSDR to _____.

◆ ◆ ◆

display the data contained within the byte chosen of the general register

14. Within storage and display operations, only the _____ byte, or byte 2, of the MSAR is useful to the operator.

◆ ◆ ◆

rightmost

15. Byte 2 of the MSAR is divided into two 4-bit halves, referred to as _____ .

◆ ◆ ◆

group C and group D

16. The data displayed by the group C half of the MSAR represents _____ .

◆ ◆ ◆

the number of the general register accessed

17. The Group D half of the MSAR will display _____ .

◆ ◆ ◆

the number of the byte entered, within the general register

18. Within general register operations, depression of the STORE pushbutton will cause the MSDR to display _____ .

◆ ◆ ◆

the byte of data entered into the general register

In the IBM System/360 Series, internal CPU registers serve a variety of purposes. Although each CPU register will serve a specific purpose in the IBM Model 30, they have the following characteristics in common:

Internal CPU Registers

Their purpose and use

1. Alphabetic characters are used to identify all internal CPU registers (i.e., G, I, J, etc.).
2. Internal registers are 2 bytes in length (16 bits).

In general, internal CPU registers are accessed only during a "hands-on" debugging effort by the programmer. To perform such a debugging operation, the programmer would first have to inform the operator what use he has made of each register and which particular registers he wishes to access. Once the operator is in possession of this information, he can access the appropriate register to provide the required data to the programmer.

Knowledge of the internal CPU registers can serve the operator as an invaluable basis for understanding how a computer system functions. Table 16-2 details the purpose of selected internal CPU registers.

Table 16-2. Selected Internal CPU Registers

Register	These Registers . . .
I and J	are combined to contain the address of the next instruction to be executed by the computer.
G, U, and V	are combined to create one computer instruction. The G register contains the operational code (op code) of an instruction. The op code directs the computer to complete a specific activity (i.e., add two numbers, move data from one storage area to another). Registers U and V store the operands, that is the data that is to be operated on, in the manner described by the op code.

The display of data

In most instances, it is the computer operator's task to display the contents of the various CPU registers, while the programmer, for the most part, is only concerned with the specifics of the data stored within these registers. Thus, the display operation is uniquely suited for these activities. The steps employed to display data stored within an internal CPU register, though similar in concept to those procedures previously discussed, differs slightly. The procedure and illustration which follow (Figure 16-11) outline those steps used when data is to be displayed from an internal CPU register.

1. Depress the STOP pushbutton. The MAN indicator light will light.
2. Set switch E to the alphabetic character that corresponds to the letter of the internal CPU register to be displayed. The letter corresponding to that register should appear against the black background behind switch E.
3. Depress the DISPLAY pushbutton.
4. Examine the A- and B-REGISTER displays.

The A- and B-REGISTER displays are constructed similarly to the MSDR and are, therefore, read in the same manner. Converting the displayed data from its hexadecimal format, we will obtain a representation of the bytes of data stored at the selected CPU register.

Self-study exercise 16-5

1. All internal CPU registers are identified by _____ and are _____ bytes long.

◆ ◆ ◆

alphabetic characters
2

2. Generally, internal CPU registers are accessed only during a(n) _____ effort by the programmer.

◆ ◆ ◆

"hands-on" debugging

3. Knowledge of the purpose of the various internal CPU registers serves as an invaluable basis for _____ how a computer system _____.

◆ ◆ ◆

understanding
functions

Figure 16-11
The Sequence of Steps
Employed in the Display
of Data of a CPU
Register

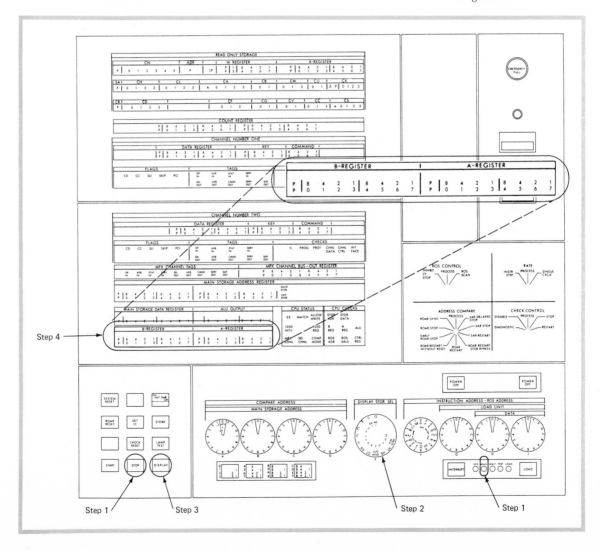

4. Internal CPU registers I and J are combined to contain the _____ of the next instruction to be executed by the computer.

◆ ◆ ◆

address

5. Internal CPU registers G, U, and V are _____ to create _____ computer instruction.

◆ ◆ ◆

combined
one

6. When the internal registers G, U, and V are combined, the G register contains the _____ of the instruction, while registers U and V store the _____ .

◆ ◆ ◆

operational code, or op code
operands or data to be operated on

7. During the display of data involved in a CPU register, the switch E setting _____ to the alphabetic character of the internal register to be displayed.

◆ ◆ ◆

corresponds

8. For display operations involving the CPU registers, the _____ will display a representation of the bytes of data stored at the selected CPU register.

◆ ◆ ◆

A- and B-REGISTERS

Single-instruction Processing   At periodic intervals, all computing systems undergo a rigorous maintenance examination. All components within the system are calibrated to ensure that they are functioning within their prescribed technical specifications. This very necessary examination and recalibration of equipment,

span. Unfortunately, this operational concept is beyond the scope of this text and will not be discussed.

We are, however, concerned with the processing of a vast quantity of programs and/or data in predetermined batches. This form of processing is referred to as *batch processing* and will be discussed in detail in Chapter 18.

Job schedules are employed within both the previously mentioned modes of processing. The schedule employed indicates those programs to be processed. For either processing mode, the entire sequence of programs is designed to be processed within a predetermined period of time.

Though computer operators are required to use the job schedules, they are not responsible for the preparation of these forms. This responsibility is assigned to a group of people within a data processing department typically referred to as the *I/O control group*.

The I/O control group (IOCG) is an integral and necessary part of a DP facility. The title assigned to this group varies slightly, and one may find them referred to by the terms *I/O control, control section,* or *data control section.* Nevertheless, the functions of this group are clearly defined:

Input/Output control group (IOCG)

1. Prepare the schedule indicating the jobs to be processed
2. Make available to the operator all supplies and resources required to process each particular application

The IOCG must be aware of the computer jobs to be processed in a given shift or day. It is their responsibility to prepare the schedules, both daily-run and regularly scheduled types, such that all job requirements for processing will be satisfied, on time. The computer operator, when checking in for work, will be given a schedule of activities for his shift.

The second responsibility of the IOCG is of particular importance to the operator. The IOCG is responsible for making all supplies required for each particular application available to the computer operator. These supplies include any magnetic tapes or disks, card files, test data, special paper or forms, etc., required to process the jobs to be run during a given shift. Here, the basic idea is to provide the operator with all the materials required for processing, thereby permitting a continuous job stream to be established and maintained. We must remember that the operator's prime responsibility is control over, and interaction with, the system. Anything that detracts from this purpose certainly diminishes his effectiveness. In essence, the IOCG makes it possible for the operator to process jobs continuously, while minimizing the time lost due to error or not having the application ready for processing.

As we have indicated, the operator will receive each job to be processed complete with all materials or supplies. Accompanying each job will be a form stipulating the specific nature of the job and any special instructions to be followed. This form, referred to as a *transmittal form*, is discussed in the next section.

Self-study exercise 17-1

1. A computer operator normally works a(n) _____ shift.

◆ ◆ ◆

8-hour

2. Within each shift, a(n) _____ of activities must be established.

◆ ◆ ◆

schedule

3. Jobs to be run on the computer are classified into _____ types, namely _____ .

◆ ◆ ◆

2
regularly scheduled and daily-run

4. A regularly scheduled job is processed _____ .

◆ ◆ ◆

at the same time, every time

5. Daily-run applications may be processed _____ .

◆ ◆ ◆

at any time

6. A run book is composed of _____ schedules.

◆ ◆ ◆

regularly scheduled and daily-run

7. Both regularly scheduled and daily-run forms should contain _____.

◆ ◆ ◆

the time of day an activity must commence, an estimate of the time required to complete the activity, those computer programs required for each application, a narrative of the task, and the overall sequence of jobs to be processed

8. Multiprogramming defines the ability of the computer to _____.

◆ ◆ ◆

process more than one program concurrently or in the same time span

9. The processing of programs and/or data in predetermined batches is referred to as _____.

◆ ◆ ◆

batch processing

10. The I/O control group (IOCG) is a(n) _____ component of a DP facility.

◆ ◆ ◆

integral

11. The function of the IOCG is _____.

◆ ◆ ◆

to prepare the schedule of jobs to be processed and to make available to the operator all resources and supplies required to process a particular application

12. The IOCG will prepare both types of job schedules—_____ and _____.

◆ ◆ ◆

regularly scheduled
daily-run

13. The supplies provided to the operator may include _____.

♦ ♦ ♦

magnetic tapes or disks, card files, test data, special paper forms,
etc.

14. The IOCG's activities make it possible for the operator to _____ to
the computer system.

♦ ♦ ♦

devote his full attention

Transmittal Form   To prepare himself for the next job to be processed, the operator need only glance at the run schedule. The schedule will provide a general job description, but does not have the individual particulars of each job. The form containing these specifics is referred to as a *transmittal form* (or slip), and one must be made available for every job. Figure 17-3 depicts a typical transmittal slip.

After determining the next application for processing, the operator must examine the transmittal slip and acquaint himself with any special instructions or procedures associated with this job. That is, the information on the transmittal form should answer such questions as what specific tapes are to be used during processing, where is the resulting output to be sent, is the program to be executed, etc. The operator then cross-references the transmittal slip and any supplies forwarded with it. A completed transmittal slip is illustrated in Figure 17-4.

Once the operator receives the transmittal slip, he immediately records its receipt. This is accomplished through use of a time stamp—a device similar to a time clock which records the current date and time of day. This information is stamped in the Time Stamp Operations Reception Desk area of the form (lower lefthand corner). This procedure provides documentation of the fact that the slip and materials were received by the operator, in addition to providing documentation of the order in which the slips were received.

Examination of the entire form will reveal the following:

1. *Program #* _____. This entry clearly identifies the program to be used during processing by its identification number.
2. *Machine Type.* The computer configuration in which the program must be run is indicated. For example, the program might require processing in a 1400 Series mode or in a 360 Series mode.
3. *Operation Type.* The nature of the type of processing required

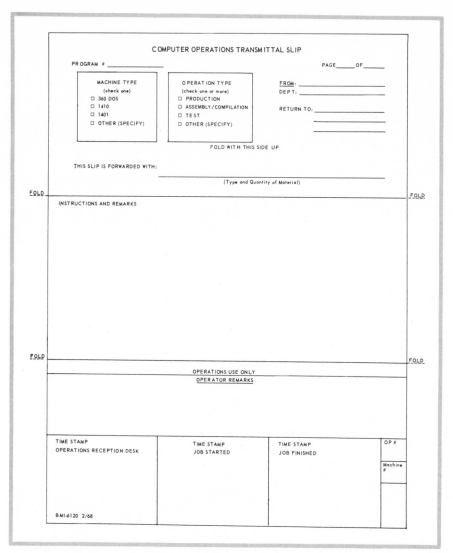

COMPUTER OPERATIONS TRANSMITTAL SLIP

PROGRAM # _____

PAGE _____ OF _____

MACHINE TYPE
(check one)
☐ 360 DOS
☐ 1410
☐ 1401
☐ OTHER (SPECIFY)

OPERATION TYPE
(check one or more)
☐ PRODUCTION
☐ ASSEMBLY/COMPILATION
☐ TEST
☐ OTHER (SPECIFY)

FROM: _____
DEPT: _____

RETURN TO: _____
_____
_____

FOLD WITH THIS SIDE UP

THIS SLIP IS FORWARDED WITH: _____

(Type and Quantity of Material)

FOLD   FOLD

INSTRUCTIONS AND REMARKS

FOLD   FOLD

OPERATIONS USE ONLY
OPERATOR REMARKS

TIME STAMP
OPERATIONS RECEPTION DESK

TIME STAMP
JOB STARTED

TIME STAMP
JOB FINISHED

OP #

Machine #

BMI-6120 2/68

Figure 17-3
A Typical Transmittal Slip

for the problem program is defined. *Production* is marked when one desires to indicate that the problem program is functionally operational and can be directly inserted into the *job stream* (normal flow of processing). *Assembly/Compilation* is marked when one desires to indicate to the operator that the problem program is to be assembled or compiled as the programmer is running the program in order to detect any coding errors. The *Test* box is checked when the programmer desires that his pro-

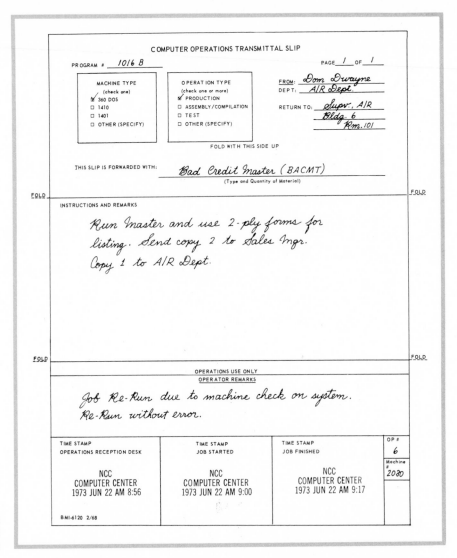

COMPUTER OPERATIONS TRANSMITTAL SLIP

PROGRAM #   _1016 B_   PAGE _1_ OF _1_

MACHINE TYPE
(check one)
☑ 360 DOS
☐ 1410
☐ 1401
☐ OTHER (SPECIFY)

OPERATION TYPE
(check one or more)
☑ PRODUCTION
☐ ASSEMBLY/COMPILATION
☐ TEST
☐ OTHER (SPECIFY)

FROM: _Dom Dwayne_
DEPT: _A/R Dept._

RETURN TO: _Supv., A/R_
Bldg. 6
_Rm. 101_

FOLD WITH THIS SIDE UP

THIS SLIP IS FORWARDED WITH: _Bad Credit Master (BACMT)_
(Type and Quantity of Material)

FOLD   FOLD

INSTRUCTIONS AND REMARKS

Run Master and use 2-ply forms for listing. Send copy 2 to Sales Mgr. Copy 1 to A/R Dept.

FOLD   FOLD

OPERATIONS USE ONLY
OPERATOR REMARKS

Job Re-Run due to machine check on system. Re-Run without error.

TIME STAMP OPERATIONS RECEPTION DESK	TIME STAMP JOB STARTED	TIME STAMP JOB FINISHED	OP # _6_
NCC COMPUTER CENTER 1973 JUN 22 AM 8:56	NCC COMPUTER CENTER 1973 JUN 22 AM 9:00	NCC COMPUTER CENTER 1973 JUN 22 AM 9:17	Machine # _2030_
BMI-6120 2/68			

Figure 17-4
A Completed Transmittal Slip

gram be executed or run with actual data. In order that all aspects of the program may be completely tested, it is essential that the operator make ready all peripheral devices (card read/punch, printer, tape drives, disk drives, etc.) that will be required by the program in the course of its execution. The *Other* setting typically is used to define such activities as preventative maintenance, the generation of new or updated system control programs (supervisors), etc. It is also noteworthy that more than one operation type may be selected on a single transmittal slip. For example, it is not uncommon for a programmer to check both Assembly/ Compilation and Test. In so doing, he indicated to the operator that he does not expect any coding errors, and should he be correct (no coding errors), he wishes the program executed.

4. *From/To.* The requesting department is identified, as well as the receiver of the output.

5. *This Slip Is Forwarded With.* All the items which accompanied the transmittal slip are indicated here—for example, control cards submitted by the requesting department, sample labels, error message sheets, etc.

6. *Instructions and Remarks.* Any special instructions requested by the user will be indicated. For example, use two-ply paper, use mailing labels, run completely if no errors exist after compilation, etc.

7. *Operator Remarks.* Any special conditions or actions will be noted by operator. These remarks might indicate that the problem program "bombed" (did not run) because of incorrect data cards, improper JCL, an equipment malfunction, etc.

8. *Job Started/Finished.* Notes the actual times of day when processing was started and completed.

At the completion of the processing of the problem program, this form, accompanied by any documents, tapes, etc., produced during processing, is returned to the IOCG. The transmittal slip is then filed for future reference. For example, it may be subsequently used should statistics indicating computer utilization by the various departments be compiled.

Thus, the transmittal slip enables the operator to maintain a status on the jobs undergoing processing. In addition to following the directions indicated on transmittal slips, another responsibility of the computer operator is to record the manner in which the computer is utilized. Our next section discusses how the operator records the activities completed within the system.

Self-study exercise 17-2

1. The specifics of each particular application to be processed are described on a(n) _____ .

◆ ◆ ◆

transmittal slip

2. A transmittal slip must accompany and be provided for _____ .

◆ ◆ ◆

each and every job to be run

3. Accompanying the transmittal slip are _____.

♦ ♦ ♦

any supplies required within the processing of the respective job

4. Receipt of the transmittal slip is recorded through use of a(n) _____.

♦ ♦ ♦

time stamp

5. In defining the type of operation via the transmittal slip, *Production* is marked to _____.

♦ ♦ ♦

indicate that the problem program is functionally operational and may be employed directly within a job stream

6. The Test box is checked when a program is to be executed employing _____.

♦ ♦ ♦

actual data and all the required peripheral devices

7. A programmer (may/may not) check the Test and Assembly/Compilation operation boxes on the transmittal slip.

♦ ♦ ♦

may

8. Any special conditions or actions will be noted by the _____ on the transmittal slip.

♦ ♦ ♦

operator

9. After processing, the transmittal slip is retained by the _____.

♦ ♦ ♦

IOCG

10. The transmittal slip enables the operator to _____.

♦ ♦ ♦

maintain a status on the jobs undergoing processing

One of the activities for which the operator is responsible is the maintenance of records detailing how the computer is used, that is, what jobs are run at what time and what quantity of computer time is expended in their processing. The figures recorded by the operator are utilized in determining how efficiently the computer has been used.

A form employed to record the activities of the computer is referred to as a *computer log*. Once again, the actual format of this form will vary between companies, with most logs being similar in appearance to the one illustrated in Figure 17-5. Generally, this log is kept within easy reach of the computer operator, usually near or on the console. Thus, every activity of the system can be easily identified and recorded.

**Recording
the Activities of
the System**

Computer log

Figure 17-5
A Typical Computer Log

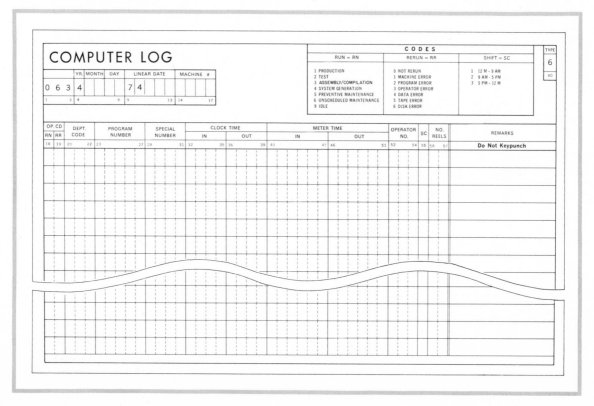

After an initial examination of the computer log, two facts should be readily apparent to the reader: (1) codes used in completing the form are stated on the form itself; (2) beneath each heading is a series of numbers which may range from 1 through 80. These numbers indicate the card columns into which the data, placed within that area on the form, will eventually be keypunched. As previously stated, data removed from this form will be used in calculating how efficiently the system has been used.

Referring to Figure 17-5, let us discuss the various entries possible on the computer log.

1. *063* is the department number assigned to the DP department.
2. *Yr/Month/Day* the 4 is fixed and represents the year 1974, while two-digit numbers are used to designate the month and day (i.e., 0531 represents May 31; 1026 represents October 26; etc.).
3. *Linear Date* notes the actual day of the year using a *Julian date* format. This format identifies the days of the year in a consecutive format. Thus, January 1 is 001, and December 31 would be 365 or 366. The prefixed digits 74 represent the year 1974.
4. *Machine #* identifies the computer employed in processing. This number will change in large DP installations where more than one computer exists.
5. *OP. CD* (operation code) identifies the manner in which a program is processed. (The codes to be used are provided in the table at the upper righthand corner of the computer log.) The RN (run) code describes what type of operations took place. Run code numbers 4, 5, and 6 must be specified by the DP center. The RR (rerun) code notes the type of error, should one be encountered, that caused the problem program to bomb. SYS GEN (system generation) defines the process by which the capabilities of the system, in the form of the supervisor control program, are altered. For the most part, computer configurations are usually upgraded to provide the system with a greater processing potential. Maintenance of the system may be regularly scheduled by the DP center or performed on an unscheduled basis whenever the system malfunctions.
6. *Department Code* identifies the department requesting the computerized activity by its code number.
7. *Program Number* identifies the program employed in processing the particular application.
8. *Special Number* further identifies the program being used.
9. *Clock Time* indicates the times of day using a 24-hour format. The IN time notes the time the job was input to the system, while the OUT time indicates when the job was removed from

the system. An entry of 1655 (IN) to 1710 (OUT) would represent 4:55 P.M. to 5:10 P.M., inclusive.

10. *Meter Time* represents readings taken from the USE meter on the console. Similarly, IN denotes when the job was started, while OUT indicates the time of completion.

11. *Operator No.* identifies the operator currently on shift and completing the log.

12. *SC* notes one of the three work shifts possible. The codes used for this category are described on the form.

13. *No. Reels* denotes the number of magnetic tape reels used during the processing of the specific application. The use of a disk pack during processing would be noted by an entry of 00 for the number of reels and a comment in the Remarks field.

14. *Remarks* provides for any descriptive comments made by the operator.

A completed computer log is illustrated in Figure 17-6. From Figure 17-6, we may note the following:

1. The job was run on September 30, 1974. Thus, the entries are 0930 for month/day and 273 for the linear, or Julian, date.

Figure 17-6
A Partially Completed
Computer Log

COMPUTER LOG

CODES			TYPE
RUN = RN	RERUN = RR	SHIFT = SC	6

1 PRODUCTION	0 NOT RERUN	1 12 M - 9 AM
2 TEST	1 MACHINE ERROR	2 9 AM - 5 PM
3 ASSEMBLY/COMPILATION	2 PROGRAM ERROR	3 5 PM - 12 M
4 SYSTEM GENERATION	3 OPERATOR ERROR	
5 PREVENTIVE MAINTENANCE	4 DATA ERROR	
6 UNSCHEDULED MAINTENANCE	5 TAPE ERROR	
9 IDLE	6 DISK ERROR	

YR. MONTH DAY LINEAR DATE MACHINE #

0 6 3 4 0 9 3 0 7 4 2 7 3 2 0 3 0

| OP. CD | DEPT. | PROGRAM | SPECIAL | CLOCK TIME | | METER TIME | | OPERATOR | SC | NO. | REMARKS |
RN	RR	CODE	NUMBER	NUMBER	IN	OUT	IN	OUT	NO.		REELS	Do Not Keypunch
1 0	1 0 6	0 1 0 1 8		1 7 0 5	1 7 2 0	0 1 2 6 3 3	0 1 2 6 7 8	0 1 2 3	0 0		
2 2	3 2 2	1 0 0 1 2	T 0 0 3	1 7 2 0	1 7 2 3	0 1 2 6 7 8	0 1 2 6 8 0	0 1 2 3	0 0		*Job to be re-run. prog. error*
1 0	2 0 0	0 0 1 1 3		1 7 2 3	1 8 1 2	0 1 2 6 8 0	0 1 2 7 7 3	0 1 2 3	0 2		*A/R update and dump onto tape*
1 5	2 0 0	0 0 1 1 4		1 8 1 2	1 8 1 3	0 1 2 7 7 3	0 1 2 7 7 4	0 1 2 3	0 1		*Tape drive specified down - reassy in JCL*
1 0	2 0 0	0 0 1 1 4		1 8 1 5	1 8 2 9	0 1 2 7 7 4	0 1 2 8 0 3	0 1 2 3	0 1		*Tape to printer of A/R job*
9 0				1 8 2 9	1 9 0 0						*Tapes not supplied / mis/u*

2.   The machine number is 2030, indicating an IBM 360 Series Model 30.
3.   Operator 012 was operator on the third shift.

Jobs 1 and 3 were run without incident. Job 2 was a test run that was not processed due to a program error. The program was removed from the system and will be rerun later, after the error has been diagnosed and corrected.

Job 4 was interrupted and had to be rerun. When initially run, the tape device specified in the program was inoperative. After adjustment of the tape drive, the program was rerun to completion. Job 4 employed one of the two tapes created by job 3.

The system remained idle for approximately 30 minutes, because the tapes required for the next job were misplaced or misfiled. In the interim, the operator researched the error condition encountered in job 2.

Error messages   Though we would like to believe all jobs run without error, there are occasions when the problem program is not processed to completion. When this occurs, at many DP installations the operator makes no attempt to debug, alter, or rerun that program. Instead, the aborted program, complete with all the data that was forwarded with it, is returned to the programmer via the IOCG.

In other installations, however, the operator is expected to rerun the program. The rerunning of a program is dependent upon three factors:

1.   The priority assigned to the program application (i.e., a weekly payroll, a daily accounts receivable update, audit of a bank's mortgage accounts, etc.)
2.   Whether the program was previously operational
3.   That all the errors possible when processing this program have been detailed and recorded

In essence, we are attempting to ensure that the program was running previously and can be returned to a completely operational state. The cataloging of errors possible with this program is a definite plus for the operator. If and when an error does occur, the operator need only reference the error listing for this program. The actions required of the operator to handle the error state will be outlined subsequently.

The programmer is responsible for the rectification and documentation of all error conditions. When the program is considered operationally sound, it is forwarded to the IOCG for subsequent storage and use in the system. Accompanying the completed program is its respective list of errors. This list will be kept on file in the computer room and is available to the operator.

PROGRAM NUMBER *BA008*	PROGRAM NAME *Assessment Update*		STEP *N/A*
APPLICATION NUMBER *103-6*	APPLICATION NAME *Update*		COMPUTER SYSTEM *360/30*
SYSTEM CODE *—*	SYSTEM NAME *Assessment File*		DATE PREPARED *9/29/73*
CODED MESSAGE	PRINTED MESSAGE	REASON FOR MESSAGE - REPLY OR ACTION REQUIRED	
Console 001	*Error 1*	*No cards in reader - Put input cards in Reader - Restart*	
Console 002	*" 2*	*First card not control card for program start - Re-read, Restart*	
Console 003	*" 3*	*Error in type of run - c/c 23-25 of control program card, correct - Restart*	
Console 004	*" 4*	*No master tape records on tape - Check Master input tape*	
Console 005	*" 5*	*Code names do not match, c/c 31-34, control card, Re-check & start*	
Console 006	*" 6*	*No data supplied by cards, Check card reader - Restart*	

Figure 17-7
A Completed Message List Noting Error Messages for a Specific Program Application

The error listing is prepared using a *message list* form, a completed copy of which is illustrated in Figure 17-7. Should the processing of a particular program be interrupted, the operator would be alerted to the existence of an error state via the console typewriter. He should then take those corrective actions noted within the message list relating to the program interrupted. It must be noted, however, that the errors currently under discussion result from check procedures which have been built into the problem program by the programmer. The error messages produced by these check procedures should not be confused with error messages that are generated by supervisor or other control programs (i.e., errors resulting from an incorrectly written program, the misassignment of I/O devices, inoperative peripheral devices, etc.). Error messages generated by the computing system will be discussed in the next chapter.

Self-study exercise 17-3

1. The computer log is used to record _____.

◆ ◆ ◆

the activities of the computer

2. The computer log is kept within _____.

♦ ♦ ♦

easy reach of the computer operator

3. Printed on the computer log are _____ employed for its completion.

♦ ♦ ♦

codes

4. Data written into the computer log will eventually be _____ and the cards produced will be employed in calculating _____.

♦ ♦ ♦

keypunched
the efficiency of the system's use

5. With a Julian date format, January 31, 1974, would appear as _____.

♦ ♦ ♦

74031 where 74 is the year and 031 is the day of the year

Questions 6 to 14 below refer to a computer log form.
6. The RN (run) code describes _____.

♦ ♦ ♦

what type of processing took place

7. The _____ code notes the type of error encountered in a program that did not run.

♦ ♦ ♦

RR(rerun)

8. Alteration of the capabilities of a computer system is defined as a(n) _____ operation.

♦ ♦ ♦

SYS GEN (system generation)

9. The requesting department is identified by its _____ .

◆ ◆ ◆

   code number

10. Identification of the programs employed during processing is accomplished through the _____ and _____ code number.

◆ ◆ ◆

   program
   special

11. Clock times are represented using a(n) _____ format.

◆ ◆ ◆

   24-hour

12. With a 24-hour format, 9:15 P.M. is represented as _____ .

◆ ◆ ◆

   2115

13. Meter readings are taken from the _____ on the console.

◆ ◆ ◆

   USE meter

14. The number of tape reels used during the processing of a problem program is noted in the area designated as _____ .

◆ ◆ ◆

   No. Reels

15. The rerunning of a problem program in which errors were encountered depends on _____ .

◆ ◆ ◆

   the priority assigned to the program application, whether the program was previously operational, and the detailing of all possible program errors

16. The cataloging of errors in a program is the responsibility of the _____ and is directed to the _____ .

◆ ◆ ◆

programmer
computer operator

17. When an error is encountered in processing a program, the operator can reference _____ for direction.

◆ ◆ ◆

the program's error listing

18. The list of errors for a program is documented employing a(n) _____ form.

◆ ◆ ◆

message list

19. A completed message list _____ an operational program with both being forwarded to the _____ .

◆ ◆ ◆

accompanies
IOCG

20. The message list is retained on file in the _____ .

◆ ◆ ◆

computer room

21. After being alerted to an error state via the _____ , the operator would examine the message list for the _____ .

◆ ◆ ◆

console
corrective actions that should be taken

As we have already discussed, output from program processing may take the form of a printed document, magnetic tapes, a magnetic disk, or a series of punched cards. In all cases, it is the operator's responsibility to identify the various outputs and initiate their correct distribution. These outputs are returned to the IOCG, accompanied by the original transmittal slip. The IOCG then forwards them to the requesting departments or individuals.

Documenting the Results of Processing

Computer-produced printouts and punched cards are easily handled by the operator. Each is readily identified by the operator. Both types of output are subsequently forwarded to the IOCG with the original transmittal slip attached. Prior to forwarding, however, the operator should cross-reference labels on the transmittal slip against headings on the printout or printed data on the cards. This double check ensures that the correct output is being issued to the proper department.

Printouts and punched cards

With the vast majority of DP installations, the creation and updating of magnetic tapes is a regular occurrence. The original tapes required for processing are supplied by the IOCG and accompany the transmittal form. Since these tapes are produced through processing, the operator must immediately identify and label them. This is a function of considerable importance over which the operator must exercise extreme care. A mislabeled tape may result in unnecessary confusion and an unwarranted reprocessing cycle.

Magnetic tapes

As the tape is removed from the tape drive, a label on which identification information is recorded is applied to the side of the reel. Figure 17-8 illustrates some of the tape labels available for the operator's use. Note that each label, for the most part, will provide documentation of the following:

1. (*Job No., File No.* or *Serial No.*) identifies the specific tape reel by an ID number.
2. *Title* (*Application*) provides a verbal narrative describing the purpose of the tape.
3. *Date Written* (*Creation Date*) indicates the actual date (month/day/year) when the tape was originally created.
4. (*Purge Date, Retention Date* or *Scratch Date*) notes the date (month/day/year) until which the file placed on this tape is valid and then should be erased, altered or re-created.
5. *Reel_____ of_____* (*Reel No._____/of_____*) indicates when more than one tape is used to represent the contents of one file. It provides the number of this reel with relation to the others in that group (e.g., Reel 2 of 5, Reel 1 of 3, Reel 6 of 20, etc.).

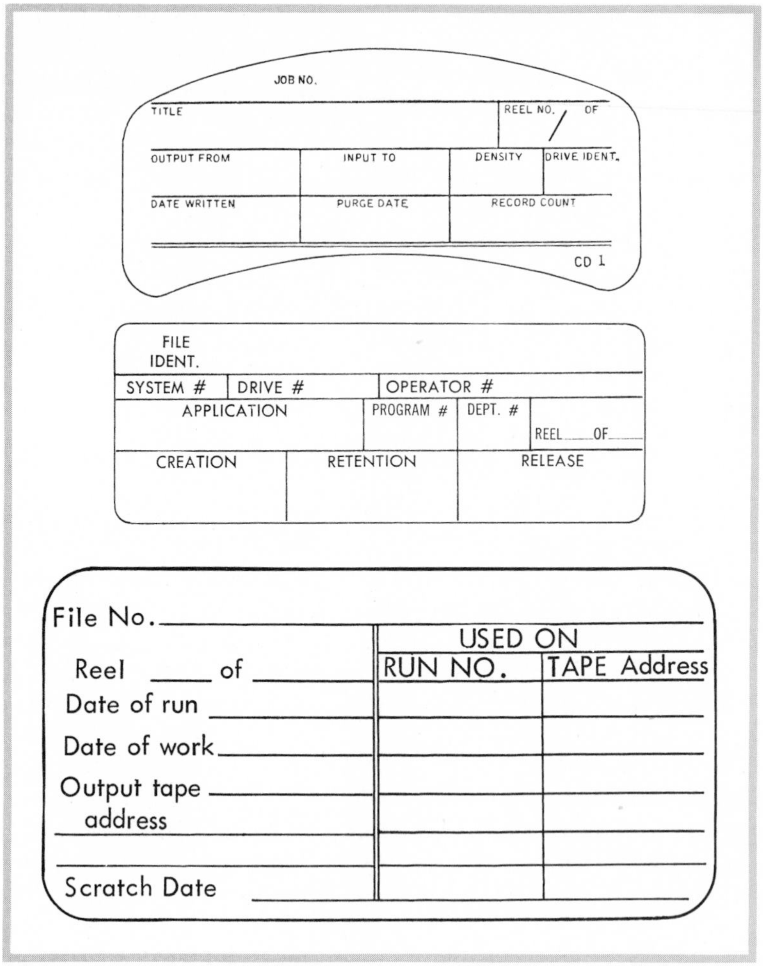

JOB NO.

TITLE

REEL NO. / OF

OUTPUT FROM | INPUT TO | DENSITY | DRIVE IDENT.

DATE WRITTEN | PURGE DATE | RECORD COUNT

CD 1

FILE IDENT.

SYSTEM # | DRIVE # | OPERATOR #

APPLICATION | PROGRAM # | DEPT. #

REEL____OF____

CREATION | RETENTION | RELEASE

File No.____

	USED ON	
Reel ____ of ____	RUN NO.	TAPE Address
Date of run ____		
Date of work____		
Output tape ____ address		
Scratch Date ____		

Figure 17-8
Examples of the Various
Types of Tape Labels That
May Be Employed in a
DP Center

In addition to affixing the completed label on the tape reel, the operator documents the existence of the new tape on the transmittal slip and computer log sheet. These items would be subsequently cross-checked by the IOCG.

Magnetic disks Magnetic disks are operationally handled by the operator in a manner similar to a tape. The major difference is that a smaller quantity of disks are handled by the operator. As with magnetic tapes, the new disk must be identified and labeled immediately after processing. In many DP installations, tape labels are applied to the dust cover of the disk pack with the identifying data recorded directly on them. Many facilities find these tape labels sufficient for their use. Disk labels do exist, however; an example is shown in Figure 17-9. Regardless of the type of label used, the operator should always ensure that the appropriate plastic dust cover is matched with the respective magnetic disk. Occasionally there occurs an accidental mixing of dust covers and disk packs, causing untold confusion. This can easily occur during processing when one or more disks are involved. Cross-referencing labels applied to the dust cover and those internally applied to the disk greatly diminishes the occurrence of this error.

The information recorded on a disk label is similar to the data recorded on a magnetic tape label. As with a magnetic tape, the operator must document the recording of new information on the magnetic disk in the computer log and transmittal slip.

Self-study exercise 17-4

1. The computer operator must _____ the output from all processing.

♦   ♦   ♦

identify

2. The outputs of processing are distributed by the _____ .

♦   ♦   ♦

IOCG

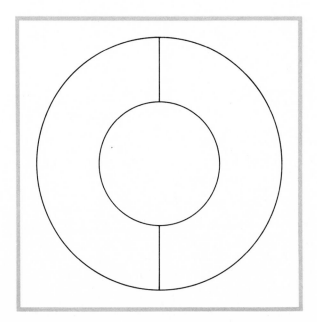

Figure 17-9
An Example of the Disk
Labels Applied to the
Outside of the Dust Cover
and Interior of the Disk

3. Printouts and punch cards are computer outputs that are _____ identified by the operator.

♦ ♦ ♦

readily

4. Despite the form of computer output, the operator should _____ the output and narrative on the corresponding transmittal slip.

♦ ♦ ♦

cross-reference

5. After creation of a magnetic tape, the operator should immediately _____ .

♦ ♦ ♦

identify and label the tape

6. Tape labels, in general, will provide the following data: _____ .

♦ ♦ ♦

file number, title, creation date, retention date, and reel _____ *of* _____

7. The file number on a tape label identifies the _____ .

♦ ♦ ♦

tape reel by an ID number

8. A narrative of the tape's purpose is provided on the tape label in the _____ entry.

♦ ♦ ♦

title

9. The creation date indicates the date the tape was _____ .

♦ ♦ ♦

originally written

10. The label entry which notes the date until which the tape file may be used is called the _____.

♦ ♦ ♦

purge date, retention date or scratch date

11. The creation of a new tape would be recorded on the _____.

♦ ♦ ♦

transmittal slip and computer log

12. A(n) _____ quantity of magnetic disks is handled by the operator, in general, than magnetic tapes.

♦ ♦ ♦

smaller

13. Magnetic disks should be _____ and _____ immediately after creation.

♦ ♦ ♦

identified
labeled

14. At many DP installations, tape labels are _____ to disk packs for the purpose of identification; however, disk labels do _____.

♦ ♦ ♦

applied
exist

15. To ensure that a disk pack and dust cover have not been mixed, the operator should _____.

♦ ♦ ♦

cross-reference the labels applied to the dust cover and disk pack

Most DP centers maintain an extensive number of magnetic tapes. Out of necessity, these tapes must be identified and properly cataloged. In general, any ordered collection of magnetic tapes is referred to as a *tape library,* **Tape Libraries** and the individual responsible for these tapes is called a *tape librarian.* In larger installations, the tape library is maintained by more than one person. We should not underestimate the importance of this task, for the volume of tapes employed within a system may be considerable. The tape librarian issues all tapes required for processing and receives all tapes created as a result of processing. It is possible for a job to become delayed because of a mix-up of tape reels and never reach the computer room. As you can imagine, the cataloging of tapes is a tedious, but critical, task and an integral part of the IOCG's function.

In some smaller installations, however, the operator may become more closely involved in the tape library function. As a result, it is imperative that he have a working knowledge of the forms that might be used. Figure 17-10 illustrates one such form.

This form, referred to as *file history,* enables the tape librarian to maintain a record on the status of a tape. Thus, as the tape reels are issued and returned, a record is kept. The entries on this form are similar to those we have previously discussed with reference to tape labels.

It is quite common for a magnetic tape to be reused, once it has been purged or after the file contained on the tape has exceeded its retention date. The tape will be reissued for processing, and new data will be recorded on it. In many instances, the tape reel will retain its original identification

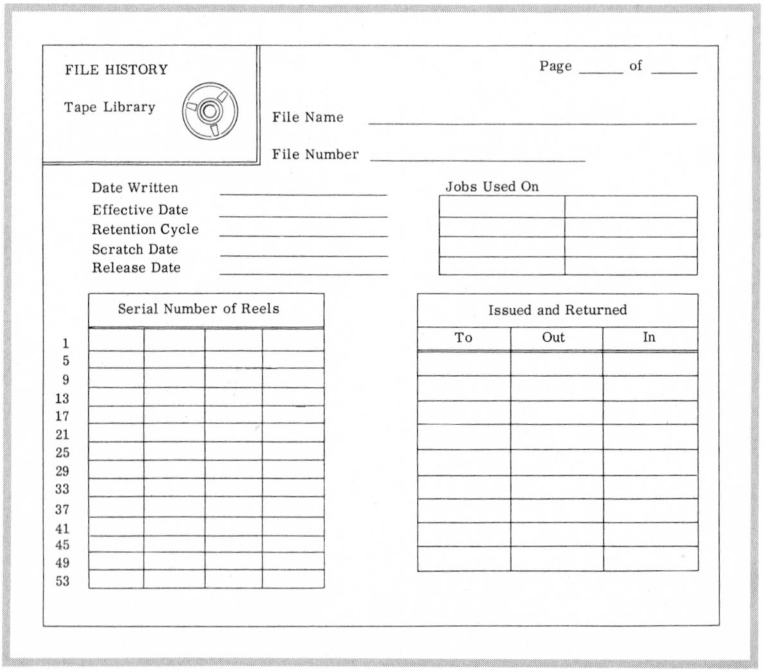

FILE HISTORY

Tape Library

Page ____ of ____

File Name ____

File Number ____

Date Written ____
Effective Date ____
Retention Cycle ____
Scratch Date ____
Release Date ____

Jobs Used On

Serial Number of Reels

1
5
9
13
17
21
25
29
33
37
41
45
49
53

Issued and Returned

To	Out	In

Figure 17-10
A Typical File History Form

```
┌─────────────────────────────────────────────────────────┐
│                                                         │
│  ┌───────────────────────────────────────────────────┐ │
│  │                    TAPE LIBRARY                    │ │
│  │        Tapes available as of this date ──────────  │ │
│  ├─────────────┬──────────────┬────────┬─────────────┤ │
│  │Reel serial no.│ Reissued to │  Date  │   For job   │ │
│  ├─────────────┼──────────────┼────────┼─────────────┤ │
│  │             │              │        │             │ │
│  └─────────────┴──────────────┴────────┴─────────────┘ │
│                                                         │
└─────────────────────────────────────────────────────────┘
```

Figure 17-11
A Tape Reissue Form

number. To overcome this problem, the tape must be reregistered to its new application. This reregistration is accomplished through use of a form, as illustrated in Figure 17-11. And so, as the tape is reissued from the tape library, it is registered to the new job. This form lists all the tapes available for reissuance, as well as documenting their new status. It should be pointed out that the ability to reuse magnetic tapes represents a tremendous saving to the DP center.

One additional point needs clarification. We have discussed two tasks in this section and implied that they are the responsibility of the operator—those operations involving the use of forms illustrated in Figures 17-10 and 17-11. In the majority of cases, however, these tasks are the assigned responsibilities of the tape librarian. We have introduced these topics in the event that the operator is required to interact with the tape librarian and must therefore have a working knowledge of these types of forms.

Self-study exercise 17-5

1. A(n) _____ number of magnetic tapes may be used in a DP center.

◆ ◆ ◆

large

2. After processing, all tapes must be _____ and _____.

◆ ◆ ◆

identified
cataloged

3. Tapes are stored and maintained within a(n) _____ under the supervision of a(n) _____ .

◆ ◆ ◆

tape library
tape librarian

4. A form which enables the tape librarian to maintain a record on the status of a tape is referred to as a(n) _____ .

◆ ◆ ◆

file history

5. A file history records the _____ .

◆ ◆ ◆

issue and receipt of tape reel(s)

6. Magnetic tapes may be reused after _____ or after the original file has _____ .

◆ ◆ ◆

purging (removal of all records from a tape)
exceeded its retention date

7. In either of the above cases, the magnetic tape may _____ its original identification number.

◆ ◆ ◆

retain

8. As a tape is reissued, it is _____ to its new application.

◆ ◆ ◆

registered

9. The cataloging of tapes is a(n) _____ task within automated processing of data.

◆ ◆ ◆

critical

True-false exercise

1. Despite the workload, all companies will establish a 24-hour, three-shift operation within their DP facilities.
2. The format of all run books is exactly the same.
3. On a regularly scheduled job run sheet, no estimates of times required for completion are provided.
4. No deviation is permitted from a regularly scheduled job run sheet.
5. The IOCG provides the operator with all the resources and supplies to process a program.
6. The Test box is checked on a transmittal slip when a program is processed employing actual data and with full support of the entire computer system.
7. The requesting programmer may not check both the Test and Assembly/Compilation boxes on the transmittal slip.
8. Data recorded on most computer logs will eventually be keypunched.
9. On a computer log, the RR code indicates the manner in which the problem program was rerun.
10. Once a program is operational and before it may be fully integrated into a job stream, the programmer must document all possible error states relating to the program.
11. The label identifying a newly created tape is applied by the IOCG as the tape is received with its transmittal slip.

Fill-in exercise

1. Newly hired operators should _____ themselves with each of the forms used at their DP facilities.
2. Computer applications are classified into two types: _____ and _____ .
3. All schedules of jobs to be processed are listed in a(n) _____ .
4. All job schedules are prepared by the _____ .
5. The operator records the receipt of a transmittal slip through use of a(n) _____ .
6. To indicate that a program should be run to detect coding errors, the _____ is checked on a transmittal form.
7. The _____ code on a computer log describes the manner in which a program was processed.
8. Maintenance of the computer may be _____ scheduled or performed on a(n) _____ basis.
9. The Clock Time entry on a computer log notes the time of day jobs were _____ to and _____ from the system.
10. The form listing the possible errors that may occur within the processing of a program is called a(n) _____ .
11. Punched cards and printouts are easily _____ by the operator for the purpose of distribution.

12. The day on which a tape is actually written is referred to as the _____ .
13. The operator will _____ the existence of a newly created disk on the computer log and transmittal slip.
14. An ordered collection of tapes is referred to as a(n) _____ .
15. The person responsible for a company's collection of tapes is a(n) _____ .

Multiple-choice exercise

1. A regularly scheduled job could be
   a. the processing of a payroll
   b. the weekly update of series of charge accounts in a department store
   c. the monthly issuance of checks to vendors in payment of goods received
   d. the daily update of an inventory file
   e. all the above
2. A daily-run application could be
   a. the operational test of a program
   b. the biweekly test of customer account credit limits
   c. the compilation/assembly of a problem program
   d. a and c
   e. b and c
3. The IOCG is designed to
   a. assist the operator in his filing of tapes resulting from processing
   b. minimize total operator time lost due to improperly prepared applications
   c. provide the operator with job schedules only
   d. supervise all control activities of the computer room
   e. none of the above
4. A transmittal form
   a. provides the particulars of each job to be processed
   b. indicates the next job to be processed
   c. stipulates special instructions or procedures for jobs
   d. a and c
   e. b and c
5. On a transmittal form, the Production box is marked to indicate that
   a. no errors exist in the problem program
   b. the program is functionally operational
   c. the program may be directly inserted in the existing job stream
   d. all the above
   e. none of the above

6. A computer log records the activities
   a. engaged in by the operator
   b. for which the computer is used
   c. of the DP facility
   d. all the above
   e. none of the above

7. The term *SYS GEN* defines the process by which
   a. power is generated to the system
   b. the capabilities of the system are altered
   c. the system generates new data for the installation
   d. *a* and *b*
   e. *b* and *c*

8. Employing a Julian date format, the date February 26, 1974, would appear as
   a. 056
   b. 057
   c. 1056
   d. 4056
   e. 4057

9. With the computer log, USE meter readings note
   a. the amount of CPU time utilized by the problem program
   b. the time of day at which the job was input
   c. the time required to process the job from input to output within the system
   d. all the above
   e. none of the above

10. When an operationally sound program is sent to the IOCG, accompanying the program is
    a. a message list
    b. a complete listing of the program
    c. the complete deck of program cards, including JCL cards
    d. a narrative noting use, special conditions, remarks, etc.
    e. all the above

11. The purge date for a magnetic tape indicates the date on which
    a. the tape is cleaned
    b. the label on the tape is changed
    c. data must be added to the tape
    d. invalid data must be removed from the tape
    e. none of the above

12. A file history is designed to record
    a. the receipt of newly created tapes only
    b. the issuance of tapes only
    c. newly registered, rerun tapes

d. a and b

e. b and c

Discussion questions

1. Briefly discuss the differences between the two methods of scheduling jobs.
2. Discuss the functions of the IOCG.
3. Outline and discuss the various entries required on a transmittal slip. How does the transmittal slip assist the operator?
4. Discuss the available entries employed on the transmittal slip to indicate the type of processing required (i.e., Test, Production, etc.).
5. The following narrative describes a portion of the operator's actions during the midnight shift.

    Operator (M01) was instructed to use the IBM 360/System machine #2030, for processing on February 3, 1974.

    Job 1. For the Payroll Dept. (#301)—special run of vacation checks. Program #0131P, version #101. Job input at 12:40 A.M.; run for 12 minutes. CPU time used—105321 to 105349.

    Job 2. For Personnel Dept. (#241)—create new personnel master tapes. Use program #120P. Input at 1:03 A.M., off of system 1:58. Meter time recorded 105349 to 105422. A total of three tapes produced.

    Using the computer log format described in this chapter, work up the appropriate entries that would be entered on the log by the operator.
6. Create a new tape label format of your own design. Ensure that the appropriate data is contained on your label and is not greater in size than a 2 by 4 in. rectangle.
7. Discuss each of the entries on your tape label or the labels provided in the text.
8. Briefly discuss the purpose of a tape library and tape librarian. Why is it important that a DP center catalog tapes, disks, etc.?
9. Discuss the use of a file history form and a reissue form.

OPERATING IN A BATCH ENVIRONMENT

CHAPTER 18

Introduction   The previous chapters have served to introduce and describe the varied aspects of, and devices employed within, an automated data processing (DP) system. In addition, we have discussed the operational use of those components which constitute a computer system. The purpose of this chapter is to tie together all these discussions, and thus, provide a comprehensive picture of the operator's role in the everyday functions of a DP facility. In this way, the reader will view these concepts as a whole instead of as a disjointed series of topics.

To introduce these points properly, we must frame our discussions within an operating environment, that is, a set of procedures employed within a DP center that defines how data should be handled. To this end, we will employ a *batch processing* environment as the vehicle for our discussions.

Batch Processing   We may deduce from the general use of the word *batch* that a large quantity of programs and/or data are involved in the completion of batch processing. This fact is the basis of any batch processing operation. Programs and/or data are accumulated over a set period of time, and then processed. The required processing will generally be scheduled at regular and frequent intervals, thereby permitting the derived results to remain pertinent and useful.

For example, a major oil company may elect to process data for all its credit/charge-card sales for New York on Tuesday mornings. Thus, all customer charge sales slips and customer payment receipt slips would be accumulated from Tuesday P.M. to Monday P.M. During this period of a week, this data would be prepared for entry into the system. On Tuesday morning, this "batch" of data would be completely processed. The result of this processing would be made available to management and other requesting departments, as well as permitting the processing of other programs dependent upon these results. This subsequent set of programs would be scheduled for processing in an appropriate order. The scheduling of these programs for processing could be accomplished on a regularly scheduled or daily-run basis.

The grouping of these related programs, the scheduling of their processing, and the gathering and batching of data are the responsibilities of the IOCG (I/O control group). For every job, however, it is the operator's responsibility to ready the computer system so that each job may be processed to completion. This is one of the primary tasks of the operator. Our next section deals with this discussion.

Self-study exercise 18-1

1. Batch processing involves a(n) _____ of programs and/or data.

◆ ◆ ◆

large quantity

2. In batch processing, data is _____ over a set period of time and then _____ .

◆ ◆ ◆

accumulated
processed

3. The required batch processing is scheduled at _____ .

◆ ◆ ◆

regular intervals

4. The results derived through batch processing must be _____ .

◆ ◆ ◆

pertinent and useful

5. Once an initial batch of data is processed, other related programs (may/may not) be scheduled for processing.

◆ ◆ ◆

may

As you should now realize, the operator has the prime responsibility for maintaining the computing system in an operational state. That is, he is responsible for the continuous and efficient processing of all types of program applications. In this respect, it is essential that he acquaint himself with the status of the system prior to his working shift. Thus, before he can assume control of the shift, he should be aware of the operational state of the computer. This information can generally be obtained from the operator currently on shift, the DP shift supervisor, the computer logs and run schedules, or by initially monitoring the activities of the system.

Setting Up for Processing

The current shift

In essence, the operator must examine those indicators that will reveal possible trouble spots or system malfunctions. For example,

1. What maintenance activities were accomplished, if any, on the previous shifts?
2. What devices or pieces of equipment have not been operable?
3. What maintenance activities are scheduled on this shift?
4. Are any scheduled applications on this shift normally troublesome, difficult to handle, or prone to producing errors? (There are some jobs which, because of the type of data they require or because of the nature of the processing involved, will induce a greater frequency of error. This may be especially true when raw source data is input into the system, test programs are being run, equipment malfunctions require the reprocessing of jobs, etc.)

In the determination of these factors, the operator must survey the breadth of activities required during his upcoming shift.

When possible, the operator assumes control of a shift at the completion of the job being processed. In most instances, the computer operator is present prior to the beginning of his shift and overlaps with the existing operator. This acquaints him with the jobs being run and provides a continuity between shifts and operators.

The first shift Thus far, we have discussed the operator who is entering into, and will continue from, an existing shift. The question arises, What does the first shift operator do? The initial responsibility of the first shift operator is to POWER ON the system and thereby render it usable. A representative of the IOCG, in all likelihood, will be on shift with the operator. In any case, the operator must be provided with any necessary run schedules, transmittal slips, tapes, disks, supplies, etc., to initiate processing.

With the completion of the POWER ON sequence for all units of the system, the operator begins IPL (initial program load) and readies the system for processing. After examining the run schedule, he determines the first job to be processed and locates its transmittal slip. The appropriate cards, tapes, paper forms, etc., are made ready within the system. The operator then *visually* rechecks the entire system and ensures that all peripheral online units are in a ready state. Entry of the appropriate JCL cards commences the processing of jobs.

An outline of this procedure is:

1. Determine the status of the system. If the system is running, prepare the next application for processing, and ensure that it can run to completion. If the system is down, take the appro-

priate steps to bring the system to an operational state (reIPL, hit the 1052's REQUEST key, POWER ON sequence, etc.).

2. Ensure that all devices are in their ready states, prepared to process, or are currently processing data.

3. If the system is not processing, load into the card reader the appropriate cards to commence processing. If the system is processing, load the next job to be processed, when possible.

4. Continuously monitor the console and all online units for error conditions.

As each of the various jobs are run to completion, the operator should reacquaint himself with the next application to be processed. The operator should always cross-reference the run schedule and transmittal slip. All the supplies forwarded with the transmittal slip must be present and accounted for. If a discrepancy is found, the operator immediately contacts the IOCG in order to determine a means of rectifying the error situation. The purpose of these activities is to ensure that the next job to be processed will be input to the computer system with a minimum of, or no, delay.

The upcoming application

As a job is completed, the operator temporarily places it aside, only long enough to note that the next application has been satisfactorily input to the system. Afterward, the completed job, with its results and transmittal slip, is forwarded to the IOCG.

These actions are implemented in an effort to increase the speed and efficiency of job throughput (input, processing, and output). Another facet of the operator's responsibility is the requirement to direct the system's activities during processing. The next section discusses some of the various procedures employed by the operator to control the efficient processing of jobs through the system.

Self-study exercise 18-2

1. The operator has the _____ of maintaining the computing system in an operational state.

♦ ♦ ♦

prime responsibility

2. Prior to assuming control of his shift, the operator _____ himself with the _____ of the computer.

♦ ♦ ♦

acquaints
status

3. The operator gains information relating to the status of the shift from
_____ .

◆ ◆ ◆

the operator on shift, the DP shift supervisor, computer logs, run
schedules, and personal observations of the system

4. The operator entering on a shift is usually present _____ and will
overlap the existing operator.

◆ ◆ ◆

prior to the beginning of his shift

5. The first shift operator is responsible for _____ to the system and
making it available for use.

◆ ◆ ◆

supplying power (or powering on)

6. Accompanying the operator onto the first shift should be a representative of the _____ .

◆ ◆ ◆

IOCG (I/O control group)

7. After completion of the POWER ON sequence, the operator begins
to _____ the system and readies the computer for processing.

◆ ◆ ◆

IPL

8. Prior to the input of the first application, the operator _____ the entire
system and ensures that all units are in a(n) _____ state.

◆ ◆ ◆

visually rechecks
ready

9. With the system in a ready state, entry of the required _____ will commence the processing of jobs.

♦ ♦ ♦

JCL cards

10. During the completion of any application, the operator should acquaint himself with the _____.

♦ ♦ ♦

next application to be processed

11. The operator must cross-reference the _____.

♦ ♦ ♦

run schedule and transmittal slip

12. All supplies forwarded with the transmittal slip must be _____.

♦ ♦ ♦

accounted for

13. When discrepancies are noted, the _____ must be contacted and this condition _____.

♦ ♦ ♦

IOCG
rectified

14. As jobs are completed, the results of processing are forwarded to the _____, accompanied by the respective _____.

♦ ♦ ♦

IOCG
transmittal slips

15. The ultimate purpose of all operator actions is to _____ the speed and efficiency of _____.

♦ ♦ ♦

increase
job throughput

Operator-initiated
Activities

Invalid input data

As we have previously mentioned, the input of data to an automated DP system often makes use of a card reading device. It, therefore, stands to reason that the card reader represents one of the first devices within the computer configuration that could alert the operator to the existence of an error. We shall, therefore, begin by discussing those errors that could be discovered as punched cards are input to the computer system.

Initially and prior to the placement of a problem program deck into the card reading device, the operator would be wise to visually check two items, namely,

1. The proper placement of JCL cards into the program
2. That all the cards within the program deck are correctly positioned for input into the card reader (i.e., with the 12 edge face up, etc.)

It is not practical or feasible for the operator to check the data punched into every card. Besides, the card reader will read-check every card as it passes beneath the card feed mechanism, on an IBM 2540 for example. In the majority of cases, read-check errors result from cards having an improper number of punches in one card column, from an improperly keyed card, or as the result of an equipment malfunction.

Therefore, when a punched card is read, a read-check is performed. Any errors noted will cause the lighting of the READ CHECK indicator light on the card reading device. This will also cause the reading of program cards to cease immediately; the operator then examines the improperly read card. The card to be examined is the *last* card found in the stacker receiving the input cards after a nonprocess runout.

The operator should examine this card column by column, searching for an improperly punched character code (too many or too few punches in one card column) or a set of punches between columns on the card. Both these errors can result from a malfunctioning keypunch. Of assistance to an operator is a device, similar to a large template, referred to as a *card gauge* (see Figure 18-1).

The card in question should be laid (face up) on top of the card gauge. Numbers printed on the gauge show through the punched holes on the card. The operator ensures that the holes punched onto the card are in alignment with the precalibrated numbers on the card gauge. Punched character codes are easily read, and punches improperly keyed out of their assigned card column can be readily noticed.

The operator also checks the card for any type of mutilation (i.e., a wrinkle along the surface of the card, a bent 9 or 12 edge, a nick or extra hole on the card, etc.). Any mutilation of a card can result in the card being improperly read.

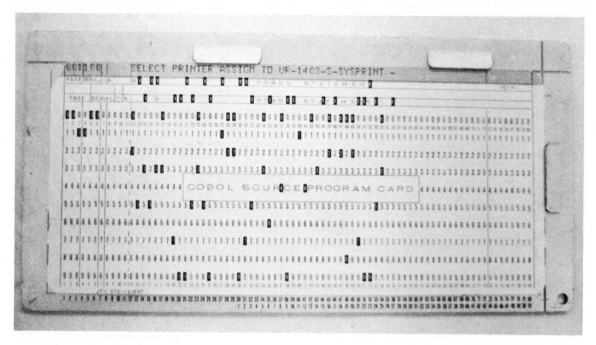

Figure 18-1
Card Gauge

A special form of read-check is a *validity check*. This error is noted by the activation of the VALIDITY CHECK light. This type of error results when more than one punch is found in rows 1 to 7 of a single card column.

Last, a read-check error will occur when cards are not properly joggled and aligned prior to their placement onto the unit's card slide. Though the card has been correctly keypunched, it will not pass beneath the card feed mechanism properly and thus results in a read-check error as the card reader considers that card to be improperly keyed. Rejoggling and rereading the entire deck of cards will rectify this condition.

In all cases, when a read-check error is indicated, the problem program should be aborted. The abort sequence may be automatically accomplished by the supervisor control program or manually under command of the operator. After a checking for errors and correction of those errors that are found, the corrected program may be reread, and if there are no other errors, the problem program can now be run to completion. Should the problem program still not run to completion, the entire program deck should be returned to the IOCG.

With the successful reading of program cards, processing of the problem program may begin. The time expended in processing a particular problem program is a function of the type of application. That is, if the program has

Detecting a program loop

a series of intricate mathematical manipulations, much processing will be required before any type of output will be forthcoming. For example, in our prior discussions, we noted that a scientific-oriented problem has complex internal arithmetic manipulations and results in a relatively small amount of output. Thus, much CPU time is expended during the completion of the required mathematical operations. As a result, the operator must wait a considerable amount of time before the results of processing are available. To the unskilled eye, it may appear as if little, or no, processing is taking place. The operator, however, should be well aware that processing is occurring.

There are occasions, however, when the time allotted to this type of processing activity must be checked by the operator. Each problem program must be apportioned a certain quantity of time in which to complete its execution. Very few programs will require the millions of manipulations which can be completed on a large computer system in approximately 10 minutes. Thus, if a program has not produced an output after this or any other specified period of time, the operator can assume either that additional time is yet required or that something has gone amiss in processing this application. If more than 10 minutes is required to process this job, for example, this fact should have been stated on the transmittal slip. If this was not done and the program execution has exceeded 10 minutes, the problem program can be considered to have entered an *iterative* or *continuous loop.*

The phrase *iterative* or *continuous loop* is used to define a set of repetitive operations, that is, a series of program instructions which will be executed by the computer over and over again—ad infinitum. It is feasible to assume that if the operator did not intervene, processing could continue indefinitely. Thus, it is imperative that the computer operator be capable of recognizing and determining when the system has entered this type of a loop so that a minimum of time will be lost.

This type of loop occurs quite often when programs are being tested or compiled/assembled and run—especially for the first time. When a computer has entered an iterative loop, the operator should observe many of the indicators below:

1. The SYS (system) indicator light on the console remains lit.
2. The USE meter on the console continues to run.
3. No output has occurred for a considerable period of time.
4. The same panel lights will flash repetitively in a recognizable pattern.
5. An I/O device reacts in a repetitive, nonproductive pattern (i.e., tape reels that are read, rewound, read, etc., with no results of processing).

The operator observing these activities could readily assume that the computer has entered a continuous loop. Should the operator desire to further verify that an iterative loop has been encountered, he employs a single-instruction processing sequence (Chapter 16). The procedure employed is:

1. Depress the STOP pushbutton on the console.
2. Set the RATE dial to the INSN STEP setting (turn one position to the left).
3. Press the START pushbutton on the console.
4. Record the address of the next instruction to be executed that appears in the B- and A-REGISTER displays.
5. Repeat step 4 as many times as required.

Since the computer is assumed to have entered a loop, the address originally recorded will eventually be redisplayed in the B- and A-REGISTER displays. If this does occur, our assumption will be confirmed. If after a period of time the original instruction address does not reappear, the program should be returned to normal processing.

Upon discovery of the fact that the problem program has entered a continuous loop, the operator aborts the job, i.e., stops the program from running and removes it from the system. He must not, however, destroy the record which documents the instruction address sequence. This listing is of value to the problem programmer and is forwarded with the respective transmittal slip.

It must be noted, however, that some computer systems have a capability to test automatically for the presence of a continuous loop. These systems employ an internal timing device to record the time expended by a job in processing. The entry of each job into the computer is recorded and temporarily stored. If, after a predetermined quantity of time, either no output is forthcoming or the program has exceeded the allotted number of minutes available for processing any job, it is automatically aborted. Not all systems are established to function under this type of operational feature. It is therefore necessary for a newly employed operator to inquire whether the installation has this operating capability.

The correcting of job control or data cards and the tracing of an iterative loop are actions resulting from the operator's monitoring of the system. The operator is able to discern through his observations the existence of an error state. More frequently, however, the system will generate a message to the operator defining some type of error condition. These types of messages are of paramount importance to the operator and will be discussed in the following section.

Self-study exercise 18-3

1. The card reader represents one of the first devices which could _____.

◆ ◆ ◆

recognize the existence of an error and alert the operator

2. Prior to the placement of a program deck into the card reader, the operator should check the _____.

◆ ◆ ◆

positioning of cards within the deck and the JCL cards included in the program deck

3. The operator (should/should not) check every data card in a program deck.

◆ ◆ ◆

should not

4. A read-check is performed on _____.

◆ ◆ ◆

all cards read by the card reader

5. A read-check is signaled by activation of a card reader's _____ light.

◆ ◆ ◆

READ CHECK

6. The card to be examined in the case of a read-check is the _____ after performing a nonprocess runout.

◆ ◆ ◆

last card found in the stacker receiving input cards

7. The operator should examine the card in question for _____.

◆ ◆ ◆

improperly punched character codes, punches entered between card columns, and mutilation of any type

8. Both of these errors may be caused by _____.

◆ ◆ ◆

a malfunctioning keypunch

9. A device employed to check the alignment of punches is a(n) _____.

◆ ◆ ◆

card gauge

10. A special form of a read-check is a(n) _____.

◆ ◆ ◆

validity check

11. A validity check results when _____ of a card column.

◆ ◆ ◆

more than one punch is found in rows 1 to 7

12. A read-check may occur as cards pass improperly beneath the _____.

◆ ◆ ◆

card feed mechanism

13. When a read-check error is found, the problem program should be _____.

◆ ◆ ◆

aborted

14. After a read-check, if the errors are corrected on the card, the program may be _____.

◆ ◆ ◆

rerun

15. If a program continues to incur read-checks, it should be _____ to the IOCG.

♦ ♦ ♦

returned

16. With cards successfully read, processing may _____.

♦ ♦ ♦

commence

17. The time expended in processing a program is a(n) _____.

♦ ♦ ♦

function of the type of application

18. Processing may occur _____ any visible output.

♦ ♦ ♦

without

19. All problem programs must be apportioned a _____ for processing.

♦ ♦ ♦

specific quantity of time

20. As a rule of thumb, the operator should allow _____ for a job to run to completion.

♦ ♦ ♦

10 minutes

21. A job requiring more than 10 minutes for processing would have this fact noted _____.

♦ ♦ ♦

on its transmittal slip

22. If a job is not intended to run for a long period of time, but does, the operator may assume it has entered a(n) _____.

♦ ♦ ♦

continuous or iterative loop

23. A continuous or iterative loop is _____.

♦ ♦ ♦

a set of repetitive operations

24. If a program has entered a continuous loop, the operator must _____ and _____ the job.

♦ ♦ ♦

intervene
abort

25. Loops are encountered when programs are being _____.

♦ ♦ ♦

tested or compiled/assembled and run

26. The operator can employ _____ to determine if a program has entered an iterative loop.

♦ ♦ ♦

single-instruction processing

27. With the discovery that a program is in a loop, the operator should _____.

♦ ♦ ♦

abort that job

28. The record of activities documented during single-instruction processing should not be _____, as it is of value to the _____.

♦ ♦ ♦

destroyed
programmer

29. Some computer systems automatically _____ for the presence of program loops through use of a(n) _____.

◆ ◆ ◆

test

timing device

System-generated Messages

You may recall from the previous chapter that we discussed a form referred to as a message list. This list documented a series of programmer-determined error messages that were possible with a specific program application. These errors are generated by the problem program itself, since it checks all the data cards being input. In this section, however, we shall concern ourselves with a different type of error message, one which is generated by the computer system. That is, we shall concern ourselves with those errors generated by the supervisor control program or a computer language compiler. The computer system records and documents the detection of such conditions in the form of *diagnostic messages*. For the purposes of our discussion, we will separate these messages into two types: *program* and *equipment diagnostic messages*.

Program diagnostic messages

During the compilation and running of a program, the program will interact with both the compiler and the supervisor. The compiler will scrutinize the problem program for errors in syntax, that is, errors in the manner in which the program was physically written. It ensures that the programmer, in writing the program, has adhered to all the rules established for that language. In particular, the supervisor will scan the program to ensure that the I/O devices and procedures are correctly assigned, appropriate JCL cards were input, data and program cards or statements are not missing.

This type of diagnostic error can be noted on the system's printer, the console typewriter, or both. For the most part, however, the majority of compiler-generated errors will be output on the system's printer. Supervisor error messages will be evenly divided between the console typewriter and printer. Regardless of the output device employed, the message will be available to the computer operator.

The operator must be capable of responding to an error condition when it is noted. To this end, error messages must be defined using a standard format. To interpret the various codes, the operator will utilize two of the manufacturer's technical manuals—the *Operator's Guide* and the *Error Message Book*. When the existence of an error is signaled via the console, the operator should cross-reference the error message in both manuals. The Error Message Book will define the error and the action required by the operator. The Operator's Guide will note the cause of the error and its effect on the system. The operator should then take the necessary action described by the Error Message Book. Of course, these actions would be adapted to the specific computer system within which the operator is working.

Diagnostic messages in FORTRAN are given the notation *ILF FORTRAN—Diagnostic messages,* whereas in COBOL the phrase *ILA— Compiler Diagnostic messages* is used. Figure 18-2 illustrates a page from a FORTRAN diagnostic manual. The message printed on either the console typewriter or a printer would follow the same format. For example, the message would be printed by the console typewriter and then be referenced in the diagnostic manual by exactly the same message format.

For the vast majority of systems, once an error (serious enough to affect processing) is noted, the supervisor will automatically cancel that program and cease its processing.

Equipment diagnostic messages serve quite a different purpose for the operator. They are designed to alert the operator to online peripheral units which are inoperable. The unit may be inoperable as a result of the operator's failure to supply power or improperly ready the unit for processing, the failure of an internal component within the unit, etc.

Equipment diagnostic messages

The appropriate error message will be transmitted through the console typewriter. In general, the format for the error message will appear as below:

XXXXX   NARRATIVE

Five-digit ID   Details of the error message
code

The operator, once alerted by the error message, will turn his attention to the specified unit of equipment. Let us consider a specific example to assist our discussions.

Occasionally, when powering up the system, the operator will fail to activate one of the online I/O units. In the case of our example, let us assume that this unit was the line printer. When the system attempts to access the printer and determines that it is in a nonready state, the system will cause an error message to be issued via the console typewriter. The error message will indicate that operator intervention is required and identify the device—the printer. That error message might appear as

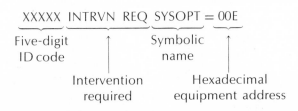

COMPILER DIAGNOSTIC MESSAGES

Two types of compiler diagnostic messages are generated—error/warning messages and status messages.

COMPILER ERROR/WARNING MESSAGES

The following text contains a description of compiler error/warning messages. The message is shown with an explanation, and any compiler or user action that is required.

ILF001I   ILLEGAL TYPE

Explanation: The variable in an assigned GO TO statement is not an integer variable; or the variable in an assignment statement to the left of the equal sign is of logical type and the expression on the right side does not correspond; or an argument in a reference to an IBM-supplied subprogram is not the type required by the subprogram.
(Error level-8)

ILF002I   LABEL

Explanation: The label required in the statement *following* the GO TO, STOP, RETURN, and arithmetic IF statements has been omitted.
(Error level-0)

ILF003I   NAME LENGTH

Explanation: The name of a variable, COMMON block, NAMELIST, or subprogram exceeds six characters; or two variable names appear in an expression without a separating operation symbol.
(Error level-4)

ILF004I   COMMA

Explanation: The comma required in the statement has been omitted.
(Error level-0)

ILF005I   ILLEGAL LABEL

Explanation: Invalid use of a statement label; for example, an attempt is made to branch to the label of a FORMAT statement; a statement label referenced in a READ or WRITE statement and occurring *after* the READ or WRITE statement is not the label of a FORMAT statement.
(Error level-8)

ILF006I   DUPLICATE LABEL

Explanation: The label appearing in the label field of a statement has previously been defined.
(Error level-8)

ILF007I   ID CONFLICT

Explanation: The name of a variable or subprogram has been used in conflict with the type that was previously defined for the variable or subprogram.

Examples: The name listed in a CALL statement is the name of a variable; a single name appears more than once in the dummy list of a statement function; a name listed in an EXTERNAL statement has been defined in another context.
(Error level-8)

ILF008I   ALLOCATION

Explanation: Storage allocation cannot be performed because of an inconsistency between the present usage of a variable name and some prior usage of that name.

Examples: A name listed in a COMMON block has been listed in another COMMON block; a variable listed in an EQUIVALENCE statement is followed by more than seven subscripts.
(Error level-8)

Figure 18-2
Sample FORTRAN
Diagnostic Messages

The five-digit ID code identifies the type of error message (the operator could reference this code in the manufacturer's Error Message Book). The term *SYSOPT* is the symbolic name noting the SYStem's OutPuT device—the line printer (i.e., a card reader could be referenced by the term *SYSIPT,* or SYStem InPuT). The number 00E is the hexadecimal representation of the address assigned by the system to the line printer (these digits can vary for different computer systems and manufacturers).

This error message alerts the operator to the necessity of his intervention at the line printer. After noting such a message, the operator then makes a visual inspection of the printer. He makes certain that there is a full supply of paper available, the feed clutch is engaged, the carriage control tape is mounted and engaged, etc. His last action is the depression of the START key on the printer's console. When the READY indicator light turns on, the operator's intervention has been successful, and processing can be resumed.

In the majority of cases, the operator's intervention will satisfactorily handle equipment errors. If the operator is unable to return the device to its ready state, he should note this condition in the computer log and contact the shift supervisor.

Prior to that, however, the operator should cancel the program application from the system.

Self-study exercise 18-4

1. For a program application, a message list records a series of _____.

◆ ◆ ◆

programmer-determined errors

2. Errors noted by the supervisor or a compiler are documented in the form of _____.

◆ ◆ ◆

diagnostic messages

3. Errors in syntax represent errors _____.

◆ ◆ ◆

in the manner in which the program was written

4. The _____ checks the problem program for errors in syntax.

◆ ◆ ◆

compiler

5. The supervisor will scan the program to ensure that _____ .

♦ ♦ ♦

I/O devices and procedures are correctly assigned, appropriate JCL were input, data cards were provided, and program statements are not missing

6. The majority of compiler-generated errors are output on the _____ .

♦ ♦ ♦

system's printer

7. Assisting the operator in the interpretation of diagnostic messages are two manufacturer's technical manuals—_____ and _____ .

♦ ♦ ♦

the Operator's Guide
Error Message Book

8. After an error is noted via the console, the operator should _____ .

♦ ♦ ♦

cross-reference the error message in both manuals

9. The _____ will define the error and indicate those actions required by the operator.

♦ ♦ ♦

Error Message Book

10. The Operator's Guide will note _____ .

♦ ♦ ♦

the cause of the error and its effect on the system

11. Diagnostic messages in FORTRAN are given the notation _____ .

♦ ♦ ♦

ILF FORTRAN—Diagnostic messages

12. In COBOL, diagnostic messages carry the notation _____.

◆ ◆ ◆

ILA—Compiler Diagnostic messages

13. Equipment error messages are designed to _____.

◆ ◆ ◆

alert the operator to an online unit which is inoperable

14. Once the system has recognized that an error exists, the appropriate error message _____.

◆ ◆ ◆

will be issued via the console typewriter

15. After noting the equipment error message, the operator will _____.

◆ ◆ ◆

turn his attention to the specific peripheral unit

16. An equipment diagnostic message should contain _____.

◆ ◆ ◆

a number ID code, a narrative requesting intervention, the device's symbolic name, and the address of the specified peripheral device

17. In the majority of cases, the operator's intervention of the unit (will/will not) satisfy most equipment errors.

◆ ◆ ◆

will

18. If the device specified by the diagnostic message remains inoperable, the operator should _____.

◆ ◆ ◆

contact his superior and abort the job from the system

The Cancel Operation The purpose of the *cancel operation* is to halt the processing of the problem program and remove that application from the system. The canceling of a program can be effected either by the supervisor control program or at the operator's discretion. As previously mentioned, should the supervisor program determine, after compilation, that a problem program is not executable, it will abort that job. That is, the supervisor will direct the computer to cancel that problem program and thereby halt its processing. For most systems, this type of cancel operation is automatically instituted by the supervisor.

The operator-initiated cancel operation is available for those conditions where the operator must intervene within processing and flush a job from the system. The operator may be required to cancel:

1. An application that has entered a continuous loop
2. A dump operation requested by a program's JCL
3. A program which has accessed a restricted, but unprotected, storage area and interfered with the supervisor
4. Any job currently running on the system

Prior to discussing each separately, let us discuss a general procedure that could be employed in all the above cases.

General procedure In almost every case, the cancel operation is initiated through the use of the console typewriter. The procedure utilized in the cancel operation is completed in exactly the same manner as any communication from the IBM 1052 Printer Keyboard. Incorporating these steps into the general cancel operation, the procedure is completed via the 1052, as follows:

1. Depress the REQUEST pushbutton on the 1052's console. The ATTN light will turn on.
2. Await activation of the PROCD light.
3. Enter the following command, beginning with print entry position 1: CANCEL.
4. After keying the character L, simultaneously depress the ALTN CODING and EOB (5) keys.

Upon completion of that entry, the computer initiates the cancel operation. In some systems, upon the completion of this operation the computer issues the following statement via the 1052:

EOJ JOB (*Program name or ID number*)

This transmission verifies the identity of the application just canceled. The operator then records the cancellation of this job on the computer log and respective transmittal slip.

Let us now consider how the cancel operation is employed in the other operational states encountered by the operator.

Initially, the operator must determine that the problem program has entered a loop by implementing those measures necessary to verify this fact. After this is accomplished, the operator interrupts the processing of that job and initiates a cancel operation. The previously outlined general procedure is employed.

Canceling a program loop

The dump option is exercised through JCL. As you may recall from Chapter 8, the printout created from a dump operation provides us with a picture of main storage. Depending upon the size of the program and the speed of the printer, the output of a dump may involve a considerable amount of time. For those instances when the operator is required to abort a dump operation, the CANCEL DUMP command is provided.

Canceling a dump

    The general procedure used to execute the cancel operation is used. The only change in the procedure is the command issued by the operator. Instead of the word *CANCEL,* the phrase *CANCEL DUMP* is substituted and keyed in. This results in the initiation of the cancel operation, thereby aborting the output of the dump.

We may also remember from Chapter 8 that the supervisor must reside in the lower address positions of main storage for the CPU to enter a supervisor state. All I/O operations are executable only when the CPU is in its supervisor state. It is therefore possible to conclude that if the supervisor control program is disturbed, altered, or tampered with, the processing of any and all subsequent jobs will be affected. Thus, other jobs cannot and will not be processed correctly, if they can be processed at all.

Cancel and reIPL

    Quite frequently during the compilation, assembly, and test of a job, the problem program bombs the supervisor. That is, on systems where the supervisor is stored in unprotected storage locations, the program enters the lower-numbered storage positions and alters the contents of those positions. The result is the altering of some instructions and commands within the supervisor control program. Thus, the system cannot continue processing, and the IPL sequence must be reinitiated. Here, the IPL operation retrieves the supervisor from the auxiliary storage device and restores the supervisor into main storage—in its proper instructional format.

    Indications that the problem program has interfered with supervisor are:

1. The system has entered a continuous loop.
2. The computing system is suddenly reacting erratically to normal operator-initiated commands.

3. The computer has entered a perpetual wait state, where nothing is being processed. The WAIT indicator light on the computer's console remains lit and does not flicker.
4. No I/O activity has occurred for a considerable length of time.

To alleviate this problem, the operator initiates a cancel operation and subsequent to its completion, reIPLs the system. If the system does not respond to the cancel command, the operator must:

1. Complete the POWER OFF sequence required for the system.
2. POWER ON the system.
3. Initiate the prescribed IPL operation.

In all cases, this sequence of steps returns the computing system to its fully operational state.

Canceling any job During processing, the operator may cancel any application being run. The program being canceled need not have an error in it, since occasionally the operator may be directed to remove that application from the computing system for other reasons. For example, the operator could be instructed to process a high-priority job immediately. Unable to wait for the completion of the current problem program, the operator is, therefore, required to abort it. Once the old program has been canceled, processing of the high-priority application may commence.

The general procedure described in a prior section can be used to cancel any program in the midst of processing. As a result of this operation, the problem program is canceled and flushed from the system.

One final point must be made relating to the cancellation of any type of program. The last set of instructions of the cancel operation is designed to initiate the input of the next program to be processed. This set of instructions is referred to as the End-Of-Job, or EOJ, commands. After the cancellation of the current problem, the EOJ commands will direct the computer to read data relating to the next application available for processing. As a result of these commands, the new application will enter processing directly, thus assisting the operator in establishing and maintaining an efficient, continuous job stream.

Self-study exercise 18-5

1. The purpose of the cancel operation is _____ .

to stop the processing of a problem program and remove that application from the system

2. The _____ or _____ may direct the cancellation of a program.

◆ ◆ ◆

supervisor control program
operator

3. The supervisor program may request a cancel operation at _____ during the processing of a program, but only after it has determined that the program is _____ .

◆ ◆ ◆

any time
unexecutable

4. The operator may _____ in the processing of any job and cancel it from the system.

◆ ◆ ◆

intervene

5. The operator may be required to cancel a job because _____ .

◆ ◆ ◆

the application has entered a continuous loop, a dump is re-quested, the program's JCL is not required, a program has entered a restricted area and interfered with the supervisor, or another job must be placed on the system

6. In general, cancel operations are initiated via the _____ .

◆ ◆ ◆

console typewriter

7. After canceling a job, the operator should record the program's cancel-lation on the _____ .

◆ ◆ ◆

computer log and transmittal slip

8. After determining that a program loop exists, the operator should _____ .

♦ ♦ ♦

interrupt processing of that job and initiate a cancel operation

9. To prevent the completion of a JCL-requested dump, the _____ command is employed in the cancel operation.

♦ ♦ ♦

CANCEL DUMP

10. Occasionally, during the _____ of a job, the problem program bombs the supervisor.

♦ ♦ ♦

compilation, assembly, and testing

11. After the supervisor has been altered, it is rendered _____ and cannot _____ .

♦ ♦ ♦

ineffective
control processing

12. Indications that a program has interfered with the supervisor are _____ .

♦ ♦ ♦

the system has entered a continuous loop, the computing system is suddenly reacting erratically to normal operator-initiated commands, the WAIT indicator light remains lit, and no I/O activity has occurred for a considerable length of time

13. The operator, upon noticing the above behavior of the system, should _____ the problem program.

♦ ♦ ♦

cancel

14. If the cancel operation is ineffective, the operator should _____ .

◆ ◆ ◆

reIPL the system

15. At times, the operator might be directed to cancel one job to _____ .

◆ ◆ ◆

run another job with a higher priority

16. The EOJ commands are the _____ set of instructions of the _____ .

◆ ◆ ◆

last
cancel operation

17. The EOJ commands are designed to _____ of the _____ job to be processed.

◆ ◆ ◆

initiate the input
next

Throughout the text, we have made one point clear—the operator is required to react quickly to any eventualities which may affect the processing capabilities of the system. To accomplish this task readily, the operator must have a working knowledge of the operational aspects of his job. That is, he must understand what procedures to follow when specific errors arise, where the technical manuals are kept, where the supplies required for processing are stored (i.e., carriage control tapes, paper, etc.), who to contact when equipment errors are noted, and what forms are employed for what purpose.

A general knowledge of "what to do" is particularly important to the newly hired computer operator. All new operators must adjust themselves to their new environments and learn where things are located, as well as what should be done with them.

To assist himself in this reorientation process, it is a good idea for the newly hired operator to prepare some form of computer room checklist. Employing this checklist, the operator can quickly ascertain what he knows or does not know with relation to his job. From the checklist, the

Computer Room Checklist

operator can develop a guideline of those operational aspects with which he must familiarize himself.

The following checklist is provided as an example of a computer room checklist which might be employed by a newly hired operator.

COMPUTER ROOM CHECKLIST

1. Locate and understand the purpose, use, and function of the following:
   _____ All reference manuals
   _____ Tape library
   _____ Disk pack storage
   _____ Printer paper storage
   _____ Carriage control tape storage
   _____ Card storage
   _____ Room temperature gauge
   _____ Room humidity gauge
   _____ Log sheets
   _____ Run schedules
   _____ Time stamp
   _____ IOCG drop area
   _____ Time-of-day clock
   _____ Tape file protect rings
   _____ All power switches/outlets

2. Perform the following:
   _____ Load a tape
   _____ Unload a tape
   _____ Mount a disk pack
   _____ Unmount a disk pack
   _____ Change forms on printer, teletype terminal, console typewriter
   _____ Retrieve a tape from the tape library
   _____ Assist in setting up the next job

3. With relation to the console, locate and familiarize yourself with the purpose and use of each of the following:
   _____ EMERGENCY PULL switch
   _____ POWER ON key
   _____ POWER OFF key
   _____ INTERRUPT key
   _____ WAIT light
   _____ MANUAL light
   _____ SYSTEM light
   _____ TEST light
   _____ LOAD light
   _____ LOAD UNIT switches
   _____ LOAD key

_____ SYSTEM RESET key
_____ STOP key
_____ ROTARY RATE switch
_____ START key
_____ DISPLAY key
_____ STORE key
_____ USE meters

4. Complete and record the results of a lamp test.
5. Record the model numbers of the devices available within the computing system:
   Card reader _____
   Card punch _____
   Tape unit(s) _____
   Disk unit(s) _____
   Printer(s) _____
   Console typewriter _____
   Terminal(s), if any, _____
6. Obtain the system assignments of each of the above devices for the available computer configuration.
7. Locate the load point marker on a reel of tape.
8. Record readings from the USE meters on the console.
9. For the printer, locate the following:
   _____ POWER ON
   _____ POWER OFF
   _____ RAISE COVER
   _____ LOWER COVER
   _____ Carriage control unit
   _____ Carriage control tape
   _____ Carriage control tape unit brushes
   _____ Print unit release lever
   _____ Print unit
   _____ Feed clutch
   _____ Line spacing settings
   _____ Vertical print adjustment control
   _____ Righthand tractor vernier control
   _____ Paper advance knob
   _____ Guide bar
   _____ Horizontal adjustment knob
   _____ Lefthand and righthand tractor latch
   _____ Print line indicator
   _____ Lateral print vernier
   _____ Print density setting
   _____ Outer guide gate
   _____ Inner guide gate
   _____ Stacker area

10.   Where is the RATE switch set?
11.   Find the EOB and CANCEL keys on the console typewriter.
12.   Describe the procedure used to cancel an incorrect transmission input via the console typewriter.
13.   Outline the IPL sequence required by the system.
14.   Describe and record the various JCL options available with the system.
15.   Outline the procedure employed on this system to cancel a job. Does the system automatically cancel jobs containing errors? If so, record the type of errors to which it will respond.
16.   Examine the type of tape and disk ID labels used.
17.   Document the procedure to be followed when an equipment malfunction is noted. If the device is inoperative, who is to be contacted?
18.   Where is the IOCG located? What are their responsibilities and relation to the operator?

Self-study exercise 18-6

1. The operator is required to _____ to all the operating states _____ by the system.

◆   ◆   ◆

react quickly
assumed

2. For the operator to interact efficiently with the system, he must have a(n) _____ of the operational aspects of his job.

◆   ◆   ◆

working knowledge

3. Newly hired operators should orient themselves to _____.

◆   ◆   ◆

their new environments

4. A _____ will assist the operator in the orientation process.

◆   ◆   ◆

checklist

5. From a computer room checklist, the operator can develop a(n) _____ of those activities with which he must _____ himself.

◆ ◆ ◆

guideline
familiarize

True-false exercise

1. Batch processing normally involves a large quantity of data.
2. The computer operator, upon entering his work shift, need only consult with the operator currently on shift.
3. The operator should have knowledge of all maintenance activities completed within the system.
4. The first-shift computer operator assumes the responsibilities for the IOCG.
5. After the POWER ON sequence, all online units should be in a ready state.
6. The operator should always reacquaint himself with the next application to be processed.
7. If an error is found that relates to the next job to be processed, the operator should rectify this error solely by himself.
8. A card gauge is designed to check the size of a punched card.
9. A validity check ensures that only one punch is placed in rows 1 to 7 in one card column.
10. Programs causing read-checks are never rerun by the operator.
11. All programs should expend the same computer time in processing.
12. When no output results from a program, the program is *not* undergoing processing.
13. A continuous loop is allowed to run to completion.
14. Program diagnostics note errors in syntax and equipment malfunctions.
15. Equipment diagnostic messages alert the operator to inoperative online peripheral devices.
16. A cancel operation will flush a program from the system.
17. A program dump cannot be canceled once it has been initiated via JCL cards.
18. A computer room checklist is of assistance to the newly hired operator.
19. The checklist assists the new operator as he acquaints himself with his new work environment.

Fill-in exercise

1. Batch processing is _____ at regular and frequent intervals.
2. It is essential that the operator acquaint himself with the _____ of the system prior to his shift.

3. The oncoming shift operator should _____ the existing shift operator's work schedule.
4. An operator preparing to assume control of the first shift must _____ and _____ the system, thereby readying it for processing.
5. Prior to the input of the first application to the computer, the operator should _____ check the entire system.
6. The card reader is often one of the _____ system devices to sense an error in the problem program.
7. When a read-check is noted, the card to be examined is the _____ card in the stacker receiving cards after the performance of a non-process runout.
8. The improper joggling of cards may result in a(n) _____ when the cards are subsequently read.
9. A(n) _____ indicates that the computer is completing the same instructions repeatedly.
10. A continuous loop defines a set of _____.
11. On some systems, a(n) _____ device is employed to check continuous program loops.
12. Error messages generated by the supervisor or compiler are called _____.
13. To interpret program-generated diagnostics, the operator can use technical manuals—_____ and _____.
14. Equipment diagnostics adhere to a predetermined _____.
15. If the supervisor has been altered by a problem program, the operator will be required to _____ the system.
16. At the completion of a cancel operation, the _____ initiate the input of the next program to be processed.

Discussion questions

1. Briefly discuss those signs that will indicate the existence of possible system trouble spots to the operator. Cite an illustration for each example given.
2. Discuss the activities required of the computer operator
   a.   Coming onto an existing shift
   b.   Initiating the day's first shift
3. Outline and discuss those procedures employed by the operator coming onto his shift.
4. Discuss two tasks the operator should perform while inputting data to the card reader.
5. Briefly discuss those factors which may signal the existence of a continuous program loop.
6. Outline and discuss the procedure employed to document the exist-

ence of an iterative loop. What purpose do the A- and B-REGISTER displays serve?

7. Briefly discuss program and equipment diagnostic messages. Cite an example for each.

8. Outline and discuss the procedure required to cancel a job. Give examples of conditions where the cancel operation might be utilized.

9. Discuss those factors which indicate that the problem program has interfered with or altered an instruction composing the supervisor.

GLOSSARY OF DATA PROCESSING TERMS

APPENDIX A*

Absolute Address (1) An *address* that is permanently assigned by the machine designer to a *storage location*.
(2) A pattern of *characters* that identifies a unique storage location without further modification.
(3) Synonymous with machine address, specific address.

Absolute Coding Coding that uses *machine instructions* with *absolute addresses*. Synonymous with specific coding.

Access Arm A part of a *disc storage* unit that is used to hold one or more reading and writing *heads*.

Access Time (1) The time interval between the instant at which *data* are called for from a *storage device* and the instant delivery begins.
(2) The time interval between the instant at which data are requested to be stored and the instant at which storage is started.

Accounting Machine (1) A keyboard actuated machine that prepares accounting *records*.
(2) A machine that *reads data* from external *storage* media, such as cards or tapes, and automatically produces accounting records or tabulations, usually on continuous forms.

Accumulator A *register* in which the result of an arithmetic or logic *operation* is formed.

Accuracy The degree of freedom from *error,* that is, the degree of conformity to truth or to a rule. Accuracy is contrasted with precision. For example, four-place *numerals* are less precise than six-place numerals, nevertheless a properly computed four-place numeral might be more accurate than an improperly computed six-place numeral.

Acoustic Delay Line A *delay line* whose operation is based on the time of propagation of sound waves in a given *medium*. Synonymous with sonic delay line.

Adder (1) A device whose *output* is a representation of the sum of the quantities represented by its *inputs*.
(2) See *half-adder*.

Address   (1) An identification, as represented by a name, *label*, or number, for a *register*, location in *storage*, or any other *data* source or destination such as the location of a station in a communication network.
(2) Loosely, any part of an *instruction* that specifies the location of an *operand* for the instruction.

Address Format   (1) The arrangement of the *address parts* of an *instruction*. The expression "plus-one" is frequently used to indicate that one of the addresses specifies the location of the next instruction to be executed, such as one-plus-one, two-plus-one, three-plus-one, four-plus-one.
(2) The arrangement of the parts of a *single address*, such as those required for identifying *channel, module, track,* etc. in a disc system.

Address Register   A *register* in which an *address* is *stored*.

ADP   *Automatic data processing.*

ALGOL   ALGOrithmic Language. A *language* primarily used to express *computer programs* by *algorithms*.

Algorithm   (SC1) A prescribed set of well-defined rules or *processes* for the solution of a problem in a finite number of steps, e.g., a full statement of an arithmetic procedure for evaluating sin x to a stated *precision*. Contrast with *heuristic*.

Algorithmic Language   A *language* designed for expressing *algorithms*.

Alphabet   (1) An ordered set of all the *letters* and associated marks used in a *language*.
(2) An ordered set of *symbols* used in a language, e.g., the Morse code alphabet, the 128 characters of the *ASCII* alphabet.

Alphabetic Code   (SC1) A *code* whose *code set* consists only of *letters* and associated *special characters*.

Alphanumeric   Pertaining to a *character set* that contains *letters, digits,* and usually other *characters* such as punctuation marks. Synonymous with alphameric.

Analog Computer   (1) (SC1) A *computer* in which *analog* representation of *data* is mainly used.
(2) A computer that operates on analog data by performing physical processes on these data. Contrast with *digital computer*.

Analysis   The methodical investigation of a problem, and the separation of the problem into smaller related units for further detailed study.

Analyst   (SC1) A person who defines problems and develops *algorithms* and *procedures* for their solution.

Aperture   (1) An opening in a *data medium* or device such as a card or *magnetic core;* e.g., the aperture in an aperture card combining a microfilm with a *punched card* or a *multiple aperture core.*
(2) A part of a *mask* that permits retention of the corresponding portions of *data.*

Arbitrary Sequence Computer   (SC1) A *computer* in which each *instruction* determines explicitly the *location* of the next instruction to be executed.

Argument   An independent variable. For example, in looking up a quantity in a *table,* the *number,* or any of the numbers, that identifies the *location* of the desired value.

Arithmetic Shift   (1) A *shift* that does not affect the *sign position.*
(2) A *shift* that is equivalent to the multiplication of a *number* by a positive or negative integral power of the *radix.*

Arithmetic Unit   The unit of a computing system that contains the circuits that perform arithmetic *operations.*

Artificial Language   A *language* based on a set of prescribed rules that are established prior to its usage. Contrast with *natural language.*

ASCII (American National Standard Code for Information Interchange, X3.4–1968)   The standard *code,* using a coded *character set* consisting of 7-bit coded characters (8 bits including *parity check*), used for information interchange among *data processing systems,* communication systems, and associated equipment. The ASCII set consists of *control characters* and *graphic characters.* Synonymous with USASCII.

Assemble   To prepare a *machine language program* from a symbolic language program by substituting *absolute operation codes* for symbolic operation codes and *absolute* or relocatable addresses for *symbolic addresses.*

Assembler A *computer program* that *assembles.*

Associative Storage A *storage device* in which storage *locations* are identified by their contents, not by names or positions. Synonymous with content addressed storage. Contrast with *parallel search storage.*

Asynchronous Computer (SC1) A *computer* in which each *event* or the performance of each *operation* starts as a result of a *signal* generated by the completion of the previous event or operation, or by the availability of the parts of the computer required for the next event or operation. Contrast with *synchronous computer.*

Automatic (SC1) Pertaining to a process or device that, under specified conditions, functions without intervention by a human operator.

Automatic Computer A *computer* that can perform a sequence of *operations* without intervention by a human *operator.*

Automatic Data Processing (1) (SC1) *Data processing* largely performed by *automatic* means.
(2) (SC1) By extension, the discipline which deals with methods and techniques related to data processing performed by automatic means.
(3) Pertaining to data processing equipment such as *electrical accounting machines* and *electronic data processing* equipment.
Abbreviated ADP.

Automation (1) (SC1) The implementation of processes by *automatic* means.
(2) The theory, art, or technique of making a process more *automatic.*
(3) The investigation, design, development, and application of methods of rendering processes *automatic,* self-moving, or self-controlling.
(4) (SC1) The conversion of a procedure, a process, or equipment to *automatic* operation.

Auxiliary Operation An *offline operation* performed by equipment not under control of the *central processing unit.*

Auxiliary Storage (1) A *storage* that supplements another storage. Contrast with *main storage.*
(2) In *flowcharting,* an *offline operation* performed

by equipment not under control of the *central processing unit*.

Available Time   Time other than *maintenance time*. Available time consists of *idle time* and *operating time*. Operating time consists of *development time*, *production time*, and *makeup time*. Contrast with *maintenance time*.

Background Processing   The *automatic* execution of lower priority *computer programs* when higher priority programs are not using the system resources. Contrast with *foreground processing*.

Base   (1) A reference value.
(2) A *number* that is multiplied by itself as many times as indicated by an *exponent*.
(3) Same as *radix*.
(4) See *floating-point base*.

Base Address   A given *address* from which an *absolute address* is derived by combination with a *relative address*.

Batch Processing   (1) Pertaining to the technique of executing a set of *computer programs* such that each is completed before the next program of the set is started.
(2) Pertaining to the sequential input of *computer programs* or *data*.
(3) Loosely, the execution of *computer programs* serially.

Baud   A unit of signalling speed equal to the number of *discrete* conditions or signal events per second. For example, one baud equals one-half dot cycle per second in Morse code, one bit per second in a train of binary signals, and one 3-bit value per second in a train of signals each of which can assume one of eight different states.

BCD   *Binary-coded decimal notation*.

Beginning-of-tape Marker   A marker on a *magnetic tape* used to indicate the beginning of the permissible recording area, e.g., a photo reflective strip, a transparent section of tape.

Benchmark Problem   A problem used to evaluate the performance of *hardware* or *software* or both.

Binary (1) Pertaining to a characteristic or property involving a selection, choice, or condition in which there are two possibilities.
(2) Pertaining to the *number representation system* with a *radix* of two.

Binary-coded Decimal Notation *Positional notation* in which the individual *decimal digits* expressing a *number* in *decimal notation* are each represented by a *binary numeral*, e.g., the number twenty-three is represented by 0010 0011 in the 8-4-2-1 type of binary-coded decimal notation and by 10111 in *binary notation*. Abbreviated BCD.

Binary Digit (1) In *binary notation*, either of the characters, 0 or 1.
(2) See *equivalent binary digits*.
Abbreviated bit.

Binary Notation *Fixed radix notation* where the *radix* is two. For example, in *binary notation* the *numeral* 110.01 represents the number 1 × 2 squared plus 1 × 2 to the first power plus 1 × 2 to the minus 2 power, that is, six and a quarter.

Binary Numeral A *binary* representation of a *number*, e.g., "101" is a binary numeral and a "V" is the equivalent Roman numeral.

Bit (1) A *binary digit.*
(2) Same as Shannon.
(3) See *check bit, information bits, parity bit, sign bit.*

Blank Character Same as *space character.*

Block (1) A set of things, such as *words, characters,* or *digits* handled as a unit.
(2) A collection of contiguous *records* recorded as a unit. Blocks are separated by *block gaps* and each block may contain one or more records.
(3) A group of bits, or n-ary digits, *transmitted* as a unit. An encoding procedure is generally applied to the group of bits or n-ary digits for error-control purposes.
(4) A group of contiguous characters recorded as a unit.

Block Diagram A diagram of a *system,* instrument, or *computer* in which the principal parts are represented by suitably associated geometrical figures to show both the basic functions and the functional relationships among the parts. Contrast with *flowchart*.

Block Gap   An area on a *data medium* used to indicate the end of a *block* or *record*. Synonymous with interblock gap.

Block Length   A measure of the size of a *block*, usually specified in units such as *records, words, computer words,* or *characters*.

Bootstrap   A technique or device designed to bring itself into a desired state by means of its own action, e.g., a machine *routine* whose first few *instructions* are sufficient to bring the rest of itself into the computer from an *input device*. Contrast with *initial program loader (IPL)*.

Buffer   (1) A *routine* or *storage* used to compensate for a difference in rate of flow of *data,* or time of occurrence of events, when transmitting data from one device to another.
(2) An isolating circuit used to prevent a driven circuit from influencing the driving circuit.

Bug   A *mistake* or *malfunction*.

Business Data Processing   (1) (SC1) Use of *automatic data processing* in accounting or management.
(2) *Data processing* for business purposes, e.g., recording and summarizing the financial transactions of a business.
(3) Synonymous with administrative data processing.

Byte   A sequence of adjacent *binary digits* operated upon as a unit and usually shorter than a *computer word*.

Calculator   (1) (SC1) A *data processor* especially suitable for performing arithmetical *operations* which requires frequent intervention by a human *operator*.
(2) Generally and historically, a device for carrying out logic and arithmetic digital operations of any kind.

Call   (1) To transfer control to a specified *closed subroutine*.
(2) In communications, the action performed by the

calling party, or the operations necessary in making a call, or the effective use made of a connection between two stations.
(3) Synonymous with cue.

Card Column A single line of *punch positions* parallel to the short edge of a $3\frac{1}{4}$ by $7\frac{3}{8}$ inch *punched card*.

Card Hopper The portion of a card processing machine that holds the cards to be processed and makes them available to a card feed mechanism. Contrast with *card stacker*.

Card Row A single line of *punch positions* parallel to the long edge of a $3\frac{1}{4}$ by $7\frac{3}{8}$ inch *punched card*.

Card Stacker The portion of a card processing machine that receives processed cards. Contrast with *card hopper*.

Carriage Control Tape A tape that contains line feed control *data* for a printing device.

Cathode Ray Storage An *electrostatic storage* device that utilizes a cathode ray beam for access to the *data*.

Central Processing Unit (SC1) A unit of a *computer* that includes the circuits controlling the interpretation and execution of *instructions*. Synonymous with main frame. Abbreviated CPU.

Chain Printer A printer in which the type slugs are carried by the links of a revolving chain.

Channel (1) A path along which *signals* can be sent, e.g., *data* channel, *output* channel.
(2) The portion of a *storage medium* that is accessible to a given reading or writing station, e.g., *track, band*.
(3) In communication, a means of one way transmission. Several channels may share common equipment. For example, in frequency multiplexing carrier systems, each channel uses a particular frequency band that is reserved for it. Contrast with *circuit*.

Character A *letter, digit,* or other *symbol* that is used as part of the organization, control, or representation of *data*. A character is often in the form of a spatial arrangement of adjacent or connected strokes.

Character Printer A device that prints a single *character* at a time. Contrast with *line printer*.

Character Recognition The identification of graphic, phonic, or other *characters* by *automatic* means. See *magnetic ink character recognition, optical character recognition*.

Check Bit A *binary check digit*, e.g., a *parity bit*.

Clear To place one or more *storage* locations into a prescribed state, usually zero or the *space character*.

Clock (1) A device that generates periodic *signals* used for synchronization.
(2) A device that measures and indicates time.
(3) A *register* whose content changes at regular intervals in such a way as to measure time.

Clock Pulse A synchronization *signal* provided by a clock.

COBOL (COmmon Business Oriented Language) A *business data processing* language.

Code (1) (SC1) A set of unambiguous rules specifying the way in which *data* may be represented, e.g., the set of correspondences in the standard code for information interchange. Synonymous with *coding scheme*.
(2) (SC1) In telecommunications, a system of rules and conventions according to which the *signals* representing *data* can be formed, transmitted, received, and processed.
(3) (SC1) In *data processing,* to represent data or a *computer program* in a symbolic form that can be accepted by a *data processor*.
(4) To write a *routine*.
(5) Same as *code set*.
(6) Same as *encode*.
(7) A *set* of *items,* such as abbreviations, representing the members of another set.
(8) Same as *code value*.

Collate To combine *items* from two or more ordered sets into one set having a specified order not necessarily the same as any of the original sets. Contrast with *merge*.

Collating Sequence An ordering assigned to a set of *items,* such that any two sets in that assigned order can be *collated*.

Collator A device to *collate, merge,* or *match* sets of *punched cards* or other *documents*.

Column   A vertical arrangement of *characters* or other expressions.

Column Binary   Pertaining to the *binary* representation of *data* on cards in which the *significances* of *punch positions* are assigned along *card columns*. For example, each column in a 12-row card may be used to represent 12 consecutive *bits*. Synonymous with Chinese binary. Contrast with *row binary*.

Column Split   Pertaining to the sensing or punching of *punched card* data in a manner that permits certain *punch positions* within a single *column* to be ignored or treated separately from the other punch positions of the same column.

Communication Link   The physical means of connecting one location to another for the purpose of transmitting and receiving *data*.

Compile   To prepare a *machine language* program from a *computer program* written in another *programming language* by making use of the overall logic structure of the program, or generating more than one *machine instruction* for each symbolic *statement,* or both, as well as performing the function of an *assembler*.

Compiler   A program that *compiles*.

Computer   (SC1) A *data processor* that can perform substantial computation, including numerous arithmetic or logic operations, without intervention by a human *operator* during the *run*.

Computer Instruction   A *machine instruction* for a specific *computer*.

Computer Program   A series of *instructions* or *statements,* in a form acceptable to a *computer,* prepared in order to achieve a certain result.

Computer Word   A sequence of *bits* or *characters* treated as a unit and capable of being *stored* in one *computer location*. Synonymous with machine word.

Concurrent   Pertaining to the occurrence of two or more *events* or activities within the same specified interval of time. Contrast with *consecutive, sequential, simultaneous*.

Connector (1) (SC1) On a *flowchart,* the means of representing the convergence of more than one *flowline* into one, or the divergence of one flowline into more than one. It may also represent a break in a single flowline for continuation in another area.
(2) A means of representing on a *flowchart* a break in a line of flow.

Consecutive Pertaining to the occurrence of two *sequential* events without the intervention of any other such event. Contrast with *concurrent, sequential, simultaneous.*

Console That part of a *computer* used for communication between the *operator* or *maintenance* engineer and the computer.

Control Character A *character* whose occurrence in a particular context initiates, modifies, or stops a *control operation,* e.g., a character that controls *carriage return,* a character that controls transmission of *data* over communication networks. A control character may be recorded for use in a subsequent action. It may in some circumstances have a graphic representation. Contrast with *graphic character.*

Control Panel (1) A part of a *computer console* that contains manual controls.
(2) Same as *plugboard.*

Corrective Maintenance *Maintenance* specifically intended to eliminate an existing *fault.* It may occur as either *emergency maintenance* or *deferred maintenance.* Contrast with *preventive maintenance.* Corrective maintenance and preventive maintenance are both performed during *maintenance time.*

CPU *Central Processing Unit.*

CRT Display *Cathode Ray Tube display.*

Cycle (1) An interval of space or time in which one *set* of *events* or phenomena is completed.
(2) Any set of *operations* that is repeated regularly in the same *sequence.* The operations may be subject to variations on each repetition.

Data (1) (SC1) A representation of facts, concepts, or *instructions* in a formalized manner suitable for communication, interpretation, or processing by human or automatic means.

(2) Any representations such as *characters* or *analog* quantities to which meaning is or might be assigned.

Data Flowchart (SC1) A *flowchart* representing the path of *data* through a problem solution. It defines the major phases of the *processing* as well as the various *data media* used. Synonymous with data flow diagram.

Data Signalling Rate In communications, the *data* transmission capacity of a set of *parallel channels*. The data signalling rate is expressed in bits per second.

Debug To detect, locate, and remove *mistakes* from a *routine* or *malfunctions* from a *computer*. Synonymous with troubleshoot.

Decimal (1) Pertaining to a characteristic or property involving a selection, choice, or condition in which there are ten possibilities.

(2) Pertaining to the *number representation system* with a *radix* of ten.

(3) See *binary-coded decimal notation*.

Decimal Notation A *fixed radix notation* where the *radix* is ten. For example, in decimal notation, the *numeral* 576.2 represents the *number* 5×10 squared plus 7×10 to the first power plus 6×10 to the zero power plus 2×10 to the minus 1 power.

Decimal Numeral A *decimal* representation of a *number*.

Decision Table A *table* of all contingencies that are to be considered in the description of a problem, together with the actions to be taken. Decision tables are sometimes used in place of *flowcharts* for problem description and documentation.

Deck A collection of *punched cards*. Synonymous with card deck.

Detail File Same as *transaction file*.

Diagnostic Pertaining to the detection and isolation of a *malfunction* or *mistake*.

Digit A *symbol* that represents one of the non-negative integers smaller than the radix. For example, in *deci-*

mal notation, a digit is one of the *characters* from 0 to 9. Synonymous with numeric character.

Digital Computer (1) (SC1) A *computer* in which *discrete* representation of *data* is mainly used.
(2) A *computer* that operates on *discrete data* by performing arithmetic and logic processes on these data. Contrast with *analog computer.*

Direct Access (1) Pertaining to the process of obtaining *data* from, or placing data into, *storage* where the time required for such access is independent of the *location* of the data most recently obtained or placed in storage.
(2) Pertaining to a *storage* device in which the *access time* is effectively independent of the location of the *data.*
(3) Synonymous with random access (1).
(4) Contrast with *serial access.*

Display A visual presentation of *data.*

Documentation (1) The creating, collecting, organizing, storing, citing, and disseminating of *documents* or the *information* recorded in documents.
(2) A collection of *documents* or *information* on a given subject.

Downtime The time interval during which a device is *malfunctioning.*

Dump (1) To copy the contents of all or part of a *storage,* usually from an internal storage into an external storage.
(2) A process as in (1).
(3) The *data* resulting from the process as in (1).

Duplex In communications, pertaining to a simultaneous two way independent *transmission* in both directions. Contrast with *half duplex.* Synonymous with full duplex.

Duplicate To *copy* so that the result remains in the same physical form as the source, e.g., to make a new *punched card* with the same pattern of holes as an original punched card. Contrast with *copy.*

Dynamic Storage A device *storing data* in a manner that permits the data to move or vary with time such that the specified data are not always available for recovery. *Magnetic drum* and *disc* storage are nonvolatile dynamic storage. An *acoustic delay line* is a volatile dynamic storage.

EAM   *Electrical Accounting Machine.*

EDP   *Electronic Data Processing.*

Electrical Accounting Machine   Pertaining to *data processing* equipment that is predominantly electromechanical such as a keypunch, mechanical *sorter, collator,* and *tabulator.* Abbreviated *EAM.*

Electronic Data Processing   (1) (SC1) *Data processing* largely performed by electronic devices.
(2) Pertaining to *data processing* equipment that is predominantly electronic such as an electronic *digital computer.*
Abbreviated EDP.

Eleven-punch   A punch in the second *row* from the top, on a *Hollerith punched card.* Synonymous with x-punch.

Emulate   To imitate one *system* with another such that the imitating system accepts the same *data,* executes the same *programs,* and achieves the same results as the imitated system. Contrast with *simulate.*

Encode   To apply a set of unambiguous rules specifying the way in which *data* may be represented such that a subsequent *decoding* is possible. Synonymous with code (6).

End-of-tape Marker   A marker on a *magnetic tape* used to indicate the end of the permissible recording area, e.g., a photo reflective strip, a transparent section of tape, a particular bit pattern.

End of Transmission Block Character   A *communication control character* used to indicate the end of a *block of data* where data are divided into blocks for *transmission* purposes. Abbreviated *ETB.*

End of Transmission Character   A *communication control character* used to indicate the conclusion of a *transmission* which may have included one or more *texts* and any associated *headings.* Abbreviated *EOT.*

Equivalent Binary Digits The *number* of *binary digits* required to express in *binary notation* a *numeral* expressed in another *number representation system*. For example, approximately $3\frac{1}{3}$ times the number of *decimal digits* is required to express a *decimal numeral* as a *binary numeral*.

Error Any discrepancy between a computed, observed, or measured quantity and the true, specified, or theoretically correct value or condition.

Exponent In a *floating point representation*, the *numeral*, of a pair of numerals representing a *number*, that indicates the power to which the *base* is raised.

Ferrite An iron compound frequently used in the construction of *magnetic cores*.

Field In a *record*, a specified area used for a particular category of *data*, e.g., a group of card columns used to represent a wage rate, a set of *bit* locations in a *computer word* used to express the *address* of the *operand*.

File A collection of related *records* treated as a unit. For example, one line of an invoice may form an *item*, a complete invoice may form a *record*, the complete set of such records may form a file, the collection of inventory control files may form a *library*, and the libraries used by an organization are known as its *data bank*.

File Maintenance The activity of keeping a *file* up to date by adding, changing, or deleting *data*.

Floating Point Representation A *number representation system* in which each *number*, as represented by a pair of *numerals*, equals one of those numerals times a power of an implicit fixed positive integer *base* where the power is equal to the implicit base raised to the *exponent* represented by the other numeral.

Common Notation	A Floating Point Representation
0.0001234 or $(0.1234) \times (10^{-3})$	1234 -03

Contrast with *variable point representation*.

Flowchart (1) (SC1) A graphical representation for the definition, analysis, or solution of a problem, in which *symbols* are used to represent *operations, data,* flow, equipment, etc. Contrast with *block diagram.*
(2) See *data flowchart, programming flowchart.*

Flowchart Symbol (SC1) A *symbol* used to represent *operations, data,* flow, or equipment on a *flowchart.*

Flowline (SC1) On a *flowchart,* a line representing a connecting path between *flowchart symbols,* e.g., a line to indicate a transfer of *data* or control.

Foreground Processing The *automatic* execution of the *computer programs* that have been designed to preempt the use of the computing facilities. Usually a *real time* program. Contrast with *background processing.*

Format The arrangement of *data.*

FORTRAN (FORmula TRANslating system) A *language* primarily used to express *computer programs* by arithmetic formulas.

Full Duplex Same as *duplex.*

General Purpose Computer (SC1) A *computer* that is designed to handle a wide variety of problems.

Half-adder A combinational *logic element* having two *outputs,* S and C, and two *inputs,* A and B, such that the outputs are related to the inputs according to the following table.

input		output	
A	B	C	S
0	0	0	0
0	1	0	1
1	0	0	1
1	1	1	0

S denotes "Sum Without Carry," C denotes "Carry." Two half-adders may be used for performing *binary* addition.

Half Duplex In communications, pertaining to an alternate, one way at a time, independent transmission. Contrast with *duplex.*

Half-word A contiguous sequence of *bits* or *characters* which comprises half a *computer word* and is capable of being addressed as a unit.

Hardware (SC1) Physical equipment, as opposed to the *computer program* or method of use, e.g., mechanical, magnetic, electrical, or electronic devices. Contrast with *software.*

Head A device that *reads, writes,* or *erases data* on a storage *medium,* e.g., a small electromagnet used to read, write, or erase data on a *magnetic drum* or *tape,* or the set of perforating, reading, or marking devices used for punching, reading, or printing on paper tape.

Heuristic Pertaining to exploratory methods of problem solving in which solutions are discovered by evaluation of the progress made toward the final result. Contrast with *algorithm.*

Hexadecimal Same as *sexadecimal.*

Hollerith Pertaining to a particular type of *code* or *punched card* utilizing 12 *rows* per *column* and usually 80 columns per card.

Hopper See *card hopper.*

Idle Time That part of *available time* during which the *hardware* is not being used. Contrast with *operating time.*

Index (1) An ordered reference list of the contents of a *file* or *document* together with *keys* or reference notations for identification or location of those contents.
(2) To prepare a list as in (1).
(3) A *symbol* or a *numeral* used to identify a particular quantity in an *array* of similar quantities. For example, the terms of an array represented by X_1, $X_2, \ldots, X_{100}$ have the indexes $1, 2, \ldots, 100$ respectively.
(4) To move a machine part to a predetermined position, or by a predetermined amount, on a *quantized* scale.
(5) See *index register.*

Index Register   A *register* whose content may be added to or subtracted from the *operand address* prior to or during the execution of a *computer instruction.* Synonymous with b box.

Indirect Address   An *address* that specifies a *storage* location that contains either a *direct address* or another indirect address. Synonymous with multilevel address. Contrast with *direct address.*

Information Bits   In *telecommunications,* those *bits* which are generated by the *data source* and which are not used for error control by the *data transmission* system.

Information Processing   (SC1) Same as *data processing.*

Information Retrieval   (SC1) The methods and *procedures* for recovering specific *information* from stored *data.*

Initial Program Loader   The procedure that causes the initial part of an *operating system* or other *program* to be loaded such that the program can then proceed under its own control. Contrast with *bootstrap.* Abbreviated *IPL.*

Initialize   To set *counters, switches,* and *addresses* to zero or other starting values at the beginning of, or at prescribed points in, a computer *routine.* Synonymous with prestore.

Input Device   The device or collective set of devices used for conveying *data* into another device.

Input/Output   Pertaining to either *input* or *output,* or both.

Inquiry Station   *Data* terminal equipment used for inquiry into a *data processing* system.

Instruction   A *statement* that specifies an *operation* and the values or locations of its *operands.*

Instruction Address   The *address* that must be used to *fetch* an *instruction.*

Instruction Register   A *register* that stores an *instruction* for execution.

Integrated Data Processing   (SC1) *Data processing* in which the coordination of *data* acquisition and all other stages of data processing is achieved in a coherent system, e.g., a *business data processing* system in which data for orders and buying are combined to accomplish the functions of scheduling, invoicing, and accounting. Abbreviated IDP.

Interblock Gap Same as *block gap*.

Interface A shared boundary. An interface might be a *hardware* component to link two devices or it might be a portion of *storage* or *registers accessed* by two or more *computer programs*.

Internal Storage Addressable *storage* directly controlled by the *central processing unit* of a *digital computer*.

Interpreter (1) A *computer program* that *translates* and executes each *source language* statement before translating and executing the next one.
(2) A device that prints on a *punched card* the *data* already punched in the card.

Inter-record Gap Same as *record gap*.

Interrupt To stop a *process* in such a way that it can be resumed.

I/O An abbreviation for *input/output*.

IPL *Initial program loader*.

ISO International Organization for Standardization.

Item (1) In general, one member of a group, e.g., a *record* may contain a number of items such as *fields* or groups of fields; a *file* may consist of a number of items such as records; a *table* may consist of a number of items such as entries.
(2) A collection of related *characters*, treated as a unit.

Job A specified group of tasks prescribed as a unit of work for a *computer*. By extension, a job usually includes all necessary *computer programs, linkages, files,* and *instructions* to the *operating system*.

Job Control Statement A *statement* in a *job* that is used in identifying the job or describing its requirements to the *operating system*.

K   (1) An abbreviation for the prefix kilo, i.e., 1000 in decimal notation.
(2) Loosely, when referring to storage capacity, two to the tenth power, 1024 in *decimal notation.*

Keypunch   A keypunch actuated device that punches holes in a card to represent *data.*

Label   One or more *characters* used to identify a *statement* or an *item* of *data* in a *computer program.*

Laced Card   A *punched card* that has a lace-like appearance, usually without information content.

Latency   The time between the completion of the interpretation of an *address* and the start of the actual transfer from the addressed *location.* Latency includes the *delay* associated with access to *storage devices* such as *magnetic drums* and *delay lines.*

Leader   The blank section of tape at the beginning of a reel of tape.

Left-justify   (1) To adjust the printing positions of *characters* on a page so that the left margin of the page is regular.
(2) By extension, to *shift* the contents of a *register* so that the most significant *digit* is at some specified position of the register.

Library   (1) A collection of organized *information* used for study and reference.
(2) A collection of related *files.* For example, one line of an invoice may form an *item,* a complete invoice may form a file, the collection of inventory control files may form a library, and the libraries used by an organization are known as its *data bank.*
(3) See *program library.*

Library Routine   A proven *routine* that is maintained in a *program library.*

Line Printer   A device that prints all *characters* of a line as a unit. Contrast with *character printer.*

Linear Programming   (1) (SC1) In *operations research,* a procedure for locating the maximum or minimum of a linear *function* of *variables* that are subject to linear constraints.

(2) Synonymous with linear optimization. Abbreviated LP.

Linkage In *programming, coding* that connects two separately coded *routines.*

Load In *programming,* to enter *data* into *storage* or working *registers.*

Load-and-go An operating technique in which there are no stops between the *loading* and execution phases of a *program,* and which may include *assembling* or *compiling.*

Location Any place in which *data* may be *stored.*

Logical Record A collection of *items* independent of their physical environment. Portions of the same logical *record* may be located in different physical records.

Loop A *sequence* of *instructions* that is executed repeatedly until a terminal condition prevails.

Machine Address Same as *absolute address.*

Machine Code An *operation code* that a machine is designed to recognize.

Machine Language A *language* that is used directly by a machine.

Machine Readable Medium A *medium* that can convey *data* to a given sensing device. Synonymous with automated data medium.

Macro Instruction An *instruction* in a *source language* that is equivalent to a specified *sequence* of *machine instructions.*

Magnetic Card A card with a magnetic surface on which *data* can be *stored* by selective magnetization of portions of the flat surface.

Magnetic Core A configuration of magnetic material that is, or is intended to be, placed in a spatial relationship to current-carrying conductors and whose magnetic properties are essential to its use. It may be used to concentrate an induced magnetic field as in a transformer induction coil, or armature, to retain a magnetic polarization for the purpose of *storing* data, or for its nonlinear properties as in a *logic element*. It may be made of such material as iron, iron oxide, or ferrite and in such shapes as wires, tapes, toroids, rods, or thin film.

Magnetic Disc A flat circular plate with a magnetic surface on which *data* can be *stored* by selective magnetization of portions of the flat surface.

Magnetic Drum A right circular cylinder with a magnetic surface on which *data* can be *stored* by selective magnetization of portions of the curved surface.

Magnetic Ink Character Recognition The machine recognition of characters printed with magnetic ink. Contrast with *optical character recognition*. Abbreviated *MICR*.

Magnetic Tape (1) A tape with a magnetic surface on which *data* can be *stored* by selective polarization of portions of the surface.
(2) A tape of magnetic material used as the constituent in some forms of *magnetic cores*.

Magnetic Thin Film A layer of magnetic material, usually less than one micron thick, often used for logic or storage elements.

Main Frame (SC1) Same as *central processing unit*.

Main Storage The general-purpose *storage* of a *computer*. Usually, main storage can be *accessed* directly by the operating *registers*. Contrast with *auxiliary storage*.

Maintenance Any activity intended to eliminate *faults* or to keep *hardware* or *programs* in satisfactory working condition, including tests, measurements, replacements, adjustments, and repairs.

Management Information System (1) (SC1) Management performed with the aid of *automatic data processing*. Abbreviated *MIS*.
(2) An *information system* designed to aid in the performance of management *functions*.

Mark Sensing The electrical sensing of manually recorded conductive marks on a nonconductive surface.

Mass Storage Device A device having a large *storage capacity*, e.g., *magnetic disc, magnetic drum*.

Match To *check* for identity between two or more *items* of *data*. Contrast with *hit*.

Medium The material, or configuration thereof, on which *data* are recorded, e.g., paper tape, cards, *magnetic tape*. Synonymous with data medium.

Memory Same as *storage*.

Merge To combine *items* from two or more similarly ordered sets into one set that is arranged in the same order. Contrast with *collate*.

MICR *Magnetic Ink Character Recognition.*

MIS *Management Information System.*

Mnemonic Symbol A *symbol* chosen to assist the human memory, e.g., an abbreviation such as "mpy" for "multiply."

Modem (MOdulator-DEModulator) A device that modulates and demodulates signals transmitted over communication facilities.

Multiple Aperture Core A *magnetic core* with two or more holes through which wires may be passed and around which magnetic flux may exist. Multiple aperture cores may be used for *nondestructive reading*.

Multiple Punching Punching more than one hole in the same column of a *punched card* by means of more than one keystroke.

Multiplex To *interleave* or simultaneously *transmit* two or more messages on a single *channel*.

Multiprocessing (1) Pertaining to the simultaneous execution of two or more *computer programs* or *sequences of instructions* by a *computer* or *computer network*.
(2) Loosely, *parallel processing*.

Multiprogramming Pertaining to the *concurrent* execution of two or more *programs* by a *computer*.

Natural Language A *language* whose rules reflect and describe current usage rather than prescribe usage. Contrast with *artificial language*.

Number (1) A mathematical entity that may indicate quantity or amount of units.
(2) Loosely, a *numeral*.

Number Representation System An agreed set of *symbols* and rules for *number representation*. Synonymous with numeral system, numeration system.

Numeral (1) A discrete representation of a *number*. For example, twelve, 12, XII, 1100 are four different numerals that represent the same number.
(2) A numeric word that represents a *number*.
(3) See *binary numeral, decimal numeral.*

Numeral Analysis The study of methods of obtaining useful quantitative solutions to problems that have been expressed mathematically, including the study of the *errors* and bounds on errors in obtaining such solutions.

Numeric Character Same as *digit*.

Object Code *Output* from a *compiler* or *assembler* which is itself executable *machine code* or is suitable for processing to produce executable machine code.

Object Program A fully *compiled* or *assembled program* that is ready to be *loaded* into the *computer*. Synonymous with target program. Contrast with *source program*.

OCR *Optical character recognition.*

Octal (1) Pertaining to a characteristic or property involving a selection, choice, or condition in which there are eight possibilities.
(2) Pertaining to the *number representation system* with a *radix* of eight.

Offline Pertaining to equipment or devices not under control of the *central processing unit*.

Offline Storage *Storage* not under control of the *central processing unit*.

Online (1) Pertaining to equipment or devices under control of the *central processing unit*.
(2) Pertaining to a user's ability to interact with a *computer*.

Online Storage   *Storage* under control of the *central processing unit.*

Operand   That which is operated upon. An operand is usually identified by an *address part* of an *instruction.*

Operating System   (SC1) *Software* which controls the execution of *computer programs* and which may provide scheduling, *debugging,* input/output control, accounting, *compilation, storage* assignment, *data* management, and related services.

Operating Time   That part of *available time* during which the *hardware* is operating and assumed to be yielding correct results. It includes *development time, production time,* and *makeup time.* Contrast with *idle time.*

Operation   (1) A defined action, namely, the act of obtaining a result from one or more *operands* in accordance with a rule that completely specifies the result for any permissible combination of operands.
(2) The *set* of such acts specified by such a rule, or the rule itself.
(3) The act specified by a single *computer instruction.*
(4) A *program* step undertaken or executed by a *computer,* e.g., addition, multiplication, *extraction,* comparison, *shift, transfer.* The operation is usually specified by the *operator* part of an instruction.
(5) The event or specific action performed by a *logic element.*

Operation Code   A *code* that represents specific operations. Synonymous with instruction code.

Operations Research   The use of the scientific method to provide criteria for decisions concerning the actions of people, machines, and other resources in a system involving repeatable operations. Synonymous with operations analysis. Abbreviated OR.

Operator   (1) In the description of a *process,* that which indicates the action to be performed on *operands.*
(2) A person who operates a machine.

Optical Character Recognition   The machine identification of printed *characters* through use of light-sensitive devices. Contrast with *magnetic ink character recognition.* Abbreviated *OCR.*

Optical Scanner   (1) A device that scans optically and usually generates an *analog* or *digital signal.*
(2) A device that optically scans printed or written *data* and generates their *digital representations.*

Output Device   (SC1) The device or collective set of devices used for conveying *data* out of another device.

Overflow   (1) That portion of the result of an *operation* that exceeds the capacity of the intended unit of *storage.*
(2) Pertaining to the generation of overflow as in (1).
(3) Contrast with *underflow.*

Overlay   The technique of repeatedly using the same blocks of internal *storage* during different stages of a *program.* When one *routine* is no longer needed in storage, another routine can replace all or part of it.

Pack   To compress *data* in a *storage* medium by taking advantage of known characteristics of the data, in such a way that the original data can be recovered, e.g., to compress data in a storage medium by making use of *bit* or *byte* locations that would otherwise go unused.

Parallel   (1) Pertaining to the *concurrent* or *simultaneous* occurrence of two or more related activities in multiple devices or *channels.*
(2) Pertaining to the simultaneity of two or more *processes.*
(3) Pertaining to the simultaneous processing of the individual parts of a whole, such as the *bits* of a *character* and the characters of a *word,* using separate facilities for the various parts.
(4) Contrast with *serial.*

Parallel Search Storage   A *storage device* in which one or more parts of all storage *locations* are queried *simultaneously.* Contrast with *associative storage.*

Parallel Transmission   In *telecommunications,* the *simultaneous transmission* of a certain number of *signal* elements constituting the same telegraph or *data* signal. For example, use of a *code* according to which each signal is characterized by a combination of three out of twelve frequencies simultaneously transmitted over the *channel.* Contrast with *serial transmission.*

Parity Bit   A *check bit* appended to an *array* of *binary digits* to make the sum of all the binary digits, including the check bit, always odd or always even.

Parity Check   A *check* that tests whether the number of ones (or zeros) in an *array* of *binary digits* is odd or even. Synonymous with odd-even check.

Peripheral Equipment   (SC1) In a *data processing* system, any unit of equipment, distinct from the *central processing unit,* which may provide the system with outside communication.

Plugboard   A perforated board into which plugs are manually inserted to control the *operation* of equipment. Synonymous with control panel (2).

Positional Notation   (SC1) A *numeration system* in which a *number* is represented by means of an ordered *set* of *digits,* such that the value contributed by each digit depends upon its position as well as upon its value. Synonymous with positional representation.

Precision   The degree of discrimination with which a quantity is stated. For example, a three-digit *numeral* discriminates among 1000 possibilities.

Preventive Maintenance   *Maintenance* specifically intended to prevent *faults* from occurring during subsequent *operation.* Contrast with *corrective maintenance.* Corrective maintenance and preventive maintenance are both performed during *maintenance time.*

Printer   See *chain printer, character printer, line printer.*

Problem Description   (1) (SC1) In *information processing,* a statement of a problem. The statement may also include a description of the method of solution, the procedures and *algorithms,* etc.
(2) A statement of a problem. The statement may also include a description of the method of solution, the solution itself, the transformations of *data,* and the relationship of procedures, data, constraints, and environment.

Problem Oriented Language   A *programming language* designed for the convenient expression of a given class of problems.

Procedure Oriented Language A *programming language* designed for the convenient expression of procedures used in the solution of a wide class of problems.

Processor (1) In *hardware,* a *data processor.*
(2) In *software,* a *computer program* that includes the *compiling, assembling, translating,* and related functions for a specific *programming language, COBOL* processor, *FORTRAN* processor.

Program (1) (SC1) A series of actions proposed in order to achieve a certain result.
(2) Loosely, a *routine.*
(3) To design, write, and test a program as in (1).
(4) Loosely, to write a *routine.*

Program Library A collection of available *computer programs* and *routines.*

Programmer (SC1) A person mainly involved in designing, writing, and testing *computer programs.*

Programming (SC1) The design, the writing, and testing of a *program.*

Programming Flowchart (SC1) A *flowchart* representing the sequence of *operations* in a *program.*

Programming Language A *language* used to prepare *computer* programs.

Punch (1) A perforation, as in a *punched card* or paper tape.
(2) See *digit punch, keypunch, eleven punch, spot punch, twelve punch, zone punch.*

Punched Card (1) A card *punched* with a pattern of holes to represent *data.*
(2) A card as in (1) before being *punched.*

Punched Tape A tape on which a pattern of holes or cuts is used to represent *data.*

Punch Position A defined *location* on a card or tape where a hole may be *punched.*

Queued Access Method Any access method that automatically synchronizes the *transfer* of *data* between the *program* using the access method and *input/output* devices, thereby eliminating delays for input/output *operation.*

Radix   (SC1) In *positional representation,* that integer, if it exists, by which the *significance* of the *digit place* must be multiplied to give the significance of the next higher digit place. For example, in *decimal notation,* the radix of each place is ten; in a *biquinary code,* the radix of the fives place is two. Synonymous with base (3).

Random Access   (1) Same as *direct access.*
(2) In COBOL, an *access mode* in which specific *logical records* are obtained from or placed into a *mass storage file* in a nonsequential manner.

Read   To acquire or interpret *data* from a storage device, a *data medium,* or any other source.

Real Time   (1) Pertaining to the actual time during which a physical *process* transpires.
(2) Pertaining to the performance of a computation during the actual time that the related physical *process* transpires, in order that results of the computation can be used in guiding the physical process.

Record   (1) A collection of related *items* of *data,* treated as a unit, for example, one line of an invoice may form a record; a complete set of such records may form a *file.*
(2) See *logical record, variable-length record.*

Record Gap   An area on a *data medium* used to indicate the end of a *block* or *record.* Synonymous with inter-record gap.

Recording Density   The number of *bits* in a single linear *track* measured per unit of length of the recording *medium.*

Record Layout   The arrangement and structure of *data* in a *record,* including the *sequence* and size of its components. By extension, a record layout might be the description thereof.

Record Length   A measure of the size of a *record,* usually specified in units such as *words* or *characters.*

Register   A device capable of *storing* a specified amount of *data* such as one *word.*

Remote Access   Pertaining to communication with a *data processing* facility by one or more stations that are distant from that facility.

Reproduce   To prepare a duplicate of stored information, especially for punched cards, punched paper tape, or magnetic tape. (IBM definition)

Response Time   The elapsed time between the generation of a message at a terminal and the receipt of a reply in case of an inquiry or receipt of message by addressee. (IBM definition)

Rewind   To return a magnetic or paper tape to its beginning. (IBM definition)

Right-justify   (1) To adjust the printing *positions* of *characters* on a page so that the right margin of the page is regular. (2) To *shift* the contents of a *register* so that the least *significant digit* is at some specified *position* of the register. Contrast with *normalize*.

Routine   (SC1) An ordered set of *instructions* that may have some general or frequent use.

Row   A horizontal arrangement of *characters* or other expressions.

Row Binary   Pertaining to the *binary* representation of *data* on cards in which the *significances* of *punch positions* are assigned along *card rows*. For example, each row in an 80-column card may be used to represent 80 consecutive *binary digits*. Contrast with *column binary*.

Run   A single, continuous performance of a *computer program* or *routine*.

Scheduled Maintenance   *Maintenance* carried out in accordance with an established plan.

Segment   (1) To divide a *computer program* into parts such that the program can be executed without the entire program being in *internal storage* at any one time. (2) A part of a *computer program* as in (1).

Sequential   Pertaining to the occurrence of *events* in time *sequence*, with little or no simultaneity or overlap of events. Contrast with *concurrent, consecutive, simultaneous.*

Sequential Computer   A *computer* in which *events* occur in time *sequence,* with little or no simultaneity or overlap of events.

Serial   (1) Pertaining to the *sequential* or *consecutive* occurrence of two or more related activities in a single device or *channel.*
(2) Pertaining to the *sequencing* of two or more *processes.*
(3) Pertaining to the *sequential processing* of the individual parts of a whole, such as the *bits* of a *character* or the characters of a *word,* using the same facilities for successive parts.
(4) Contrast with *parallel.*

Serial Access   (1) Pertaining to the *sequential* or *consecutive transmission* of *data* to or from *storage.*
(2) Pertaining to the *process* of obtaining *data* from or placing *data* into *storage,* where the *access time* is dependent upon the *location* of the data most recently obtained or placed in storage. Contrast with *direct access.*

Serial Transmission   In *telecommunications, transmission* at successive intervals of *signal* elements constituting the same telegraph or *data* signal. The *sequential* elements may be transmitted with or without interruption, provided that they are not transmitted *simultaneously.* For example, telegraph transmission by a time divided *channel.* Contrast with *parallel transmission.*

Sexadecimal   (1) Pertaining to a characteristic or property involving a selection, choice, or condition in which there are sixteen possibilities.
(2) Pertaining to the *numeration system* with a *radix* of sixteen.
(3) Synonymous with hexadecimal.

Shannon   A unit of measurement of quantity of information equal to that contained in a *message* represented by one or the other of two equally probable, exclusive, and exhaustive states.

Sight Check   A *check* performed by sighting through the holes of two or more aligned *punched cards* toward a source of light to verify the punching, e.g., to determine if a hole has been punched in a corresponding *punch position* on all cards in a deck.

Sign Bit   A *binary digit* occupying the *sign position*.

Significant Digit   A *digit* that is needed for a certain purpose, particularly one that must be kept to preserve a specific *accuracy* or *precision*.

Simulation   (SC1) The representation of certain features of the behavior of a physical or abstract *system* by the behavior of another system, e.g., the representation of physical phenomena by means of *operations* performed by a *computer* or the representation of operations of a computer by those of another computer.

Simultaneous   Pertaining to the occurrence of two or more *events* at the same instant of time. Contrast with *concurrent, consecutive, sequential.*

Single Step   Pertaining to a method of operating a *computer* in which each step is performed in response to a single manual operation.

Software   (SC1) A set of *computer programs, procedures,* and possibly associated *documentation* concerned with the *operation* of a *data processing system,* e.g., *compilers, library routines,* manuals, circuit diagrams. Contrast with *hardware.*

Solid State Component   A component whose *operation* depends on the control of electric or magnetic phenomena in solids, e.g., a transistor, crystal diode, *ferrite* core.

Sort   (1) To segregate *items* into groups according to some definite rules.
(2) Same as *order.*

Sorter   A person, device, or *computer routine* that *sorts.*

Source Language   The *language* from which a *statement* is translated.

Source Program   A *computer program* written in a *source language.* Contrast with *object program.*

Special Character   A *graphic character* that is neither a *letter,* nor a *digit,* nor a *space character.*

Stacker See *card stacker.*

Statement (1) In *computer programming,* a meaningful expression or generalized *instruction* in a *source language.*
(2) See *job control statement.*

Storage (1) Pertaining to a device into which *data* can be entered, in which they can be held, and from which they can be retrieved at a later time.
(2) Loosely, any device that can *store data.*
(3) Synonymous with memory.

Storage Capacity The amount of *data* that can be contained in a *storage device.*

Storage Device A device into which *data* can be inserted, in which they can be retained, and from which they can be retrieved.

Storage Protection An arrangement for preventing access to *storage* for either *reading,* or *writing,* or both. Synonymous with memory protection.

Stored Program Computer (SC1) A *computer* controlled by internally stored *instructions* that can synthesize, *store,* and in some cases alter instructions as though they were *data* and that can subsequently execute these instructions.

Summary Punch A card-punching operation which connects the reproducer to an accounting machine to punch totals or balance cards. To punch summary information in cards. (IBM definition)

Symbolic Coding *Coding* that uses *machine instructions* with *symbolic addresses.*

Synchronous Computer (SC1) A *computer* in which each *event,* or the performance of any basic *operation,* is constrained to start on, and usually to keep in step with, *signals* from a *clock.* Contrast with *asynchronous computer.*

System (1) (SC1) An assembly of methods, *procedures,* or techniques united by regulated interaction to form an organized whole.
(2) (SC1) An organized collection of men, *machines,* and methods required to accomplish a *set* of specific *functions.*

Tape   See *carriage control tape, magnetic tape, punched tape*.

Tape Drive   A device that moves tape past a *head.* Synonymous with tape transport.

Tape To Card   Pertaining to equipment or methods that *transmit data* from either *magnetic tape* or *punched tape* to *punched cards.*

Tape Unit   A device containing a *tape drive,* together with *reading* and *writing heads* and associated controls. Synonymous with tape deck, tape station.

Telecommunications   Pertaining to the *transmission* of *signals* over long distances, such as by telegraph, radio, or television.

Terminal   A point in a *system* or communication network at which *data* can either enter or leave.

Time Sharing   Pertaining to the *interleaved* use of the time of a device.

Track   The portion of a moving *storage medium,* such as a drum, tape, or *disc,* that is accessible to a given *reading head position.*

Transaction File   A *file* containing relatively transient *data* to be processed in combination with a *master file.* For example, in a payroll application, a transaction file indicating hours worked might be processed with a master file containing employee name and rate of pay. Synonymous with detail file.

Transmission   (1) The sending of *data* from one *location* and the receiving of data in another location, usually leaving the source of data unchanged.
(2) The sending of *data.*
(3) In *ASCII* and communications, a series of *characters* including *headings* and *texts.*

Truncate   To terminate a computational *process* in accordance with some rule, e.g., to end the evaluation of a power series at a specified term.

Twelve-punch   A *punch* in the top row of a *Hollerith punch card.* Synonymous with y-punch.

Typebar A linear type element containing all printable symbols. (IBM definition)

Unit Record Historically, a card containing one complete record. Currently, the punched card. (IBM definition)

USASCII Same as *ASCII*.

Validity Check A check that a code group is actually a character of the particular code in use. (IBM definition)

Variable A quantity that can assume any of a given *set* of values.

Variable-length Record Pertaining to a *file* in which the *records* are not uniform in length.

Verify (1) To determine whether a transcription of *data* or other *operation* has been accomplished accurately. (2) To *check* the results of *keypunching*.

Word A *character string* or a *bit string* considered as an entity.

X-punch Same as *eleven-punch*.

Y-punch Same as *twelve-punch*.

Zero Suppression The elimination of nonsignificant zeros in a *numeral*.

Zone Punch A *punch* in the eleven, twelve, or zero row of a *punched card*.

DATA PROCESSING PERIODICALS, JOURNALS, NEWSLETTERS, ASSOCIATIONS, AND MANUFACTUR-ERS

APPENDIX B

Periodicals, Journals, and Newsletters

Business Automation, 288 Park Avenue West, Elmhurst, Illinois 60126.

Communications of the ACM, 211 E. 43rd Street, New York, New York 10017.

Computers and Automation, 815 Washington Street, Newtonville, Massachusetts 02160.

Computers and Data Processing, 217 Broadway, New York, New York 10007.

Computing Newsletter For Community Colleges, University of Colorado, Colorado Springs, Colorado 80903.

Computing Reviews, 211 E. 43rd Street, New York, New York 10017.

Datamation, 1830 W. Olympic Boulevard, Los Angeles, California 90006.

Data Processing Digest, 1140 S. Robertson Boulevard, Los Angeles, California 90035.

Data Processing for Management, 22nd floor, Book Tower, Detroit, Michigan 48226.

Data Processing Magazine, 134 N. 13th Street, Philadelphia, Pennsylvania 19107.

Data Product News, McGraw-Hill Building, 1221 Avenue of the Americas, New York, New York 10020.

Journal of Accountancy, 270 Madison Avenue, New York, New York 10016.

Journal of Data Education, 247 Edythe Street, Livermore, California 94550.

Journal of Data Management, 505 Busse Highway, Park Ridge, Illinois 60068.

Journal of the ACM, 211 E. 43rd Street, New York, New York 10017.

N.A.A. Bulletin, 505 Park Avenue, New York, New York 10022.

Operations Research, Mt. Royal and Guilford Avenue, Baltimore, Maryland 21201.

Systems and Procedures Journal, 7890 Brookside Drive, Cleveland, Ohio 44138.

Associations and Other Sources

Administrative Management Society, 212 Fifth Avenue, New York, New York 10010.

American Federation of Information Processing Societies, 211 E. 43rd Street, New York, New York 10017.

American Institute of Certified Public Accountants, 666 Fifth Avenue, New York, New York 10019.

American Institute of Industrial Engineers, 345 E. 47th Street, New York, New York 10017.

American National Standards Institute, 1430 Broadway, New York, New York 10018.

Association for Computing Machinery, 211 E. 43rd Street, New York, New York 10017.

Association for Educational Data Systems, 1201 16th Street, N.W., Washington, D.C. 20036.

Association of Data Processing Service Organizations, 947 Old York Road, Abington, Pennsylvania 19001.

Business Equipment Manufacturers Association, 235 E. 42nd Street, New York, New York 10017.

Data Processing Management Association, 505 Busse Highway, Park Ridge, Illinois 60068.

Institute of Electrical and Electronics Engineers, 345 East 47th Street, New York, New York 10017.

National Association for Accountants, 505 Park Avenue, New York, New York 10022.

Operations Research Society of America, Mt. Royal and Guilford Avenue, Baltimore, Maryland 21201.

Project on Information Processing, Box 201, Montclair State College, Upper Montclair, New Jersey 07043.

Society of Data Educators, 247 Edythe Street, Livermore, California 94550.

Systems and Procedures Association, 7890 Brookside Drive, Cleveland, Ohio 44138.

Burroughs Corporation, 6071 Second Avenue, Detroit, Michigan 48202.   **Manufacturers**

Control Data Corporation, 8100 34th Avenue South, Minneapolis, Minnesota 55420.

Friden Corporation, 2350 Washington Avenue, San Leandro, California 94577.

General Electric Computer Division, P. O. Box 270, Phoenix, Arizona 85001.

General Precision Corporation, 101 W. Alameda, Burbank, California 91502.

Honeywell EDP Division, 60 Walnut Street, Wellesley Hills, Massachusetts 02181.

International Business Machines Corporation, 112 East Post Road, White Plains, New York 10601.

National Cash Register Company, Main and K Streets, Dayton, Ohio 45402.

UNIVAC Division, Sperry Rand, 1290 Avenue of the Americas, New York, New York 10009.

SELECTED BIBLIOGRAPHY APPENDIX C

American National Standard Flowchart Symbols and Their Usage in Information Processing. New York: American National Standards Institute, 1968.

Arnold, Robert R., Harold Hill, and Aylmer Nichols, *Modern Data Processing.* New York: John Wiley & Sons, Inc., 1969.

Awad, Elias M., *Automatic Data Processing.* Englewood Cliffs, N.J.: Prentice-Hall, Inc., 1970.

Becker, Joseph, and Robert M. Hayes, *Information Storage and Retrieval.* New York: John Wiley & Sons, Inc., 1967.

Brightman, Richard, Bernard Lusken, and Theodore Tilton, *Data Processing for Decision Making.* New York: The Macmillan Company, 1971.

Bureau of Navy Personnel, Navy Training Manual, NAVPERS 10264-A, Washington, D.C.

Claffey, William J., *Principles of Data Processing.* Encino, Calif.: Dickenson Publishing Company, Inc., 1967.

Clark, Frank J., *Information Processing.* Pacific Palisades, Calif.: Goodyear Publishing Co., Inc., 1970.

Crawford, F. R., *Introduction to Data Processing.* Englewood Cliffs, N.J.: Prentice-Hall, Inc., 1968.

Davis, Gordon B., *Computer Data Processing.* New York: McGraw-Hill Book Company, 1969.

————, *Introduction to Electronic Computers.* New York: McGraw-Hill Book Company, 1971.

Diebold, John, *Man and the Computer.* New York: Praeger Publishers, Inc., 1969.

Ditri, Arnold E., John C. Shaw, and William Atkins, *Managing the EDP Function.* New York: McGraw-Hill Book Company, 1971.

Elliott, C. Orville, and Roger H. Hermanson, *Introduction to Data Processing.* Homewood, Ill.: Richard D. Irwin, Inc., 1970.

Farina, Mario, *Computers, A Self-Teaching Introduction.* Englewood Cliffs, N.J.: Prentice-Hall, Inc., 1969.

Feingold, Carl, *Fundamentals of Punched Card Data Processing.* Dubuque, Iowa: Wm. C. Brown Company Publishers, 1969.

Fuori, William M., *Introduction to the Computer: The Tool of Business*. Englewood Cliffs, N.J.: Prentice-Hall, Inc., 1973.

Gray, Mox, and Keith London, *Documentation Standards*. Princeton, N.J.: Brandon/Systems Press, Inc., 1969.

Gregory, Robert H., and Richard L. Van Horn, *Automatic Data Processing Systems*. Belmont, Calif.: Wadsworth Publishing Company, Inc., 1963.

Gruenberger, Fred, *Computer and Communications*. Englewood Cliffs, N.J.: Prentice-Hall, Inc., 1968.

————, *Fourth Generation Computers*. Englewood Cliffs, N.J.: Prentice-Hall, Inc., 1970.

Gupta, Roger, *Electronic Information Processing*. New York: The Macmillan Company, 1971.

Heyel, Carl, *Computers, Office Machines, and the New Information Technology*. London: Collier-Macmillan Limited, 1969.

Hughes, Marion L., et al., *Decision Tables*. Wayne, Pa.: MDI Publications, 1968.

Joslin, Edward O., *Computer Selection*. Reading, Mass.: Addison-Wesley Publishing Company, Inc., 1968.

————, *Management and Computer Systems*. Washington, D.C.: College Readings, Inc., 1969.

Karplus, Walter J., *On-Line Computing,* New York: McGraw-Hill Book Company, 1966.

Katner, Jerome, *Management Guide to Computer System Selection and Use*. Englewood Cliffs, N.J.: Prentice-Hall, Inc., 1967.

Kovaleosky, V. A., *Character Readers and Pattern Recognition*. New York: Spartan Books, 1968.

Krauss, Leonard, *Administering and Controlling the Company Data Processing Function*. Englewood Cliffs, N.J.: Prentice-Hall, Inc., 1969.

Langenbach, Robert G., *Introduction to Automated Data Processing*. Englewood Cliffs, N.J.: Prentice-Hall, Inc., 1968.

Laurie, Edward J., *Computers and Computer Languages*. Cincinnati: South-Western Publishing Co., 1966.

Levy, Joseph, *Punched Card Data Processing*. New York: McGraw-Hill Book Company, 1968.

Martin, James, *Design of Real-Time Computer Systems*. Englewood Cliffs, N.J.: Prentice-Hall, Inc., 1967.

Sippl, Charles J., *Computer Dictionary*. Indianapolis: Howard W. Sams & Co., Inc., Publishers, 1966.

Sisson, Roger L., *A Manager's Guide to Computer Processing*. New York: John Wiley & Sons, Inc., 1967.

SRA, *Principles of Business Data Processing*. Chicago, Illinois: Science Research Associates, Inc., subsidiary of IBM, 1970.

Swanson, Robert, *An Introduction to Business Data Processing and Computer Programming*. Encino, Calif.: Dickenson Publishing Company, Inc., 1967.

Traviss, Irene, *The Computer Impact*. Englewood Cliffs, N.J.: Prentice-Hall, Inc., 1970.

Wanous, S. J., E. E. Wanous, and A. E. Hughes, *Introduction to Automated Data Processing*. Cincinnati: South-Western Publishing Co., 1968.

Weiss, Eric A., *Computer Usage Fundamentals*. New York: McGraw-Hill Book Company, 1969.

OPERATOR GUIDES

APPENDIX D

IBM 2540

OPERATOR'S GUIDE

GENERAL INFORMATION

CARDS

1. WEAR—Using cards in good condition prevents lost time due to misfeeds and jamming.
2. STORAGE—Cards should be stored in a cool, dry location, away from temperature and humidity extremes to prevent warpage.
3. HUMIDITY—Keep in location of 30-65% relative humidity to prevent feeding and stacking problems.
4. PUNCHING—Cards off-punched should be traced to the punching source and corrected immediately. Frequently checking for registration will prevent flooding files with off-punched cards and reduce reading failures.

BRUSHES

Use care to prevent damage to the read and punch brushes when removing jams. Insure that there are no damaged (bent or short) strands and that the brushes are locked in place after replacement. Brushes not locked in place will give read checks, validity checks and punch checks.

PROGRAMS

When failures are experienced, check that the correct program is being used and that the setup is as desired for this job. Check the program to see if any modifications were made, cards made over and punched incorrectly, or cards missing.

RESTART PROCEDURES

Each program should have a restart procedure to allow completion of the job in the event of an incorrectly punched detail card, a card jam or an intermittent machine failure.

RESTART PROCEDURES — STANDARD AND PFR OPERATION

INDICATIONS	RESTART PROCEDURES
Reader Feed Stop Light (Only) Sense Bit 1 — Intervention Required (Only) NOTE: If read check/bit 3 or validity check/bit 4 indications accompany feed stop/bit 1, follow procedure for read check or validity check.	1. Remove cards from stacker R1. 2. Open hopper joggler gate and remove cards from hopper. 3. Open covers and remove any jammed cards from read feed. Reconstruct any damaged cards. 4. With joggler gate open, press reader start key to clear read feed. 5. Remove cards just run out into stacker R1, place them and any reconstructed cards, in proper sequence, ahead of cards removed from hopper, and replace this deck in hopper or ahead of cards in file feed magazine. 6. Close joggler gate. 7. Press reader start key.
Reader Feed Stop Light Read Check Light Sense Bit 1 — Intervention Required (Only)	This combination of error indications accompanies a 2540 read clutch failure; there may be cards in stacker R1 that have not been read. Restart the job from the last checkpoint.
Read Check Light Sense Bit 3 — Equipment Check (If card is read and stacked with single command.)	1. Remove cards from stacker R1. Determine (perhaps with aid) from programmed message) which was last card read into processing unit, and correct any off-registration punching in it. Place this corrected card in stacker R1. 2. Open joggler gate and remove cards from hopper. 3. With joggler gate open, press reader start key to clear read feed. 4. Remove cards from stacker R1 and place them ahead of cards removed from hopper. Place this deck in hopper or ahead of cards in file feed magazine. 5. Close joggler gate. 6. Press reader start key.
Read Check Light Sense Bit 3 — Equipment Check (If stacker selection is delayed.)	1. Remove cards from stacker R1. 2. Follow steps 2-6 of preceding procedure, correcting any off-registration punching in first card run out into stacker R1.

RESTART PROCEDURES — STANDARD AND PFR OPERATION — CONTINUED

INDICATIONS	RESTART PROCEDURES
Validity Check Light Sense Bit 4 — Data Check (If card is read and stacked with single command.)	1. Remove cards from stacker R1. Determine (perhaps with aid from programmed message) which was last card read into processing unit (this card may be in another stacker) and correct any errors in this card. Place the corrected card in stacker R1. 2. Open joggler gate and remove cards from hopper. 3. With joggler gate open, press reader start key to clear read feed. 4. Remove cards from stacker R1 and place them ahead of cards removed from hopper. Place this deck in hopper or ahead of cards in file feed magazine. 5. Close joggler gate. 6. Press reader start key.
Validity Check Light Sense Bit 4 — Data Check (If stacker selection is delayed.)	1. Remove cards from stacker R1. 2. Open joggler gate and remove cards from hopper. 3. With joggler gate open, press reader start key to clear read feed. 4. Locate and correct invalid character(s) in first card in stacker R1. 5. Place corrected card ahead of cards in stacker R1 ahead of cards removed from hopper. Place this deck in hopper or ahead of cards in file feed magazine. 6. Close joggler gate. 7. Press reader start key.
Validity Check Light Punch Check Light Sense Bit 3 — Equipment Check Sense Bit 4 — Data Check (If 2540 is performing PFR read operation.)	1. Remove cards from punch hopper. 2. Press punch start key to clear punch feed. 3. Remove last three cards from stacker P1. 4. The first of these three cards may have to be reconstructed because it has been read and punched but not punch checked. 5. The second card caused the validity check. Correct it as necessary. 6. Place these three cards, after any necessary corrections, in front of the cards removed from the hopper. Place this deck in the hopper. 7. Press the punch start key. 8. Reconstruct internal data in the system as necessary to restart at the Start I/O instruction that caused the reading of the first card run out of the punch feed in step 3. NOTE: In some programs, reconstruction of internal data may not be provided for. In that case, restart the job from the last checkpoint.
Punch Feed Stop Light (Only) Sense Bit 1 — Intervention Required (Only) (If the 2540 is not performing PFR operations.)	1. Remove cards from stacker P1. 2. Remove cards from hopper. 3. Open covers and remove any jammed cards from punch feed. 4. Press punch start key to clear punch feed. 5. Discard last card punched (2540 will repunch this card automatically). 6. Replace blank cards in hopper and press punch start key. Last card will be repunched automatically and 2540 enters ready status.
Punch Feed Stop Light (Only) Sense Bit 1 — Intervention Required (Only) (If 2540 is performing PFR operation.)	1. Remove cards from stacker P1. 2. Remove cards from hopper. 3. Open covers and remove any jammed cards from punch feed. Press punch start key to clear punch feed. 4. Any card removed or run out from between punch station and punch check brushes should be reconstructed, because it has been punched but not punch checked. 5. Place reconstructed cards and cards run out into stacker P1 in proper sequence ahead of cards removed from hopper, and place this deck in hopper. 6. Press punch start key. 7. Reconstruct internal data in the system as necessary to restart at the Start I/O instruction that caused the first card removed or run out to be read at the PFR station. NOTE: In some programs, reconstruction of internal data may not be provided for. In that case, restart the job from the last checkpoint.

SEE REVERSE SIDE

IBM 2540

INDICATIONS	RESTART PROCEDURES
Punch Check Light Sense Bit 3 — Equipment Check (If 2540 is not performing PFR operation and is using stacker P1.)	1. Remove cards from hopper. 2. Press punch start key to clear punch feed. 3. Remove last four cards from stacker P1. The last two cards are blank; the first two should be discarded. 4. Replace blank cards and cards removed from hopper in hopper. 5. Reconstruct internal data in the system as necessary to restart at the Start I/O instruction that caused the first card removed from stacker P1 to be punched. NOTE: In some programs, reconstruction of internal data may not be provided for. In that case, restart the job from the last checkpoint.
Punch Check Light Sense Bit 3 — Equipment Check (If 2540 is not performing PFR operation and is not using stacker P1.)	1. Examine and correct, if necessary, error card, which is last card in stacker P1. (2540 automatically routes error card to stacker P1.) 2. Place this card in appropriate stacker. 3. Press punch start key. 4. The 2540 will force the card following the error card into stacker P1, also. Place this card in the appropriate stacker. NOTE: Because the error card and the card following it are both directed to stacker P1, the program can correct a non-PFR punch check without operator intervention by repunching both cards and directing them to appropriate stackers. The operator can then discard all cards in stacker P1 at the end of the job.
Punch Check Light Sense Bit 3 — Equipment Check (If 2540 is performing PFR operation.)	1. Remove cards from punch hopper. 2. Press punch start key to clear feed. 3. Remove last four cards from stacker P1. The last two cards are correct; pre-punching in the first two must be reconstructed. 4. Place the two reconstructed cards, the two correct cards, and the cards removed from the hopper, in that sequence, in the hopper. 5. Reconstruct internal data in the system as necessary to restart at the Start I/O instruction that caused the first reconstructed card to be read at the PFR station. NOTE: In some programs, reconstruction of internal data may not be provided for. In that case, restart the job from the last checkpoint.

RESTART PROCEDURES—2540 COMPATIBILITY OPERATION

INDICATIONS	RESTART PROCEDURES
Reader Feed Stop Light (Only) System Console Main Storage Data Register (MSDR) Display: 4F (If there is no card jam in the 2540 read feed.)	1. Remove cards from stacker R1. 2. Open joggler gate and remove cards from read hopper. 3. Open covers and remove any jammed cards from read feed. 4. With joggler gate still open, press reader start key to clear feed. Any damaged cards must be reconstructed. 5. Remove cards just run out into stacker R1. Place them and any reconstructed cards, in proper sequence, ahead of cards removed from hopper, and place this deck in hopper or ahead of cards in file feed magazine. 6. Close joggler gate. 7. Press reader start key. 8. Press system console start key.
Reader Feed Stop Light Read Check Light System Console MSDR Display: 3F (If there is no card jam in the 2540 read feed.)	This combination of error indications accompanies a 2540 read clutch failure; there may be cards in stacker R1 that have not been read. Restart the job from the last checkpoint.
Reader Feed Stop Light Read Check Light System Console MSDR Display: 3F (If there is a jam in the 2540 read feed.)	Follow the procedure for read check or validity check (the next procedure in this chart).

INDICATIONS	RESTART PROCEDURES
System Console MSDR Display: 3F (Read check or validity check has occurred, but the light has been turned off.) NOTE: This same indication can occur for PFR operation; see that procedure later in this chart if appropriate.	1. The last card in stacker R1 is error card. Correct it. 2. Open joggler gate and remove cards from hopper. 3. With joggler gate open, press reader start key to clear feed. 4. Place corrected card ahead of the three cards just run out into stocker R1. Place these four cards ahead of the cards removed from the hopper, and place this deck in the hopper or ahead of the cards in the file feed magazine. 5. Close joggler gate. 6. Press reader start key. 7. Press system console start key.
Punch Feed Stop Light (Only) System Console MSDR Display: 5F (If 2540 is not performing PFR operation.)	1. Remove cards from stacker P1. 2. Remove cards from punch hopper. 3. Open covers and remove any jammed cards from punch feed. 4. Press punch start key to clear feed. 5. Discard last card punched (2540 will repunch this card automatically). 6. Replace blank cards in hopper and press punch start key. Last card will be repunched. 7. Press system console start key.
Punch Check Light (Punch feed stop light may be on or off.) System Console MSDR Display: 5F (If 2540 is not performing PFR operation.)	1. The last card in stacker P1 caused the punch check. Correct it as necessary. Place corrected card in appropriate stacker. 2. Press system console start key.
System Console MSDR Display: 3F Punch Check Light and Validity Check Light may be on or off. (If 2540 is performing PFR operation.)	1. Remove cards from punch hopper. 2. Press punch start key to clear feed. 3. Remove last three cards from stacker P1. 4. The first of these three cards must be reconstructed because it has been read and punched but not punch checked. 5. The second card caused the error; correct it as necessary. 6. Place reconstructed card 1, corrected card 2, and card 3 in front of the cards removed from the hopper. At the front of this deck place a readily-identifiable blank card, and place this deck in the hopper. 7. Reconstruct internal data in the system as necessary to restart at the instruction that caused card 1 (see steps 4-6) to be read at the PFR station. NOTE: In some programs, reconstruction of internal data may not be provided for. In that case, restart the program from the last checkpoint. Be sure that the readily-identifiable blank card is the first card in the hopper. 8. Set the system console process switch at SINGLE CYCLE. 9. Set address 10FF in switches F, G, H, and J on the system console. 10. Press the system reset key. 11. Press ROAR reset key. 12. Press system console start key. 13. Set system console process switch at PROCESS. 14. Press 2540 punch start key. 15. At system console, perform Set IC function to address appropriate instruction. See Operator's Guide for the appropriate system. 16. Press system console start key to resume processing. 17. Remove readily-identifiable blank card inserted in step 6 when it is stacked. This card may now be punched; if it is, discard it.

Printed in U.S.A. 229-4031-0

IBM Field Engineering Division
112 East Post Road, White Plains, N. Y. 10601

IBM 2540
Card 1 of 2

IBM 2540

OPERATOR'S GUIDE

RESTART PROCEDURES — 2540 COMPATIBILITY OPERATION — CONTINUED

INDICATIONS	RESTART PROCEDURES
Punch Feed Stop Light (Only) System Console MSDR Display: 5F (If 2540 is performing PFR operation.)	1. Remove cards from stacker P1. 2. Remove cards from punch hopper. 3. Open covers and remove any jammed cards from punch feed. 4. Press punch start key to clear feed. 5. Any cards removed or run out from between punch station and punch check brushes have been punched but not punch checked. Pre-punching in these cards should be reconstructed. 6. Place any reconstructed cards and cards run out into stacker P1 in proper sequence ahead of cards removed from hopper. Place a readily-identifiable blank card ahead of this deck and place deck in hopper. 7. Perform steps 7-17 of preceding procedure in this chart.
Punch Check Light (Punch feed stop light may be on or off.) (If 2540 is performing PFR operation.)	1. Remove cards from punch hopper. 2. If punch feed stop light is on, open covers and remove any jammed cards from punch feed. Correct any damaged cards. 3. Press punch start key to clear feed. 4. Of the last four cards to enter the 2540 punch feed, the last two are correct and pre-punching in the first two must be reconstructed. 5. Place a readily-identifiable blank card, the two reconstructed cards, the two correct cards, and the cards removed from the hopper in the hopper. 6. Performs steps 7-17 of PFR punch/validity check procedure (two procedures back in this chart).

STOPPAGES

When all cards and card fragments have been removed from the punch unit, the operator replaces the die by pushing it up into the punch unit, and turning the handle. The die is improperly seated if a light tug on the handle causes it to fall.

NOTE: Runout is inactive after a jam. Cards must be removed by hand.

OPERATING AND RESTART PROCEDURES

INITIAL START

To begin operation with the 2540 reader:

1. Perform a nonprocess runout (NPRO) operation by opening the joggler gate, emptying the hopper, and pressing the reader start key to ensure that no cards are left in the feed.
2. Load the desired cards into the hopper of the file-feed magazine, and close the joggler gate. Card decks less than one-inch thick should be placed directly in the hopper with the card weight; larger decks can be placed in the file-feed magazine.
3. Press the reader start key.

To begin operation with the 2540 punch:

1. Perform a nonprocess runout (NPRO) operation by emptying the hopper and pressing the punch start key.
2. Load the desired cards into the punch hopper.
3. Press the punch start key.

RESTARTS FROM ERROR CONDITIONS

The 2540 uses the flexible System/360 command set; therefore, different external error conditions can each require different restart procedures, depending upon whether the 2540 operation is reading, punching or PFR (Punch Feed Read). If the program provides some programmed message to indicate the 2540 sense conditions (type-out, printout, system console display, etc.), the operator can use this message to determine which specific restart procedure he should follow. To locate the error card for read-check and validity-check errors, the operator should be familiar with the type of processing used by the program: that is, whether the program is reading and stacking each card with a single command, or delaying the stacker selection until the data from the card is analyzed.

The following shows the various 2540 error indications and appropriate restart procedures for standard operations, for PFR operations, and for 2540 Compatibility-mode operations. The procedures for compatibility operation assume that the I/O-Check-Stop switch on the system console is on. External indications and channel indications are included in both procedures. The programmer should display the sense indications to the operator.

NOTE: The punch end-of-file key, installed as part of the 2540 Punch-Feed-Read special feature, should not be used when the 2540 is operating in 2540 Compatibility mode.

WILL NOT RUN — POWER LIGHT ON — NO OTHER INDICATORS ON

1. Covers not properly closed. Check all covers.
2. Binding or sticking stop key.

NORMAL STOP CONDITIONS

1. Stacker light on — stacker full.
2. Chip box light on — chip box full.
3. Empty hopper.

CARD JAMMING STOP CONDITIONS

1. Transport light on — A card jam in feed rolls over the stacker area has occurred. Remove jams with care to avoid damage to card chute blades, deflectors and jam detection assembly.
2. Feed stop light on — A card failure or a card jam in the read or punch feed has occurred. Possible causes:
   a. Warped or worn cards.
   b. Piece of card, rubber band, paper clip or staple in the feed.
   c. Card weight missing or in the wrong way.
   d. Brushes not positioned properly.
   CAUTION: Use care when removing a card jam.
   a. Handle brush assemblies carefully.
   b. Remove brushes before pulling cards from feed rolls.

ERROR STOP CONDITIONS — READER CHECKS, PUNCH CHECKS OR VALIDITY CHECKS

Possible causes:
   a. Poor feeding due to warped or worn cards.
   b. Off punched cards.
   c. Invalid card code punched in card.
   d. Brush assemblies not fully latched.
   e. Bent or damaged brushes.

JAM REMOVAL

The operator can gain access to the top of the read feed, transport and stacker area, and punch feed by raising the top covers of the 2540. He can remove the read-check brushes, the read brushes and punch-check brushes, and the PFR brushes, as necessary, to free jammed cards.

If brushes must be removed, avoid contact between the brushes and any other part of the machine. Such contact can damage the brushes or blow a fuse. When replacing these brushes, the locking pins should be snapped into place before a restart is attempted. A series of reader checks or punch checks upon restarting could indicate damaged or improperly positioned brushes. Jams in the punch unit could require the operator to open the front cover of the punch feed, crank the punch clutch to a setting between 335° and 350°, remove the plastic chip funnel, and lower and remove the punch die. The die has a handle shaped like an inverted T. The operator must turn this handle until the lock at the top of the die is released, and if necessary, trip the ejection trigger on the handle to remove the die from the machine.

SEE REVERSE SIDE

IBM 2540

This OPERATOR'S GUIDE has been prepared to assist IBM customers in utilizing their machines to the fullest extent. It is intended to supplement the Reference Manual. The Reference Manual provides valuable instruction in correct usage of switches, polling and addressing formats, as well as operating instructions. The OPERATOR'S GUIDE will assist you in minimizing delay. If you're unsure of what should be done, please discuss with the Customer Engineer responsible for your service.

IBM Field Engineering Division
112 East Post Road, White Plains, N. Y. 10601

Printed in U.S.A. 229-4031-0

IBM 1403N1

OPERATOR'S GUIDE

GENERAL INFORMATION

OPERATING LIGHTS AND KEYS

START KEY

Makes printer ready for print command from CPU. A duplicate start key is located at the rear of printer for operator convenience. The start key on the 1403, attached to the System/360, also permits operation of the printer for one print cycle after the end of forms light is on until channel 1 of the carriage tape is sensed.

STOP KEY

This key stops the printer at the completion of the instruction in process. A duplicate key is located at the rear of the printer for operator's convenience.

CHECK RESET KEY

This key is used to reset a printer error indication. The start key is used to restart the operation.

LIGHTS

END OF FORMS LIGHT

This light indicates when the trailing end of the last form has reached the lower tractors or the absence of forms in the upper tractors. If an End of Forms condition occurs during a skip or while spacing within the last form in the printer, single cycle print until the next skip to a new form occurs. When the last form is skipped out, follow the procedure described for inserting new forms and determining the print line.

FORMS CHECK LIGHT

Indicates form feed trouble in the tractors.

READY LIGHT

Turns on when printer is ready to print.

PRINT CHECK LIGHT

Indicates a print error.

SYNC CHECK LIGHT

Turns on when the train is not in synchronization with the compare counter for the printer.

INDICATOR PANEL LIGHTS

GATE INTERLOCK LIGHT

Turns on when the print unit is not locked in position.

BRUSH INTERLOCK LIGHT

Turns on if the carriage tape brushes are not latched in position for operation.

SHIFT INTERLOCK LIGHT

Turns on to indicate that the manual feed clutch is not properly positioned.

THERMAL INTERLOCK LIGHT

Turns on to indicate that a thermal unit has caused a fuse to burn out. If it is on, the Customer Engineer responsible for your service should be notified.

CARRIAGE FUSE LIGHT

Turns on to indicate a blown fuse in the carriage start stop circuit.

SEE REVERSE SIDE

STOPPAGES AND FAILURES

READY FAILS TO COME ON

1. Power on light not on.
2. Forms check light on.
3. End of forms light on.
4. Print check light on.
5. Sync check light on.
6. Gate interlock light on.
7. 1416 train cartridge not locked in place.

POWER ON LIGHT FAILS TO COME ON

1. System not turned on.
2. If system is on and 1403 power on light is not on, the Customer Engineer responsible for your service should be notified.

FORMS CHECK LIGHT IS ON

1. Does printer contain properly loaded forms and are the tractor covers closed?
2. The carriage tape brushes not locked in place?
3. Manual feed clutch not locked in proper position.
4. Carriage stop key depressed.
5. Reset by depressing reset check key.

END OF FORMS LIGHT ON

1. No forms in lower and/or upper tractors.
2. Reset by depressing reset check key.

PRINT CHECK LIGHT ON

1. Print area contains unprintable character.
2. UCS buffer not loaded or loaded incorrectly. Reload UCS buffer.
3. Reset by depressing reset check key.

SYNC CHECK LIGHT ON

1. Depress reset check key and restart printer.
2. On Model 3 printers, check forms cart to insure that it is properly positioned against ground straps.

GATE INTERLOCK LIGHT ON

1. T-casting open or lock lever not in position.

SHIFT INTERLOCK LIGHT ON

1. Manual feed clutch not properly positioned.

THERMAL INTERLOCK LIGHT ON

1. Turns on to indicate a blown fuse. The Customer Engineer responsible for your service should be notified.

BRUSH INTERLOCK LIGHT ON

1. Carriage tape brushes not latched in position.

CARRIAGE FUSE LIGHT ON

1. Turns on to indicate a blown fuse in the carriage control circuits. If this light is on, the Customer Engineer responsible for your service should be notified.

IMPROPER CARRIAGE OPERATION

Inspect carriage tape for damage at the pin feed holes and wear in general. If worn, replace tape. The last hole punched in the tape should be at least four lines from the cut edge, because approximately the last half inch of the tape overlaps the glue section when the two ends are spliced. If it is necessary to punch a hole lower than four lines from the bottom of the form, the tape should be placed with the top line (immediately under the glue portion) four lines lower than the top edge of the form, before marking the channels. To compensate for the loss, the tape should then be cut four lines lower than the bottom edge of the form — to avoid having a hole punched near the glued portion of the tape.

The tape should never be punched in more than one channel in the same line. Holes in the same channel should not be spaced closer than eight lines apart.

TEARING OF FORMS AND JAMMING

Paper tension is obtained by moving the right-hand tractors slide bars via the vernier knob. Excessive tension will cause the pin feed to tear the forms with possible forms jams at the tractors. Inadequate tension can cause print quality problems (uneven density and/or wavy printing).

STACKER JAMS AND DELEAVING OF MULTI-PART FORMS

Insure that the static eliminators on the stacker are properly installed. Adjust forms guide in stacker to correct height.

On the improved stacker, lock out the unused feed rolls. Stacking can sometimes be improved by locking out some of the feed rolls on the form. This will vary with forms thickness and number of forms.

PRINT QUALITY

DENSITY SETTING

The print density control is a knob located on the upper left side of the printer frame. This knob moves the hammer bumper bar (behind the forms) closer to or farther from the train. The best possible print quality is obtained by optimizing print density. Excessive density can cause smudging. Refer to OCR section.

CHARACTER CUT-OFF, LIGHT TOPS OR BOTTOMS

The forms thickness lever is located at the right-hand end of the ribbon cover on the main casting. This lever must be set for the proper forms thickness. An improper setting can cause light printing on top or bottom and/or character cut-off. Light tops indicates the lever is too high; light bottoms indicates the lever is too low. Refer to OCR section.

LIGHT PRINTING IN A SECTION

Inspect ribbon for uneven inking and wear.

SEE REVERSE SIDE

IBM 1403N1

CARRIAGE CONTROL KEYS

RESTORE KEY

Pressing this key positions the carriage at channel 1 (home position). If the carriage feed clutch is in neutral, the forms do not move. If it is in drive, the form moves with the control tape.

CARRIAGE STOP KEY

Pressing this key stops the carriage operation and turns on the forms check light.

SPACE KEY

Pressing this key causes the carriage to advance the control tape and forms one space if the clutch is engaged. If the clutch is disengaged only the carriage tape will advance.

SINGLE CYCLE KEY (EXCEPT WHEN A PART OF SYSTEM/360)

Pressing this key operates the printer for one cycle. If the end of forms light is on, pressing this key causes printing until channel 1 in the carriage tape is sensed.

SINGLE CYCLE KEY (ON SYSTEM/360)

The single cycle key must be program supported.

COVER CONTROLS

COVER RAISE KEY

Pressing this key causes the top cover to raise. Note that the motor driven cover on the 1403N1 rises when a forms error occurs. Therefore, do not place anything on the printer cover.

COVER LOWER KEY

Pressing this key causes cover to close.

MANUAL CONTROLS

FEED CLUTCH KNOB

The feed clutch controls the carriage drive and form feeding mechanism and can be used only when the feed clutch is disengaged. When set to either neutral, automatic form feeding cannot take place.

PAPER ADVANCE KNOB

This knob positions the form vertically and can be used only when the feed clutch is disengaged.

VERTICAL PRINT ADJUSTMENT KNOB

This knob controls fine spacing adjustments of the forms at the print line. The carriage tape is not affected by this knob.

PRINT UNIT RELEASE LEVER

This lever allows the T-casting to be opened, to permit forms insertion.

RIGHT-HAND TRACTOR VERNIER KNOB

This knob controls fine adjustments in paper tension.

LATERAL PRINT VERNIER KNOB

This knob controls fine adjustments for horizontal registration of the forms.

HORIZONTAL ADJUSTMENT

When the lock lever is raised, the print mechanism unlocks and can be positioned horizontally.

OPERATOR PROCEDURES

RIBBON CHANGING

To change the ribbon on the IBM 1403 Printer:
1. Raise the printer cover.
2. Pull back and unlock the print unit release lever. Swing the print unit out.

TRAIN CLEANING

To maintain print quality, the type should be cleaned regularly. To clean the type, use the pink type cleaning paper. Remove the ribbon. Shift carriage drive to neutral. Run the ripple print pattern while manually advancing the paper by the paper advance knob until the ink residue on paper becomes light. Contact account Customer Engineer for instructions. NEVER attempt to clean type face with any other method such as cloth, brush, typewriter cleaner.

OPTICAL CHARACTER RECOGNITION

RIBBON

An OCR quality ribbon is recommended.

PRINT DENSITY CONTROL

Density settings are very important and vary with the life of the ribbon. Assuming a ribbon with a useful life of 250,000 lines, the following settings are recommended as a guide:

0 to 50,000 lines	— D Density
50,000 to 100,000 lines	— C Density
100,000 to 150,000 lines	— B Density
150,000 to 250,000 lines	— A Density

Each printing format and consequent ribbon wear is unique. Therefore, the number of lines printed at a density setting may vary.

FORMS THICKNESS CONTROL LEVER

The forms thickness must be adjusted to correspond to paper thickness. The paper supplier can furnish this information. In general, 20-24 pound bond is .004 inches thick; continuous card stock is .007 inches thick. Light tops of characters indicate the lever is too high; light bottoms indicates the lever is too low.

FORMS TRACTOR

Tractor tension must be set to keep the paper tight; however, care should be taken not to overdo this, as form tearing will result.

TRAIN CLEANING

Frequent vacuuming and type cleaning is necessary to prevent smudging. Refer to "Train Cleaning" above.

ADDITIONAL INFORMATION

Additional print quality information may be obtained from the following SRL's:

a. IBM 1403 Printer A24-3073
b. IBM 1282 Optical Reader Card Punch A24-3106
c. IBM 1418 Optical Character Reader IBM 1428 Alphanumeric Optical Reader A24-1473
d. IBM 1287 Optical Reader A21-9064
e. Print Quality Considerations, IBM 1418 and 1428, A24-1452
f. IBM 1288 Optical Reader A21-9081

PROPER USE OF RIBBONS

The type of ribbon used is very important to the print quality. Be sure to use the specified ribbon on each application. Refer to OCR section.

T-CASTING

DO NOT SLAM the T-casting. Print quality depends on the T-casting being in proper adjustment. Rough handling of the T-casting can destroy these adjustments.

TRACTORS

To avoid damage, close tractor door before moving tractor.

IBM Field Engineering Division
112 East Post Road, White Plains, N. Y., 10601

Printed in U.S.A. G 229-2135-1

IBM 1403N1

3. Open the top ribbon cover.
4. Unlatch the print line indicator ribbon shield and position it against the form.
5. Push the top ribbon roll to the right (hinged side of the print unit), lift out the left end of the ribbon roll and remove the roll from the drive end of the mechanism.
6. Slip the ribbon from under the ribbon correction sensing lever.
7. To remove the bottom roll, press the ribbon roll to the right, lower the left end of the ribbon roll, and remove it from the mechanism.
8. When replacing the ribbon in the machine, hand tighten the ribbon to remove slack from in front of the printing mechanism.

Ribbons are available in 11 inch widths, in addition to the standard 14 inches. The ribbon width lever can adjust the ribbon feed mechanism to accommodate the various ribbon widths.

FORMS INSERTION

1. Raise the front cover of the printer to gain access to the print unit and forms area.
2. Turn the feed clutch to neutral.
3. Unlock and swing back the print unit by pulling the print unit release lever toward you.
4. Set both the left-hand forms tractors slightly to the left of the first printing position. Pull the tractor until it latches in the appropriate notch. NOTE: Do not use open tractor cover to move tractor.
5. Open the left-hand tractor covers and place the forms over the pins. Close the covers.
6. Open both right-hand tractor covers.
7. Move the right-hand tractors to the desired location to line up the right side of the forms. Pull out the tractor pin latch and slide the tractor until the pin snaps into the appropriate position.
8. Turn feed clutch to 6 or 8 line drive.

TAPE CONTROLLED CARRIAGE

The tape controlled carriage controls high-speed feeding and spacing of continuous forms. The carriage is controlled by punched holes in a paper or plastic tape that corresponds in length to the length of one or more forms. Holes punched in the tape stop the form when it reaches any predetermined position.

INSERTING CARRIAGE CONTROL TAPE

1. Raise the printer cover.
2. Turn the feed clutch to neutral.
3. Move the latch on the side of the brush holder to the left and raise the assembly.
4. With the printing on the outside of the loop, place the loop over the pin feed drive wheel so the pins engage the holes in the tape.
5. Place the other end of the loop around the adjustable carriage control tape idler. Adjust the idler by loosening the locking knob and moving the idler in its track. No noticeable slack should be in the tape, but the tape should not be under tension. Test the tape by pressing the sides of the loop together. There should be some "give": if the tape is too tight, the pin feed holes will be damaged. Be sure to retighten the locking knob on the idler.
7. Lower brush assembly. A click can be heard when the latch engages.
8. Press the restore key. When the tape has returned to the home (channel 1) position, engage the feed clutch. NOTE: If there is no channel 1 punch in the carriage tape, the drive will not stop. Carriage stop must be depressed.

FORMS

Refer to SRL A24-3041 "IBM 1403 and 1443 Printers, Forms Design Considerations."

SELECTIVE TAPE LISTING FEATURE

The selective tape listing feature allows printing on individual paper tapes. These tapes can be 1.5" wide or 3.1" wide. Four 3.1" tapes or eight 1.5" tapes can be used. They can be in combinations if the wider tape uses positions 1-2, 3-4, 5-6 or 7-8. The tapes are not fed by the standard carriage, which is disconnected when this feature is used. Instead, they are fed individually by magnetic feeders under program control.

INTERMITTENT PROBLEMS

To aid in correcting intermittent problems, record all information such as:
1. Specific application that was running at the time of failure.
2. Copy of failure.
3. What should have printed.
4. Type of failure (sync check, fail to print, tear paper, etc.).
5. When failure occurred.

SEE REVERSE SIDE

TIMING THE UCS/PCS CARTRIDGE TO THE PRINTER — TRAIN PRINTERS

The slot in the type train drive gear can engage the key in the cartridge drive gear at several positions with respect to the graphics (characters) on the train. However, one and only one of these positions is correct. To insure that only this correct position is used, preparatory adjustments must be made to both the cartridge and cartridge drive mechanism.

PREPARING THE UCS/PCS TRAIN CARTRIDGE FOR INSTALLATION

To facilitate the timing of the UCS/PCS cartridge, a type slug containing the graphic (character) 1 is designated as the home position slug. The front area of this slug just above the embossed graphics is copper colored for ready identification. There may be other slugs having a 1 graphic, but they will not have this distinctive coloration. Align the graphic 1 on this marked slug with the arrow scribed on the base of the cartridge. This insures that the type train drive gear has made the necessary number of revolutions to obtain the correct type slug to PSS pulse relationship. Be careful to retain this alignment when installing the cartridge.

PREPARING THE UCS/PCS CARTRIDGE DRIVE MECHANISM TO ACCEPT UCS/PCS CARTRIDGE

To provide a universal method of timing the UCS/PCS cartridge to the printer, a new style gear cover was designed. This cover has a circular window near its center and a circular opening with a rectangular notch. To time the cartridge drive mechanism, turn the cartridge drive gear until these two conditions are met:

1. The key on the cartridge drive gear aligns with the rectangular notch.
2. The UCS/PCS pointer clamping screw is visible through the circular window.

The cartridge can now be correctly installed. Be careful to maintain the alignments indicated in these preparatory adjustments while engaging the slot in the train drive gear with the key on the cartridge drive gear. Lock the cartridge in position with its locking handles.

This OPERATOR'S GUIDE has been prepared to assist IBM customers in utilizing their machines to the fullest extent. It is intended to supplement the Reference Manual. The Reference Manual provides valuable instruction in correct usage of switches, polling and addressing formats, as well as operating instructions. The OPERATOR'S GUIDE will assist you in minimizing delay. If you're unsure of what should be done, please discuss with the Personnel responsible for your service.

IBM Field Engineering Division
112 East Post Road, White Plains, N. Y. 10601

Printed in U.S.A. G 229-2135-1

IBM 1403N1

Card 2 of 2

IBM 2311

OPERATOR'S GUIDE

GENERAL INFORMATION

DISK PACKS

1. Never mount a disk pack on a file drive that has been dropped or shows signs of physical damage. Severe damage to the file drive can result. Call the Customer Engineer responsible for your service if pack damage is suspected.
2. Never put labels anywhere on a disk pack except inside the pack center hub.
3. Never put labels on the side of the disk pack top cover. Labels can come off and cause damage to file drive.
4. Always be sure that both top and bottom covers are together.
5. Always store disk pack flat, not on edge.
6. Each pack should rest on a shelf, not on another disk pack.
7. Store disk packs in a machine room atmosphere.
8. If a disk pack must be stored in a different environment, allow two hours for adjustment to machine room atmosphere before use.

STOPPAGES

If problems are encountered in programmed operation of the disk drive, the following check list should be used:

1. Meter enable switch (should be turned to the enable position).
2. The disk pack (should be mounted and the 2311 top cover securely latched closed).
3. Start stop switch (should be on and as a result the file should be in a ready condition, green light on).
4. The 2841 meter switch should be turned on. Note: in the case of a two-channel switch operation, both meter switches should be on if both channels are to be in operation with the control unit.

If all points have been checked and found to be satisfactory, and the system is still not functioning properly, the Customer Engineer should be called to correct the situation.

SELECT LOCKS (RED INDICATOR ON)

IMPORTANT: Select lock indications may be reset by powering off the 2311 and then turning it back on. If the select lock persists, the Customer Engineer should be notified immediately.

DISK I/O ERRORS

1. Verify that disk pack is properly initialized and has correct VTOC.
2. If I/O errors persist, try back-up pack when available.
3. Never move a disk pack causing errors more than once. The disk pack may be defective and cause damage to a file drive. Call Customer Engineer and have both file drives and disk pack checked.

For further details refer to SRL A26-5756 — IBM Disk Pack Handling and Operating Procedures.

SEE REVERSE SIDE

This OPERATOR'S GUIDE has been prepared to assist IBM customers in utilizing their machines to the fullest extent. It is intended to supplement the Reference Manual. The Reference Manual provides valuable instruction in correct usage of switches, polling and addressing formats, as well as operating instructions. The OPERATOR'S GUIDE will assist you in minimizing delay. If you're unsure of what should be done, please discuss with the Customer Engineer responsible for your service.

IBM Field Engineering Division
112 East Post Road, White Plains, N. Y. 10601

Printed in U.S.A. 229-5053-0

IBM 2311

IBM 2401, 2402, 2403, 2404

OPERATOR'S GUIDE

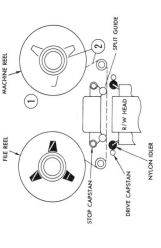

Diagram labels: MACHINE REEL, FILE REEL, SPLIT GUIDE, R/W HEAD, NYLON IDLER, STOP CAPSTAN, DRIVE CAPSTAN, (1), (2)

2401 - 2404 Tape Units

Characteristics	Model 1	Model 4	Model 1	Model 2	Model 5	Model 2	Model 3	Model 6	Model 3
Number of Tracks and Recording Method	9Track NRZI	9-Track PE	7-Track NRZI	9-Track NRZI	9-Track PE	7-Track NRZI	9-Track NRZI	9-Track PE	7-Track NRZI
Density (BPI) Bytes per inch	800	1600	800 / 556 / 200	800	1600	800 / 556 / 200	800	1600	800 / 556 / 200
Data Rate (Bytes/Sec)	30,000	60,000	30,000 / 20,850 / 7,500	60,000	120,000	60,000 / 41,700 / 15,000	90,000	180,000	90,000 / 62,500 / 22,500
Tape Speed (In/Sec)	37.5	37.5	37.5	75.0	75.0	75.0	112.5	112.5	112.5
Interblock Gap (Inches)	.75	.6	.75	.75	.6	.75	.75	.6	.75

CONTROL PANEL FUNCTIONS

Button	Status of Unit When Used	Action
load/rewind	unloaded	loads tape and rewinds to L. P.
load/rewind	loaded & not ready	rewinds to L. P.
start	loaded	turn on ready
start	loaded & not ready	turn on ready at rewind end
unload	loaded & not ready	unload tape and reset T. I.
reset	loaded & ready	turn off ready
reset	H. S. rewinding	go into L. S. rewind
reset	L. S. rewinding	stop

LOADING PROCEDURE

1. Mount file reel — place reel on hub — lock hub.
2. Thread tape through transport and over machine reel hub as shown in diagram, broken line.
3. With the left index finger, push the tape gently against the reel hub at point (1).
4. With the right index finger, pull the excess tape back over the reel hub by pushing the tape to the right at point (2).
5. Spin machine reel clockwise, winding up the tape while holding the reel release button depressed with the left hand. Continue to turn reel until the L. P. marker is several turns onto the machine.
6. Close door and/or window.
7. Push load/rewind button.
8. Push start.

UNLOADING PROCEDURE

1. Push load/rewind button (if reel is to be removed).
2. Push unload when tape stops at L. P.
3. Wind tape onto file reel with right index finger while holding reel release button depressed.
4. Loosen reel lock. Remove reel by finger pressure at the rear of the reel near the hub.
5. Attach tape end retainer and place reel in its container.

IBM no longer recommends the use of Mylar* tape on 2401, 2402, 2403, Mod 4, 5 or 6.

CLEANING PROCEDURE

(AS REQUIRED — MAXIMUM EIGHT HOURS OPERATION OR EVERY 10 FULL REEL PASSES WITH HD TAPE OR 2 REEL PASSES WITH MYLAR TAPE) MATERIALS: CLEAN LINT-FREE CLOTH, STIFF BRUSH, IBM TRANSPORT CLEANER.

1. With clean cloth moist with transport cleaner:
   a. Clean R/W heads.
   b. Clean bottom of stop capstans.
   c. Clean nylon idler.
   d. Clean drive capstans.
   e. Clean Vacuum Columns.
2. Brush bottom of split guides and visually inspect cleaner blade.
3. Visually inspect tape transport path for loose oxide or foreign matter.

CLEANING NOTES

Do not allow cleaning fluids to contact tape.
Do not load tape until all fluid used is dry.
Do not use excessive fluid.
Do not allow fluid to contact skin.
Do not wait eight hours for cleaning if visual inspection or operation indicates that cleaning is necessary.
Do not clean capstans under power.

"DO NOT" NOTES

1. Do not touch tape edge in reel openings.
2. Do not remove file protect ring without unloading drive.
3. Do not operate unit with window open.
4. Do not allow tape to touch floor.
5. Do not squeeze reel flanges.
6. Do not handle tape while smoking or eating.
7. Do not use reels that are cracked or warped.

*Trademark of E. I. DuPont de Nemour & Co., Inc.

SEE REVERSE SIDE

SUGGESTED TAPE LIBRARY IDENTIFICATION

1. Give each tape unit a number or letter identification.
2. Give each tape reel an identification code.
3. Record:
   a. Date tape received and entered to service.
   b. Date written on tape drive identification (Item 1) on reel label.
4. When problems occur, supply the Customer Engineer responsible for your service with:
   a. When and which tape unit wrote the tape (Item 3-b)
   b. Tape unit experiencing difficulty.
   c. Description of problem symptoms.
   d. Reel of tape experiencing problem.
   e. Type of error indication if possible.

This OPERATOR'S GUIDE has been prepared to assist IBM customers in utilizing their machines to the fullest extent. It is intended to supplement the Reference Manual. The Reference Manual provides valuable instruction in correct usage of switches, polling and addressing formats, as well as operating instructions. The OPERATOR'S GUIDE will assist you in minimizing delay. If you're unsure of what should be done, please discuss with the Customer Engineer responsible for your service.

IBM   Field Engineering Division
112 East Post Road, White Plains, N. Y. 10601

Printed in U.S.A.   229-2141-0

IBM 2401-2404

INDEX

(NOTE: Page numbers appearing in italics refer to text illustrations.)